Collins

Cambridge IGCSE™

Additional Maths

TEACHER'S GUIDE

Also for Cambridge IGCSE (9–1)

David Bird, Claire Powis,
Su Nicholson, Brian Speed, Colin Stobart

Collins

William Collins' dream of knowledge for all began with the publication of his first book in 1819.

A self-educated mill worker, he not only enriched millions of lives, but also founded a flourishing publishing house. Today, staying true to this spirit, Collins books are packed with inspiration, innovation and practical expertise. They place you at the centre of a world of possibility and give you exactly what you need to explore it.

Collins. Freedom to teach.

Published by Collins

An imprint of HarperCollins*Publishers*

The News Building, 1 London Bridge Street, London, SE1 9GF, UK

Macken House, 39/40 Mayor Street Upper, Dublin 1, D01 C9W8, Ireland

Browse the complete Collins catalogue at
collins.co.uk

British Library Cataloguing-in-Publication Data

A catalogue record for this publication is available from the British Library.

Authors: David Bird, Claire Powis, Su Nicholson, Brian Speed, Colin Stobart
Publisher: Elaine Higgleton
Commissioning editor: Rachael Harrison
In-house project manager: Letitia Luff
Project manager: Wendy Alderton
Copyeditor: Tim Jackson
Answer checker: Steven Matchett
Proofreader: Jo Kemp/Wendy Alderton
Illustrators: QBS/Jouve
Cover designer: Kevin Robbins and Gordon MacGilp
Cover illustrator: Ann Paganuzzi
Production controller: Lyndsey Rogers
Printed and bound in the UK using 100% Renewable Electricity at CPI Group (UK) Ltd

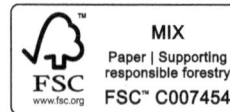

MIX
Paper | Supporting responsible forestry
FSC
www.fsc.org
FSC™ C007454

This book is produced from independently certified FSC™ paper to ensure responsible forest management . For more information visit: www.harpercollins.co.uk/green

Acknowledgements

The publishers gratefully acknowledge the permission granted to reproduce the copyright material in this book. Every effort has been made to trace copyright holders and to obtain their permission for the use of copyright material. The publishers will gladly receive any information enabling them to rectify any error or omission at the first opportunity.

Cambridge International copyright material in this publication is reproduced under licence and remains the intellectual property of Cambridge Assessment International Education.

Endorsement indicates that a resource has passed Cambridge International's rigorous quality-assurance process and is suitable to support the delivery of a Cambridge International syllabus. However, endorsed resources are not the only suitable materials available to support teaching and learning, and are not essential to be used to achieve the qualification. Resource lists found on the Cambridge International website will include this resource and other endorsed resources. Any example answers to questions taken from past question papers, practice questions, accompanying marks and mark schemes included in this resource have been written by the authors and are for guidance only. They do not replicate examination papers. In examinations the way marks are awarded may be different. Any references to assessment and/or assessment preparation are the publisher's interpretation of the syllabus requirements. Examiners will not use endorsed resources as a source of material for any assessment set by Cambridge International. While the publishers have made every attempt to ensure that advice on the qualification and its assessment is accurate, the official syllabus, specimen assessment materials and any associated assessment guidance materials produced by the awarding body are the only authoritative source of information and should always be referred to for definitive guidance. Cambridge International recommends that teachers consider using a range of teaching and learning resources based on their own professional judgement of their students' needs. Cambridge International has not paid for the production of this resource, nor does Cambridge International receive any royalties from its sale. For more information about the endorsement process, please visit www.cambridgeinternational.org/endorsed-resources

Contents

Downloads

Answers and Word files of lesson plans, resource sheets, homework and extension material can be found online at www.collins.co.uk/cambridge-international-downloads

Introduction

Welcome to the Teacher's Guide for *Collins Cambridge IGCSE™ Additional Maths* for the Cambridge IGCSE™ Additional Mathematics syllabus (0606) for examination from 2025. These resources also support the Cambridge O Level Additional Mathematics syllabus (4037).

Contents of the Teacher's Guide

The Teacher's Guide comprises two components – the printed book and downloadable files. The **printed book** has lesson plans to accompany all the topics in the Student's Book, along with resource sheets, homework and extension activity sheets and a scheme of work.

Available to **download**, is all the content from the printed book in Word format so that it can be edited to suit the needs of individual classes or departmental schemes of work.

Also available to download are:

- Answers to all exercises in the Student's Book (these also appear at the back of the Student's Book).

- Answers to homework and extension activity sheets.

Downloads are available at www.collins.co.uk/pages/cambridge-international-downloads

Lesson plans

Each topic in the Student's Book (1.1, 1.2, 1.3, etc.) is supported by a lesson plan, and each one follows the same format, making it easy to use and prepare lessons.

The following sections of the plan help in preparing lessons:

- **Key words** highlight important mathematical vocabulary.

- **IGCSE Maths prior knowledge** clearly states the knowledge that students need before they can successfully attempt the topic.

- **Learning outcomes** indicate clearly what the students should master during the lesson and are a useful way of measuring its success.

- **Cross references** to the relevant Student's Book pages make it easy to integrate the book into class teaching.

- **Common mistakes and remediation** are pinpointed so they can be recognised quickly and rectified.

- **Useful tips** help students remember key concepts easily.

- **Guidance** provides support around how to deliver activities most effectively in both the Student's Book and the Lesson plans.

- **Checking progress** provides activities or guidance on how to assess students' progress through the topic.

- These are followed by suggestions for the structure of the lesson:

- **Starters** involve the whole class and give you ideas on how to capture students' attention and interest.

- **Main lesson activities** help you lead students into exercise questions.

- **Plenaries** offer guidance on how to round off the three-part lessons.

Resource sheets, Homework sheets and Extensions Sheets mentioned in Lesson Plans can be found at the end of each chapter and online.

This book helps students to become proficient in using mathematical techniques with and without a calculator. Whilst students are allowed to use a scientific calculator in one of their examinations, they should understand the theory as well to show their working for non-calculator questions.

It is important to emphasise to students that use of graphical calculators are not permitted in the examination. Lesson plans in the Student book suggest the use of graphical calculators and apps as they are excellent tools for students to use in class and provide good preparation for the study of mathematics AS and A level mathematics. All activities can be run without calculators, but timings may need to be adjusted.

1 Functions

TOPIC:
1.1 Mappings, functions and notation

KEY WORDS:
mapping diagram, one-one, many-one, one-many, many-many, function, domain, range

IGCSE MATHS PRIOR KNOWLEDGE:
Recognise the notation that is used to describe a function

Find the inverses of simple functions

Form composite functions

Sketch and recognise the graphs of linear and quadratic equations

Learning aims:
- Understand the terms: function, domain, range (image set), one – one function, many – one function, inverse function, and composition of functions
- Find the domain and range of functions

Resources:
- Student Book: pages 4–13
- Resource sheet 1.1
- Graphical calculators and apps
- A1/flipchart paper
- Mini whiteboards

Common mistakes and remediation:
Lower-achieving students might think that f(x) means 'f times x'. Encourage students to write out the alternative notation, for example, f: $x \rightarrow x + 3$, to help their understanding.

Students might not think that other letters, apart from f(x), can be used for notation. Show students how alternative letters can be used.

Students might think that a constant function is not actually a function because they cannot see an input value. Show students how all different values in the starting data set map to the one value.

Useful tips:
Sketch a mapping to help visualise its type.

Guidance:
The starting point questions in the Student Book could be used as a short quiz before or instead of the starter activity.

To support the main activity, extra discussion about the different types of mappings, including how the domain can be restricted (for example, $x \rightarrow x^2 - 2x - 4$, $-7 \leq x \leq 5$), might be needed before students investigate for themselves.

During the main activity, encourage students to find different examples of each type of mapping, for example, trigonometric ratios.

At the end of the main activity, the large paper used by students can be displayed.

Consider questions that you could ask students as they work in groups, particularly those that encourage students to explain and justify their thinking. Also, encourage students to discuss their mathematics and reflect upon their work.

STARTER (5–10 mins)
Equipment: Resource sheet 1.1

➤ Hand out a set of cards to students, who work in groups of three or four. Explain that they will be matching pairs of cards – matching involves evaluating functions, functions and their inverses, composite functions, solving functional equations. The activity covers the function knowledge and understanding from IGCSE Mathematics.

➤ Allow them to match as many as they can in the time available. Lower-achieving students can be guided to try certain types of card first, say evaluating functions.

➤ At the end of the activity, allow time for two students from each group to move around the classroom to look at other groups' answers, while two students remain to justify their answers.

- ➢ As time allows, students can discuss any differences they see between responses to the activity.
- ➢ The importance of the activity is not so much that students complete every matching pair, but that they are reminded of the knowledge and understanding they have from IGCSE Mathematics.

MAIN LESSON ACTIVITY (40–45 mins)

Equipment: Graphical calculators and apps, A1/flipchart paper

- ➢ Using an example of a one-one mapping, create a mapping diagram, explaining that each input number maps onto an output value. In this example, define the domain (the starting data set – independent values), range (the resulting data set – dependent values), mapping notation (for example, $x \rightarrow 3x; x \in \mathbb{R}$ notation could also be used) for this diagram and explain that it is a one-one mapping (each input value has only one output value and each output value has only one input value). Ask what the mapping would look like graphically. (See guidance above.)

- ➢ Hand out a large piece of paper to students working in groups of three or four. Explain that they need to define what a one-one mapping is and try to find other possible types of mapping, recording their work on the paper. Encourage students to define the domain and range for their mappings; use mapping diagrams, correct notation and sketches. They can use graphical calculators and apps to help create the mappings. Lower-achieving students can be given, for instance, one example of each type of mapping to investigate what type it is. Higher-achieving students can be encouraged to consider mappings involving x^n, etc. Students need to create at least one example of each type of mapping. (See guidance above.)

- ➢ Put the groups of students together to discuss their findings. Make sure all the types of mapping are discussed, based on students' examples: one-one, many-one, one-many, many-many.

- ➢ Define a function (each input value can only have one output value), the function notation (for example, f: $x \rightarrow x + 3$, $f(x) = x + 3$) and introduce the geometric test for functions (using vertical lines parallel to the y-axis). Explain to students how, as they saw in the starter activity, different letters can be used to describe functions (for example, $f(x)$, $g(x)$, $h(x)$). Discuss with students that only one-one and many-one mappings are functions.

- ➢ Ask students to highlight on their paper, in some way, which mappings are functions and which are not. Ask them to add both types of function notation to the functions, for example, f: $x \rightarrow x + 3$, $f(x) = x + 3$.

- ➢ The large pieces of paper can be displayed as posters.

- ➢ Students can now do Exercise 1.1. This provides opportunities for students to identify mappings and determine the domain and range.

PLENARY (10 mins)

Equipment: Mini whiteboards or similar

- ➢ Ask students 'show me' or similar questions to explore their understanding of the lesson. Questions can be in word form or diagrammatic/graphical. Cover all the learning aims.

- ➢ For example, *Show me a one-one mapping.* (Answers could be given using notation, a mapping diagram or graphically.) *Show me the range of* $f(x) = x^2 - 2x - 4$, $-7 \leq x \leq 5$.

Homework and answers: Resource sheets, homework and extension exercises can be found at the end of this chapter and in the downloadable materials. Answers can be found in the downloadable materials.

CHECKING PROGRESS	Use the immediate feedback from the plenary to check students' progress.

1 Functions

TOPIC:

1.2 Composite functions

KEY WORDS:

composite function

IGCSE MATHS PRIOR KNOWLEDGE:

Recognise the notation that is used to describe a function

Form composite functions

Learning aims:
- Understand the terms: function, domain, range (image set), one – one function, many – one function, inverse function, and composition of functions
- Form and use composite functions
- Find the domain and range of functions

Resources:
- Student Book: pages 13–14
- Consolidation downloadable resource: Domain and range of a composite function

Common mistakes and remediation:

Students might think that fg(x) means f(x) multiplied by g(x). Encourage students to remember that f(g) is substituted into the position of the x in f(x).

Useful tips:

The values used, and then subsequently found, when evaluating a composite function (using the two-step process), can be used to check whether the composite function, shown as a single expression, is correct.

Guidance:

For the starter make clear that, for the justification, students need to use a written, diagrammatic or graphical explanation.

For the main activity, when defining a composite function, it would be useful to use a mapping diagram so that students can visualise the process. Clarify the two-step process that students can use to evaluate a composite function; for example, finding the value of f(2) then using the answer to this in g(x).

For the main activity, if necessary, provide additional opportunity for evaluating composite functions, for example, after the discussion on evaluating.

For the main activity you could ask students to make use of a graphing tool (calculator or, online tool) to and visualise confirm the *range* of a composite function.

For the main activity, think, pair, share involves a student thinking through the problem on their own for a short while, for example, one to five minutes. They then share their conclusions with their partner. After this the pair of students share their ideas with a wider group.

For the plenary, make sure new pairs of students are formed. Encourage students to explain and justify their thinking as they share their understanding.

STARTER (5–10 mins)

➢ Students work in pairs. Ask each student to create a one-one function and a many-one function and give these to their partner. The partner should justify why each one is the particular type. (See guidance above.)

MAIN LESSON ACTIVITY (40–45 mins)

➢ Using two functions from one of the students, define a composite function. Discuss what composite functions are possible and perform any possible evaluation, for example, fg(2) and gf(2). Discuss whether fg(2) and gf(2) give the same value. (See guidance above.)

➢ Discuss what single expressions the composite functions would create, for example, fg(x) and gf(x). Make sure the students understand what $f^2(x)$ means.

➢ Create an equation that needs to be solved, for example, fg(x) = 2. Students think, pair, share how to solve the equation. Groups of students should be organised in a way that supports lower-achieving students. (See guidance above.)

➢ Working in pairs and using their functions, students create all the possible composite functions as single expressions. Students should then create an equation from one of the composite functions, make sure they can solve it themselves and then give it to another group to solve. After a specified time, the solutions should be shared with their originators and checked/marked.

➢ Working in pairs, students work to identify the domain and range of their composite functions.

➢ Students can now do Exercise 1.2. This provides practice in evaluating composite functions, solving composite function equations and identifying their domain and range.

PLENARY (10 mins)

➢ Ask students, in pairs, to share their understanding from the lesson in written form. (See guidance above.)

Homework and answers: Resource sheets, homework and extension exercises can be found at the end of this chapter and in the downloadable materials. Answers can be found in the downloadable materials.

CHECKING PROGRESS	Use the written evidence from the plenary to check students' progress.

1 Functions

TOPIC:
1.3 Inverse functions

KEY WORDS:
Inverse function, self-inverse function

IGCSE MATHS PRIOR KNOWLEDGE:
Recognise the notation that is used to describe a function

Find the inverses of simple functions

Learning aims:
- Understand the terms: function, domain, range (image set), one – one function, many – one function, inverse function, and composition of functions
- Find the inverse of a one-one function
- Explain in words why a given function does not have an inverse

Resources:
- Student Book: pages 15–17
- Graphical calculators and apps
- Small pieces of paper

Common mistakes and remediation:
Students might think that all functions have inverses, so they do need to see counter examples. Also, they need to be shown how non-invertible functions can become invertible by restricting the domain.

When using the notation f^{-1}, students might think the '−1' is an exponent. Encourage students to learn $f^{-1}(x) \neq \dfrac{1}{f(x)}$.

Useful tips:
Write the function as an equation with y as the subject. Then rearrange the equation to make x the subject. Then swap x and y round. Alternatively, swap x and y first, then rearrange the equation.

Guidance:
For the main activity, the fact that the domain of a function is the range of its inverse and vice versa needs to be clear from mapping diagrams and graphically. At this stage, no mention should be made of only functions with one-one mappings having an inverse function. Students should discover this fact during the investigation.

For the main activity, if necessary, provide additional opportunities for finding the inverse of functions, for example, after the initial discussion.

During the investigation, encourage students to investigate self-inverse functions. If any students are still lacking understanding of what a function is, this should become clear as they see the one-many mappings.

For the plenary, using exit tickets means students should hand in their 'tickets', with their responses to the task on them, as they leave the class.

STARTER (5–10 mins)
➤ Ask students, in pairs, to find two functions that could create the **composite function** $fg(x) = 12 - 4x$. When the two functions have been found, arrange for students to swap their functions with another pair so the functions can be checked.

MAIN LESSON ACTIVITY (40–45 mins)

Equipment: Graphical calculators and apps

➤ Using a function found by one pair of students, discuss inverse functions. Use mapping diagrams to visualise a function and it's inverse, then represent the function graphically. Emphasise the relationship between the domains and ranges of a function and its inverse: the domain of a function is the range of its inverse and vice versa. Discuss the method for

finding the inverse of a function, for example, $f(x) = 5x + 3 \rightarrow y = 5x + 3 \rightarrow x = \dfrac{x-3}{5} \rightarrow f^{-1}(x) = \dfrac{x-3}{5}$. (See guidance above.)

➤ Working in pairs, and using graphical calculators and apps, students investigate functions and their inverses: they create a function and write down the domain and range of the function and its inverse. Encourage students to use correct notation and write down any observations they have.

➤ As students discover that a function with a many-one mapping cannot have an inverse, ask them to consider how they could arrange for the particular function to have an inverse, by restricting the domain.

➤ Lower-achieving students could be given specific functions with one-one/many-one mappings to investigate. Higher-achieving students could be encouraged to investigate more complex functions, for example, trigonometric functions.

➤ Bring the groups of students together to discuss their findings. Make sure functions with one-one mappings are

understood to be the only ones that have an inverse. Discuss self-inverse functions, for example, $\dfrac{1}{x}$, creating them with

graphical calculators and apps, if necessary. As time allows, explore $ff^{-1}(x) = f^{-1}f(x) = x$, and the inverse of a composite function, using mapping diagrams to visualise the inverse of $fg(x)$ being $g^{-1}f^{-1}(x)$.

➤ Students can now do Exercise 1.3.

➤ Questions 1 to 6 provide practice in finding the inverse of a function. (Graphical calculators and apps could be used for question 6.)

➤ Question 7 looks at self-inverse functions.

➤ Questions 8 to 10 include looking at composite functions and inverses.

PLENARY (10 mins)

Equipment: Small pieces of paper

➤ Using exit tickets, ask the students to write down a function and its inverse, a function that does not have an inverse and a self-inverse function. (See guidance above.)

Homework and answers: Resource sheets, homework and extension exercises can be found at the end of this chapter and in the downloadable materials. Answers can be found in the downloadable materials.

CHECKING PROGRESS	Use the exit tickets to check students' progress.

1 Functions

TOPIC:

1.4 Graphs of a function and its inverse

KEY WORDS:

None

IGCSE MATHS PRIOR KNOWLEDGE:

Sketch and recognise the graphs of linear and quadratic equations

Learning aims:

- Use sketch graphs to show the relationship between a function and its inverse

Resources:

- Student Book: pages 17–20
- Resource sheet 1.2
- Graphical calculators and apps
- A1/flipchart paper
- Graph paper
- Small pieces of paper

Common mistakes and remediation:

When using the notation f $^{-1}$, student might think the '−1' is an exponent. Encourage students to learn $f^{-1}(x) \neq \dfrac{1}{f(x)}$.

Useful tips:

To check inverse functions, substitute numbers from the domain into the original function to get the range, and vice versa into the inverse to get back to the original domain.

Guidance:

For the starter, encourage the students to work together on the different parts of the question.

For the main activity, as students sketch the functions on the axes, encourage them to think carefully about what scale they are using; link this to how they are actually restricting the domain of each function.

At the end of the main activity, the large paper used by students can be displayed.

Consider questions that you could ask students as they work in groups, particularly those that encourage students to explain and justify their thinking. Also, encourage students to discuss their mathematics and reflect upon their work.

For the plenary, using exit tickets means the students should hand in their 'tickets', with their responses to the task written on them, as they leave the class.

STARTER (5-10 mins)

➢ Working in groups of three or four, students answer the following question to review previous understanding. (See guidance above.)

$h(x) = \dfrac{2}{3x-1}$

a   State the domain of h(x). $\left(\text{Answer: } x \in \square, x \neq \dfrac{1}{3}\right)$

b   State the range of h(x).   (Answer: $y \in \square, y \neq 0$)

c   Work out h^{-1}(x). $\left(\text{Answer: } h^{-1}(x) = \dfrac{2}{3x} + \dfrac{1}{3}\right)$

d   State the domain of h^{-1}(x).   (Answer: $x \in \square, x \neq 0$)

e   Show that $x = 1$ for h^2(x) = 1.   (Answer: $h^2(x) = \dfrac{2(3x-1)}{7-3x} \rightarrow \dfrac{2(3x-1)}{7-3x} = 1 \rightarrow 6x-2 = 7-3x \rightarrow 9x = 9 \rightarrow x = 1$)

MAIN LESSON ACTIVITY (40–45 mins)

Equipment: Graphical calculators and apps, A1/flipchart paper, Resource sheet 1.2

➢ Hand out resource sheet 1.2 to groups of three or four students. Explain that they need to match each function with its inverse, being careful with one of the functions because it will only match if its domain is restricted. (They need to write their own restriction on the card and any restriction that occurs to the domain of the inverse.) After they have matched the cards they need to find the composite functions, using the functions and their inverses. (This will remind them of $ff^{-1}(x) = f^{-1}f(x) = x$). Lower-achieving students can be guided to match specific cards first, for example, those that emphasise asymptotes. As time allows, groups can check each other's work.

➢ Hand out a large piece of paper to each of the groups. Ask students, using graphical calculators and apps, to investigate the functions and their inverses. As they complete one function and its inverse, ask them to sketch the two functions on a set of axes. (They could use different colours for the function and for the inverse.) Encourage them to write down any observations they have.

➢ Lower-achieving students can be guided to investigate just the cards they were able to match.

➢ As students investigate, encourage them to draw on the axes of symmetry ($y = x$), mark asymptotes and highlight the symmetrical nature of self-inverse functions as they 'discover' them. Encourage students to think about the application of the axes of symmetry (how it can enable either function to be drawn when only one of them is seen) and the intersection of a function and its inverse and what this is. (See guidance above.)

➢ Bring the students together to discuss their findings. Make sure that they discuss $y = x$ being the line of reflection between a function and its inverse (and how this fact can enable either function to be drawn when only one of them is seen) and the connection with $ff^{-1}(x) = f^{-1}f(x) = x$. Also, discuss the intersection between a function and its inverse, and self-inverse functions being symmetrical about $y = x$. Discuss asymptotes, for example, for $g(x) = \dfrac{3}{x}$.

➢ As necessary, ask students to add to their sets of axes any detail they have missed.

➢ Students can now do Exercise 1.4.

➢ For question 5 they will need graph paper.

PLENARY (10 mins)

Equipment: Small pieces of paper

➢ Using exit tickets, ask the students to write down the main points of the lesson, using sketches to support what they have written. (See guidance above.)

Homework and answers: Resource sheets, homework and extension exercises can be found at the end of this chapter and in the downloadable materials. Answers can be found in the downloadable materials.

CHECKING PROGRESS	Use the exit tickets to check students' progress.

1 Functions

TOPIC:

1.5 Modulus functions

KEY WORDS:

modulus, absolute value

IGCSE MATHS PRIOR KNOWLEDGE:

Solve quadratic equations by factorising

Learning aims:

- Understand the relationship between $y = f(x)$ and $y = |f(x)|$, where $f(x)$ may be linear quadratic, cubic or trigonometric

Resources:

- Student Book: pages 20–22
- Mini whiteboards, or similar

Common mistakes and remediation:

Students might forget to consider solving both $ax + b = m$ and $ax + b = -m$. The definition of a modulus, or absolute value, needs to be clearly understood.

Useful tips:

Consider both the positive and negative case when solving modulus function equations.

Guidance:

The starter is revision of completing the square. This is needed for lesson 1.7. An example of a prompt card for a lower-achieving student would be, 'Think about reversing the $\sqrt{17}$ as a first step.'

For the main activity, twenty questions could be numeric or algebraic, for example, what is the absolute value of −5; what does $|x|$ mean, if $|x| = m$; what value does x have, if $f(x) = |2x - 4|$; what is the value of f(2); does $|x + 4| = x - 4$?

As the students work in pairs, encourage them to discuss their mathematics and reflect upon their work.

STARTER (5–10 mins)

➤ Set the students the problem below to review solving a quadratic equation by completing the square, then ask them to create their own problem. Lower-achieving students can be given prompt cards that explain the steps they need to take. Higher-achieving students could be encouraged to consider square roots involving decimals, fractions, etc. These can then be shared around the whole class. (See guidance above.)

A quadratic equation has the following solution:

$$-3 \pm \sqrt{17}$$

What is the equation?

MAIN LESSON ACTIVITY (40–45 mins)

➤ Discuss the concept of the modulus, or absolute value, of a real number (the size of the number, ignoring its sign) and the notation. This could be achieved, for instance, by considering a point q on a number line; $|q|$ being the distance of q from the origin, always positive.

The modulus is always the positive value, for example:

$$|-4| = 4, \quad |2| = 2, \quad \left|\frac{11}{2}\right| = \frac{11}{2}$$

➤ Introduce the strict definition: $|x| = \begin{cases} -x \text{ if } x < 0 \\ x \text{ if } x \geq 0 \end{cases}$ or $|x| = \sqrt{x^2}$

➤ Practise the concept of a modulus, or absolute value, using, for example, twenty questions. (See guidance above.)

➤ Discuss the modulus of a function and the notation. Discuss $|ax + b| = m$ and solving it for both $ax + b = m$ and $ax + b = -m$.

➤ Students think, pair, share whether the following equation is true:

$|5x - 3| = 5x + 3$

➤ Bring the students together to discuss their findings. For instance, discuss the use of an integer to prove the statement is not true, for example, using −2. Discuss that an absolute value cannot be negative; the right-hand number is:

$|5 \times (-2) - 3| \neq 5 \times -2 + 3$

$|-13| \neq -7$

➤ Discuss correcting the statement so that it is true.

➤ Discuss the alternative method for obtaining solutions to a modulus function by squaring each side of the equation. Ask students, in pairs, to investigate the solutions for the following equations:

$|4 - 7x| + 2 = 5$ $\left(\text{Answer: } \frac{1}{7} \text{ and } 1\right)$

$\left|\dfrac{3x+2}{x-5}\right| + 2 = -1$ (No solutions)

$|4x - 2| = 3x + 1$ $\left(\text{Answer: } \frac{1}{7} \text{ and } 3\right)$

$|x^2 - 2| = 3x - 1$ (Answer: 3.3, 0.79)

➤ Lower-achieving students can be given prompt cards that explain the steps they need to take, as in the starter.

➤ Higher-achieving students can be encouraged to consider modifying the equations to create, for instance, $|4x - 2| = |3x - 3|$. (See guidance above.)

➤ Bring the students together to discuss their findings. In particular, discuss why each of the second and third equations did not have two solutions.

➤ Students can now do Exercise 1.5.

➤ For question 3, students will need to solve quadratics by factorising.

PLENARY (10 mins)

Equipment: Mini whiteboards, or similar.

➤ Ask students 'show me' or similar questions to explore their understanding of the lesson. Cover all aspects of the learning outcome.

➤ For example, *Show me the solutions to this modulus function equation. Show me a modulus function equation that has no solutions.*

Homework and answers: Resource sheets, homework and extension exercises can be found at the end of this chapter and in the downloadable materials. Answers can be found in the downloadable materials.

CHECKING PROGRESS	Use the responses to the 'show me' questions to check students' progress.

TOPIC:

1.6 Graphs of $y = |f(x)|$ where $f(x)$ is linear

KEY WORDS:

None

IGCSE MATHS PRIOR KNOWLEDGE:

Sketch and recognise the graphs of linear and quadratic equations

Learning aims:

- Understand the relationship between $y = f(x)$ and $y = |f(x)|$, where $f(x)$ may be linear quadratic, cubic or trigonometric

Resources:

- Student Book: pages 23–25
- Graphical calculators and apps
- A1/flipchart paper

Common mistakes and remediation:

Students might only use positive x-values when plotting the graph of modulus function. Encourage them to choose both positive and negative x-values.

Useful tips:

The graph of a modulus function always has a vertical line of symmetry.

Reflect the part of the graph that is below the x-axis in the x-axis, to give the rest of the points that need plotting.

Guidance:

For the starter, do not label the graph.

For the main activity, if necessary, discuss, for example, $f(x) = |x|$, $f(x) = |ax + b|$, $f(x) = |ax + b| + c$, before students attempt the investigation.

For the main activity, if necessary, provide specific values for a, b and c to enable students to start the investigation.

During the first investigation, encourage students to remember how to draw the graph, creating a table of values, if necessary.

During the second investigation, students can modify the graphs they already have, to show the solutions to equations.

The second investigation could be combined with the first.

For the plenary, each student in the group mentions a different learning point. Then the points are summarised as, for example, a poster. The different learning points could be bulleted.

STARTER (5–10 mins)

➢ Draw the following graph of the absolute function $f(x) = |x|$.

➢ Ask the students, working in pairs, to discuss and write down as many observations as they can about the graph. (See guidance above.)

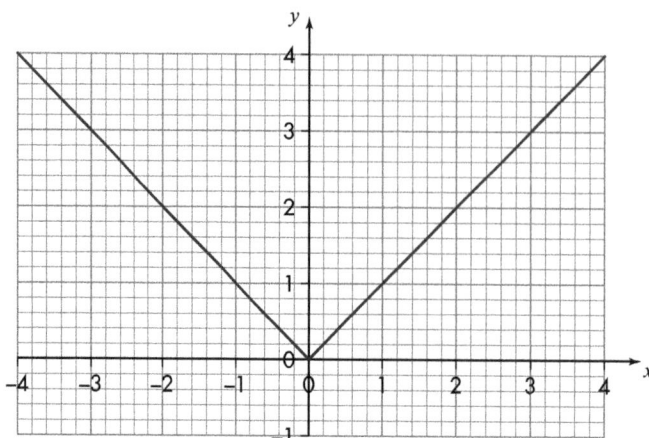

MAIN LESSON ACTIVITY (40–45 mins)

Equipment: Graphical calculators and apps

➢ Discuss students' findings from the starter. Discuss how the line is created from $y = x$ (reflecting the part of the graph that is below the x-axis in the x-axis, to give the rest of the points that need plotting) and the x-axis being a line of symmetry. Make sure it is understood to be the graph of the absolute function $f(x) = |x|$. (See guidance above.)

➢ Working in pairs, and using graphical calculators and apps, students investigate the graphs of the functions $f(x) = |x|$, $f(x) = |ax + b|$, $f(x) = |ax + b| + c$. Encourage them to consider how the graph of the function $f(x) = |x|$ is 'changed' by the addition of the constants. Also, encourage them to consider the lines of symmetry and the domains and ranges of the functions. (See guidance above.)

➢ Lower-achieving students could be given specific functions to draw, for example, functions using only positive and negative values for the constants. Higher-achieving students could be encouraged to investigate more complex functions, for example, fractional and decimal values for the constants, $f(x) = -|ax + b| + c$, x^n, trigonometgric functions.

➢ Bring students together to discuss their findings. Discuss the line of symmetry being at $y = 0$ and the value of c indicating a shift in the y-direction applied to the graph of the function.

➢ Working in pairs, and using graphical calculators and apps, students investigate solving equations of the form $|ax + b| + c = dx + e$. Encourage them to check their solutions algebraically. (See guidance above.)

➢ Lower-achieving students could be given specific equations to solve, for example, equations using only positive and negative values for the constants. Higher-achieving students could be encouraged to investigate solving more complex equations, for example, fractional and decimal values for the constants, $-|ax + b| + c = dx + e$, $|ax + b| = |dx + e|$.

➢ Bring students together to discuss their findings. Discuss the solutions to the equations being where the graphs intersect.

➢ Students can now do Exercise 1.6.

➢ Questions 1 to 3 involve drawing graphs of absolute functions.

➢ Question 4 is about recognising graphs of absolute functions.

➢ Questions 5 and 6 involve solving absolute function equations.

PLENARY (10 mins)

Equipment: A1/flipchart paper

➢ Working in groups of three or four, students produce a summary of the main learning points from the lesson, in a format of their own choice. (See guidance above.)

Homework and answers: Resource sheets, homework and extension exercises can be found at the end of this chapter and in the downloadable materials. Answers can be found in the downloadable materials.

CHECKING PROGRESS	Use the summary to check students' progress.

1 Functions

TOPIC:

1.7 Graphs of $y = |f(x)|$ where $f(x)$ is quadratic

KEY WORDS:

roots, turning point, stationary point

IGCSE MATHS PRIOR KNOWLEDGE:

Sketch and recognise the graphs of linear and quadratic equations

Learning aims:

- Understand the relationship between $y = f(x)$ and $y = |f(x)|$, where $f(x)$ may be linear quadratic, cubic or trigonometric

Resources:

- Student Book: pages 26–31
- Small pieces of paper
- Graphical calculators and apps

Common mistakes and remediation:

Lower-achieving students might have difficulties using negative values when exploring quadratic functions. Show students how negative values are substituted and manipulated.

Students might only use positive x-values when plotting the graph of modulus function. Encourage them to choose both positive and negative x-values.

Useful tips:

The graph of a modulus function always has a vertical line of symmetry.

Reflect the part of the graph that is below the x-axis in the x-axis, to give the rest of the points that need plotting.

Guidance:

For the starter, graphical calculators and apps could be used.

For the main activity, the first discussion needs enough detail for students to be able to access drawing the modulus of a quadratic function. Guidance on factorising and completing the square can be given, if necessary. Greater detail on working with quadratic functions occurs in Chapter 2.

During the first investigation encourage students to remember how to draw a graph, creating a table of values, if necessary.

During the second investigation, as time permits, suggest that students create some equations of their own that others can solve graphically. The activity provides an opportunity for students to draw/sketch the graphs of the modulus of a quadratic function without technology.

The second investigation could be combined with the first.

For the plenary, using exit tickets means students should hand in their 'tickets', with their responses to the task written on them, as they leave the class.

STARTER (5–10 mins)

➤ Working in pairs, students create their own graph of an absolute function, then give it to their partner to work out what the function is.

➤ The partner can then add an additional graph of an absolute function to the function they received, and pass it back to their partner, who should state what equation is now being represented and solve it, then checking it algebraically.

MAIN LESSON ACTIVITY (40–45 mins)

Equipment: Graphical calculators and apps

➢ Discuss drawing the graph of quadratic functions, for example, $f(x) = ax^2 + bx + c$. Discuss the parabolic shape of the graph of a quadratic function and the significant points – y-intercept, roots, minimum value, maximum value, turning point, stationary point. Discuss the line of symmetry. (See guidance above.)

➢ Display the following:

$f(x) = x^2 + 3x - 5$ $f(x) = 3x^2 - 2x - 7$ $f(x) = 4x^2 - 6x + 1$ $f(x) = x^2 - 3x - 5$

➢ Working in pairs, and using graphical calculators and apps, students investigate the graphs of the functions, identifying the significant points, and the graphs of the modulus of each function. Encourage them to consider how the graph of the function is 'changed' by the addition of the modulus.

➢ Lower-achieving students could be given 'hint' cards to remind them what to look for, for example, 'Look for the y-intercept first.' Higher-achieving students could be encouraged to investigate, for example, the addition of negative signs inside and outside the modulus.

➢ Bring the students together to discuss their findings. Discuss the minimum amount of information that is needed to draw the graph of the modulus of a function and how the method is very similar to drawing the graphs of the modulus of linear functions – reflecting the portion of the graph that is below the x-axis above the x-axis.

➢ Working in pairs, and using graphical calculators and apps, students investigate solving equations of the form $|ax^2 + bx + c| = k$, where k is a constant, by modifying the given functions. Ask them to then create their own equations, check they can solve them (using technology) and then give them to another pair of students to solve graphically but without the use of technology. Solutions are returned to be checked, using technology, if necessary. (See guidance above.)

➢ Lower-achieving students could be encouraged just to add, for example, integers as the constant. Higher-achieving students could be encouraged to investigate solving more complex equations, for example, fractional and decimal values for the constants, adding in brackets.

➢ Students can now do Exercise 1.7.

➢ Question 1 involves exploring the significant points of a curve and then sketching it.

➢ Questions 2 and 4 involve sketching the graph of an absolute quadratic function.

➢ Questions 3, 5 and 6 extend students' knowledge about completing the square, roots, stationary points and solutions to equations.

PLENARY (10 mins)

Equipment: Small pieces of paper

➢ Using exit tickets, ask the students to sketch the graph of the modulus of any quadratic function, highlighting the significant points, and then add any constant to their function, creating an equation, which they then solve graphically.

Homework and answers: Resource sheets, homework and extension exercises can be found at the end of this chapter and in the downloadable materials. Answers can be found in the downloadable materials.

CHECKING PROGRESS	Use the exit tickets to check students' progress.

Resource sheet 1.1

$fg(4) = -24$	$f(x) = 4 - 2x,$ $g(x) = x^2 - 2$
$f(x) = 4 - 2x$	$f^{-1}(x) = \dfrac{4-x}{2}$
$h(x) = 2x - 4$	$x = 2, h(x) = 0$
$f(x) = 4 - 2x$	$x = -1, f(x) = 6$
$g(x) = \dfrac{3}{x}$	$g^{-1}(x) = \dfrac{3}{x}$
$h^{-1}(x) = 4x - 7$	$h(x) = \dfrac{x+7}{4}$
$g(x) = (x - 2)^2$	$x = 2, g(x) = 0$
$h(x) = 2x - 4$	$h^{-1}(x) = \dfrac{x+4}{2}$
$x = -7, g(x) = -\dfrac{3}{7}$	$g(x) = \dfrac{3}{x}$
$f(x) = 3 + x,$ $g(x) = x^2 - 2$	$gf(x) = x^2 + 6x + 7$
$g(x) = 7x, x = \pm\sqrt{\dfrac{3}{7}}$	$g(x) = \dfrac{3}{x}$

$g(x) = x^3$	$x = 0, g(x) = 0$
$f(x) = 3 + x$	$f^{-1}(x) = x - 3$
$h(x) = 2x - 4$	$h(x) = 3x, x = -4$
$x = -3, h(x) = 1$	$h(x) = \dfrac{x+7}{4}$
$f(x) = 3 + x$	$f(x) = -\dfrac{1}{2}x, x = -2$
$gh(x) = \dfrac{3}{2x-4}$	$g(x) = \dfrac{3}{x}, h(x) = 2x - 4$
$hg(3) = 2$	$g(x) = (x-2)^2,$ $h(x) = \dfrac{x+7}{4}$

Resource sheet 1.2

$h(x) = \dfrac{x^2 + 7}{4}$	$h^{-1}(x) = \sqrt{4x - 7}$
$g(x) = \dfrac{1}{x + 1}$	$g^{-1}(x) = \dfrac{1}{x} - 1$
$h(x) = 7 - 2x$	$h^{-1}(x) = \dfrac{7 - x}{2}$
$g^{-1}(x) = \dfrac{7}{x} - 3$	$g(x) = \dfrac{7}{x + 3}$
$g(x) = \dfrac{3}{x}$	$g(x) = \dfrac{3}{x}$

Homework

1.1 Mappings, functions and notation

1   Identify the type of mapping for each function.

    a $f: x \rightarrow 3x - 1$ **b** $f(x) = x^2 + 2$ **c** $g(x) = 4^x$

    d $h(x) = 4 - 2x$ **e** $f: x \rightarrow \cos(x)$ **f** $f: x \rightarrow x^3 - 2x^2 + 2$

2   For each graph, work out the domain and range and decide whether it is the graph of a function.

a

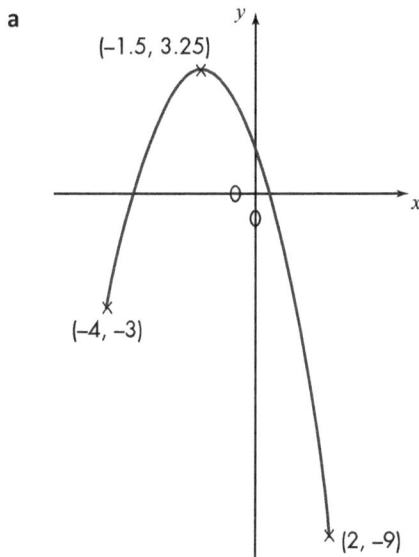

b

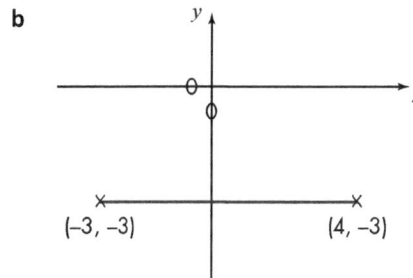

c

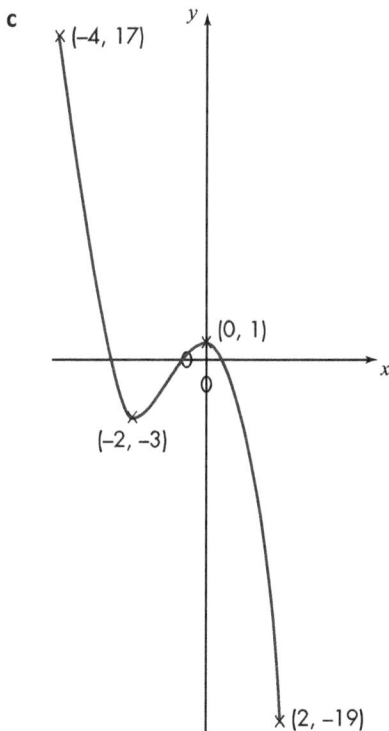

d

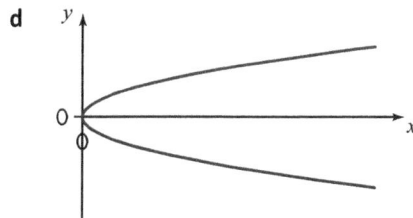

e

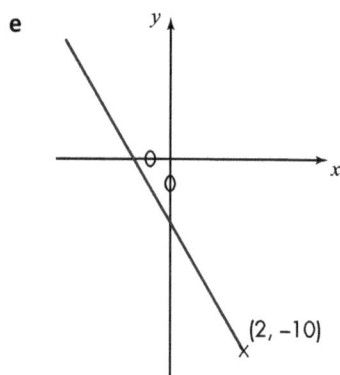

Point labeled: (2, –10)

3   Find the range for each function.

   a $f: x \rightarrow 3x - 4, -6 \leq x \leq 5$

   b $f(x) = x^3 - 3, -3.5 \leq x \leq 4$

   c $g(x) = (x - 3)^2 - 5, x \leq 0$

   d $g: x \rightarrow 4 - \dfrac{3}{x}, -4.2 \leq x \leq 8, x \neq 0$

   e $f(x) = \tan(x)$

4   Show that the equation $y^2 - 2 = 2$ does not represent a function.

5   Show that the area A of a square, when expressed as a function of the perimeter, is represented by $A = \dfrac{p^2}{16}$.

1   Functions

Homework

1.2 Composite functions

1   $f(x) = x^2 + 2$ and $g(x) = 4x - 2$. Find:

   a $fg(-3)$

   b $gf(-3)$

   c $g^2(5)$

   d $f^2(-2)$

   e $gf(x)$

   f $f^2(x)$

   g   Find the domain and range of $gf(x)$

2   $f(x) = (2x - 3)^2 - 4$ and $g(x) = \dfrac{3x + 2}{2x - 4}$.

   a   Find $fg(4)$.

   b   Find the domain and range of $fg(x)$.

3   $g(x) = 2x^2 + x$ and $h(x) = 3x - 2$. Solve for $gh(x) = 3$

4   $g(x) = ax^2 + 2$, $h(x) = 5 - 3x$ and $gh(x) = 52 - 60x + 18x^2$. Find the value of a.

5   $g(x) = bx + c$ $(b > 0)$ and $g^2(x) = 4x + 9$. Find the values of b and c.

6 You work 35 hours per week at a supermarket. You are paid an hourly salary of $12.50, plus 2% commission on the sales over $36 000.

Given the functions $f(x) = 0.02x$ and $g(x) = x - 36\,000$:

   a Form a composite function that represents your commission.

   b Find your total earnings for a week when the total sales were $52 000.

7 You manage a sports team. You want to purchase the team a new outfit from the local sports shop. You must pay 7.5% sales tax, if your purchase is over $500, and the sports shop charges a $15 delivery charge. (Delivery charges are tax free.)

   a Form a function that represents the price you pay for the outfit, if the purchase is above $500.

   b Form a function that represents the price paid to the sports shop before tax, after the delivery charge has been added on.

   c Using a composite function, show that the price paid for a $1500 outfit is $1 627.50.

   d If the state can collect taxes on delivery fees, work out the price you would pay for the outfit.

1   Functions

Homework

1.3 Inverse functions

1 For each of the following functions, find an expression for the inverse function.

   a $h(x) = (3x - 2)^2$ for $x \geq 1$ **b** $f(x) = (2x - 3)^2 + 4$ for $x < 0$

   c $h(x) = \dfrac{4x - 2}{3x}$, $x \neq 0$ **d** $g(x) = (x - 2)^3 - 2$

2 Using an example, explain why a function might not have an inverse.

3 For each of the following functions, decide if they have an inverse.

   a $f(x) = x^2 - 4$ **b** $\dfrac{3x - 1}{x^2}$ for $x \geq 1$

   c $\sqrt[3]{4x} + 2$ **d** $\dfrac{x^2 + 2x + 4}{3x}$ for $x \geq 4$

4 Using an example, explain what a self-inverse function is.

5 $h(x) = \dfrac{1}{3x + 2}$, for $1 \leq x \leq 4$

   a What is the range of h?

   b Find an expression for $h^{-1}(x)$ and write down its domain.

   c Solve $h^{-1}(x) = 2$

6 $g(x) = 3x - 2$, for $h(x) = x^3 - 2$

   a Find an expression for $g^{-1}(x)$.

   b Find an expression for $h^{-1}(x)$.

   c Show that $x = -514$ for $g^{-1}h^{-1}(x) = -2$

7 $f(x) = 2x^3 - 3$, for $x > 0$ and $g(x) = x - 1$

   a Find an expression for gf(x).

   b Find an expression for the inverse of $gf^{-1}(x)$.

Homework

1.4 Graphs of a function and its inverse

1   Copy this graph of a function $y = f(x)$ and sketch the graph of the function $y = f^{-1}(x)$. State the domain and range of $y = f^{-1}(x)$.

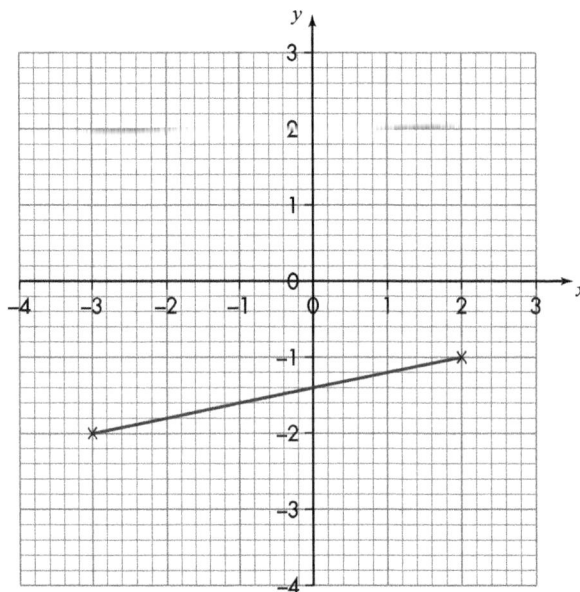

2   Copy this graph of a function $y = f(x)$ and sketch the graph of the function $y = f^{-1}(x)$. State the domain and range of $y = f^{-1}(x)$.

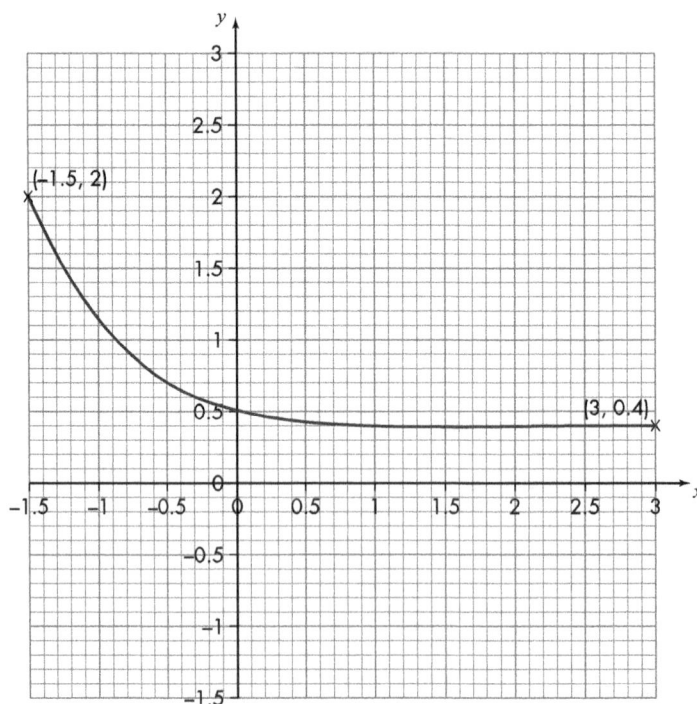

3 $f(x) = 5 - 2x$, for $-2 \leq x \leq 3$

On the same diagram, sketch the graphs of $f(x)$ and $f^{-1}(x)$.

State the domain and range of $f^{-1}(x)$.

4 $g(x) = (4 + x)^2 - 7$, for $-4 \leq x \leq 1$

On the same diagram, sketch the graphs of $g(x)$ and $g^{-1}(x)$.

State the domain and range of $g^{-1}(x)$.

Using the graphs, find the value of x for which $g(x) = g^{-1}(x)$.

5 On graph paper, draw coordinate axes for $0 \leq x \leq 1$ and $-2 \leq y \leq 1$, using the same scale on each axis.

Plot the graph of the function $h(x) = \dfrac{2}{x} - 4$.

By drawing a suitable line on the diagram, find the value of x for which $h(x) = h^{-1}(x)$.

By using algebra, check your answer.

6 $h: x \longrightarrow 3x^2 + rx + 30$. It can also be written $h: x \longrightarrow 3(x - 3)^2 + s$

a Find the values of r and s.

b What is the lowest point on the graph of the function h?

c Hence, state the range of the function h.

d Choose a suitable domain so that h^{-1} exists.

e Using your chosen domain, sketch the graphs of the functions h and h^{-1}.

f Find the value of x such that $h(x) = h^{-1}(x)$.

1 Functions

Homework

1.5 Modulus functions

1 Find the values of:

a $3 \times |-24 \times 25.6|$

b $\left| \dfrac{-32 \times 18 - 12}{25} \right| + 25.4$

c $|55 - 65| \times 8 + \dfrac{15}{4}$

d $\dfrac{2 \times |-57 \times 80.4|}{|29.4 - 52.5|}$

2 $f(x) = |3x - 4|$. Find the values of:

a $f(5)$

b $f(-7)$

c $f\left(\left| \dfrac{3}{7} \right| \right)$

d $f(-0.4)$

3 $f(x) = |x^2 - 9x - 2|$. Find the values of:

a $f(-5)$

b $f(5.4)$

c $f(2.9)$

d $f(0.24)$

4 By using examples, show that $|x| + |y| \geq |x + y|$

5 Solve:

a $|7 - 4x| = 13$

b $|5x + 3| - 2 = 8$

c $\left|\dfrac{3x - 3}{x}\right| = 5$

d $\left|\dfrac{2x + 7}{3x - 5}\right| + 7 = 8$

e $2|3x + 2| - 4 = 10$

f $3|2x - 3| + 6 = 12$

6 Solve:

a $|x^2 - 10| = 6$

b $|x^2 + 4| = 20$

c $|x^2 - 3x - 4| = 4 - x$

d $|x^2 + 3x| = 2x^2$

e $|x^2 - 2x - 2| = x + 2$

7 By using completing the square, or otherwise, solve:

a $|x^2 - 3x - 2| = x + 2$

b $|x^2 - 4x - 2| = 2x + 1$

c $|2x^2 - 11x + 2| = 3x + 2$

d $|x^2 - 9x - 2| = 2x + 2$

1 Functions

Homework

1.6 Graphs of $y = |f(x)|$ where f(x) is linear

1 Draw the graphs of:

a $f(x) = |x + 3|$

b $f(x) = |5x - 4|$

c $f(x) = |7 - x|$

d $f(x) = |5 - 8x|$

e $f(x) = -|3 - 7x|$

2 By using examples, explain why the graph of $y = |f(x)|$, where f(x) is linear, does not have an inverse.

3 Draw the graphs of:

a $f(x) = |x + 2| + 4$

b $f(x) = |3x - 2| - 3$

c $f(x) = |8 - x| + 4$

d $f(x) = |3 - 8x| + 1$

e $f(x) = -|6 - 2x| - 5$

4 For each graph, find the function $f(x) = |ax + b|$.

a

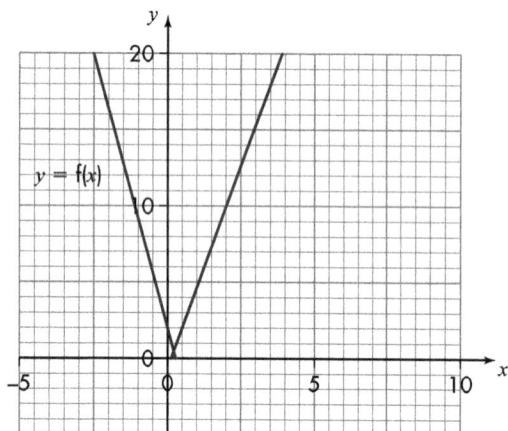

b

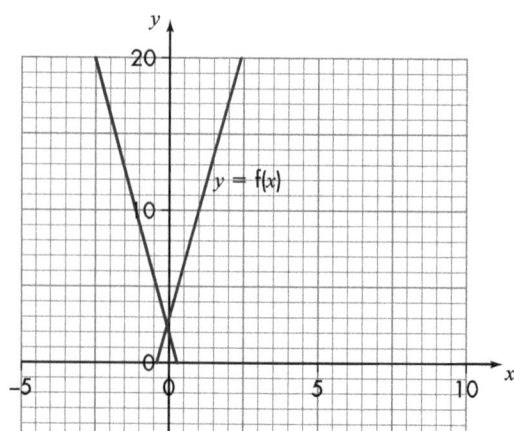

c

5. Solve the following equations by drawing appropriate graphs. Check your solutions algebraically. Compare your solutions with the answers from question 5 on homework sheet 1.5.

   a $|7 - 4x| = 13$ **b** $|5x + 3| - 2 = 8$

   c $|5x - 3| - 2 = 2x + 1$ **d** $2|3x + 2| - 4 = 10$

1 | Functions

Homework

1.7 Graphs of $y = |f(x)|$ where f(x) is quadratic

1. Draw a sketch of the graph of each modulus quadratic function and solve as directed, giving answers to 1 decimal place:

   a $f(x) = |x^2 + x - 2|$ Solve for $f(x) = 4$

   b $f(x) = |x^2 + 2x - 2|$ Solve for $f(x) = 4$

   c $f(x) = |x^2 - 5x + 4|$ Solve for $f(x) = 4$ Solve for $f(x) = 1.75$

   d $f(x) = |3x^2 - 6x - 4|$ Solve for $f(x) = 4$

2. $f(x) = |(x + 2)(x - 3)|$

   a The function has three solutions. What is the value of the function at this point?

   b The function has two solutions. What is the set of values for the function so this is true?

   c The function has four solutions. What is the set of values for the function so this is true?

3. $f(x) = |3x^2 - 2x - 4|$

   a Explain, using an appropriate value, at what point the number of solutions for the function changes from four to three, and then two.

   b What is the set of values for the function to have four solutions?

   c What is the set of values for the function to have two solutions?

4. $x^2 + px + q$ can be rewritten as $(x - 1.25)^2 - 0.8$

   a What are the values of p and q?

   b What are the coordinates of the roots and the stationary point of the function?

Extension

1.2 Composite functions

1 $f(x) = 3x$ and $g(x) = 3^x$. Find:

    a $gf(x)$ **b** $fg(x)$

2 If $f(x) = x - 3$ and $g(x) = \dfrac{1}{x+2}$. Find:

    a the domain of $gf(x)$ **b** the domain and range of $fg(x)$.

3 Complete the table using appropriate notation.

Functions	Composite	Domain	Range
f: $x \rightarrow 2x - 2$ g: $x \rightarrow x - 4$	fg		
f: $x \rightarrow x^2 + 2x$ g: $x \rightarrow x - 2$	gf		
g: $x \rightarrow 2x - 3$ h: $x \rightarrow \dfrac{1}{x}$	hg		
f: $x \rightarrow \sqrt{x} + 2$ g: $x \rightarrow x - 4$	fg		
f: $x \rightarrow x^3$ g: $x \rightarrow \sqrt{x+2}$	fg		

4 $q(x) = \sqrt{2x - 1}$ and $r(x) = 2x^2$.

    a Find the domain and range of $rq(x)$.

    b Explain why $qr(x)$ does not exist.

    c Using an example, show how $qr(x)$ could exist.

1 **Functions**

Extension

1.5 Modulus functions

1 $|ax + b| = m$ is solved for both $ax + b = m$ and $ax + b = -m$.

Determine how $|ax + b| = |cx + d|$ can be solved.

2 Solve these equations. For each one verify that your solutions are correct by substitution.

  a $|4x - 2| = |3x + 1|$

  b $|2x + 4| = |3x + 1|$

  c $|3x - 2| = |5x - 7|$

  d $|4x + 2| = |2x - 5|$

3 Investigate how $|4x - 2| = |3x + 1|$ can be solved graphically.

4 Sanjet is walking along the side of the road. Mohammed is watching him.

  If Sanjet walks forwards, Mohammed writes the distance down as a positive number.

  If Sanjet walks backwards, Mohammed writes the distance down as a negative number.

  Mohammed has recorded that Sanjet has walked p, then q, then r metres.

  a What formula represents the total distance that Sanjet has walked?

  b What does the formula $|p + q + r|$ represent?

  c How can the formula in part **a** give the same value as the formula in part **b**?

5 For each expression, using examples, determine how values change when the modulus notation is applied.

  a $\sin x$, $|\sin x|$

  b $\cos x$, $|\cos x|$

  c $\tan x$, $|\tan x|$

6 Investigate how $|\sin x|$, $|\cos x|$ and $|\tan x|$ appear graphically.

1   Functions

Extension

1.7 Graphs of $y = |f(x)|$ where f(x) is quadratic

1 Solve $|3x - 3| - |x^2 - 2x - 5| = 1$ graphically.

2 Solve $|2x - 4| = |3x^2 - 4x - 5| - 2$ graphically.

3 Draw the graph of the function $f(x) = |\sin x|$. Use degrees on the x-axis from $(0, 0)$ to $(2\pi, 0°)$

4 Draw the graph of the function $f(x) = |\cos x|$. Use degrees on the x-axis from $(0, 0)$ to $(\frac{3\pi}{2}, 0°)$

5 Draw the graph of the function $f(x) = -|\cos x|$. Use degrees on the x-axis from $(0, 0)$ to $(\frac{3\pi}{2}, 0°)$

6 Draw the graph of the function $f(x) = \left|\frac{1}{x}\right|$ with x-axis $(-6, 0)$ to $(6, 0)$

7 Investigate how to solve $|x^2 - 2x - 5| = |3x^2 - 4x - 5|$ graphically.

2 Quadratic Functions

TOPIC:

2.1 The quadratic function

KEY WORDS:

parabola, *y*-intercept, roots, minimum value, maximum value, turning point, stationary point

IGCSE MATHS PRIOR KNOWLEDGE:

Recognise, sketch and interpret graphs of quadratic equations

Identify and interpret roots, intercepts and turning points of quadratic functions graphically

Know the symmetrical property of a quadratic

Solve linear inequalities

Learning aims:

- Find the maximum or minimum value of the quadratic function f : $x \mapsto ax^2 + bx + c$ by completing the square or by differentiation
- Use the maximum or minimum value of f(x) to sketch the graph of y = f(x) or determine the range for a given domain

Resources:

- Student Book: pages 34–39
- Graphical calculators and apps
- Mini whiteboards, or similar

Common mistakes and remediation:

Lower-achieving students might have difficulties using negative values when exploring quadratic functions. Show students how negative values are substituted and manipulated.

Useful tips:

Sketch the graph of a quadratic function to help visualise it.

Guidance:

The starting point questions in the Student Book could be used as a short quiz before or instead of the starter activity.

For the starter, all students can be encouraged to consider the factorised form of their equations.

For the main activity, the first discussion will need additional examples if students have not created enough examples from the starter activity.

Consider questions that you could ask students as they work in groups, particularly those that encourage students to explain and justify their thinking. Also, encourage students to discuss their mathematics and reflect upon their work.

STARTER (5–10 mins)

➢ Display this question.

> A quadratic equation has two roots, $x = 2$ and $x = 4$.
>
> What could the graph look like?

➢ Encourage students to sketch the graphs, without a table of values. Lower-attaining students can be guided to consider the factorised form of the equation as a first step. Higher-attaining students can be guided to consider equations of the form $rx^2 - 6rx + 8r$ and $- rx^2 - 6rx + 8r$, where r is a real number. (See guidance above.)

➢ At the end of the activity, as time allows, students share their equations and discuss differences between them.

MAIN LESSON ACTIVITY (40–45 mins)

Equipment: Graphical calculators and apps

➢ Using examples from the starter, discuss the parabolic shape of the graph of a quadratic function and the significant points – *y*-intercept, roots, minimum value, maximum value, turning point, stationary point. Discuss the line of symmetry and the difference between $x^2 - 6x + 8$ and $-x^2 - 6x + 8$. Discuss the connection between $x^2 - 6x + 8$, and $rx^2 - 6rx + 8r$ and $-rx^2 - 6rx + 8r$, where r is a real number, including how the maximum and minimum values change but the roots stay the same. (See guidance above.)

➢ Discuss the general form of the quadratic function f(x) = $ax^2 + bx + c$, including the value of c giving the *y*-axis intercept.

- Students work in pairs. Explain that they need to use graphical calculators and apps to explore the graphs shown on page 34 of the Student Book, in each case writing down the coordinates of the significant points and the equation of the line of symmetry. Explain that they can explore further by making changes to the graphs, writing down any observations they have. Explain that they need to consider how they are restricting the domain, and the range that is produced, and the four questions, expressing their findings algebraically. Lower-attaining students can be given hint cards to support changing the graphs, for example, 'Change the coefficient of x^2'. Higher-attaining students can be encouraged to observe the changes that occur as the different parts of the graphs are changed consistently.

- Bring the groups of students together to discuss their findings. Make sure all four questions are discussed, with students expressing the answers to the third and fourth questions algebraically: sum of the roots is $-\dfrac{b}{a}$ and product of the roots is $\dfrac{c}{a}$.

- Discuss the two rules using any quadratic function, $ax^2 + bx + c$. Vary the values of all three constants to show how the rules change algebraically.

- Students can now do Exercise 2.1.

- Question 1 provides an opportunity for students to draw and label the significant points of the graph of a quadratic function, as well as labelling the line of symmetry and determining the range.

- Question 2 provides an opportunity for students to find the equations of quadratic graphs from sketches. Students should be encouraged to explore both using the roots and applying the two rules: sum of the roots is $-\dfrac{b}{a}$ and product of the roots is $\dfrac{c}{a}$. (One method provides a check for the other.) Students can be encouraged to substitute the minimum/maximum point to check whether answers are correct. To support part **c** students could consider assuming $a = 1$ and then adjusting the equation, using the minimum point; for example, $x^2 - 4x \rightarrow 2^2 - 4 \times 2 \neq -24 \rightarrow 6 \times (2^2 - 4 \times 2) = -24 \rightarrow 6x^2 - 24x$.

- Questions 3 to 8 provide opportunities for students to use the properties of quadratic graphs and the two rules. Question 7 could be developed by students exploring whether more than one form of the equation or graph is possible.

- Lower-achieving students can be given hint cards to support them, for example, in question 4a: 'Use the product of roots', 4b: 'Sketch the graph', 4c: 'Use substitution', 4d: 'Use substitution'.

- In all questions students can be encouraged to sketch the graphs.

PLENARY (10 mins)

Equipment: Mini whiteboards, or similar

- Ask the students 'show me' or similar questions to explore their understanding of the lesson. Questions can be in word form or diagrammatic/graphical. Cover all the learning aims.

- For example: *Show me a graph with roots 0 and 4. How can $x^2 - 6x$ be changed so that it has a maximum point?*

Homework and answers: Resource sheets, homework and extension exercises can be found at the end of this chapter and in the downloadable materials. Answers can be found in the downloadable materials.

CHECKING PROGRESS	Use the immediate feedback from the plenary to check students' progress

2 Quadratic Functions

TOPIC:

2.2 Completing the square

KEY WORDS:

completing the square

IGCSE MATHS PRIOR KNOWLEDGE:

Identify and interpret roots, intercepts and turning points of quadratic functions graphically

Learning aims:

- Find the maximum or minimum value of the quadratic function $f(x) = ax^2 + bx + c$ by completing the square
- Solve quadratic equations for real roots

Resources:

- Student Book: pages 39–42
- Resource sheet 2.1
- A1/flipchart paper
- Interactive whiteboard (optional)

Common mistakes and remediation:

Lower-achieving students might have difficulties using negative values when exploring quadratic functions. Show students how negative values are substituted and manipulated.

Students might have difficulty manipulating completing the square. Emphasise the three basic steps shown on page 39 of the Student Book.

Useful tips:

When reversing completing the square, remember that there could be a value for the coefficient of a outside the bracket: $a(x - 1) - 4$, before the procedure starts.

Guidance:

For the starter, lower-achieving students can focus on positive coefficients of x.

For the starter, think, pair, share involves students thinking through the problem on their own for a short while, for example, one to two minutes, then sharing their conclusions with a partner. After this, the pair of students share their ideas with a wider group.

For the main activity, in the first discussion include additional functions, as necessary, to develop students' understanding.

To support the card activity, if necessary, allow time for more direct instruction on the method of completing the square.

The card activity could be presented on A1/flipchart paper or interactive whiteboard, with supporting comments from the students.

For the main activity, if necessary, allow time for more direct instruction on solving equations by completing the square. This section of the main activity could be added into the original instructions for the card activity, if deemed appropriate.

Consider questions that you could ask students as they work in groups, such as those that encourage students to explain and justify their thinking. Also, encourage students to discuss their mathematics and reflect upon their work.

For the plenary, the problems that students create could be collected in (instead of sharing them immediately), checked and then distributed in another lesson for further consolidation and practice.

STARTER (5–10 mins)

➤ Display these functions.

$f(x) = x^2$ $f(x) = (x - 2)^2$ $f(x) = (4 - x)^2$ $f(x) = -(x - 2)^2$

$f(x) = -x^2 + 3$ $f(x) = (x - 1)^2 + 3$ $f(x) = -(3 + x)^2 - 2$

➤ Ask students to sketch the graph of each function and write down the coordinates of the turning point (minimum or maximum point). Lower-achieving students can be encouraged to use a table of values. (See guidance above.)

➤ Ask students to think, pair, share, explaining the relationship between the turning point (minimum or maximum point) and each function. (See guidance above.)

MAIN LESSON ACTIVITY (40–45 mins)

Equipment: Resource sheet 2.1, A1/flipchart paper or interactive whiteboard

➤ Discuss students' findings from the starter activity. Using, for example, $f(x) = (x - 1)^2 + 3$, discuss where the turning point (minimum point) can be seen in the function. (See guidance above.)

➤ Discuss the algebraic form $f(x) = (x + p)^2 \pm q$ as completing the square and ask where the turning point (minimum or maximum point) can be seen in the function. Discuss the turning point (minimum or maximum point) being equivalent to $(-p, q)$.

➤ Hand out sets of cards to groups of three or four students. Explain that they will be matching sets of cards illustrating completing the square: linking expression, form $(x + p)^2 \pm q$ and turning point. Explain that they need to label the turning point as a maximum or minimum point. (Allow them to match as many cards as they can in the time available.) Lower-attaining students can be guided to try certain types of cards first, for example, without a coefficient of x^2. Higher-attaining students could create their own sets of cards. (See guidance above.)

➤ At the end of the activity, allow time for two students from each group to move around the classroom to look at other groups' answers while two students remain to justify their answers.

➤ Bring the groups of students together to discuss their sets of cards. Discuss reversing the procedure – going from completing the square back to the original equation. Discuss the implications of the last set of cards that just use algebra. (The 'completing the square' form provides an algebraic solution to finding the values of the coefficients, and constant, in $ax^2 + bx + c$, and the turning point, when certain information is known.)

➤ Ask students to return to their cards and change the expressions into equations set equal to 0 and then continue the method to solve them. One of the equations cannot be solved. As time allows, discuss this anomaly. (See guidance above.)

➤ Students can now do Exercise 2.2.

➤ Questions 1 to 4 provide opportunities to practise completing the square and finding turning points.

➤ Questions 5 to 8 provide opportunities to use the skills from questions 1 to 4 in problem-solving contexts.

➤ Questions 5 and 7 require students to understand reversing the procedure – going from completing the square back to the original equation.

➤ Lower-attaining students can be given hint cards to support completing the square in steps, for example: 'Ignore the constant. Concentrate on $ax^2 + bx$.'

PLENARY (10 mins)

➤ Ask students to write their own equations that they can solve by completing the square, then share them with another student to solve.

➤ Ask the students to write a problem-solving question, similar to question 5 in Exercise 2.2, that they can solve and share with another student to solve.

Homework and answers: Resource sheets, homework and extension exercises can be found at the end of this chapter and in the downloadable materials. Answers can be found in the downloadable materials.

CHECKING PROGRESS	Use the written problems from the plenary to check students' progress.

TOPIC:
2.3 The quadratic formula

KEY WORDS:
factorising, discriminant

IGCSE MATHS PRIOR KNOWLEDGE:
Recognise, sketch and interpret graphs of quadratic equations

Learning aims.
- Know the conditions for f(x) = 0 to have:

  (i) two real roots, (ii) two equal roots, (iii) no real roots
- Solve quadratic equations for real roots

Resources:
- Student Book: pages 43–47
- Resource sheet 2.2
- Mini whiteboards, or similar
- A1/flipchart paper
- Graphic calculators and apps

Common mistakes and remediation:
Lower-achieving students might have difficulties using negative values when exploring quadratic functions. Show students how negative values are substituted and manipulated.

Students might have difficulty manipulating the quadratic formula or the discriminant. Emphasise the need to match up the coefficients a and b, and the constant c, in a quadratic equation carefully with the correct letters in the formula or discriminant. Emphasise the need to have the division line and the square-root symbol the correct length.

Useful tips:
When manipulating the quadratic formula, or discriminant, use negative values and inequalities carefully.

Guidance:
For the starter, the questions allow students to answer in word or diagrammatic/graphical form.

For the main activity, as students work in groups, consider questions that will encourage them to determine the relationship between the discriminant and the solutions to the equations. (Do not mention the term 'discriminant' at this point.)

To support the card activity, if necessary, allow time for more direct instruction on using the formula.

The card activity could be presented on A1/flipchart paper with supporting comments from students.

For the main activity, if necessary, allow time for more direct instruction on using the three statements about the discriminant in context.

Consider questions that you could ask students as they work in groups, particularly those that encourage students to explain and justify their thinking. Also, encourage students to discuss their mathematics and reflect upon their work.

STARTER (5–10 mins)
Equipment: mini whiteboards, or similar

➢ Ask students 'show me' or similar questions to review their understanding of the properties of quadratic functions. Questions can be in word form or diagrammatic/graphical.

➢ For example: *Show me an equation that would or could represent this graph* (a sketch of a quadratic function is shown, without numbers on the axes). *Give me the values of the x and y intercepts of y = (x − 4)(x + 3). How do you know? Show me a quadratic function that has a turning point at (4, −3). Now show me in a different form.* (See guidance above.)

MAIN LESSON ACTIVITY (40–45 mins)

Equipment: Resource sheet 2.2, A1/flipchart paper, graphic calculators and apps

➤ Hand out sets of cards to groups of three or four students. Explain that they will be matching sets of cards based on the quadratic formula: equations, formulae, roots. (The blank cards will be used after the feedback about the activity.) Explain that they can use graphical calculators and apps to see what each equation looks like graphically. Ask them to write down any observations they have. (As students match the cards, they should be encouraged to consider any connection there might be between the formula and solutions.) (See guidance above.)

➤ At the end of the activity, allow time for two students from each group to move around the classroom to look at other groups' answers while two students remain to justify their answers.

➤ Bring the groups of students together to discuss their sets of cards. Discuss the expression under the square root sign, the discriminant ($b^2 - 4ac$) (in relation to the general form of the function $ax^2 + bx + c$) and any connection there is between it and the solutions. Discuss the three statements:

$b^2 - 4ac > 0$, the equation has 2 distinct real roots

$b^2 - 4ac = 0$, the equation has 2 equal (1 distinct) real roots

$b^2 - 4ac < 0$, the equation has no real roots.

➤ Ask students to write the statements on their blank cards and then match them to each set of three cards.

➤ Bring the groups of students together to discuss using the statements in context, for example, $x^2 + 3x + g - 2 = 0$ has two different roots. What is the range of values for g? (See guidance above.)

➤ Students can now do Exercise 2.3.

➤ Question 1 provides opportunities for students to practise using the formula.

➤ Lower-attaining students can be given, for instance, extra support on matching the coefficients and constant in a quadratic equation with the letters in the formula.

➤ Questions 2 to 6 provide an opportunity to use the three statements about the discriminant in context.

PLENARY (10 mins)

➤ Ask students to write down a quadratic function, and sketch its graph, for each of the three statements about the discriminant.

Homework and answers: Resource sheets, homework and extension exercises can be found at the end of this chapter and in the downloadable materials. Answers can be found in the downloadable materials.

CHECKING PROGRESS	Use the written functions, and the sketches of their graphs, from the plenary to check students' progress.

TOPIC:

2.4 Intersection of a line and a curve

KEY WORDS:

None

IGCSE MATHS PRIOR KNOWLEDGE:

Identify and interpret roots, intercepts and turning points of quadratic functions graphically

Learning aims:

- Know the conditions for f(x) = 0 to have:

  (i)   two real roots, (ii) two equal roots, (iii) no real roots and the related conditions for a given line to: (i) intersect a given curve, (ii) be a tangent to a given curve, (iii) not intersect a given curve

- Solve quadratic equations for real roots

Resources:

- Student Book: pages 47–49
- Graphic calculators and apps

Common mistakes and remediation:

Lower-achieving students might have difficulties using negative values when exploring quadratic functions. Show students how negative values are substituted and manipulated.

Students might have difficulty manipulating the quadratic formula or the discriminant. Emphasise the need to match up the coefficients *a* and *b*, and the constant *c*, from a quadratic equation carefully, with the correct letters in the formula or discriminant. Emphasise the need to have the division line and the square root symbol the correct length, if the formula is being used.

Students might have difficulty understanding and solving inequalities, for example, dividing or multiplying by a negative value and interpreting the result. Support students with understanding the context and graphical representation of results.

Useful tips:

When using the discriminant, solving a quadratic equation by completing the square or the quadratic formula, use negative values and inequalities carefully. (Using brackets with negative values can be helpful.)

When manipulating inequalities consider the context of the problem.

Guidance:

For the main activity, as the students work in pairs, consider questions that will encourage the students to determine the relationship between the discriminant and the intersection.

For the main activity, the first problem that is discussed is Example 10 from page 48 of the Student Book: $m > -3$ or $m < -7$. The second problem: $2.5 - \sqrt{18} < q < 2.5 + \sqrt{18}$ ($-1.74 < q < 6.74$ to 3 s. f.) The two problems allow students to investigate the discriminant being < 0 (the range being outside the two solutions) and the discriminant being > 0 (the range being between the two solutions). If students are able, allow the problems to be solved without additional discussion on the use of the discriminant.

STARTER (5–10 mins)

➤ Display these equations, but not the answers.

$x^2 - 7x = 2x - 3$ $2x^2 - 3x + 4 = x + 2$ $x^2 + 12x + 44 = 1 - x$

(Answers: (0.347, 8.65)   (1)   (No solutions))

➤ Ask students to solve the equations, stating the number of solutions and the value of the discriminant. As necessary, remind students about the three discriminant statements.

MAIN LESSON ACTIVITY (40–45 mins)

Equipment: Graphic calculators and apps

➤ Students work in pairs. Explain that they need to investigate how to represent the three equations from the starter graphically, using graphic calculators and apps and confirming their own solutions. Explain that they need to write down any observations they have. (Encourage students to consider representing graphically the line, curve and the quadratic equation they solve.) (See guidance above.)

➤ Bring students together to discuss their findings. Discuss how the line and the curve intersected with each other. Discuss the tangent to the curve. Discuss the solutions of the quadratic equation they solved or tried to solve and how these are the same as the x-coordinates of the points of intersection. Discuss the use of the discriminant ($b^2 - 4ac$) in relation to the general form of the function $ax^2 + bx + c$, giving information about how curves and lines intersect and the number of solutions.

➤ Display this problem:

The line $y = mx - 2$ intersects the curve $y = x^2 - 5x - 1$ at two distinct points. Find the range of values of m.

➤ Discuss the use of the discriminant ($b^2 - 4ac$) in relation to the general form of the function $ax^2 + bx + c$, in solving the problem. (See guidance above.)

➤ Students work in pairs to solve the problem. Explain that they need to investigate ways of representing their solution graphically, using graphic calculators and apps. Encourage students to consider substituting their solutions for m back into the problem and then representing the information graphically. Encourage them to interpret the inequality graphically by plotting the curve and shading their solution. (See guidance above.)

➤ Display this problem:

The line $y = 2.5x - 0.5$ does not cross the curve $y = 3x^2 + qx + 1$. What is the range of values for q?

➤ Discuss the use of the discriminant ($b^2 - 4ac$) in relation to the general form of the function $ax^2 + bx + c$, in solving the problem. (See guidance above.)

➤ Students work in pairs to solve the problem. Explain that they need to investigate ways of representing their solution graphically, using graphic calculators and apps. Encourage students to consider substituting their solutions for q back into the problem and then representing the information graphically. Encourage them to interpret the inequality graphically by plotting the curve and shading their solution. (See guidance above.)

➤ Bring students together to discuss their solutions to the problems. Discuss how they represented the inequality graphically. Discuss the discriminant being > 0 (the range being outside the two solutions) and the discriminant being < 0 (the range being between the two solutions).

➤ Students can now do Exercise 2.4.

➤ Questions 1 to 3 provide opportunities for investigating tangents.

➤ Questions 4 and 5 provide opportunities for investigating two distinct solutions.

➤ Questions 6 and 7 provide opportunities for investigating no solutions.

PLENARY (5–10 mins)

➤ Ask students to explain briefly what they have understood from the lesson to another person, whom they did not work with on the problems.

Homework and answers: Resource sheets, homework and extension exercises can be found at the end of this chapter and in the downloadable materials. Answers can be found in the downloadable materials.

CHECKING PROGRESS	Use the verbal feedback to partners in the plenary to check students' progress.

2 Quadratic Functions

TOPIC:

2.5 Quadratic inequalities

KEY WORDS:

None

IGCSE MATHS PRIOR KNOWLEDGE:

Solve linear inequalities

Learning aims:
- Find the solution set for a quadratic inequality either graphically or algebraically
- Know the conditions for f(x) = 0 to have:

  (i) two real roots (ii) two equal roots (iii) no real roots
- Solve quadratic equations for real roots

Resources:
- Student Book: pages 50–52
- Graphic calculators and apps

Common mistakes and remediation:

Lower-achieving students might have difficulties using negative values when exploring quadratic functions. Show students how negative values are substituted and manipulated.

Students might have difficulty manipulating the quadratic formula. Emphasise the need to match up the coefficients **a** and **b**, and the constant **c**, from a quadratic equation carefully, with the correct letters in the formula. Emphasise the need to have the division line and the square root symbol the correct length in the formula.

Students might have difficulty understanding and solving inequalities, for example, dividing or multiplying by a negative value and interpreting the result. Support students in understanding context and graphical representation of results.

Useful tips:

When solving a quadratic inequality by completing the square or the quadratic formula, use negative values and inequalities carefully.

When manipulating inequalities consider the context of the problem.

Guidance:

For the starter, encourage students to use two different colours, or similar, for shading the inequalities. The activity is about shading the curve rather than the appropriate values on the x-axis.

For the main activity, when students first work in pairs, allow them to experiment with how they can represent the solutions on a number line. Four solutions are: $x < 1$ and $x > 8$, $1 < x < 8$, $-1 < x < 4$, $x < -1$ and $x > 4$.

For the main activity, when students modify the inequalities, remind them that they need to ask for solutions be shown on a number line as well.

For the main activity, the modulus quadratic inequality solution is $0 \leq x \leq 1$ and $4 \leq x \leq 5$. As necessary, more examples of this type of inequality could be given to enrich student comprehension.

For the main activity, when students modify the modulus quadratic inequality, remind them that they need to ask for solutions be shown on a number line as well.

STARTER (5–10 mins)

➤ Display these functions and inequalities.

$f(x) = x^2 - 7x - 8$ $g(x) = 3x - x^2 + 4$

$x^2 - 7x - 8 > 0$ $x^2 - 7x - 8 < 0$ $3x - x^2 + 4 > 0$ $3x - x^2 + 4 < 0$

Ask students to draw the graphs of the functions and then shade them to represent the inequalities. (See guidance above.)

MAIN LESSON ACTIVITY (40–45 mins)

Equipment: Graphic calculators and apps

➤ Students work in pairs. Explain that they need to solve the four inequalities, using their shading of the inequalities to support how they could represent their solution on a number line. (See guidance above.)

➤ Bring students together to discuss their solutions. Discuss the four different solutions to the inequalities and how students represented them on a number line. Discuss the difference between representing $<$ and $\leq$ and $>$ and $\geq$ on the number line.

➤ Students work in pairs. Ask them to modify the four original inequalities (so that there are additions to the right-hand side of the inequality), check they can solve them and then pass them to another pair of students to solve them. Solutions are returned to be checked. (Students can be encouraged to modify the inequalities so that they can, and cannot, be factorised. They can use graphical calculators and apps to support the process of modifying/checking their solutions). Lower-achieving students can be guided, for example, to just use integers to modify the inequalities. Higher-attaining students can be guided, for example, to use any number and brackets. (See guidance above.)

➤ Display this inequality.

$|x^2 - 5x + 2| \leq 2$

➤ Students work in pairs. Explain that they need to solve the inequality, being careful to consider how they will represent the solution on a number line. (See guidance above.)

➤ Bring students together to discuss their solutions. Discuss modifying inequalities to include an absolute (modulus) value. Discuss representing the solution on a number line.

➤ Students work in pairs. Ask them to modify the absolute quadratic inequality, check they can solve it themselves and then pass it to another pair of students to solve it. (Students can be encouraged to modify the inequalities so that they can, and cannot, be factorised. They can use graphical calculators and apps to support the process of modifying and checking their solutions). Lower-achieving students can be guided, for example, to just use integers to modify the inequalities. Higher-achieving students can be guided, for example, to use any number and brackets. (See guidance above.)

➤ Students can now do Exercise 2.5.

➤ Questions 1 and 2 provide opportunities for solving quadratic inequalities.

➤ Questions 3 provides opportunities for solving modulus quadratic inequalities.

➤ Questions 4 and 5 provide opportunities for problem solving and extension.

PLENARY (10 mins)

➤ Ask the students to explain briefly what they have understood from the lesson to another person, who they did not work with on the problems. Alternatively, use a quick quiz to cover the main learning points from the lesson.

Homework and answers: Resource sheets, homework and extension exercises can be found at the end of this chapter and in the downloadable materials. Answers can be found in the downloadable materials.

CHECKING PROGRESS	Use the verbal feedback to partners in the plenary to check students' progress. Alternatively, use the responses from the quick quiz to check students' progress.

Resource sheet 2.1

Completing the square

$x^2 + 4x + 3$	$(x + 2)^2 - 1$	$(-2, -1)$
$x^2 + 5x + 1$	$(x + 2.5)^2 - 5.25$	$(-2, -5.25)$
$2x^2 - 3x$	$2(x - 0.75)^2 - 1.125$	$(0.75, -1.125)$
$12x - x^2 + 4$	$-(x - 6)^2 + 40$	$(6, 40)$
$3x^2 + 6x - 7$	$3(x + 1)^2 - 10$	$(-1, -10)$
$3x - 2x^2 - 4$	$-2(x - 0.75)^2 - 2.875$	$(0.75, -2.875)$
$ax^2 + bx + c$	$a\left(x + \dfrac{b}{2a}\right)^2 + c - \dfrac{b^2}{4a}$	$\left(-\dfrac{b}{2a}, c - \dfrac{b^2}{4a}\right)$

Resource sheet 2.2

The quadratic formula

$x^2 + 5x - 2 = 0$	$x = \dfrac{-5 \pm \sqrt{5^2 - 4 \times 1 \times -2}}{2 \times 1}$	$x = 0.37$ $x = -5.37$
$x^2 - 8x + 16 = 0$	$x = \dfrac{8 \pm \sqrt{(-8)^2 - 4 \times 1 \times 16}}{2 \times 1}$	$x = 4$ $x = 4$
$x^2 + 5x + 8 = 0$	$x = \dfrac{-5 \pm \sqrt{5^2 - 4 \times 1 \times 8}}{2 \times 1}$	No solutions
$3x - 5x^2 - 8 = 0$	$x = \dfrac{3 \pm \sqrt{3^2 - 4 \times -5 \times -8}}{2 \times -5}$	No solutions
$-9x - 3x^2 + 1 = 0$	$x = \dfrac{-9 \pm \sqrt{(-9)^2 - 4 \times -3 \times 1}}{2 \times -3}$	$x = -3.11$ $x = 0.11$
$2x - 4x^2 + 8 = 0$	$x = \dfrac{-2 \pm \sqrt{2^2 - 4 \times -4 \times 8}}{2 \times -4}$	$x = -1.19$ $x = 1.69$

2 Quadratic Functions

Homework

2.1 The quadratic function

1   Draw a graph of each function. Mark the coordinates of the significant points. Draw and label the line of symmetry and determine the range.

   a $y = -2x^2$, for $-4 \leq x \leq 4$

   b $y = x^2 - 3x$, for $-3 \leq x \leq 6$

   c $y = -2.5x^2 - 1.5x$, for $-2 \leq x \leq 2$

   d $y = -2x^2 - 3x + 2$, for $-2.5 \leq x \leq 1$

2   Each sketch shows the roots of the quadratic equation and the coordinates of the minimum or maximum point. For each one, work out the equation of the graph.

   a
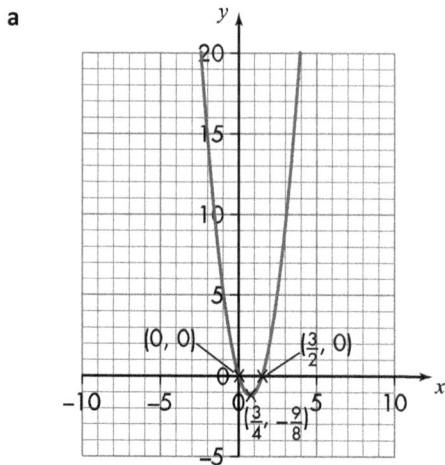

   b
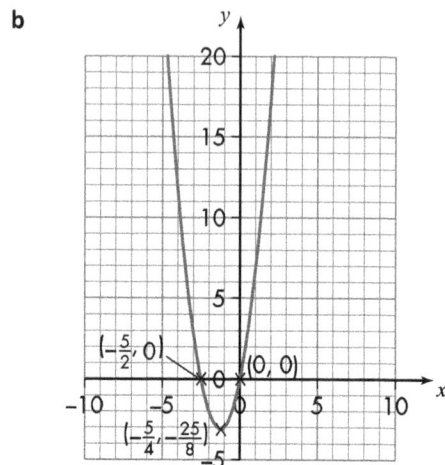

   c
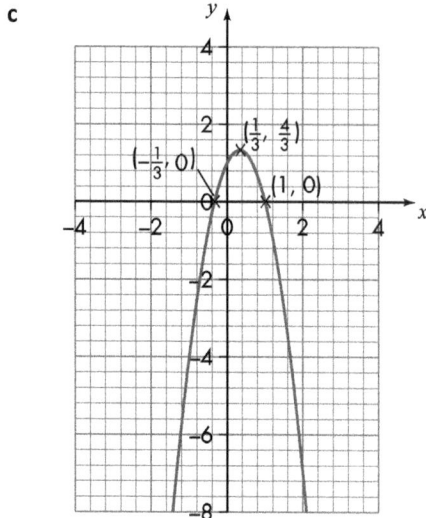

3   Here are some properties of quadratic graphs. In each case, use the information to work out the equation of the graph.

   a   Roots $x = 0$ and $x = 3$, minimum point $(1.5, -2.25)$

   b   Roots $x = -2$ and $x = 3$, minimum point $(0.5, -6.25)$

   c   One root $x = -3$

   d   Roots $x = -\dfrac{5}{3}$ and $x = 1$, maximum point $\left(-\dfrac{1}{3}, \dfrac{16}{3}\right)$

4   The graph of $y = x^2 - 4x + c$ crosses the x-axis at $(5, 0)$ and $(-1, 0)$.

   a   What is the value of c?

   b   What is the equation of the line of symmetry?

   c   What are the coordinates of the y-intercept?

   d   What are the coordinates of the minimum point?

5   The graph of $y = -x^2 + bx + c$ crosses the x-axis at $(1, 0)$ and $(-4, 0)$.

    a   What is the value of b?

    b   What is the value of c?

    c   What are the coordinates of the y-intercept?

    d   What are the coordinates of the maximum point?

6   One root of the graph of $y = x^2 + bx - 4$ is $x = 2$.

    a   What is the value of b?

    b   What are the coordinates of the minimum point?

7   One root of the graph of $y = -3x^2 + x + c$ is $x = 1$.

    a   Work out the other root.

    b   Work out the value of c.

2   Quadratic Functions

Homework

2.2 Completing the square

1   State whether the turning point is a maximum or minimum point and give its coordinates. When y takes the value of zero decide if the equation has any solution.

    a $y = (x + 2)^2 - 3$ **b** $y = (x - 3)^2 - 5$ **c** $y = (-2 - x)^2 + 3$

    d $y = 3(x + 3)^2 - 6$ **e** $y = -3(x + 3)^2$ **f** $y = -(1 - 2x)^2 - 3$

2   Convert each of these expressions to the format $(x + a)^2 \pm b$ and state the coordinates of the turning point of its graph.

    a $x^2 - 4x + 2$ **b** $2x^2 - 3x$ **c** $x^2 + 8x + 6$

    d $5x - x^2 - 11$ **e** $-8x - 16x^2 - 4$ **f** $ax^2 + bx + c$

3   Change each of the expressions in question 2 into an equation by setting it equal to 0 and solve by completing the square or factorising. Clearly state if there is no solution.

4   $f(x) = 3x^2 + 8x - 6$

    a   Rewrite the function in the form $f(x) = a(x + p)^2 + q$, then find the values of a, p and q.

    b   What are the coordinates of the turning point?

    c   What is the range of $f(x)$?

5   The function $f(x) = ax^2 + bx - 5$ has a minimum value of -2 when $x = -7$. Find the values of a and b.

6   An equation of the form $y = ax^2 + bx + c$ has a minimum value of -12.5 when $x = 4$.

    The point $(0, -4)$ is on the curve.

    Work out the values of a and b.

7   A ball is kicked across a field. The arc through which the ball travelled before hitting the ground is given by the function $p(d) = 3d - 0.05d^2$, where d is the horizontal distance travelled, in metres.

    a   What is the maximum height that the ball reaches?

    b   How far does the ball travel across the field horizontally?

Homework

2.3 The quadratic formula

1   Use the quadratic formula to solve these equations, if possible, giving answers correct to 2 d.p.
For each equation, state the value of the discriminant and the number of real roots.

   a $9x^2 - 12x + 4 = 0$ **b** $x^2 - 3x + 4 = 0$ **c** $4x^2 - 5x + 2 = 0$

   d $4x - x^2 + 11 = 0$ **e** $-9x - 15x^2 - 4 = 0$

2 $9x^2 - nx + 4$ has two different roots. Find the range of values of n.

3   Each equation has two different roots. Find the range of values of n in each case.

   a $x^2 + 7x - n - 1 = 0$

   b $-4x^2 - 8x + n - 2 = 0$

   c $2x^2 + 3x + 2 - n = 0$

4   Each equation has two equal roots. Find the range of values of n in each case.

   a $nx^2 + 56x + 49 = 0$

   b $4x^2 - 20x + n - 7 = 0$

5   Each equation has no real roots. Find the range of values of n in each case.

   a $3x^2 - 5x + c + 2 = 0$

   b $4x^2 - 3x = c - 2$

   c $3(c + 2)x^2 = 3(x - 3)$

Homework

2.4 Intersection of a line and a curve

1   The line $y = 3x - c$ is a tangent to the curve $y = x^2 - 12x + 4$.
What is the value of c?

2   The line $y = mx - 5$ is a tangent to the curve $y = 2x^2 + 3x - 3$.
What are the values of m?

3   The line $y = 4x - 35$ is a tangent to the curve $y = 0.5x^2 - 4x + c$.
What is the y-intercept of the curve?

4   The line $y = 4x - 3$ intersects the curve $y = x^2 - kx + 5$ at two distinct points.
What is the range of the values of k?

5   The line $y = 3x - 2.5$ does not cross the curve $y = px^2 - 4x - 20$.
What is the range of the values for p?

6 The line $y = -1.5x + 3.5$ does not cross the curve $y = -x^2 - qx - 10$.

What is the range of values for q?

7 The line $y = -4.2$ intersects the curve $y = x^2 + 2x - 3.5$ at two distinct points, A and B.

What is the length of the line segment AB?

8 The line $y + 3.5x + 4 = 0$ intersects the curve $y + x^2 - x - 5 = 0$ at two distinct points, C and D.

What is the length of the line segment CD?

9 The line $y + 1.25x = 5$ intersects the circle $x^2 + y^2 - 10y = 16$ at two distinct points, E and F.

What is the length of the line segment EF?

2   Quadratic Functions

Homework

2.5 Quadratic inequalities

1 Solve these inequalities.

  a $(x - 5)(x - 2) > 0$ **b** $(x + 3)(x - 7) < 0$ **c** $(x + 0.5)(3x - 4) \geq 0$

  d $x^2 + 2x - 8 < 0$ **e** $6x^2 - 6 \geq 5x$

2 Solve these inequalities.

  a $(x + 6)(x - 2) < 3(4x - 3)$ **b** $x^2 + 9x - 4 \leq 6x - 2$

  c $(x - 7)^2 - 4 < 2 + 3x$ **d** $(2x + 4)^2 \leq (2 - x)^2$

3 Solve these inequalities.

  a $|x^2 - 2x - 4| \leq 4$ **b** $|x^2 + 4x - 5| < 7$

  c $|x^2 - 3x - 12| > 7$ **d** $|2x^2 - 7.5x - 3| \leq 5$

4 A conference room has a perimeter of 120 m. At least 50 tables, each with an area of 1.5 m², can fit in the room.

What could the length and width of the room be?

5 Solve the inequalities $x^2 - 4x \leq 5$ and $3(x^2 - 2x - 6) \leq 0$.

Extension

2.1 The quadratic function

1 The general form of the quadratic function is $ax^2 + bx + c$. An equation is created: $ax^2 + bx + c = 0$

The roots of this equation are r and s, such that $(x - r)(x - s) = 0$.

Show that $x^2 - (r + s)x + rs = x^2 + \dfrac{b}{a}x + \dfrac{c}{a}$, when $a = 1$.

2 The roots of the equation $ax^2 + bx + c = 0$ are the reciprocal of each other. What is the relationship between a and c?

3 For each quadratic equation, write down the sum and product of the roots.

   a $x^2 - 4x + 3 = 0$

   b $-3x^2 - 7x + 3 = 0$

   c $x(x - 7) = x - 5$

   d $\dfrac{x - 1}{3} = \dfrac{4}{x - 2}$

   e $x^2 + rx - r^2 = 0$

   f $sx^2 - x(s - 2) + s = 0$

4 The equation $3x^2 - 8x + 3 = 0$ has roots r and s. Work out the values of:

   a $\dfrac{1}{r} + \dfrac{1}{s}$

   b $\dfrac{1}{rs}$

   c $(r + 1)(s + 1)$

   d $r^2 + s^2$

   e $r^2s + rs^2$

   f $(r - s)^2$

   g $\dfrac{r}{s} + \dfrac{s}{r}$

   h $\dfrac{1}{r + 1} + \dfrac{1}{s + 1}$

5 The equation $2x^2 - 3x - 7 = 0$ has roots t and q. Find the equation for each set of roots:

   a $t + 1, q + 1$

   b $\dfrac{1}{t}, \dfrac{1}{q}$

   c t^2, q^2

   d $\dfrac{t}{q}, \dfrac{q}{t}$

6 The equation $4x^2 + 3x - 2 = 0$ has roots s and t. Find the equation that has roots that are the reciprocals of s and t.

7 The equation $3x^2 + x - 1 = 0$ has roots a and b. Find the equation that has roots that are double a and b.

8 The equation $4x^2 + 3x - k = 0$ has roots that differ by two. What is the value of k?

Extension

2.3 The quadratic formula

1   The general form of the quadratic function is $ax^2 + bx + c$. An equation is created:

$ax^2 + bx + c = 0$

Rewrite the equation in the form $a(x + p)^2 + q = 0$ and hence make x the subject of the equation.

2   For each equation, write down the type of roots it has but do not solve it.

    a $2x^2 - 4x + 5 = 0$ **b** $-2x^2 - 3x + 2 = 0$ **c** $4x^2 - 7x - 1 = 0$

    d $x^2 - 14x + 49 = 0$ **e** $-(x - 7)^2 - 4 = 0$ **f** $(x - 10)^2 = 0$

3   What values can r have so that $4x^2 - rx + 9$ is a perfect square?

4   Explain why $r^2p^2 + 3 = rp - p^2$ has non-real roots when r is a real number.

5   Show that $r = s$ if the equation $r^2x^2 + sx + 0.25 = 0$ has equal roots.

6   Show that the roots of $x^2 - 3x - 8$ are irrational.

7   Show that $(x + s)(x + t) = 4r^2$ has real roots for all real values of r, s and t.

| 2 | **Quadratic Functions** |

Extension

2.5 Quadratic inequalities

1   $3x - 1 < x^2 - 5 < 14$

Show that the solution to this statement is $-\sqrt{19} < x < -1$ and $4 < x < \sqrt{19}$.

2   $\dfrac{(x - 2)^2}{x + 4} < 1$

Find the values that make this statement true.

3   What is the set of values for which $\dfrac{x^2 + 58}{x} > 16$ is true?

4   Consider $\dfrac{5x + 1}{x^2 + 3}$, where x is real.

Show that the statement $-1.29 \le \dfrac{5x + 1}{x^2 + 3} \le 1.62$ is true.

5 Consider $\dfrac{5(x-3)^2}{3x^2+7}$, where x is real.

Show that the statement $-0.708 \le \dfrac{5(x-3)^2}{3x^2+7} \le 2.38$ is true.

6 What is the range of values of x such that each function is positive? Give your answers to two decimal places.

    a $f(x) = x^2 + 5x - 7$
    b $g(x) = -x^2 - 10x + 3$
    c $h(x) = \dfrac{f(x)}{g(x)}$

7 What is the range of values of x such that each function is negative?

    a $f(x) = 2x^2 - 5x - 10$
    b $g(x) = \dfrac{x-3}{(x-2)(x-1)}$

8 The constant a has a value such that the function $f(x) = x^2 + 5x + a + 4$ is never negative.

What type of roots does the equation $y = (x^2 + 3)(a - 2)$ have? Find the value of a such that the equation has two equal (one distinct) real roots.

3 Factors of Polynomials

TOPIC:
3.1 The factor theorem

KEY WORDS:
polynomial, variable, cubic, factor theorem, quotient, divisor, long division method, grid method

IGCSE MATHS PRIOR KNOWLEDGE:
Factorise quadratic expressions

Solve quadratic equations by factorisation, the quadratic formula, completing the square

Learning aims:
- Know and use the factor and remainder theorem
- Find factors of polynomials
- Solve cubic equations

Resources:
- Student Book: pages 58–64
- Resource sheet 3.1
- Black pens
- Mini whiteboards and pens
- Stopwatch

Common mistakes and remediation:
Students are often unclear about the difference between a factor of a polynomial and a root of a polynomial equation – clear and consistent use of terminology helps here.

When using the long division method, students often make errors with signs on the subtractions. It can be useful to put in the subtraction sign and brackets to help students deal with negative terms, and distinguish clearly between subtraction and negative terms.

Useful tips:
Students often find the long division method of finding factors quite intimidating. It may be useful to complete a numerical example of long division first, to remind them of the algorithm or process.

Some students may have seen long division set out slightly differently (in some countries the divisor is written on the right).

Some students find it helpful if teachers use different colours, particularly to clarify the subtractions and to show steps when modelling examples.

Guidance:
Students often find this topic initially quite challenging, as it requires confident algebraic manipulation, so it is better not to rush the initial steps and to ensure that students have a clear understanding of the process.

Students need to be clear about the difference between being asked to demonstrate that a linear bracket is a factor of a polynomial, **fully factorising** a polynomial expression and using the factor theorem to **solve** a polynomial equation.

Where possible, show examples and working without a using calculator, so students become familiar with the processes of solving these types of problems without calculators. They can then check solutions using calculators, developing efficient use.

STARTER (5 mins)

Equipment: Resource sheet 3.1, stopwatch

➤ Let students work in pairs to identify the quadratic equation, factorisation or solution for the examples on the sheet. Students fill in the gaps on the sheet, using black pen – any teacher support or assistance can then be shown in a different colour. An electronic stopwatch timer can be used to give pace to the activity.

➤ Check students' solutions and understanding of factorising and factors of quadratics. Emphasise the idea of a factor and a root of an equation and how they are connected.

MAIN LESSON ACTIVITY (50 mins)

Equipment: Mini whiteboards and pens

➤ Take the third example from the starter sheet and work backwards (as in the example on page 58 of the Student Book, leading to $x^2 - x - 20 = 0$) to show how solutions of a quadratic equation, such as $x = -\frac{2}{3}$ and $x = 4$, give $(3x + 2)(x - 4) = 0$, which multiplies out to $3x^2 - 10x - 8 = 0$ and, when writing this as a function, $f(x) = 3x^2 - 10x - 8$, $f\left(-\frac{2}{3}\right) = 0$ and $f(4) = 0$. Get students to check these results by calculation.

➤ Give each student one example from the starter activity, write the polynomial in function form and check that the x-values found give a result of 0. Differentiate who does which example by support or challenge required. Check results.

➤ Give the formal definition of the factor theorem:

> If $f(x)$ is a polynomial and a value a can be found so that $f(a) = 0$, then $x = a$ is a solution of the equation $f(x) = 0$ and $x - a$ is a factor of the polynomial.

Give the reminder: If $ax - b$ is a factor of the polynomial then $f\left(\frac{b}{a}\right) = 0$.

➤ Students should copy both of these into their books for future reference.

➤ Introduce the idea of dividing by a factor with a simple numerical example, for example, $640 \div 20 = 32$ to introduce the terms quotient (32) and divisor (20).

➤ Write a parallel example, such as $(x^2 - x - 6) = (x - 3)(x + 2)$, so $(x^2 - x - 6) \div (x - 3) = (x + 2)$, and use this to check that students know which is the quotient and which is the divisor.

➤ Get students to write further examples, either from the starter questions or their own, on mini whiteboards and hold them up for checking.

➤ Show students how to obtain this answer by long division. It can be useful to work the numerical example alongside the algebraic one so that students can compare the numerical and algebraic processes. Encourage students to compare the two and ask questions if they are unclear on the algorithm.

➤ Complete one example from Exercise 3.1, question 1 with the students, checking their understanding of the method each step of the way. Then set students one or two further parts of question 1 to complete independently, using long division. Lower-achieving students may need further practice.

➤ Get feedback from students, or check their solutions.

➤ Introduce the grid method as an alternative approach, solving one of the questions previously set for the grid method. (Students can follow, using their mini whiteboards, to try it out.)

➤ Get students to compare advantages and disadvantages of each method of factorising cubic, in a short discussion. Ensure they record a copy of each method.

➤ Write Exercise 3.1, question 2a on the board. Ask: *How will you factorise this expression?*

Where will you start? With some guided questioning, students should be able to relate this to $f(a) = 0 \rightarrow x - a$ is a factor. Get students to identify factors and factorise.

➤ Give the students a problem such as: '$x^3 - 2x + c$ has a factor $(x - 2)$. What is the value of c? How can you check your solution?'. Ask them to discuss and solve in pairs. ($c = -4$)

➤ Set students further questions from Exercise 3.1, differentiating and selecting appropriate ones to ensure all have the opportunity to practise methods and solve equations. Lower-achieving students may need support in consistently applying methods accurately. Challenge higher-achieving students to answer later questions in the exercise independently.

PLENARY (5–10 mins)

Equipment: Mini whiteboards and pens

➢ Using mini whiteboards, get students to solve the equation $2x^3 - 8x^2 + 6x - 3 = 0$, displaying their methods and solutions on boards to enable quick checking of methods and solutions. Which methods do they find easiest? Why?

➢ Refer to Problem solving 3.1 question 2. Without necessarily working it out, can students predict why some values may not be valid? What approach would they take to working out this question? Ask higher-achieving students to find a solution.

Homework and answers: Resource sheets, homework and extension exercises can be found at the end of this chapter and in the downloadable materials. Answers can be found in the downloadable materials.

CHECKING PROGRESS	Students work in pairs. Give each pair of students a pair of cubic polynomial expressions and ask them to find all the linear factors and hence the common factors of their pair of polynomials. For example:
	
	 Set A: $x^3 + 5x^2 - 2x - 24$ and $x^3 - 2x^2 - 9x + 18$
	         (common factors $(x - 2)$ and $(x + 3)$)
	
	 Set B: $2x^3 + 11x^2 - 7x - 6$ and $2x^3 - 7x^2 + 7x - 2$
	         (common factor $(x - 1)$)
	
	 Set C: $6x^3 - 17x^2 + 11x - 2$ and $6x^3 - 19x^2 + 16x - 4$
	         (common factors $(2x - 1)$ and $(x - 2)$)
	
	 Ask students in their pairs to make up cubic equations using any of their linear factors. Then the pairs swap equations and challenge other pairs to solve them. Allow peer assessment of solutions.
	
	 Collect in the mini-posters after they have been checked. A glance at these should provide enough feedback as to whether students understand the concept of differentiation to obtain the various kinematics equations.

3 Factors of Polynomials

TOPIC:
3.2 The remainder theorem

KEY WORDS:
remainder, remainder theorem, dividend

IGCSE MATHS PRIOR KNOWLEDGE:
Factorise quadratic expressions

Solve quadratic equations by:

- factorisation
- the quadratic formula
- completing the square

Learning aims:
- Know and use the factor and remainder theorem

Resources:
- Student Book: pages 64–67
- A3 paper and pens
- Stopwatch

Common mistakes and remediation:
Substitutions involving negative numbers or coefficients always provide opportunities for errors – encourage students always to check signs carefully, write their work down and use brackets when substituting negative values for x. This is one case in which 'working it out in your head' should probably be discouraged. If students are using calculators, ensure they distinguish clearly between a minus and a negative (a good opportunity to reinforce squaring negative numbers).

Useful tips:
Clear setting out of examples encourages clear thinking, particularly for questions leading to simultaneous equations.

Guidance:
As for the factor theorem, relating this to an accessible numerical example supports students' understanding of the theorem in the early stages.

As far as possible, model non-calculator methods and approaches.

STARTER (5–10 mins)
➤ Write a cubic polynomial such as $2x^3 + x^2 - 25x + 12$ on the board. Ask students to identify potential linear factors of the polynomial, listing them on the board as the students give them. (Be sure to choose a polynomial that will have an appropriate number of potential factors.)

➤ Share out the potential factors among students (one or two each) and ask them to check if it is a factor or not – they will need to justify their answers.

➤ Students identify factors and explain why other linear expressions are not factors.

➤ Show the fully factorised polynomial as a function and remind students that the factors show which values of x will make the polynomial 0.

MAIN LESSON ACTIVITY (40–45 mins)

Equipment: A3 paper and pens, stopwatch

➢ Explain that in this lesson students will be focusing on what happens when a polynomial does not divide exactly.

➢ Give an example of when numbers do not divide exactly, such as $637 \div 20 = 31$ remainder 17.

➢ Show that this can be rewritten as $637 = 20 \times 31 + 17$.

➢ Match this to an algebraic example. You could use the starter again here, for example,
$2x^3 + x^2 - 25x + 12 = (x - 1)(2x^2 + 3x - 22) - 10$, then ask students to check the value when $x = 1$ is substituted into the polynomial.

➢ Introduce the remainder theorem. Link it to the previous example to explain why it works.

➢ Model examples of questions, asking students to identify methods and approaches at each step of the way. Include questions of the type:

   • Find the remainder when $f(x) = 2x^3 - 3x^2 - 11x + 6$ is divided by $(x - 2)$.

   • When $f(x) = 3x^3 - 6x^2 + ax - 2$ is divided by $(x + 1)$ the remainder is -18. Work out the value of a.

   • When $f(x) = ax^3 + bx^2 - 10x + a$ is divided by $(x + 1)$ the remainder is 3, and when it is divided by $(3x - 1)$ the remainder is -1. Find the values of a and b.

   Alternatively, give each student an example of each type of question, differentiating by support or challenge required, and ask them to prepare a model answer to share with the class. Selected students then model answers for the class or share in small groups.

➢ Set students selected questions from Exercise 3.2, questions 1 and 2, with a short time limit. Ensure students have the opportunity to tackle both non-calculator and calculator questions.

➢ Arrange students in pairs or threes, provide A3 paper and pens. Differentiating by support or challenge required, give groups one of the Exercise 3.2 questions 3–6 to solve and provide a model answer. Set an appropriate time limit using an electronic stopwatch or similar to provide pace.

➢ At the end of the time limit, rotate the solutions to the next group for checking and peer assessment. The second group adds any corrections and additional comments.

➢ Rotate to third group for final checking and feedback.

➢ Groups give feedback to each other.

➢ Ensure that students record at least one model answer for each type of question.

PLENARY (10 mins)

➢ With students remaining in their groups, use Problem solving 3.2, question 1 to check their understanding and application of the remainder theorem.

➢ Check students' reasoning and understanding through questioning.

➢ Ask students to recap key features of the factor and remainder theorems.

Homework and answers: Resource sheets, homework and extension exercises can be found at the end of this chapter and in the downloadable materials. Answers can be found in the downloadable materials.

CHECKING PROGRESS	Ask students to construct questions of the form $f(x) = 3x^3 + jx^2 + 8x + k$. When $f(x)$ is divided by $(x + 1)$ there is a remainder of -4. When $f(x)$ is divided by $(x - 2)$ there is a remainder of 80. Find the values of the constants j and k. They should use their own polynomial and linear expressions, making sure they know the correct solutions. Students then challenge each other to solve their problems accurately.

3   Factors and Polynomials

Resource sheet 3.1

Starter activity

Complete the table.

No.	Equation	Factorisation	Solution
1	$x^2 - 8x + 12 = 0$		
2		$(2x - 3)(x + 4) = 0$	
3			$x = -\dfrac{3}{2}, x = 4$
4	$8x^2 = 15 - 14x$		
5		$(2x - 1)(x + 3)(x - 4) = 0$	

Solution

No.	Equation	Factorisation	Solution
1	$x^2 - 8x + 12 = 0$	$(x - 2)(x - 6) = 0$	$x = 2, x = 6$
2	$2x^2 + 5x - 12 = 0$	$(2x - 3)(x + 4) = 0$	$x = \dfrac{3}{2}, x = -4$
3	$2x^2 - 5x - 12 = 0$	$(2x + 3)(x - 4) = 0$	$x = -\dfrac{3}{2}, x = 4$
4	$8x^2 = 15 - 14x$	$(4x - 3)(2x + 5) = 0$	$x = \dfrac{3}{4}, x = -\dfrac{5}{2}$
5	$2x^3 - 3x^2 - 23x + 12 = 0$	$(2x - 1)(x + 3)(x - 4) = 0$	$x = \dfrac{1}{2}, x = -3, x = 4$

3   Factors of Polynomials

Homework

3.1 The factor theorem

1   [NC] Find the quotient obtained by dividing:

    a $x^3 - 2x^2 - 5x + 6$ by $x - 3$ **b** $x^3 + 4x^2 - x - 4$ by $x + 4$

    c $x^3 + 7x^2 + 4x - 12$ by $x + 2$ **d** $4x^3 - 8x^2 - x + 2$ by $x - 2$

2   [NC] By finding a linear factor first, fully factorise:

    a $x^3 - 3x^2 - 6x + 8$ **b** $2x^3 - x^2 - 13x - 6$

    c $x^3 - x^2 - 9x + 9$ **d** $x^3 + 8$

3   Solve the equations.

    a $x^3 + 6x^2 + 13x + 10 = 0$ **b** $2x^3 + x^2 - 2x - 1 = 0$

    c $x^3 - 19x + 30 = 0$ **d** $4x(2x + 1) = 48 - x^3$

4   [NC] Demonstrate that $(x + 1)$ is a factor of $x^3 + 2x^2 - x - 2$, and hence write $f(x) = x^3 + 2x^2 - x - 2$ as a product of three linear factors.

5 $f(x) = x^3 - 2x^2 + px + q$

    Given that $(x - 1)$ and $(x + 2)$ are factors of $f(x)$:

    a   demonstrate that $p = -5$ and find the value of q **b**   express $f(x)$ as a product of linear factors.

6 $x^3 - ax^2 + bx + 18$ has factors $(x - 6)$ and $(x + 1)$.

    a   find the values of a and b

    b   find the remaining factor of the expression.

3 Factors of Polynomials

Homework

3.2 The remainder theorem

1   [NC] Find the remainder when:
   a $f(x) = x^3 + 3x^2 - 4x + 6$ is divided by $(x - 2)$
   b $f(x) = 2x^3 + 6x^2 + 8x + 12$ is divided by $(x + 3)$
   c $f(x) = 4x^3 + 4x^2 - 3x + 5$ is divided $(2x - 1)$

2   Calculate the value of a if:
   a   when $f(x) = x^3 + 3x^2 + ax - 2$ is divided by $(x + 1)$ the remainder is 5
   b   when $f(x) = 2x^3 + ax^2 - 3x + 1$ is divided by $(x - 3)$ the remainder is 82
   c   when $f(x) = ax^3 - 3x^2 + 3x - 3$ is divided by $(2x - 1)$ the remainder is -2

3   [NC] $f(x) = ax^3 + bx^2 + bx + 3$
   a   Given that $(x + 1)$ is a factor of $f(x)$, find the value of a.
   b   Given that when $f(x)$ is divided by $(x - 1)$ the remainder is 4, find the value of b.

4   $f(x) = 3x^3 - 5x^2 + mx + n$
   Given that when $f(x)$ is divided by $(x + 1)$ the remainder is 6 and that when $f(x)$ is divided by $(x - 3)$ the remainder is 26, find the values of m and n.

5   [NC] $f(x) = x^3 + 2x^2 - ax - 10$
   Given that the remainder when $f(x)$ is divided by $(x - 3)$ and the remainder when $f(x)$ is divided by $(x + 1)$ are equal:
   a   find the value of the constant a
   b   find the remainder when $f(x)$ is divided by $(x + 2)$

Extension

3.1 The factor theorem

1.   [NC] Given that $(x - 2)$ is a factor of $g(x) = x^3 - 3x^2 + kx - 8$, find the value of k.

2.   [NC] Given that $x^3 - 6x^2 + px + q$ can be factorised to give $(x + r)^3$, work out the values of p, q and r.

3.   The diagram shows the curve with the equation $y = 2x^3 - 5x^2 - 28x + 15$.

   a   State the coordinates of the point A where the curve crosses the y-axis.

   The curve crosses the x-axis at the points B, C and D.

   b   Given that B has coordinates $(-3, 0)$, find the coordinates of the points C and D.

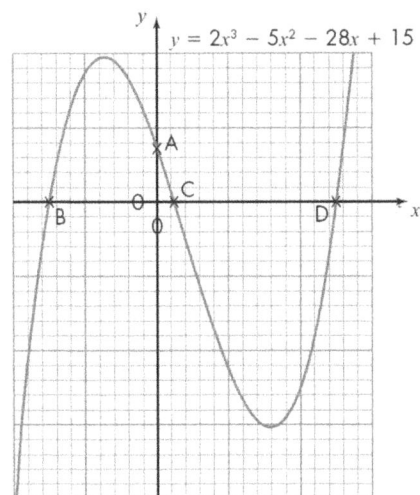

4.   A cuboid has sides of lengths x cm, $(x + 3)$ cm and $(x - 4)$ cm. Given that its volume is 108 cm³, find the integer value of x.

5.   [NC] A square-based pyramid has a base of side length $(x - 2)$ cm and a perpendicular height of x cm. Given that its volume is 15 cm³, find the integer value of x.

Extension

3.2 The remainder theorem

1.   [NC] $f(x) = x^3 - 5x + 3$

   a   Given that when $f(x)$ is divided by $(2x - a)$, where a is a constant, the remainder is 1, show that $a^3 - 20a + 16 = 0$.

   b   Given also that when $f(x)$ is divided by $(x + a)$ the remainder is -41, find the value of a.

2. $f(x) = x^3 - 3x^2 - 18x + 12$

   a   Find the remainder when $f(x)$ is divided by $(x - 4)$.

   Given that $g(x) = f(x) + k$, and that $(x - 4)$ is a factor of $g(x)$:

   b   State the value of the constant k.

   c   Solve the equation $g(x) = 0$.

3. $f(x) = 2x^3 + bx^2 + cx + d$, where b, c and d are constants.

   Given that when $f(x)$ is divided by $(x - 1)$ or $(x - 2)$ the remainder is -30, and when $f(x)$ is divided by $(x + 1)$ the remainder is 12, find the values of b, c and d.

4 Equations, Inequalities and Graphs

TOPIC:
4.1 Solving absolute-value linear equations

KEY WORDS:
absolute value, modulus

IGCSE MATHS PRIOR KNOWLEDGE:
Solve simple linear equations with one unknown variable

Learning aims:
- Solve equations of the type

  $|ax + b| = c \ (c \geqslant 0)$

  $|ax + b| = cx + d$

  $|ax + b| = |cx + d|$

  $|ax^2 + bx + c| = d$

  using algebraic or graphical methods

Resources:
- Student Book: pages 72–77
- Mini whiteboards, or similar
- A1/flipchart paper
- Graphical calculators and apps
- Small pieces of paper

Common mistakes and remediation:
Students might forget to consider solving both $ax + b = m$ and $ax + b = -m$. The definition of a modulus, or absolute value, needs to be clearly understood.

Useful tips:
Consider both the positive and negative case when solving absolute-value equations.

Consider only two cases when solving equations of the form $|ax + b| = |cx + d|$.

Guidance:
The starter is a revision of solving linear equations using twenty questions, for example: *Give me the value of x that satisfies 2x + 3 = 7. What is the solution to 7(x + 2) = 9? Show me a diagram that solves 3(x + 2) = −2(x − 4).*

For the main activity, the spider diagram style activity provides an opportunity for students to evaluate their understanding of absolute values, absolute functions, etc. (as seen in Chapters 1 and 2 of the Student Book) and for checking student progress. The paper could be displayed as posters at the end of the activity.

During the discussion of the 'final' paper, additional examples showing how to solve equations of the form $|ax + b| = c$, algebraically or graphically, could be given if students have not included them on the paper.

As the students work in pairs, encourage them to discuss their mathematics and reflect upon their work.

For the plenary, using 'exit tickets' means students hand in their 'tickets', with their responses to the task written on them, as they leave.

STARTER (5–10 mins)
Equipment: Mini whiteboards, or similar

➢ Practise the concept of solving linear equations using, for example, twenty questions. (See guidance above.)

MAIN LESSON ACTIVITY (40–45 mins)

Equipment: A1/flipchart paper, graphical calculators and apps

➢ Display on the board: $|x|$

➢ Students work in groups of three or four. They write the modulus of x ($|x|$) in the centre of an A1/flipchart sheet of paper. Using a spider diagram style, or similar, students write down everything they know about absolute values, for example, a definition, a calculation, a graph, the method for drawing the graph of a modulus function, a practical example, an equation and a solution.

➢ After an allocated time, groups join up with other groups to compare and share ideas. Anything that one group has and another doesn't can be written on the paper, but a group is not allowed to add something that they do not understand. They must have it explained, and check it, before they add it to their own paper. All groups must see all papers by the end of the activity, so that every group has the same content. (See guidance above.)

➢ Bring students together to discuss the 'final' paper. Statements can be picked from the paper for different groups to explain or justify. (As necessary, discuss how to graph absolute functions, for example, producing a table of values, reflecting the line below the x-axis.) (See guidance above.)

➢ Display these modulus statement (but not the answers) on the board:

$|3x - 2| = |4x + 8|$ $\left(\text{Answer: } x = -10, x = -\dfrac{6}{7}\right)$

$2|3x - 1| = |5x - 4|$ $\left(\text{Answer: } x = -2, x = \dfrac{6}{11}\right)$

The first might be considered by lower-achieving students, the second by higher-achieving students.

➢ Working in pairs, students investigate how the equation can be solved, using graphical calculators and apps, as necessary; ask them to sketch their version of the equation.

Encourage students to consider all the different combinations, for example, $3x - 2 = (4x - 8)$, $3x - 2 = -(4x - 8)$, $-(3x - 2) = (4x - 8)$, and whether they are all necessary.

➢ Lower-achieving students could be given hint cards that explain steps they need to consider, for example: 'compare positive with negative for both sides of the equation'. Higher-achieving students could be encouraged to consider equations of the form $|ax^2 + bx + c| = |dx^2 + ex + f|$.

➢ Bring students together to discuss their findings. Discuss the possibilities and establish that only two are necessary. (The Student Book encourages $ax + b = cx + d$, $ax + b = -(cx + d)$.)

➢ Students can now do Exercise 4.1.

➢ Question 1 provides opportunities for solving equations of the form $|ax + b| = c$ algebraically.

➢ Question 2 provides opportunities for solving equations of the form $|ax + b| = c$ graphically.

➢ Question 3 provides opportunities for solving equations of the form $|ax + b| = |cx + d|$ algebraically.

➢ Question 4 provides opportunities for solving equations of the form $|ax + b| = |cx + d|$ graphically.

PLENARY (10 mins)

Equipment: Small pieces of paper

➢ Display on the board:

$|3x - 4| = 2$ $\left(x = 2, x = \dfrac{2}{3}\right)$ $|3x - 4| = 2|5x + 4|$ $\left(x = -\dfrac{4}{13}, x = -\dfrac{12}{7}\right)$

➢ Distribute exit tickets and ask the students to solve both equations, writing down their answers, both algebraically and graphically, if time permits. (See guidance above.)

Homework and answers: Resource sheets, homework and extension exercises can be found at the end of this chapter and in the downloadable materials. Answers can be found in the downloadable materials.

CHECKING PROGRESS	Use the exit tickets to check students' progress.

TOPIC:

4.2 Solving absolute-value linear inequalities

KEY WORDS:

critical values

IGCSE MATHS PRIOR KNOWLEDGE:

Solve simple linear inequalities

Learning aims:
- Solve graphically or algebraically inequalities of the type

$k|ax + b| > c \ (c \geqslant 0)$

$k|ax + b| \leqslant c \ (c > 0)$

$k|ax + b| \leqslant |cx + d|$

where $k > 0$

$|ax + b| \leqslant |cx + d$

$|ax^2 + bx + c| > d$

$|ax^2 + bx^2 + c| \leqslant d$

Resources:
- Student Book: pages 77–84
- Graphical calculators and apps
- Mini whiteboards, or similar

Common mistakes and remediation:

Students might forget to consider solving both $ax + b = m$ and $ax + b = -m$. The definition of a modulus, or absolute value, needs to be clearly understood.

Students might have difficulty understanding and solving inequalities, for example, dividing or multiplying by a negative value and interpreting the result. Support students in understanding context and graphical representation of results.

Useful tips:

Consider both the positive and negative case when solving absolute-value inequalities.

Consider only two cases when solving absolute-value inequalities of the form $|ax + b| = |cx + d|$.

When manipulating inequalities consider the context of the problem.

Consider carefully the two critical values that are generated from an inequality. Use a value as a test to decide whether the solution set lies inside (between) or outside these two values.

Guidance:

For the main activity, think, pair, share involves students thinking through the problem on their own for a short while, for example, one to five minutes, then sharing their conclusions with a partner. After this the pair of students share their ideas with a wider group.

For the main activity, as necessary, provide more support on how to draw the inequalities graphically.

Consider questions that you could ask students as they work in pairs, particularly those that encourage students to explain and justify their thinking. Also, encourage students to discuss their mathematics and reflect upon their work.

STARTER (5–10 mins)

➢ Display on the board:

$|3x - 2| = a$ $|3x - 2| = |ax + b|$

➢ Ask students to replace the letters in each equation, make sure their new equations can be solved, then share them with another student, explaining how each equation is solved, including by graphical representation. Anything that is not clear or understood can be challenged.

MAIN LESSON ACTIVITY (40–45 mins)

Equipment: Graphical calculators and apps

➢ Display on the board:

$|x| < 1$ $\qquad$ $|x| > 1$ $\qquad$ $|ax + b| \leq c$ $\qquad$ $|ax + b| \geq c$

➢ Ask students to think, pair, share how they think the solution set for each inequality could be expressed on a number line and in written form, for example, $-1 < x < 1$, $x < -1$ and $x > 1$, $-c \leq ax + b \leq c$, $ax + b < -c$ and $ax + b > c$. (See guidance above.)

➢ Bring students together to discuss their conclusions. Discuss how they would solve $|ax + b| \leq c$ and $|ax + b| \geq c$, for example, $-c \leq ax + b$ and $ax + b \leq c$, $ax + b < -c$ and $ax + b > c$. Discuss the fact that the two values that are generated from each pair of inequalities are critical values and are the limits of a solution. Discuss how to decide whether the solution set lies inside (between) or outside the critical values. Discuss the value of testing, by substitution into the original inequality, to confirm where the solution set is.

➢ Display these inequalities, but not the answers:

$\|3x - 2\| \leq 7$	$\left(\text{Answer: } -1\dfrac{2}{3} \leq x \leq 3\right)$
$\|2x - 3\| + 3 \geq 7$	(Answer: $x \leq -0.5$ and $x \geq 3.5$)
$\dfrac{\|2x - 4\|}{3} < 7$	(Answer: $-8.5 \leq x \leq 12.5$)
$3\|4x + 5\| < \|2x - 1\|$	(Answer: $-1.6 < x < -1$)
$\|3x - 2\| \geq \|4x + 8\|$	$\left(\text{Answer: } -10 \leq x \leq -\dfrac{6}{7}\right)$
$\dfrac{\|2x - 4\|}{3} < \|4x + 8\|$	$\left(\text{Answer: } -2.8 > x \text{ and } x > -1\dfrac{3}{7}\right)$

➢ Working in pairs, students solve the first three inequalities. For the fourth, fifth and sixth inequality, ask the students to investigate how the inequality could be solved. (For all the inequalities, encourage them to express solution sets on number lines, and in written form, and investigate how the solution of each inequality could be found graphically; graphical calculators and apps can be used, as necessary. Encourage the use of testing (by substitution into the original inequality) to confirm where the solution set is.) (See guidance above.)

➢ Bring students together to discuss their solutions and findings. Discuss how the fourth and fifth inequalities could be solved. For easier access to solving these inequalities, discuss solving them as equations, and then testing (by substitution into the original inequality) to confirm where the solution set is.

➢ Students can now do Exercise 4.2.

➢ Question 1 provides opportunities for solving inequalities (where the absolute value is on one side of the inequality) algebraically.

➢ Question 2 provides opportunities for solving inequalities (where the absolute value is on one side of the inequality) graphically.

➢ Question 3 provides opportunities for solving inequalities (where the absolute value is on both sides of the inequality) algebraically.

➢ Question 4 provides opportunities for solving inequalities (where the absolute value is on both sides of the inequality) graphically.

PLENARY (10 mins)

➢ Ask students 'show me' or similar questions to explore their understanding of the lesson. Questions can be in word form or diagrammatic or graphical. Cover all the learning aims.

➢ For example: *Show me the solution to $|3x - 2| \leq 7$. What would the solution to $|3x - 2| \geq |4x + 8|$ look like graphically?*

Homework and answers: Resource sheets, homework and extension exercises can be found at the end of this chapter and in the downloadable materials. Answers can be found in the downloadable materials.

CHECKING PROGRESS	Use the 'show me' questions to check students' progress.

4 Equations, Inequalities and Graphs

TOPIC:
4.3 Solving cubic inequalities graphically

KEY WORDS:
derivative, differentiation, turning points

IGCSE MATHS PRIOR KNOWLEDGE:
Solve quadratic equations by factorising, by completing the square or by using the quadratic formula

Learning aims:
- Solve graphically cubic inequalities of the form: $f(x) > d$, $f(x) \leqslant$ and $f(x) < d$ where $f(x)$ is a product of three linear factors and d is a constant.

Resources:
- Student Book: pages 84–89
- Resource sheet 4.1
- Graphic calculators and apps
- A1/flipchart paper

Common mistakes and remediation:
Lower-achieving students might have difficulties using negative values when exploring cubic functions. Show students how negative values are substituted and manipulated.

Students might have difficulty with sketching a graph. Emphasise how to obtain the shape of a graph from any information that is given.

Students might have difficulty with the manipulations involved in completing the square. Emphasise the three basic steps shown in Chapter 2 of the Student Book, on page 39.

Students might have difficulty manipulating the numbers when using the quadratic formula. Emphasise the need to match up the coefficients a and b, and the constant c, in a quadratic equation carefully with the correct letters in the formula. Emphasise the need to have the division line and the square root symbol the correct length.

Useful tips:
When expressing a cubic expression in full, use negative values carefully.

When manipulating the quadratic formula, use negative values carefully.

When substituting values for x into a factorised cubic, use values around zero carefully.

Guidance:
For the starter, when curve sketching, support students by encouraging them to find the solutions to the quadratic and the turning point.

For the starter, students might need support with the factorised form.

For the main activity, during the first task, encourage students to consider how the graphs could be drawn without technology or tables of values.

For the main activity, the alternative exercise approach could involve, for example, posters.

For the plenary, each student in the group mentions a different learning point. Then the points are summarised, for example as a poster.

As students to work in pairs, or larger groups, encourage them to discuss their mathematics and reflect upon their work.

STARTER (5–10 mins)
- Display on the board:

  $-0.5x^2 - 4.5x - 7 < 0$

- Ask students to sketch the graph of this quadratic inequality, highlighting the solution set and any significant points on the graph, such as turning points (maximum or minimum), y-intercept, roots. (See guidance above.)
- Ask students to write the inequality in its factorised form, for example, $-0.5(x + 7)(x + 2) < 0$ and write the solution set on a number line and in written form: $x < -7$ and $x > -2$. (See guidance above.)

MAIN LESSON ACTIVITY (40–45 mins)

Equipment: Resource sheet 4.1, graphic calculators and apps, A1/flipchart paper

➢ Display on the board these inequalities, but not the answers.

$x^3 - 2x^2 - x + 2 < 0$ (Answer: $(x-1)(x-2)(x+1)$, $x < -1$ and $1 < x < 2$)

$x^3 - 2x^2 - x + 2 > 0$ (Answer: $(x-1)(x-2)(x+1)$, $-1 < x < 1$ and $x > 2$)

$3x^3 + 8x^2 + 3x - 2 < 0$ $\left(\text{Answer: } (x+2)(x+1)(3x-1), x < -2 \text{ and } -1 < x < \dfrac{1}{3}\right)$

$2x^3 - 12x^2 + 22x - 12 < 0$ (Answer: $2(x-1)(x-2)(x-3)$, $x < 1$ and $2 < x < 3$)

$2x^3 - 12x^2 + 22x - 12 > 0$ (Answer: $2(x-1)(x-2)(x-3)$, $1 < x < 2$ and $x > 3$)

$3x^3 - 12x^2 + 3x + 18 < 2$ (Answer: $3(x+1)(x-2)(x-3)$, $x < -0.943$ and $1.80 < x < 3.14$)

➢ Working in pairs, using graphic calculators and apps, students find the factorised form and solution sets for the inequalities. Encourage students to use the technology to create the graphs and then create their own sketches of them, shading the solution sets. Encourage them to write out the factorised form and write the solution sets on a number line and in written form, for example, $x < 1$ and $2 < x < 3$ for $2x^3 - 12x^2 + 22x - 12 < 0$. (See guidance above.)

➢ Discuss students' solutions, including the shading. Discuss the factorised form of the four cubic inequalities and the general form of a factorised cubic inequality, for example, $k(x-a)(x-b)(x-c) \leq d$. Discuss the minimum amount of information needed to draw a graph of a cubic inequality, without technology or a table of values, for example, the y-intercept, critical values (roots) and turning points.

➢ Discuss the turning points (where the gradient of the curve is zero) and how to obtain their approximate values by assuming that the curves are normally close to being symmetrical.

➢ Hand out Resource sheet 4.1 to students working in groups of four. Explain that the task is to find turning points for cubic inequalities. Ask students to sketch the cubic inequalities, shading the solution sets and write the solution sets on a number line and in written form.

Answers: $(x-3)(x-2)(x-1) < 0$ $x < 1, 2 < x < 3$

$(x+2)(x+3)(x+4) < 0$ $x < -4, -3 < x < -2$

$0.5(x-1)(x+2)(x+2.5) < 0$ $x < -2.5, -2 < x < 1$

$(x-2)(x+2)(x-1) > 0$ $-2 < x < 1, x > 2$

$(x-2)(x+1)(x-4) > 0$ $-1 < x < 2, x > 2$

$(x+4)(x+1)(x-1) > 0$ $-4 < x < -1, x > 1$

➢ At the end of the activity, allow time for two students to move around the classroom to look at other groups' answers, while two students remain to justify answers. As time allows, the five inequalities could be checked using graphic calculators and apps.

➢ Students can now do Exercise 4.3.

➢ Questions 1 to 3 provide opportunities for solving cubic inequalities graphically.

➢ Questions 4 to 6 provide opportunities for solving more challenging cubic inequalities graphically. You may want to discuss having a negative value for k.

➢ One option for approaching the exercise is to have the students work in groups of three or four and allocate each group a question, which they answer on A1/flipchart paper. As well as answering the question, writing out all appropriate steps, students can highlight and label all significant points on the graph. (See guidance above.)

PLENARY (10 mins)

Equipment: A1/flipchart paper

➢ Working in groups of three or four, students produce a summary of the main learning points from the lesson. (See guidance above.)

Homework and answers: Resource sheets, homework and extension exercises can be found at the end of this chapter and in the downloadable materials. Answers can be found in the downloadable materials.

CHECKING PROGRESS	Use the summary of the learning points to check students' progress.

4   Equations, Inequalities and Graphs

TOPIC:
4.4 Graphs of polynomials and their moduli

KEY WORDS:
polynomial

IGCSE MATHS PRIOR KNOWLEDGE:
Solve quadratic equations by factorising, by completing the square or by using the quadratic formula

Learning aims:
- Sketch the graphs of cubic polynomials and their moduli, when given as a product of three linear factors

Resources:
- Student Book: pages 89–95
- Resource sheet 4.2
- A1/flipchart paper

Common mistakes and remediation:
Lower-achieving students might have difficulties using negative values when exploring cubic functions. Show students how negative values are substituted and manipulated.

Students might have difficulty with sketching a graph. Emphasise how to identify the shape of a graph from any information that is given.

Students might have difficulty manipulating the numbers when completing the square. Emphasise the three basic steps shown in Chapter 2 of the Student Book, on page 39.

Students might have difficulty manipulating the numbers in the quadratic formula. Emphasise the need to match up the coefficients a and b, and the constant c, in a quadratic equation carefully with the correct letters in the formula. Emphasise the need to have the division line and the square root symbol the correct length.

Useful tips:
When expressing a cubic expression in full, use negative values carefully.

When manipulating the quadratic formula, use negative values carefully.

When substituting values for x into a factorised cubic, use values around zero carefully.

Guidance:
For the starter, for the curve sketching, support students by encouraging them to use the minimum amount of information needed to draw a graph of a cubic inequality: the y-intercept, critical values (roots) and turning points. Remind students of the steps for finding the turning points:

$$\text{factorised form} \rightarrow \text{full expression} \rightarrow \frac{dy}{dx} \rightarrow \text{solving quadratic} \rightarrow \text{substitution}$$

For the main activity, think, pair, share involves students thinking through the problem on their own for a short while, for example, one to five minutes, then sharing their conclusions with their partner. After this the pair of students share their ideas with a wider group.

For the main activity, the discussion from the starter should support the discussion.

For the main activity, the task of creating sets of cards is time dependent. Three sets of cards is the recommended number.

For the plenary, each student in the group mentions a different learning point. Then the points are summarised as, for example, a poster.

Consider questions that you could ask students as they work in pairs, particularly those that encourage students to explain and justify their thinking. Also, encourage students to discuss their mathematics and reflect upon their work.

STARTER (5–10 mins)

➤ Display this inequality, but not the answer:

$(x-1)(x-2)(x-5) < 0$ (Answer: $x < 1$ and $2 < x < 5$)

➤ Ask students to sketch the graph of this cubic inequality, highlighting the solution set and any significant points on the graph, for example, turning points (maximum/minimum), y-intercept, roots. (See guidance above.)

➤ Ask students to write the solution set on a number line and in written form.

MAIN LESSON ACTIVITY (40–45 mins)

Equipment: Resource sheet 4.2

➤ Discuss the starter. As necessary, discuss the minimum amount of information needed to draw a graph of a cubic inequality, without technology or a table of values, for example, y-intercept, critical values (roots) and turning points.

➤ Display this inequality:

$y = |(x-1)(x-2)(x-5)|$

➤ Ask students to think, pair, share what they think the sketch of the graph of the equation would look like. (See guidance above.)

➤ Bring students together to discuss their conclusions. Discuss the term polynomial. Discuss the method for drawing the graph of a modulus of a cubic polynomial, for example, reflecting the curve that is below the x-axis. (Emphasise that all the other methods discussed for the starter are still valid.)

➤ Hand out a set of cards to students working in pairs. Explain that the cards involve them matching cubic modulus equations with their graphs. They need to match the five sets of cards. As necessary, discuss what steps are needed for the task. Lower-achieving students could be given hint cards to support the matching, for example, 'Find the y-intercept as a first step.' (Hint cards can be withdrawn when students are ready to work independently.)

➤ At the end of the activity, allow time for students to move around the classroom to look at other groups' answers.

➤ Bring students together to discuss their solutions.

➤ Hand out a set of blank cards to students working in pairs. Explain that they need to create sets of cards for the same activity, for another pair of students to match. Discuss, as necessary, what steps the students think they need to go through to create the cards, for example, starting with the roots, testing the cards actually work. Lower-achieving students could be given hint cards to support the steps that are needed to create the cards. (See guidance above.)

➤ Students can now do Exercise 4.4 (questions 1 – 4).

➤ Questions 1 to 3 provide opportunities for drawing the graphs of cubic modulus equations.

➤ Question 4 provides opportunities for drawing the graph of a more challenging cubic modulus equations.

➤ Display the graph of $y = |(x-2)(x+2)(x-1)|$ (without showing the equation)

➤ Ask students to think, pair, share what they think the equation that would produce this graph might be. Ask students to think of the process they have been following to get a sketch from an equation and apply the ideas in reverse.

➤ Display the graph of $y = |2(x-1)(x+3)(2x-1)|$ (without showing the equation)

➤ Once again ask students to work out what the originating equation might be. Remind students that factors should be integer values.

➤ Students can now do the final question of Exercise 4.4.

PLENARY (10 mins)

Equipment: A1/flipchart paper

➤ Use a quick quiz to cover the main learning points from the lesson.

Homework and answers: Resource sheets, homework and extension exercises can be found at the end of this chapter and in the downloadable materials. Answers can be found in the downloadable materials.

CHECKING PROGRESS	Use the responses from the quick quiz to check students' progress

TOPIC:

4.5 Solving quadratic equations by substitution

KEY WORDS:

quartic equation, radical equation

IGCSE MATHS PRIOR KNOWLEDGE:

Solve quadratic equations by factorising, by completing the square or by using the quadratic formula

Learning aims:	Resources:
• Use substitution to form and solve a quadratic equation in order to solve a related equation	• Student Book: pages 95–99 • Mini whiteboards, or similar • Graphic calculators and apps

Common mistakes and remediation:

Students might have difficulty manipulating the numbers when completing the square. Emphasise the three basic steps shown in Chapter 2 of the Student Book, on page 39.

Students might have difficulty manipulating the numbers when using the quadratic formula. Emphasise the need to match up the coefficients a and b, and the constant c, in a quadratic equation carefully with the correct letters in the formula. Emphasise the need to have the division line and the square root symbol the correct length.

Useful tips:

When manipulating the quadratic formula, use negative values carefully.

Guidance:

For the starter, for the first quadratic equation, one student in the pair uses the formula and the other completes the square. They can swap methods for the second quadratic equation.

For the main activity, include as many 'show me' questions as necessary to support understanding suitable substitution.

For the plenary, the created equations could be used for another task, for example, a starter, formative test.

Consider questions that you could ask students as they work in pairs, particularly those that encourage students to explain and justify their thinking. Also, encourage students to discuss their mathematics and reflect upon their work.

STARTER (5–10 mins)

➢ Display this equation on the board, but not the answer:

$x^2 + 4x - 6 = 0$ (Answer: $x = -5.16$, $x = 1.16$)

➢ Students work in pairs. Ask each student to solve this quadratic equation, either using the formula or by completing the square. They then swap and check solutions.

➢ Ask each student to create another quadratic equation, using a different variable, for their partner to solve using either method. They then swap and check solutions.

MAIN LESSON ACTIVITY (40–45 mins)

Equipment: Mini whiteboards, or similar, graphic calculators and apps

➤ Ask students 'show me' or similar questions to develop their understanding of variables and powers, for example: *Show me a variable to the power of 8. Write x^4 in another way.* (for example, $x^2 \times x^2$) *Convince me that x^2 is a factor of x^6. If u was a substitute for x^2, what would x^4 be?, x^6?, x^{10}? $u = k$ and $u = x^2$, what would x equal?*

➤ Display these questions, on the board, but not the answers:

$x^4 - 3x^2 + 2 = 0$	(Answer: $x = -1.41, -1, 1, 1.41$)
$4x^4 - 3x^2 + 0.5 = 0$	(Answer: $x = -0.707, -0.5, 0.5, 0.707$)
$2x^4 - 10x^2 + 6 = 0$	(Answer: $x = -2.07, -0.835, 0.835, 2.07$)
$3x^6 + 2x^3 - 5 = 0$	(Answer: $x = -1.19, 1$)
$x^{10} - 5x^5 + 6 = 0$	(Answer: $x = 1.25, 1.15$)

➤ Students work in pairs. Ask them to investigate how the equations could be rewritten, substituting in variables with lower powers, for example, $x^4 - 3x^2 + 2 = 0$ becomes $u^2 - 3u + 2 = 0$ where $u = x^2$. Ask if they could solve the original equations because of this substitution. (Encourage them to consider solving the rewritten equations, using suitable substitution and the connection between the solutions and the original variable, for example, $u = 1 \rightarrow x^2 = 1 \rightarrow x = 1$.) They can use graphic calculators and apps to check their solutions.

➤ Bring students together to discuss their findings. Discuss $x^4 - 3x^2 + 2 = 0$, which is called a quartic equation. Discuss changing $x^4 - 3x^2 + 2 = 0$ to become $u^2 - 3u + 2 = 0$, then solving $u^2 - 3u + 2 = 0$, which leads to a solution of $x^4 - 3x^2 + 2 = 0$.

➤ As part of the discussion, display this procedure to support solving the original equation:

examine terms $\rightarrow$ substitute variable $\rightarrow$ solve quadratic $\rightarrow$ compare solutions $\rightarrow$ find original variable

➤ Display these functions (but not the answers):

$4x - 11\sqrt{x} + 6 = 0$	(Answer: $x = 0.563, 4$)
$5x - 12\sqrt{x} + 5 = 0$	(Answer: $x = 0.288, 3.47$)
$(x^2 - x)^2 = 6(x^2 - x) = 0$	(Answer: $x = -2, 0, 1, 3$)
$(x^2 - x)^2 - 5(x^2 - x) = 0$	(Answer: $x = -1.79, 0, 1, 2.79$)

➤ Students work in pairs. Ask them to investigate how the equations could be rewritten, using suitable substitutions, and solved. They can use graphic calculators and apps to check their solutions.

➤ Bring students together to discuss their solutions.

➤ Students can now do Exercise 4.5.

➤ Questions 1 to 6 provide opportunities for using suitable substitutions to solve equations.

➤ Questions 7 and 8 provide opportunities for using suitable substitutions to solve more challenging equations.

➤ Q9 is an extension type question for higher-achieving students – make reference to Chapter 6 for working with logarithms.

PLENARY (10 mins)

➤ Each student needs to create an equation that can be solved by using suitable substitution. It is then solved by a student who has not been a partner to the creator of the equation. Students swap and check solutions.

Homework and answers: Resource sheets, homework and extension exercises can be found at the end of this chapter and in the downloadable materials. Answers can be found in the downloadable materials.

CHECKING PROGRESS	Use the created equations to check students' progress.

Resource sheet 4.1

Solving cubic inequalities graphically

$(x-3)(x-2)(x-1) < 0$
$(x-2)(x+2)(x-1) > 0$
$(x+2)(x+3)(x+4) < 0$
$(x-2)(x+1)(x-4) > 0$
$0.25(x+1)(x+2)(x+3) < 0$
$(x+4)(x+1)(x-1) > 0$

4   Equations, Inequalities and Graphs

Resource sheet 4.2

Graphs of polynomials and their moduli

$y = |(x-3)(x-2)(x-1)|$	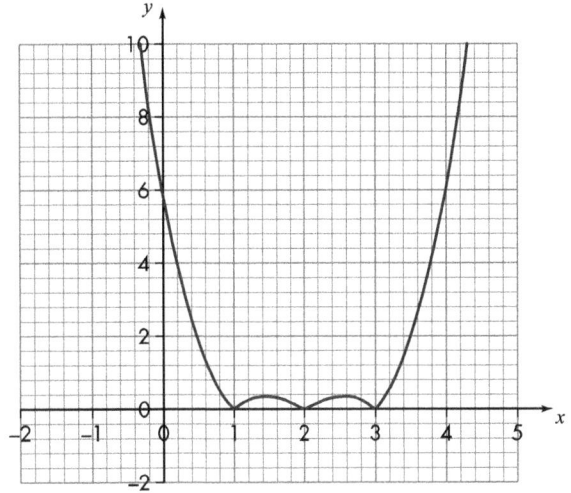
$y = |(x-4)(x+3)(x-2)|$	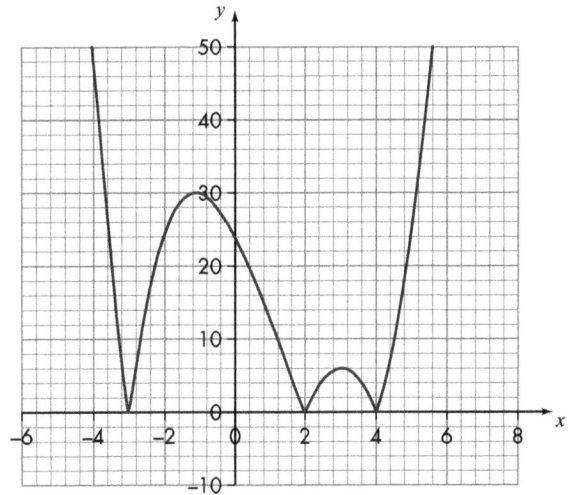
$y = |(x-2)(x+5)(x-6)|$	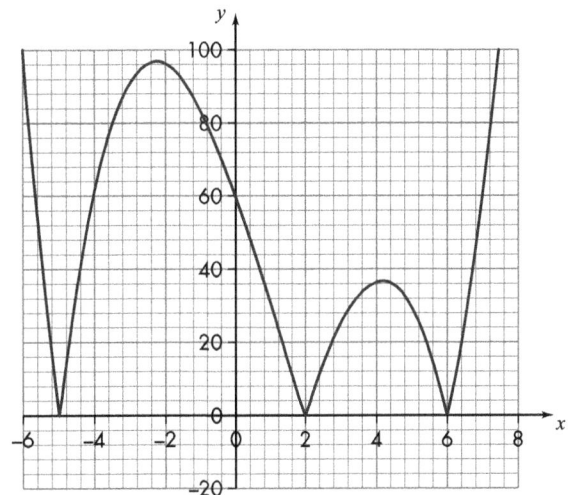

$y = \|0.5(x-1)(x-2)(x-4)\|$	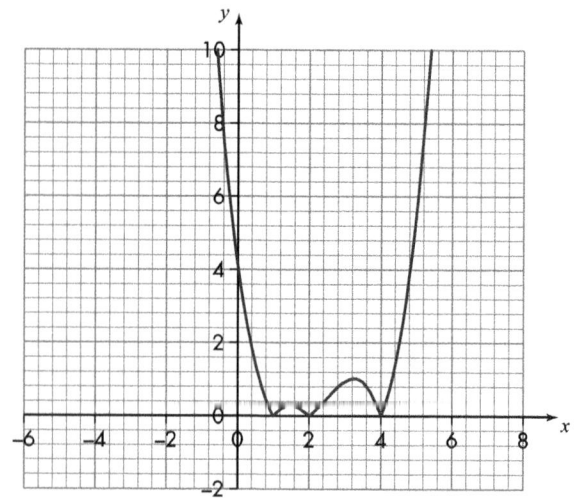
$y = \|0.25(x-3)(x+2)(x-1)\|$	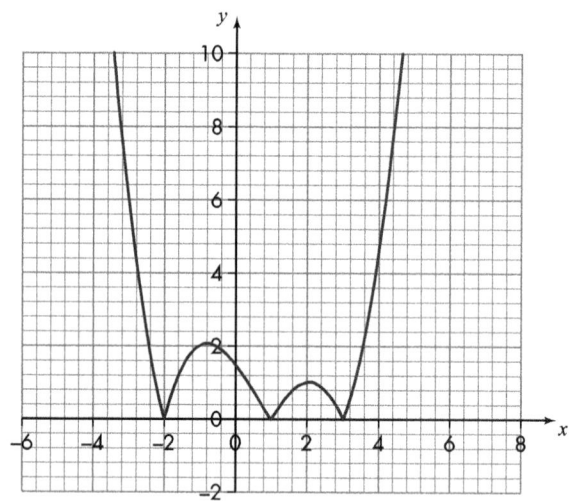

4   Equations, Inequalities and Graphs

Homework

4.1 Solving absolute-value linear equations

1   Solve these equations algebraically.

    a $|4x - 2| = 3$ **b** $|3x - 4| = 7$

    c $\left|\dfrac{x-5}{3}\right| = 8$ **d** $4\,|0.25x - 5| = 0$

2   Solve these equations by plotting graphs.

    a $|3x - 2| = 2$ **b** $|4x + 2| = 8$

    c $3\,|x - 5.5| = 2$ **d** $\left|\dfrac{2x+4}{3}\right| = 4$

3   Solve these equations algebraically.

    a $|2x - 2| = |3x + 8|$ **b** $|3x + 2| = |5 - x|$

    c $0.25\,|x + 3| = 4\,|0.25x - 3|$ **d** $\left|\dfrac{3x+1}{3}\right| = \left|\dfrac{x-3}{4}\right|$

    e $\left|\dfrac{4(x+4)}{7}\right| = \left|\dfrac{2x-5}{4}\right|$

4   Solve these equations by plotting graphs, giving answers to 1 decimal place.

    a $|0.6x - 3| = |2x - 1|$ **b** $|2.5x - 6| = |0.8x + 2|$

    c $\left|\dfrac{3x-2}{4}\right| = \left|\dfrac{x-3}{5}\right|$ **d** $\left|\dfrac{4x+1}{2}\right| = \left|\dfrac{3x-2}{4}\right|$

4   Equations, Inequalities and Graphs

Homework

4.2 Solving absolute-value linear inequalities

1   Solve these inequalities algebraically.

    a $|5x - 4| > 5$ **b** $|3x + 4| < 7$

    c $\left|\dfrac{2x-5}{3}\right| \geq 7$ **d** $|4x + 3| - 2 \leq 0$

    e $4\,|2x - 3| < 6$

2   Solve these inequalities by plotting graphs.

    a $|3x - 2| > 7$ **b** $|2x - 4| < 5$

    c $0.4\,|x - 5| \leq 0.8$ **d** $\left|\dfrac{3x-5}{4}\right| \geq 2$

3   Solve these inequalities algebraically.

    a $|3x+4| \geq |x-4|$ **b** $|4x-3| < |x+2|$

    c $|6x-7| > |3x+2|$ **d** $|6-x| > |3+x|$

    e $6|2x-1| > 3|2x+5|$

4   Solve these inequalities by plotting graphs, giving answers to 1 decimal place where necessary.

    a $|2x-3| > |3x-4|$ **b** $|6x-9| < |x+4|$

    c $\left|\dfrac{4x+2}{3}\right| \leq |2x-4|$ **d** $\left|\dfrac{x+2}{3}\right| \geq \left|\dfrac{3x+2}{2}\right|$

    e $2\left|\dfrac{3x+5}{2}\right| < 3|5x-1|$

4	**Equations, Inequalities and Graphs**

Homework

4.3 Solving cubic inequalities graphically

Solve these inequalities graphically.

a $(x+2)(x+3)(x+5) \leq 0$ **b** $(x-2)(x+3)(x-5) > 0$

c $2(x-1)(x+3)(x+4) < 0$ **d** $(x+2)(x-2.5)(x-3.5) \leq 2$

e $(x-1)(x-2)(x+3) > 3$ **f** $0.5(x-1)(x-2)(x+3) > 1$

g $0.25(x-1)(x-2)(x+3.5) < 3$ **h** $0.4(x-1)(x+2)(x-3.5) < 2.5$

i $(x+2)(x-3)(x+1) > 0$ **j** $0.2(x-1)(x-2)(x+2.5) > 0$

4	**Equations, Inequalities and Graphs**

Homework

4.4 Graphs of polynomials and their moduli

1   Sketch the graph of each equation.

    a $y = |(x+1)(x+2)(x-3)|$

    b $y = |(x-2)(x-3)(x-5)|$

    c $y = |0.5(x-1)(x-3)(x+4)|$

    d $y = |0.25(x+2)(x-2.5)(x-3.5)|$

    e $y = |1.5(x-1)(x+2)(x+3)|$

2   Create five of your own cubic moduli equations and sketch their graphs.

3 In each case the graph of $y = |f(x)|$, $f(x)$ is a cubic function.

    a Find the possible expressions for f(x) in factorised form.

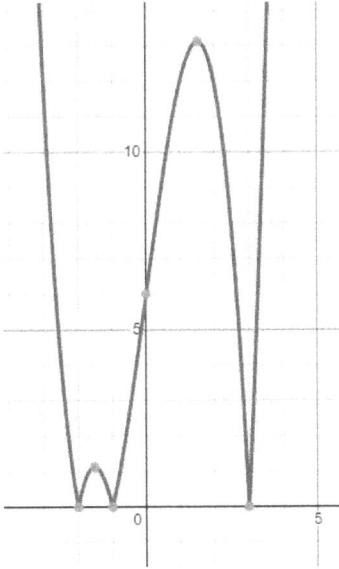

    b Find the possible expressions for f(x) in factorised form.

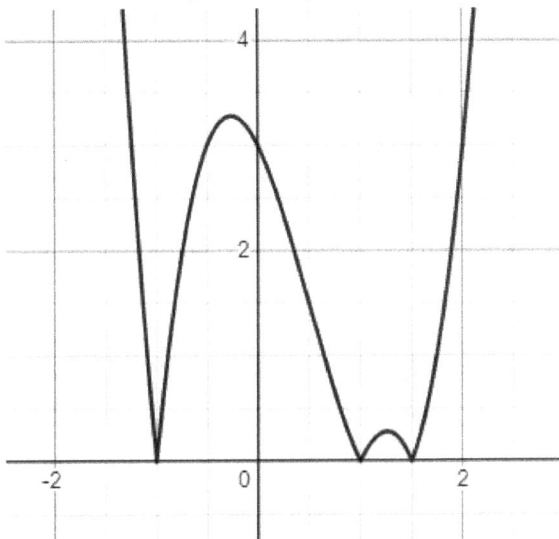

4   Equations, Inequalities and Graphs

Homework

4.5 Solving quadratic equations by substitution

1 Use a suitable substitution to solve each equation.

    a $x^4 - 3x^2 + 2 = 0$

    b $2x^4 - 4x^2 + 2 = 0$

    c $2w^4 + 5w^2 - 4 = 0$

    d $4x - 9\sqrt{x} + 5 = 0$

    e $5x - 12\sqrt{x} = 7$

    f $2(x^2 - x)^2 = 0.5(x^2 - x)$

    g $(x^2 - x)^2 = 7(x^2 - x)$

2 Create five of your own equations and, using a suitable substitution, solve them. Use suitable technology to check the solutions.

Extension

4.2 Solving absolute-value linear inequalities

1 Solve these inequalities algebraically, giving answers to 1 decimal place when necessary.
   Check your answers by drawing graphs of the modulus expressions.

   a $|x| \geq |x^2 - 5|$

   b $|x| < |x^2 - 8x + 5|$

   c $|\sin x| + 1 < |\cos x| + 1$ for $0 \leq x \leq \pi$

   d $|x - 2| > |x^2 + 4x - 3|$

   e $|x - 2| - 5 \leq 1 - |x^2 + 4x + 1|$

   f $|x^2 + 4x + 5| \geq |x^3 + 2|$

2 Create five of your own inequalities, solving them algebraically, and checking them by drawing graphs of the modulus expressions.

3 Consider this inequality: $|(x-2)^2| > |x^2 + 3x - 2|$

   a Solve: $(x - 2)^2 > x^2 + 3x - 2$

   Now, consider $(x - 2)^2 > -(x^2 + 3x - 2)$

   b Plot $(x - 2)^2$ and $x^2 + 3x - 2$ as two separate curves on the same axis. What do you notice?
   How could you use algebra to identify that this would happen?

   c What is the answer to the original inequality?

Extension

4.3 Solving cubic inequalities graphically

1 Solve these cubic inequalities graphically, giving answers to 1 decimal place when necessary.

   a $1.1(x + 2)(x + 3)(x + 5) \leq 2$

   b $1.5(x - 2)(x + 3)(x - 5) > 3$

   c $-0.5(x - 1)(x + 3)(x + 4) < 3$

   d $-0.75(x + 2)(x - 2.5)(x - 3.5) \geq -4$

2 Create five of your own, positive and negative, cubic inequalities, solving them graphically.

3 Create a card-matching exercise that could support the understanding of this topic.

Extension

4.5 Solving quadratic equations by substitution

Investigate using the factor theorem to factorise expressions such as:

$x^3 - 3x^2 + 3x - 8$

$x^4 - 2$

$x^4 - 3x^3 + 3x^2 - 8x + 2$

5 Simultaneous Equations

TOPIC:
5.1 Simultaneous equations

KEY WORDS:
simultaneous equation, substitution, linear, non-linear, quadratic

IGCSE MATHS PRIOR KNOWLEDGE:
Solve simultaneous linear equations in two unknowns

Solve simultaneous equations involving one linear and one quadratic

---

Learning aims:
- Solve simultaneous equations in two unknowns by elimination or substitution

Resources:
- Student Book: pages 104–107
- Resource sheet 5.1

Common mistakes and remediation:
Students sometimes make mistakes with signs when rearranging the linear equation as they are focusing on the substitution – try to get them in the habit of checking.

Signs are also often a problem when simplifying or solving simultaneous equations. Encourage students to distinguish between a subtraction and a negative number.

Useful tips:
Using brackets when substituting a linear term into a more complex equation avoids errors with signs.

Encourage clear setting out at each stage and labelling of equations to avoid confusion.

Guidance:
Encourage students to get into the habit of writing each step of their solution clearly.

A first step in solving by rearrangement and substitution is to look for the easiest substitution to use. Encourage students to consider both variables before starting to solve an equation.

For contextual questions, students may need support to identify and allocate letters to variables and then construct equations.

STARTER (5–10 mins)
Equipment: Resource sheet 5.1
- ➤ Do not give the topic of the lesson at this stage.
- ➤ Divide the students into pairs and give each pair one question from the resource sheet (early questions for lower-achieving students, later questions for higher-achieving students). It doesn't matter if some pairs have the same question.
- ➤ Give the students 2–3 minutes to try to solve the problem.
- ➤ Display one of the questions and ask students for their solution and explanation as to how they found the answer.
- ➤ Repeat for other questions.
- ➤ Ask students to guess the topic of the lesson.
- ➤ If time, ask students to recap the main features of simultaneous equations.
- ➤ **Answers**
- ➤ **1** 42 and 28
- ➤ **2** Muffin: $1.25, doughnut: $1.50
- ➤ **3** Red: 16 g, yellow: 30 g
- ➤ **4** Alex: 21, Ben: 7
- ➤ **5** 7 and −2

MAIN LESSON ACTIVITY (45 mins)

➤ Write an example of simultaneous equations with one linear and one quadratic, such as $y = x^2 - 2$, $y = 2x + 1$, or Example 1 or 2 from the Student Book. Ask students for suggestions as to how to solve the problem. Use appropriate suggestions to model a solution.

➤ Make sure all steps of the solution are written and that there is a clear structure:

  - Rearrange the linear equation.

  - Substitute into the quadratic equation, using brackets to ensure signs are taken into account.

  - Simplify to find solutions.

  - Substitute back into the linear equation to find the second values.

  - Check that **both** solutions work in **both** equations.

  - Write pairs of solutions clearly – emphasise the need to pair the solutions correctly.

➤ Complete a second example, such as $x^2 + y^2 = 25$ and $y - x = -1$, asking students to describe the process each step of the way, to reinforce their understanding of the process.

➤ Ask students to complete a third example of the form $x + y = 9$, $xy = 8$. Students may need support to see how a quadratic equation is formed in simultaneous equations such as these.

➤ For one of the examples, use substitution of the 'other' variable to show that whichever way the variables are substituted, the solutions are the same. Alternatively, ask students to complete this individually to check their understanding of the process.

➤ Set students questions from Exercise 5.1. Higher-attaining students may need only to complete one part of the earlier questions before moving on, while lower-attaining students may need to complete more parts to consolidate their understanding.

➤ Ensure students have the opportunity to tackle problem solving and contextual questions such as those that are given later in the exercise. They may initially need some support in setting up equations and deciding variables.

PLENARY (5–10 mins)

➤ Ask students to write points for a 'help sheet' for students tackling this topic. Ask: *What are the key points to remember? What advice would you give?*

➤ Review key points and clarify any uncertainties either with individual students or the whole class as the feedback requires.

➤ If time allows, a short peer assessment of each other's advice could consolidate methods and approaches.

Homework and answers: Resource sheets, homework and extension exercises can be found at the end of this chapter and in the downloadable materials. Answers can be found in the downloadable materials.

CHECKING PROGRESS	Play simultaneous equations consequences.
	Start by asking students to choose two numbers. They write these at the top of a piece of paper and hand it on to the next student. (Move the papers clockwise around the room or in some other sensible organised order. Groups of 4 can work well.)
	The second student writes a linear and a quadratic equation that are both true for the two numbers, then folds the paper so that the numbers cannot be seen (but the equations can). They then hand the paper on to the third student.
	The third student solves the equations (without cheating!) and hands the paper on to the fourth student.
	The fourth student checks the solution and, if it is not correct, analyses the errors and passes it back to the third student.
	Encourage students to be challenging in the equations they construct.

5 Simultaneous Equations

TOPIC:

5.2 Interpreting and solving simultaneous equations graphically

KEY WORDS:

intersection, points of intersection, tangent, graphically

IGCSE MATHS PRIOR KNOWLEDGE:

Solve simultaneous linear equations in two unknowns

Solve simultaneous equations involving one linear and one quadratic

---

Learning aims:

- Solve simultaneous equations in two unknowns by elimination or substitution

Resources:

- Student Book: pages 108–112
- Mini whiteboards and pens
- Graphing software
- Graphical calculators

Common mistakes and remediation:

Students sometimes find it hard to draw the graphs to be able to solve problems graphically. They need to know the basic shapes of graphs and how to use factorisation to find axis intercepts.

Useful tips:

Using graphing software helps the flow of this topic and encourages students more quickly to develop a 'feel' for graphical solutions.

The 'Trace' function for graphs on graphical calculators can also be used to check solutions if students have them available.

Guidance:

For this topic students need to have a reasonable awareness of the shapes of graphs and the number of potential intersections, but do not spend so much time on drawing graphs that it detracts from the main theme of the lesson. Graph sketching and identifying of key points are skills to be encouraged here.

STARTER (5–10 mins)

Equipment: Mini whiteboards and pens, graphing software or use of graphical calculators optional

- ➢ Students work individually.
- ➢ Ask students to draw a set of axes, then a range of graphs. After each graph, ask them to hold up their boards for you to check their graphs and points of intersection with axes, then clear the axes for the next graph.
- ➢ As well as the standard $y = x$, $y = x^2$ and $y = x^3$, include simple linear graphs, quadratics such as $y = (x - 2)^2$, $y = x^2 - 4x + 3$ and cubic such as $x^3 + 1$.
- ➢ Challenge students to draw the graph of $x^2 + y^2 = 4$.
- ➢ Graphical software could be used to check sketches of graphs.
- ➢ If you do not have mini whiteboards available, a simpler version of this exercise can be done with students drawing shapes in the air.

MAIN LESSON ACTIVITY (45 mins)

Equipment: Mini whiteboards and pens, graphing software

➢ Ask students to draw a set of axes then a pair of linear graphs such as $y = 2x + 1$ and $y = -2x - 3$ and identify the point of intersection. Ask them to explain why only one point of intersection is possible. Relate back to the simultaneous equations.

➢ Show them the graph of a quadratic such as $y = x^2 - 4x + 3$ (using graphical software, or show how to sketch by factorising and identifying axes intersections). Ask them how many points of intersection are possible with a linear graph, then ask them to suggest possible lines to give two, one or no points of intersection.

➢ For each line, ask students to identify the points of intersection on the graph and state that these are the solution to the simultaneous equations formed by the quadratic and their linear graph.

➢ Ask the students to check that the points of intersection are correct algebraically, with one-third of the class checking the two-point line, one-third of the class checking the single-intersection line and the remaining one-third of the class checking the no-intersections line. Get feedback from students.

➢ For the example for no points of intersection, show students how this can be proved using the discriminant of the resulting quadratic equation (a similar process to Example 3 in the Student Book).

➢ Ensure that students record quick sketches of possible outcomes for the intersection of a linear graph and a quadratic curve. Encourage them to consider negative quadratic curves as well.

➢ Give the students the graph $x^2 + y^2 = 25$ and again ask them to work in pairs, identifying possible lines with two, one or no points of intersection. Ensure that students identify the points of intersection and recognise that these are solutions to the simultaneous equations formed by the circle and the straight lines. Encourage higher-achieving students to use negative or fractional coefficients in their linear graphs.

➢ Set students selected questions from Exercise 5.2, ensuring that they tackle a range of question types. Lower-achieving students may need more consolidation of earlier questions, whereas higher-achieving students should be set the later questions, requiring interpretation and explanation of answers.

PLENARY (5–10 mins)

Equipment: Graphing software

➢ Show the students the graph of $x^2 + y^2 = 16$ and the question: 'Find the exact value of m for which the line $y = mx + 6$ is a tangent to the curve.'

➢ Ask students what the question is asking them to do. Ask: *How would you go about solving it? How would you explain to a fellow student who had missed the lesson?*

➢ Choose one student to come to the board to model a solution – they can only write what the rest of the class tell them. The other students provide instructions and help develop a model solution.

➢ Students may need to be made aware that as $m^2 = \dfrac{5}{4}$, they will need to consider two possible values of m, but wait to see if they realise this before telling them.

➢ Ask students to use graphing software to check their solution.

Homework and answers: Resource sheets, homework and extension exercises can be found at the end of this chapter and in the downloadable materials. Answers can be found in the downloadable materials.

CHECKING PROGRESS	Create a selection of linear equations and quadratic equations in various forms.
	On the board, draw a grid with the linear equations across the top and the quadratic equations down the side. This can be done in a 'Jeopardy game' style, with different points for different equation combinations.
	Give a clear time limit.
	Students select one linear and one quadratic equation at a time, then sketch the graphs to obtain values for intersections and hence solutions to the equations as simultaneous equations. As they find solutions, they write them on the board and claim the points (students' initials can be used to keep track of whose solution is whose). Teacher wipes off any incorrect answers.
	The student with the most points at the end of the time wins the game.
	If you want individual feedback on progress, students can also be given a printed copy of the table on which to record their answers, which can be collected in for checking at the end.

Resource sheet 5.1

Starter activity

Questions

1   The sum of two numbers is 70 and the difference between them is 14. What are the two numbers?

2   In a café, 2 muffins and 3 doughnuts cost $7.00, but 4 muffins and 1 doughnut costs £6.50. What is the cost of a muffin and the cost of a doughnut?

3   A box contains only red and yellow blocks. Find the weight if each type of block if 9 red blocks and 6 yellow blocks weigh 324 g and 5 red blocks and 4 yellow blocks weigh 200 g

4   The sum of Alex and Ben's ages is 28. In seven years' time Alex will be twice as old as Ben. How old are they each now?

5   Huma thinks of two numbers. When she doubles the first number and adds treble the second number she gets an answer of 8. When she trebles the first number and subtracts the second number she gets an answer of 23. What are the two numbers?

5 Simultaneous Equations

Homework

5.1 Simultaneous equations

1 **[NC]** Use the substitution method to solve these pairs of linear simultaneous equations.

    a $a - 7b = 23$
              $3a + 9b = 9$

    b $-5c + 6d = 44$
              $9c + 7d = -8$

2 **[NC]** Solve these pairs of simultaneous equations.

    a $y = x^2 - 3x + 2$
              $y = x + 7$

    b $y = 2x^2 + 7x - 4$
              $y = 3x - 4$

3 Solve these pairs of simultaneous equations.

    a $x^2 + y^2 = 13$
              $2y - x = 4$

    b $x^2 - y^2 = 0$
              $x + 2y = 8$

    c $3x^2 - xy = 24$
              $x + y = 4$

4 **[NC]** Find the coordinates of the points where the graphs of $x^2 + y^2 - 5y = 5$ and $x = 2y - 5$ intersect.

5 Given that $x^2 + y^2 = 136$ and $y = 3x - 4$, demonstrate that $5x^2 - 12x - 60 = 0$.

6 A rectangle has sides $(x + 4)$ cm and $(y - 2)$ cm. Its perimeter is 20 cm and its area is 21 cm^2. What are the values of x and y?

7 **[NC]** A square ended cuboid has the volume x^2y, where x and y are side lengths. A cuboid of this type for which $y = 3x$ has a volume of 192 cm^2. Find the values of x and y.

5   Simultaneous Equations

Homework

5.2 Interpreting and solving simultaneous equations graphically

1   Use graphical methods to find the solutions to these pairs of simultaneous equations. Your solutions may be approximate or exact. In this question, suitable ranges for the axes are given.

   a $y = x^2 - x - 2$ and $y = 2x - 2$ ($-5 < x < 5$, $-10 < y < 10$)

   b $y = x^2 + 4x - 12$ and $y = -2x - 3$ ($-8 < x < 3$, $-10 < y < 12$)

   c $x^2 + y^2 = 16$ and $y = 2x - 1$ ($-5 < x < 5$, $-5 < y < 5$)

   d $y^2 = 9 - x^2$ and $2x + y = 3$ ($-4 < x < 4$, $-4 < y < 4$)

   e $y = x(x - 3)(x + 2)$ and $y = x + 1$ ($-4 < x < 4$, $-10 < y < 10$)

2   Solve the simultaneous equations $x^2 + y^2 = 8$ and $x + y = 4$ graphically ($-4 < x < 4$, $-4 < y < 4$).

   a   What is special about the intersection of these two graphs?

   b   Prove your solution algebraically.

3   State how many pairs of solutions these simultaneous equations have. Justify your answer in each case using an appropriate quadratic equation and finding the discriminant.

   a $y = x^2 - 4x + 3$ and $y = 2x - 1$

   b $y = x^2 + 8x + 5$ and $y = 3x - 4$

   c $y = 2x^2 - 2x + 1$ and $y = 5(x + 2)$

   d $y = 3x^2 - 2x + 1$ and $y = 3x - 5$

   e $x^2 + y^2 = 8$ and $y = 3x + 7$

4   Solve the simultaneous equations $y = 2x^2 - 1$ and $4x + y + 3 = 0$.

5   A ball is thrown in the air modelling the curve $y = -x^2 + 6x - 4$. A laser pointer is held to model the line $y = \frac{3}{2}x - 3$. At what height is the ball illuminated by the laser pointer? (Use metres as units.) Illustrate your answer graphically.

5 Simultaneous Equations

Extension

5.1 Simultaneous equations

1 Find the coordinates of the points where the graphs of $x^2 + y^2 - 2x - 24 = 0$ and $x = 2y - 9$ intersect.

2 Solve the simultaneous equations $x + y = 3$ and $x^2 + xy + 2y^2 + x + 2y = 12$.

3 Solve the simultaneous equations $x + \dfrac{1}{y} = 1$ and $y + \dfrac{1}{x} = 4$.

4 A large L-shaped room has sides of lengths as shown below. Given that it has a floor area of 198 m^2 and that $xy = 42$, find the perimeter of the room.

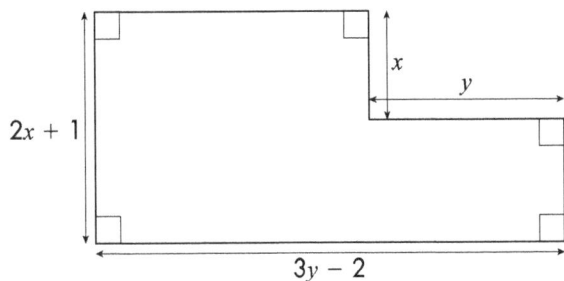

5 Solve the simultaneous equations $x^2 + y^2 = 5$ and $\dfrac{1}{x^2} + \dfrac{1}{y^2} = \dfrac{5}{4}$.

Extension

5.2 Interpreting and solving simultaneous equations graphically

1   The diagram shows the graphs of $y = x^2 - 4x + 1$ and $y = x - 3$.

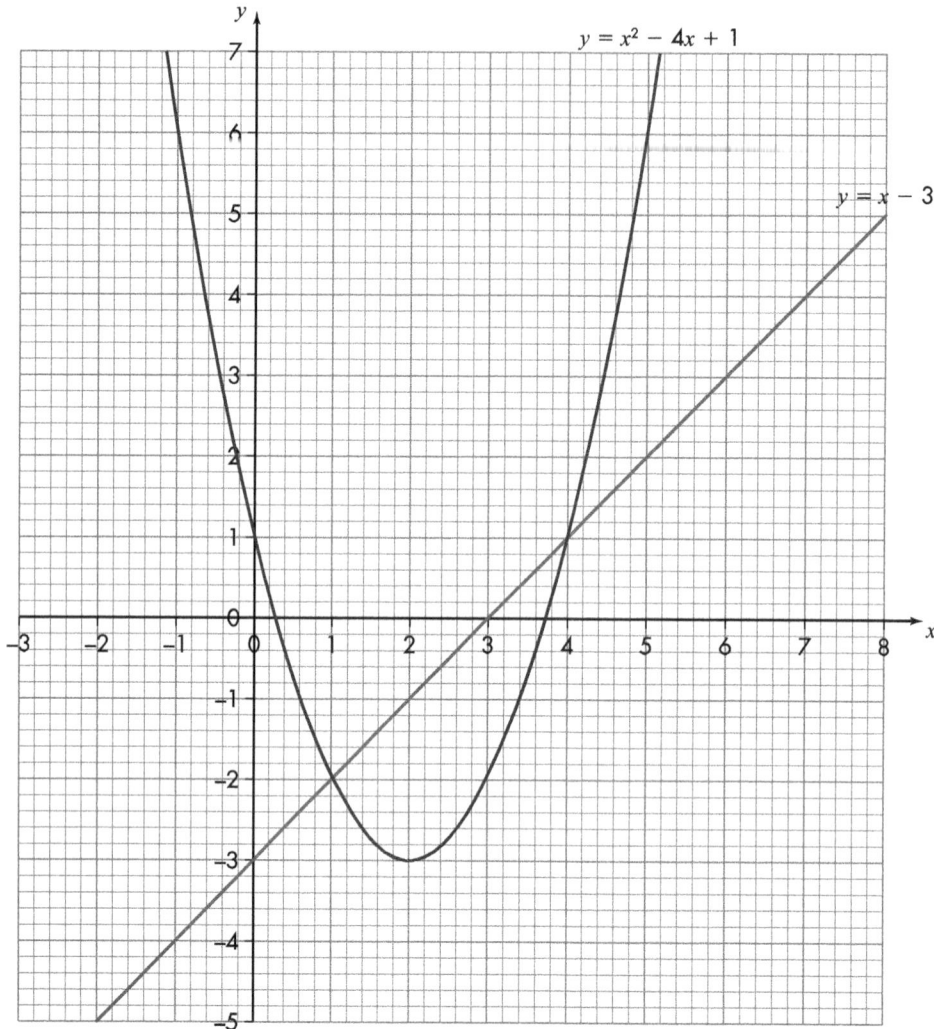

Use the graph to solve the following equations.

a $x^2 - 5x + 4 = 0$ b $x^2 - 4x + 1 = 2$ c $x^2 - 4x = 3$

Demonstrate clearly how you obtained your answers.

2   Draw the graph of $y = x^2 - 3x - 10$.

a   Solve $x^2 - 3x - 10 = 0$.

b   By drawing a suitable line solve $x^2 - 3x - 4 = 0$

c   By drawing a suitable line solve $x^2 - 4x - 6 = 0$

3 The diagram below shows the graphs of A: $y = x^3 - 2x^2 + 1$, B: $2x - 2y + 1 = 0$ and C: $x + 2y = 1$.

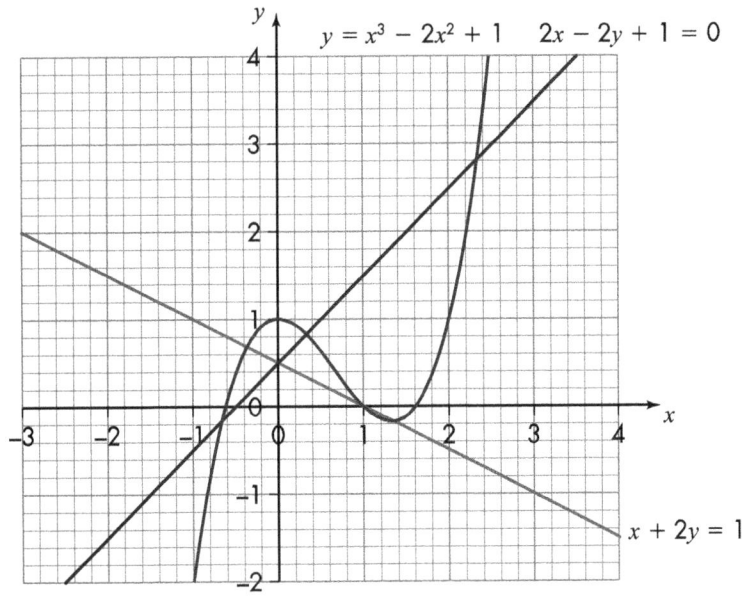

$y = x^3 - 2x^2 + 1$ $2x - 2y + 1 = 0$

$x + 2y = 1$

Find the points of intersection of the lines.

What other equations can you create and solve using these lines? Create challenging questions for a partner.

6 Logarithmic and Exponential Functions

TOPIC:

6.1 Properties of exponential functions and their graphs

KEY WORDS:

the number e, domain, range, asymptote, growth, exponential growth, decay, exponential decay, half-life, exponential functions, base

IGCSE MATHS PRIOR KNOWLEDGE:

Use the laws of indices

Work with the properties of inverse functions

Solve simultaneous equations

Solve quadratic equations

Learning aims:

- Know and use simple properties and graphs of the logarithmic and exponential functions, including $\ln x$ and e^x

Resources:

- Student Book: pages 118–121
- Whiteboards, or similar
- Graphical calculators and apps
- Small pieces of paper

Common mistakes and remediation:

A common misconception for graphs of functions of the form $y = a^x$ where $a > 0$, is that y is negative for negative values of x. Graphical calculators or online graph tools can be used to draw functions of the form $y = a^x$ where $a > 0$, and demonstrate that $y > 0$ for all values of x. Students need to understand that the negative x-axis is an asymptote for exponential graphs of this form. They should know that an asymptote is a straight line that a curve approaches but never meets or crosses. Students should also be taught that it is important when drawing sketches of exponential functions, they make sure their curve does not veer away from any asymptotes.

Useful tips:

Remember that $a^0 = 1$.

Guidance:

The starter is revision of content from IGCSE, using twenty questions, for example, *Show me the simplified version of $3x^2y \times 4x^5y^3$. What is the inverse of f(x) = 4x − 3? What are the solutions of $x^2 + 7x − 18 = 0$?*

For the main activity, think, pair, share involves students thinking through the problem on their own for a short while, for example, one to five minutes, then sharing their conclusions with their partner. After this the pairs of students share their ideas with a wider group.

For the think, pair, share activity, encourage students to devise some 'tips' that would enable another student to sketch the function.

As students work in pairs, encourage them to discuss their mathematics and reflect upon their work.

For the plenary, using exit tickets means that students should hand in their 'tickets', with their responses to the task written on them, as they leave.

Questions involving working with logarithmic and exponential functions can be calculator or non-calculator.

Note: Encourage students to explore the nature of graphical functions using graphical calculators or relevant IT, but remind them that these aids may not be used in the examination.

STARTER (5–10 mins)

Equipment: Mini whiteboards, or similar

➤ Practise manipulating indices, finding inverses of functions, sketching graphs of functions and their inverses, solving simultaneous equations, solving quadratic equations, using, for example, twenty questions. (See guidance above.)

MAIN LESSON ACTIVITY (40–45 mins)

Equipment: Graphical calculators and apps

➤ Using think, pair, share, ask students to consider the exponential function $f(x) = ka^{nx} + b$, where n, k, a and b are integers and $a > 0$. Ask them to consider, for example, how the function could be represented graphically with different values for the integers. Ask: *What is the easiest way to sketch the function? What happens if $a < 1$? Does the function intercept the axes, any asymptotes that exist, the domain and range of the function?* (Graphical calculators and apps can be used to support this activity.) (See guidance above.)

Bring students together to discuss their conclusions. Discuss the variety of different forms of the function $f(x) = ka^{nx} + b$, where k, a, n and b are integers and $a > 0$, beginning with $f(x) = a^x$. Discuss $a < 1$ and $a > 1$, domains, ranges, asymptotes, intersecting the axes. Discuss growth and exponential growth, decay and exponential decay/half-life and real-life applications of exponential functions.

➤ Display these instructions, but not the answers.

   $y = k(2^x) + c$, given $y = 7$ when $x = 0$ and $y = 2$ when $x = -1$ (Answer: $k = 10$, $c = -3$)

   $y = k(3^x) + c$, given $y = 3$ when $x = 0$ and $y = 7$ when $x = 1$ (Answer: $k = 2$, $c = 1$)

   $y = k(5^x) + c$, given $y = 5.5$ when $x = 0$ and $y = 3.5$ when $x = -1$ (Answer: $k = 2.5$, $c = 3$)

➤ Working in pairs, students investigate how the values of k and c could be found. Lower-achieving students could be given hint cards to support them in starting the activity, for example, 'Substitute $x = 0$ as a first step.'

Bring students together to discuss their findings. Emphasise substituting $x = 0$ and the need for using simultaneous equations.

➤ Discuss a standard method for expressing exponential functions in terms of the number e.

Display:

   $y = 2e^{4x}$ $y = 2e^{3x} + 1$ $y = 2e^{3x} - 1$

➤ Working in pairs, students sketch the graph of each function, checking their answers on graphical calculators and apps. Encourage them to state the equation of any asymptote and the coordinates of the point of intersection with the y-axis. Ask students to investigate different values for the three expressions, using positive and negative values for x. Lower-achieving students could just substitute positive values for x.

Students can now do Exercise 6.1.

➤ Questions 1 and 2 provide opportunities for graphing exponential functions.

Question 3 provides opportunities for evaluating expressions of the form ke^{nx+c}

➤ Questions 4 and 5 provide opportunities for finding the values of k and c in expressions of the form $y = k(a^x) + c$.

Question 6 provides the opportunity for problem solving.

PLENARY (10 mins)

Equipment: Small pieces of paper, or similar

➤ Use exit tickets. Ask students to write down three main learning points from the lesson. (See guidance above.)

Homework and answers: Resource sheets, homework and extension exercises can be found at the end of this chapter and in the downloadable materials. Answers can be found in the downloadable materials.

CHECKING PROGRESS	Use the exit tickets to check students' progress.

TOPIC:

6.2 Properties of logarithmic functions and their graphs

KEY WORDS:

base, exponent, power, index, exponential form, logarithmic form, logarithmic functions, Naperian or natural logarithm, common logarithm, inverse, the number e, domain, range, asymptote

IGCSE MATHS PRIOR KNOWLEDGE:

Use the laws of indices

Work with the properties of inverse functions

Learning aims:

- Know and use simple properties and graphs of the logarithmic and exponential functions, including $\ln x$ and e^x

Resources:

- Student Book: pages 121–126
- Graphical calculators and apps
- Mini whiteboards

Common mistakes and remediation:

- Students sometimes have difficulty recognising the relationship between logarithms and exponentials as inverse functions. As an introduction, graphical calculators or online graph tools can be used to draw a function and its inverse on the same axes to demonstrate reflection in the line $y = x$. This can then be shown to apply to the graphs of $y = e^x$ and $y = \ln x$, as well as $y = 10^x$ and $y = \log x$. In each case, the relationship between the asymptotes and the intercepts on the x-axis and y-axis can be highlighted. Discussion should also relate to the connection between the domain and range of a function and its inverse.

Useful tips:

If $y = a^x$ then $\log_a y = x$

$a = a^1$ this means $\log_a a = 1$

$1 = a^0$ this means $\log_a 1 = 0$

The graphs of $y = e^x$ and $y = \ln x$ are inverse functions. The graphs are reflected in the line $y = x$

Graph of $y = e^x$	Graph of $y = \ln x$
$e^x > 0$ for all values of x	$\ln x > 0$ only exists for $x > 0$
passes through (0, 1)	passes through (1, 0)
equation of asymptote $y = 0$	equation of asymptote $x = 0$

Guidance:

For the main activity, as students investigate graphing with technology, encourage them to consider how they would sketch the logarithmic functions, for example, by considering points of intersection and asymptotes. Encourage them to think about using, for example, $\log_e 1 = 0$. (At this point $\ln x$ for $\log_e x$ has not been introduced.) Do not mention inverses at this point.

For the main activity, discuss the use of the calculator after the investigation with technology.

For Exercise 6.2, cards could be produced for question 11 to allow for further group work.

As students work in pairs, encourage them to discuss their mathematics and reflect upon their work.

STARTER (5–10 mins)

Equipment: Graphical calculators and apps

➢ Display: $f(x) = 2e^{2x}$ $\quad\quad$ $g(x) = 2e^{-2x} - 3$ $\quad\quad$ $h(x) = -1.5e^x + 1$

➢ Ask the students to sketch the graphs of the functions, labelling any asymptotes with their equation and labelling the coordinates of the point of intersection with the y-axis.

➢ Ask students to use graphical calculators and apps to check their graphs.

➢ As time allows, ask students to investigate different values for each function, using positive and negative values for x.

MAIN LESSON ACTIVITY (40–45 mins)

Equipment: Graphical calculators and apps

➢ Display:

$32 = 2^5$ $\quad\quad$ $10\,000 = 10^4$ $\quad\quad$ $81 = 3^4$ $\quad\quad$ $64 = 4^3$ $\quad\quad$ $15.625 = 2.5^3$

$1 = e^0$ $\quad\quad$ $e = e^1$ $\quad\quad$ $y = a^x$ $\quad\quad$ $y = e^x$

➢ Discuss power, exponent, index and base for $32 = 2^5$. Discuss exponential form. Introduce the logarithmic form, 'log base 2 of 32 is 5'.

➢ Working in pairs, students write all seven expressions in logarithmic form then create five of their own logarithmic expressions, that can be evaluated without the use of a calculator, (as relevant, discuss the evaluation of a logarithmic expression). Another pair of students can evaluate them. Answers are returned to be checked.

➢ Display these questions, but not the answers.

$\log_2 x = 7$ $\quad\quad$ $\log_2 x = 10$ $\quad\quad$ $\log_4 x = 5$ $\quad\quad$ $\log_6 x = 4$ $\quad\quad$ $\log_{1.5} x = 4$

(Answers: 128 $\quad\quad\quad\quad$ 1024 $\quad\quad\quad\quad$ 1024 $\quad\quad\quad\quad$ 1296 $\quad\quad\quad\quad$ 5.0625)

➢ Working in pairs, students find the value of x in each expression, without the use of a calculator.

➢ Display these equations.

$y = 2^x$ $\quad\quad$ $y = 10^x$ $\quad\quad$ $y = 3^x$ $\quad\quad$ $y = e^x$ $\quad\quad$ $2y = e^{\frac{x}{3}}$ $\quad\quad$ $y + 2 = e^{\frac{x}{3}}$ $\quad\quad$ $y = \dfrac{e^{\frac{x}{3}} + 2}{2}$

➢ Working in pairs, using graphical calculators and apps, students draw the graphs of each equation then investigate drawing graphs after converting them into logarithmic form. Encourage them to write down any observations they have, for example, asymptotes, points of intersection. Lower-achieving students could be given, for example, hint cards to support using logarithms, such as: 'Swap x and y round after creating the logarithm form.' (See guidance above.)

➢ Bring students together to discuss their findings. Discuss inverses, $\log_{10} x$ (common logarithm) being written as $\log x$ or $\lg x$, $\log_e x$ (Naperian or natural logarithm) being written as $\ln x$. Discuss the use of $\ln 1 = 0$ and $\ln x$ only existing for $x > 0$ when sketching equations such as $y = 4\ln(2x - 3)$. A visual aid could support this discussion. (See guidance above.)

➢ Students can now do Exercise 6.2.

➢ Questions 1 and 2 provide opportunities for writing expressions in logarithmic and exponential form.

➢ Questions 3 and 4 provide opportunities for evaluating logarithms and finding the value of x in expressions.

➢ Questions 5 to 7 provide opportunities for manipulating logarithms.

➢ Questions 8 to 11 provide opportunities for investigating graphs of exponential and logarithmic functions.

PLENARY (10 mins)

Equipment: Mini whiteboards, or similar

➢ Ask students 'show me' or similar questions to explore their understanding of the lesson. Cover all aspects of the learning outcome.

➢ For example, *Show me the logarithmic form of $81 = 3^4$. Show me a logarithmic function that intersects the x-axis at (1,0).*

Homework and answers: Resource sheets, homework and extension exercises can be found at the end of this chapter and in the downloadable materials. Answers can be found in the downloadable materials.

CHECKING PROGRESS	Use the 'show me' questions to check students' progress.

6 Logarithmic and Exponential Functions

TOPIC:

6.3 Laws of logarithms

KEY WORDS:

base, power

IGCSE MATHS PRIOR KNOWLEDGE:

Use the laws of indices

Work with the properties of inverse functions

Solve simultaneous equations

Solve quadratic equations

Learning aims:	Resources:
• Know and use the laws of logarithms, including change of base of logarithms	• Student Book: pages 126–129
	• Graphical calculators and apps
	• A1/flipchart paper, or similar

Common mistakes and remediation:

Students sometimes have difficulty converting between logarithmic and exponential form. It is useful to relate the connection between powers of 10 and log. For example:

$10^0 = 1$ so log 1 = 0

$10^1 = 10$ so log 10 = 1   etc

Students may need reminding about using the quadratic formula. Emphasise the need to take care when identifying the values of the coefficients a and b, and the constant c, in a quadratic equation $ax^2 + bx + c = 0$ and substituting correctly in the formula.

Useful tips:

Remember to think carefully about the order when manipulating the laws of logarithms.

When solving equations involving logarithms and constants you can make use of the fact $\log_a a = 1$ to write, for example, 3 as $3 \log_a a$.

Guidance:

For the main activity, use twenty questions, for example, *Solve these simultaneous equations using substitution. Solve this quadratic equation using the formula.*

For the main activity, the paper could be displayed as posters.

For the main activity, when discussing $\log_8 (2x + 1) + \log_8 (x - 2) = 2 + \log_8 2$, discuss why there is only one positive solution for the value of x, by considering $\log_a x$ only exists for x > 0. So, in this example, both $(2x + 1) > 0$ and $(x - 2) > 0$ which means the solution for *x* must be > 2.

Consider questions that you could ask students as they work in groups, particularly those that encourage students to explain and justify their thinking. Also, encourage students to discuss their mathematics and reflect upon their work.

STARTER (5–10 mins)

Equipment: Graphical calculators and apps

➤ Display: $f(x) = \ln (4x)$ $g(x) = 3\ln (2x + 1)$ $h(x) = 2\ln (2x - 1)$

➤ Ask students to sketch the graphs of the functions, labelling any asymptotes with their equation and labelling the coordinates of the points of intersection with the *x*-axis.

➤ Ask students to use graphical calculators and apps to check their graphs.

➤ As time allows, ask students to graph the inverses of each of the functions on the same set of axes, using graphical calculators and apps.

MAIN LESSON ACTIVITY (40–45 mins)

Equipment: A1/flipchart paper, or similar

➤ Using twenty questions, or similar, ask students to solve some simultaneous and quadratic equations.

➤ Display:

$$\log_a b = x \qquad\qquad \log_a \square = \square \qquad\qquad \square = a \qquad\qquad c = \square^y$$

$$\log_a bc = \square \qquad\qquad \log_a \frac{b}{c} = \square \qquad\qquad \log_a b^2 = \square \qquad\qquad \log_a c^2 = \square$$

➤ Working in groups of three or four, students complete the questions in the first line, then investigate completing those in the second line. Ask students to produce a summary of their investigation on A1/flipchart paper. Lower-achieving students could be given be further cards that need completing, for example, $bc = a \times a$ (See guidance above.)

➤ Bring students together to discuss their findings. Discuss the three laws:

$$\log_a bc = \log_a b + \log_a c \qquad\qquad \log_a \frac{b}{c} = \log_a b - \log_a c \qquad\qquad \log_a b^2 = 2 \log_a b$$

➤ Display these questions, but not the answers.

➤ Express in terms of $\log_a x$, $\log_a y$ and $\log_a z$: $\qquad \log_a (xy^2 z) \qquad\qquad \log_a \dfrac{xy}{z^2}$

(Answers: $\log_a x + 2 \log_a y + \log_a z \qquad\qquad \log_a x + \log_a y - 2 \log_a z$)

Write as single logarithm: $\quad 4 + \log_a 5 \qquad$ (Answer: $\log_a 5a^4$)

Find the value of x for which: $\quad \log_2 (x - 1) - \log_2 (x - 2) = \log_2 2 \qquad$ (Answer: $x = 3$)

Solve: $\quad \log_8 (2x + 1) + \log_8 (x - 2) = 2 + \log_8 2 \qquad$ (Answer: $x = 8.85$ to 3 s.f.)

➤ Working in groups of three or four, students investigate using the three laws of logarithms to solve the problems. Encourage them to consider, for example, applying the laws in reverse. Lower-achieving students could be given, for example, hint cards to provide support for solving the problems, such as: 'Use law 3 first'.

➤ Bring students together to discuss their findings. Discuss the application of the laws in each context. (See guidance above.)

➤ Students can now do Exercise 6.3.

➤ Questions 1 to 3 provide opportunities for practising the laws.

➤ Questions 4 to 6 provide opportunities for finding the value of unknowns and logarithmic expressions.

➤ Questions 7 to 9 provide opportunities for solving equations.

➤ Question 10 provides opportunities for solving a simultaneous equation.

PLENARY (10 mins)

➤ Ask students to write a logarithmic equation that they can solve and give to another student to solve. Lower-achieving students could be encouraged to write, for example, an equation of the form $\log_8 (2x + 1) = 2$. Higher-achieving students could be encouraged to write an equation that makes use of the quadratic formula when solving it.

Homework and answers: Resource sheets, homework and extension exercises can be found at the end of this chapter and in the downloadable materials. Answers can be found in the downloadable materials.

CHECKING PROGRESS	Use the written problems from the plenary to check students' progress.

6 Logarithmic and Exponential Functions

TOPIC:

6.4 Changing the base of a logarithm

KEY WORD:

base

IGCSE MATHS PRIOR KNOWLEDGE:

Use the laws of indices

Learning aims:
- Know and use the laws of logarithms, including change of base of logarithms

Resources:
- Student Book: pages 129–130
- Small pieces of paper, or similar

Common mistakes and remediation:

Students sometimes have difficulty converting between logarithmic and exponential form. It is useful to relate the connection between powers of 10 and log. For example:

$10^0 = 1$ so $\log 1 = 0$

$10^1 = 10$ so $\log 10 = 1$ etc

Useful tips:

Remember, for example, $(\log_a a)^2$ means $\log_a a \times \log_a a$.

Guidance:

For the main activity, the spider diagram requires the student responses to be placed around the 7, for example:

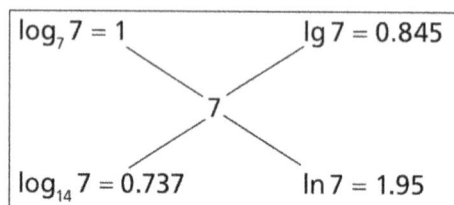

$$\log_7 7 = 1 \qquad \lg 7 = 0.845$$
$$7$$
$$\log_{14} 7 = 0.737 \qquad \ln 7 = 1.95$$

For the main activity, when the students are solving the problems, encourage the technique of converting equations to linear form to support solving them, for example, when solving $4 \log_2 x + 3 \log_4 x - 5 = 0$.

Consider questions that you could ask students as they work in groups, particularly those that encourage students to explain and justify their thinking. Also, encourage students to discuss their mathematics and reflect upon their work.

For the plenary, using exit tickets means the students should hand in their 'tickets', with their responses to the task written on them, as they leave.

STARTER (5–10 mins)

➢ Working in groups of three, students each choose one of the three laws of logarithms and explain it to their group, creating simultaneous equations that use the law when they are solved.

MAIN LESSON ACTIVITY (40–45 mins)

➤ Display on the board: 7

➤ By creating a spider diagram, or similar, discuss the value of the log of 7 in a variety of bases, for example, $\log_3 7$, $\log_7 7$, $\log 7$, $\ln 7$. (See guidance above.)

➤ Using one of the students' responses, replacing their value with letter x, display, for example,

$$\log_3 7 = x$$

$$3^x = 7$$

➤ Working in groups of two, students investigate finding the value of the log of 3^x in a variety of bases.

➤ Bring students together to discuss their findings. Discuss finding the value of the log of 3^x by using the value of the log of 7.

➤ Using one of the students' examples, display, for example:

$$\log_4 3^x = \log_4 7$$

➤ Working in groups of two, students investigate finding the value of x.

➤ Bring students together to discuss their findings. Display:

$$\log_4 3^x = \log_4 7$$

$$x \log_4 3 = \log_4 7$$

$$x = \frac{\log_4 7}{\log_4 3}$$

➤ Discuss the base of x, changing from base 3 to base 4. Discuss the general form for changing the base of a logarithm, for example, $\log_a b = \dfrac{\log_c b}{\log_c a}$ Discuss the special case when $c = b$, for example, $\log_a b = \dfrac{\log_b b}{\log_b a} = \dfrac{1}{\log_b a}$, because $\log_b b = 1$.

➤ Display on the board these questions, but not the answers.

By converting to log base e, calculate, to three significant figures, the value of $\log_4 14$.

(Answer: 1.90)

Solve this equation, giving the answers to 3 s.f. $x = \dfrac{1}{\log_{16} x}$.

(Answer: $x = 7.10$ or $x = 0.141$)

Solve this equation, giving the answer to 3 s.f. $4 \log_2 x + 3 \log_4 x - 5 = 0$

(Answer: 1.88)

Given that $\log_9 8 = p$, express $\log_3 24$ in terms of p. (Answer: $2p + 1$)

➤ Working in groups of three or four, students investigate using the general form for changing the base of a logarithm to solve the problems. Lower-achieving students could be given, for example, hint cards to provide support for solving the problems, such as: '$(\log_a a)^2$ means $\log_a a \times \log_a a$.' (See guidance above.)

➤ Students can now do Exercise 6.4.

➤ Questions 1 to 3 and 6 provide opportunities for practising the use of the general form.

➤ Questions 4, 5 and 7 to 9 provide opportunities for solving equations.

➤ Question 10 provides an opportunity to solve a simultaneous equation.

PLENARY (10 mins)

Equipment: Small pieces of paper, or similar

➤ Using exit tickets, ask the students to write down three main learning points from the lesson. (See guidance above.)

Homework and answers: Resource sheets, homework and extension exercises can be found at the end of this chapter and in the downloadable materials. Answers can be found in the downloadable materials.

CHECKING PROGRESS	Use the written problems from the plenary to check students' progress.

6 Logarithmic and Exponential Functions

TOPIC:

6.5 Equations of the form $a^x = b$

KEY WORDS:

taking logs

IGCSE MATHS PRIOR KNOWLEDGE:

Use the laws of indices

Solve quadratic equations

Learning aims:

- Solve equations of the form $a^x = b$

Resources:

- Student Book: pages 131–132
- Resource sheet 6.1

Common mistakes and remediation:

Students sometimes have difficulty converting between logarithmic and exponential form. It is useful to relate the connection between powers of 10 and log. For example:

$10^0 = 1$ so log 1 = 0

$10^1 = 10$ so log 10 = 1   etc

Students may need reminding about using the quadratic formula. Emphasise the need to take care when identifying the values of the coefficients a and b, and the constant c, in a quadratic equation $ax^2 + bx + c = 0$ and substituting correctly in the formula.

Useful tips:

ln e $= 1$

For $a > 0$, a^x is positive for all values of x, so if $a^x < 0$ there are no real solutions for x.

ln $e^{nx} = nx$ ln e $= nx$

An equation such as $6e^{3k} - 6e^{-3k} - 5 = 0$ can be solved by first substituting $y = e^{3k}$ to find the value of y and subsequently the value of x.

Guidance:

For the main activity, think, pair, share involves students thinking through the problem on their own for a short while, for example, one to five minutes, then sharing their conclusions with their partner. After this, the pairs of students share their ideas with a wider group.

For the main activity, when students are solving more complex exponential equations, encourage the use of substitution in the solution. For example, use $y = e^{3k}$ to support solving $4e^{6k} - 2e^{3k} - 5 = 0$. Remind them of the laws of indices and their use with exponentials. For example, $e^{3k} \times e^{3k} = e^{3k+3k} = e^{6k}$ so if $y = e^{3k}$ then $y^2 = e^{6k}$

For the main activity, an alternative to the second group work exercise is the use of Resource sheet 6.1, a card-matching exercise involving equations that requires students to use their skills in substituting and solving quadratics. The cards include blank areas that the students have to complete. Answers for the blanks: 1.5, −0.458, −0.837, 2.

Consider questions that you could ask students as they work in groups, particularly those that encourage students to explain and justify their thinking. Also, encourage students to discuss their mathematics and reflect upon their work.

STARTER (5–10 mins)

➤ Display these logarithms, but not the answers.

$\log_4 1$	$\log_4 7$	$\log_6 3$	$\log_9 12$	$\log_9 0.5$
(Answers: 0	1.40	0.613	1.13	−0.315)

$$\log_3 x = \frac{1}{\log_9 x} \qquad\qquad 3\log_2 x + 3\log_4 x - 6 = 0$$

(Answers: 4.73 or 0.211   2.52)

➤ Ask students to find the value of each of the logarithms and solve the two equations, by changing the base of the logarithm.

MAIN LESSON ACTIVITY (40–45 mins)

➤ Display these problems, but not the answers.

$5^x = 76$	$4^x = 9$	$a^x = b$
(Answers: 2.69	1.58)	

➤ Students think, pair, share how to find the value of x.

➤ Bring students together to discuss their findings. Discuss taking logs of both sides (include discussion of which base/s would be the easiest to use.)

➤ Display these questions but not the answers.

Solve $300 = e^{2.5t}$, giving the answer to 3 s.f.   (Answer: 2.28)

Solve $12e^{3x} = 9$, giving the answer to 3 s.f.   (Answer: −0.0959)

Solve the equation $5^{p+2} - 3 = 0.8$, giving the answer to 3 s.f.   (Answer: −1.17)

Solve this equation, giving the answer to 3 s.f.

$$4e^{4x} + 5e^{2x} = 6 \qquad\qquad\qquad \text{(Answer: −0.144)}$$

➤ Working in groups of three or four, students investigate solving the problems. Lower-achieving students could be encouraged to consider the steps that are needed to solve the problems. (See guidance above.)

➤ Bring students together to discuss their findings.

➤ Working in groups of three or four, students create their own equations, similar to $4e^{4x} + 5e^{2x} = 6$, that require substitution of a variable in solving them. These can then be swapped with those of another group to be solved. Solutions are then returned to be checked. (Encourage students to consider the solutions to the equation involving the variable, as a first step in creating their equations, for example, $(5y - 2)(y - 3)$.) Lower-achieving students could create equations where the quadratic equation involving the variable is factorised. Higher-achieving students could create equations where the quadratic equation involving the variable cannot be factorised. (See guidance above.)

➤ Students can now do Exercise 6.5.

➤ Questions 1 and 2 provide opportunities for practising taking logs of both sides.

➤ Question 3 to 6 provide opportunities for solving equations.

PLENARY (10 mins)

➤ Ask students to explain briefly to another person what they have understood from the lesson, using examples where necessary.

Homework and answers: Resource sheets, homework and extension exercises can be found at the end of this chapter and in the downloadable materials. Answers can be found in the downloadable materials.

CHECKING PROGRESS	Use the verbal feedback to partners in the plenary to check students' progress.

6   Logarithmic and Exponential Functions

Resource sheet 6.1

Equations of the form $a^x = b$

$\dfrac{1}{3}$ ln _____	$6e^{3k} - 5 - 6e^{-3k} = 0$
0.549 or _____	$5e^{4x} - 17e^{2x} + 6 = 0$
_____	$8e^{3k} - 2e^{-3k} + 24 = 0$
$\dfrac{1}{2}$ ln 2 or $\dfrac{1}{2}$ ln 3	
$\dfrac{1}{2}$ (ln _____ − 1)	$3e^{(2x+1)^2} - 5e^{(2x+1)} = 2$

6   Logarithmic and Exponential Functions

Homework

6.1 Properties of exponential functions and their graphs

1   **[NC]** Sketch and label the graphs of each pair of functions on the same axes. In each case, give the equation of the asymptote, the coordinates of the point of intersection with the y-axis, the domain and range of the functions.

   a $y = 3e^x$ and $y = 3e^{-x}$ **b** $y = 2e^{2x}$ and $y = 2e^{-2x}$

   c $y = 2e^{3x}$ and $y = 2e^{-3x}$ **d** $y = 8e^{5x} + 1$ and $y = 10e^{-5x} - 1$

2   **[NC]** $y = k(2^x) + c$

   Given $y = 8$ when $x = 0$ and $y = 17$ when $x = 2$

   a   Find the value of k and the value of c.

   b   Find the value of y when $x = 1$.

3   **[NC]** $y = k(2^x) + c$

   Given $y = 5$ when $x = 0$ and $y = 7$ when $x = -2$

   a   Find the value of k and the value of c.

   b   Find the value of y when $x = 2$.

4   Calculate the value of each expression for the given value of x. Give your answer to 3 significant figures.

   a $5e^{3x+1}$ when $x = 2$ **b** $5e^{3x+1}$ when $x = -2$

   c $2.5e^{1.5x-1}$ when $x = 3$ **d** $3.5e^{3.5x-3}$ when $x = -2$

5   The variables S and x are such that $S = 400 + 3e^{x+4}$

   a   Find the value of S when $x = 4$, correct to 2 decimal places.

   b   Find the value of S when $x = -6$, correct to 2 decimal places.

6 $B = 400 + 200e^{0.4t}$ where B equals the number of bacteria after t days of observation.

   a   Find the number of bacteria at the start of the observation.

   b   Find the number of bacteria after 8 days of observation.

6 Logarithmic and Exponential Functions

Homework

6.2 Properties of logarithmic functions and their graphs

1   [NC] Write these expressions in logarithmic form.

   a $8^4 = 4096$

   b $4^{-3} = \dfrac{1}{64}$

   c $5^{-4} = 0.0016$

   d $x^g = 0.197$

   e $x^z = t$

2   [NC] Write these expressions in exponential form.

   a $\log_5 125 = 3$

   b $\log_3 243 = 5$

   c $\log_7 2401 = 4$

   d $\log_6 7776 = 5$

   e $\log_d b = t$

3   [NC] Given that $p = \lg 36$, express these in terms of p.

   a $\lg 6$

   b $\lg 216$

   c $\lg \sqrt{6}$

4   [NC] Sketch the graphs of the following functions, stating the equation of any asymptotes and the coordinates of the point of intersection with the x-axis.

   a $f(x) = \ln(3x)$

   b $g(x) = 4\ln(2x + 1)$

   c $h(x) = 2\ln(2x - 3)$

5   Evaluate these expressions, giving the answers to 3 significant figures if necessary.

   a $\log_3 45$

   b $\log_2 23$

   c $\log_4 0.8$

   d $\log_2 2^4$

   e $11^{\lg 5}$

6   Find the value of x in each equation, giving the answer to 3 significant figures if necessary.

   a $\log_3 x = -3$

   b $\log_4 x = 7$

   c $\log_5 x = -2.5$

   d $\lg x = 7$

   e $\lg x = 0.756$

7   Find the value of x, giving the answer to 3 significant figures.

   a $\ln(3x - 5) = 4$

   b $\ln(2x - 3) = 4.5$

   c $\ln(3.5x + 4) = 7.2$

6   Logarithmic and Exponential Functions

Homework

6.3 Laws of logarithms

1   **[NC]** Express in terms of $\log_a x$, $\log_a y$, $\log_a z$.

    a $\log_a (x^2 yz)$
               b $\log_a \dfrac{xy}{z}$

    c $\log_a \dfrac{x^2}{yz}$
               d $\log_a \left(x^2 z^3 \sqrt{y} \right)$

2   **[NC]** Write $3 + \log_a 4$ as a single logarithm.

3   **[NC]** Given that $4 \log_a x - 2 \log_a y = 2$, express a in terms of x and y.

4   **[NC]** Solve $2 \log_3 (x) - \log_3 (2x + 7) = 2$

5   **[NC]** Solve $\log_a 2z^2 + \log_a 16 + \log_a 32z - \log_a 64z = 2 \log_a 8$

6   **[NC]** Solve the simultaneous equations.

$\log_2 (x + 4y) = 4 + \log_2 x$

$\log_2 (2x + 5) = 3$

7   Solve $\log_2(x - 2) - 2 \log_2(x - 3) = \log_2 4$. Give your answer to 2 decimal places.

8   Solve $\log_q 512 = 4 - \log_q 64$. Give your answer to 3 significant figures.

6 Logarithmic and Exponential Functions

Homework

6.4 Changing the base of a logarithm

1   **[NC]** Find the value of $\log_{16} 64$ by first changing the base to $\log_4$.

2   **[NC]** Find the value of $3 \log_{25} 5$ by first changing the base to $\log_5$.

3   **[NC]** Given that $\log_{16} 10 = p$, express $\log_8 20$ in terms of p.

4   **[NC]** Express $\dfrac{\log_y b}{\log_b c}$ as a single logarithm.

5   **[NC]** Find k, given $\log_4 x = k \log_2 x$ for all $x > 0$.

6   By converting to base e, calculate, to 3 significant figures, the value of:
    a $\log_6 14$ b $3 \log_4 7$ c $4 \log_3 8$

7   Solve these equations for x. Give your answer to 3 significant figures where appropriate:
    a $\log_x 3 = \log_3 x$ b $\log_3 x = \dfrac{1}{\log_{27} x}$ c $4 \log_{16} x + 3 \log_4 x - 5 = 0$

8   Solve the equation $2 \log_2 x + \log_4 x - 3 = 0$. Give your answer to 3 significant figures.

6 Logarithmic and Exponential Functions

Homework

6.5 Equations of the form $a^x = b$

1 Solve the following equations, giving the answers to 2 decimal places.

    a $2^x = 25$ **b** $7^x = 36$

    c $32^x = 7$ **d** $29.4^x = 10$

2 Solve $8e^{4x} = 9$, give your answer to 3 significant figures.

3 Solve $6e^{-3x} = 9$, give your answer to 3 significant figures.

4 Solve $100 = 50e^{0.01t}$, give your answer to 3 significant figures.

5 Solve $5^{p+2} - 1 = 0.8$, give your answer to 2 decimal places.

6 Solve $6^{n+4} - 7 = 1.9$, give your answer to 2 decimal places.

7 Solve the equation $3(6^{2x}) - 6^x = 8$, give your answer to 3 significant figures.

8 Given that $y = 5x^2$, show that $\log_5 y = 1 + 2 \log_5 x$

    Hence, or otherwise, solve the equation $1 + 2 \log_5 x = \log_5 (3x + 12)$

    Give your answers to 3 significant figures.

9 Using the substitution $y = e^{4k}$ or otherwise, solve the equation $7e^{4k} - 7e^{-4k} + 50 = 0$

    Give your answer in the form $a \ln b$ where a and b are constants.

Extension

6.1 Properties of exponential functions and their graphs

1   The mathematical constant e is an irrational number 2.71828 …

Exponential functions can be expressed in terms of e.

The compound interest formula from IGCSE is given as:

$P\left(1+\dfrac{r}{100}\right)^{n}$ where P is the initial value, r is the rate of interest and n is the number of years.

So, $1 invested for 1 year at 100% interest would be $1\times\left(1+\dfrac{100}{100}\right)^{1}=\$2$

If the 100% interest was split so 50% interest was received every 6 months, the formula would then be

$1\times\left(1+\dfrac{50}{100}\right)^{2}=\$2.25$

If the 100% interest was split so 25% interest was received every 3 months, the formula would then be .

$1\times\left(1+\dfrac{25}{100}\right)^{4}=\$2.44...$

Investigate what happens to the initial investment if the interest is split further over the year.

2   Investigate how initial investments develop with different rates of interest that are split over one year.

3   What happens to investments with different interest rates and different time periods?

4   Mohammed has 200 kg of crystals that grow continuously. A single crystal doubles in size in 24 hours. What will the weight of crystals be after 8 days?

5   100 kg of radioactive material looks like it continuously decays at a rate of 50% per year. How much material will there be at the end of 5 years?

6   Logarithmic and Exponential Functions

Extension

6.2 Properties of logarithmic functions and their graphs

1   Investigate the use of logarithms in real-life contexts.

Some examples to investigate would be:

Richter scale, decibels, radioactive decay, population growth.

2   Produce a summary of your investigation in the form of a presentation, webpage, video or similar.

3   Produce an explanation of exponents and logarithms that uses non-mathematical terminology.

Extension

6.5 Equations of the form $a^x = b$

1. Investigate differentiation of exponential and logarithmic functions.

2. Produce a summary of your investigation in the form of a presentation, webpage, video or similar.

TOPIC:
7.1 Interpreting equations of the form $y = mx + c$

KEY WORDS:
Cartesian, coordinates, variable, constant, y-intercept, gradient

IGCSE MATHS PRIOR KNOWLEDGE:
Draw straight-line graphs

Work out the gradient of a straight-line

Learning aims:	Resources:
• Use the equation of a straight-line	• Student Book: pages 138–142 • Resource sheet 7.1 • Small pieces of paper, or similar

Common mistakes and remediation:

A common error for students in working out the gradient, is to divide the difference in x-values by the difference in y-values. This can be addressed by referring to the gradient formula as the 'change in y, divided by the change in x' which can be helpful to refer back to when the students learn about differentiation. Another common reference is to describe the gradient calculation as 'rise over run'. Reinforce that, working from left to right, 'uphill' lines have a positive gradient and 'downhill' lines have a negative gradient.

Useful tips:

Be careful when manipulating negative values. Remember $- \times - = +$.

Guidance:

The starter is revision of content from the IGCSE, in the form of a card-matching exercise.

For the main activity, the spider diagram requires student responses to be placed around the words, for example:

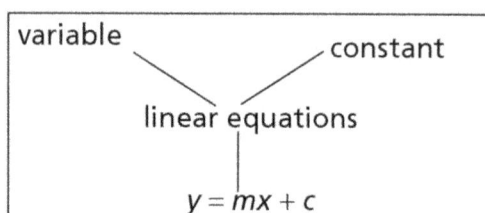

As students work in pairs, encourage them to discuss their mathematics and reflect upon their work.

For the plenary, using exit tickets means the students should hand in their 'tickets', with their responses to the task written on them, as they leave.

STARTER (5–10 mins)

Equipment: Resource sheet 7.1

➤ Working in pairs, students match the cards. (Do not give any information about content unless students are really struggling.)

MAIN LESSON ACTIVITY (40–45 mins)

➤ Display, near the centre of the board, the term: linear equations

➤ Discuss all the details that the students can remember about linear equations, for example, Cartesian, coordinates, constants, gradient, to create a spider diagram, or similar. (See guidance above.)

➤ Display this information, but not the answers, on the board.

$A(3, 4)$ and $B(7, 9)$ $A(2, 4)$ and $B(-7, 9)$ $A(-8, 4)$ and $B(-5, -6)$

$$\left(\text{Answer: } \frac{5}{4}, 4y = 5x + 1 \qquad -\frac{5}{9}, 9y = -5x + 46 \qquad -3\frac{1}{3}, 3y = -10x - 68 \right)$$

➢ Working in pairs, students write down the gradient of the line AB for each pair of coordinates and work out an equation of the line AB.

➢ Bring students together to discuss their methods and solutions. Discuss the general method for finding the gradient $m = \dfrac{y_2 - y_1}{x_2 - x_1}$ and the equation $y - y_1 = m(x - x_1)$.

➢ Working in pairs, students check the equations of the lines by using the equation.

➢ Display these questions, but not the answers.

The gradient of the line joining the points with coordinates $(-4, p)$ and $(2p, 7)$ is $\dfrac{3}{2}$. Find the value of p.

$$\left(\text{Answer: } p = \frac{1}{4} \right)$$

The gradient of the line joining the points with coordinates $(7, p)$ and $(3p, 8)$ is $\dfrac{1}{2}$. Find the value of p.

$$\left(\text{Answer: } p = 4\frac{3}{5} \right)$$

The gradient of the line joining the points with coordinates $(p, 8)$ and $(2, -3p)$ is $-\dfrac{1}{2}$. Find the value of p.

$$\left(\text{Answer: } p = -\frac{2}{2} \right)$$

➢ Working in pairs, students investigate how the value of p can be found.

➢ Bring students together to discuss their findings. Discuss using $m = \dfrac{y_2 - y_1}{x_2 - x_1}$ and simultaneous equations as a suitable method.

➢ Students can now do Exercise 7.1.

➢ Question 1 provides opportunities for finding equations of straight-lines drawn on a grid.

➢ Question 2 provides opportunities to use the general method for finding the gradient of the line joining two points.

➢ Questions 3, 5 and 6 provide opportunities to use the formula $y - y_1 = m(x - x_1)$.

➢ Question 4 provides an opportunity to use the formula $m = \dfrac{y_2 - y_1}{x_2 - x_1}$ for problem solving.

➢ Question 7 provides opportunities for problem solving.

PLENARY (10 mins)

Equipment: Small pieces of paper, or similar

➢ Ask students to write down two pairs of coordinates and find the equation of the line that joins them. (See guidance above.)

Homework and answers: Resource sheets, homework and extension exercises can be found at the end of this chapter and in the downloadable materials. Answers can be found in the downloadable materials.

CHECKING PROGRESS	Use the exit tickets to check students' progress.

TOPIC:

7.2 Transforming relationships of the form $y = ax^n$ and $y = ab^x$ to linear form

KEY WORDS:

transform, take logs, linearisation, plot, experimental data

IGCSE MATHS PRIOR KNOWLEDGE:

Draw straight-line graphs

Work out the gradient of a straight-line

Learning aims:

- Transform given relationships to and from straight-line form, including determining unknown constants by calculating the gradient or intercept of the transformed graph

Resources:

- Student Book: pages 143–150
- Graphical calculators and apps
- Spreadsheet software
- Mini whiteboards, or similar

Common mistakes and remediation:

A common error for students in working out the gradient, is to divide the difference in x-values by the difference in y-values. This can be addressed by referring to the gradient formula as the 'change in y, divided by the change in x' which can be helpful to refer back to when the students learn about differentiation. Another common reference is to describe the gradient calculation as 'rise over run'. Reinforce that, working from left to right, 'uphill' lines have a positive gradient and 'downhill' lines have a negative gradient.

Useful tips:

Remember:

- $\log_{10} x$ can be written as $\lg x$
- $\log_e x$ can be written as $\ln x$
- if $y = a^x$ then $\log_a y = x$
- if $y = 10^x$ then $\lg y = x$
- If $y = e^x$ then $\ln y = x$
- the laws of logarithms
  - Law 1: $\log_a AB = \log_a A + \log_a B$
  - Law 2: $\log_a \dfrac{A}{B} = \log_a A - \log_a B$
  - Law 3: $\log_a A^n = n\log_a A$

Be careful when manipulating negative values. Remember $- \times - = +$.

Guidance:

For the starter, make sure students work independently when manipulating the logarithmic expressions.

For the main activity, think, pair, share requires students to think through the problem on their own for a short while, for example, one to five minutes, then share their conclusions with their partner. After this, the pair of students share their ideas with a wider group.

For the main activity, spreadsheet software provides opportunities for data to be manipulated accurately, accurate graphs to be created, etc. Trend lines can be used to find, for example, y-intercepts.

For the main activity, as time allows, both activities for which students work in pairs could be extended by students creating their own data for questions that can then be shared for others to manipulate.

As the students work in pairs, encourage them to discuss their mathematics and reflect upon their work.

Note: Encourage students to explore the nature of graphical functions using graphical calculators or relevant IT, but remind them that these aids may not be used in the examination.

STARTER (5–10 mins)

➤ Display these logarithmic expressions.

$\qquad$ ln 36 $\qquad$ ln 15 $\qquad$ ln 25 $\qquad$ ln 9 $\qquad$ ln 64

➤ Ask students to rewrite each logarithm in different ways, using the three laws of logarithms. (Students can consider, for example, ln 36 = ln (6 × 6) = ln 6 + ln 6, ln 36 = ln 72 − ln 2, ln 36 = 2 ln 6.)

MAIN LESSON ACTIVITY (40–45 mins)

Equipment: Graphical calculators and apps, spreadsheet software

➤ Display these equations.

$\qquad$ $y = 3x^2$ $\qquad$ $y = 5x^3$ $\qquad$ $y = 4x^{-2}$ $\qquad$ $y = 3.5^2$ $\qquad$ $y = ax^n$ $\qquad$ $y = ab^x$

➤ Using think, pair, share, students consider how logarithms could be used to transform each equation into linear form. Encourage students to think about, for example, using natural or common logarithms, producing tables of data that can be manipulated using logarithms to create new data, plotting the new data, the gradient and y-intercept of the new straight-line graph, the relationship of the gradient and y-intercept to the original exponential equation. (Graphical calculators and apps, spreadsheet software, or similar, can be used to support this activity.)

➤ Bring students together to discuss their conclusions. Discuss transforming $y = ax^n$ by taking common logs, or natural logs, on both sides to linearise the equation. Discuss the order the laws of logarithms should be used. If considering common logs: lg y = lg ax^n, lg y = lg a + lg x^n, lg y = lg a + n lg x, comparing lg y = lg a + n lg x with $y = mx + c$ and identifying the y-intercept as the constant term and the gradient as the coefficient of lg x. Discuss how the values of a and n can be found. Repeat for equation $y = ab^x$ and compare e.g. ln y = x ln b with $y = mx + c$

➤ Display this question, but not the answer, on the board.

The variables q and p are connected by the equation $q = kp^n$, where k and n are constants.

The table shows values of p and q.

p	2	4	6	8
q	62.5	15.6	6.9	3.9

Work out the values of k and n. $\qquad$ (Answer: $n \approx -2$, $k \approx 250$, $q = 250p^{-2}$)

➤ Working in pairs, students investigate, without using technology, linearising the equation by using common logarithms, creating a new table of data and drawing a straight-line graph. Ask them to find the values of k and n from their graphs. Lower-achieving students could be given, for example, hint cards to provide support for the correct use of the laws of logarithms. (Encourage students to think about the accuracy of the logarithms. Work can be checked using graphical calculators and apps, spreadsheet software, or similar.)

➤ Bring students together to discuss their findings. Discuss methods for finding the gradient and the y-intercept from the straight-line graph. Discuss finding the values of k and n, and the accuracy of the values.

➤ Display this question, but not the answer, on the board.

The variables y and x are connected by the equation $y = ab^x$, where a and b are constants.

The table shows values of x and y.

x	2	4	6	8
y	64	16	4	1

Work out the values of a and b.

$$\left(\text{Answer: } b \approx \frac{1}{2}, \ a \approx 256, \ y = 256 \times \left(\frac{1}{2}\right)^x \right)$$

➤ Working in pairs, students investigate, without using technology, linearising the equation by using common logarithms, creating a new table of data and drawing a straight-line graph. Ask them to find the values of a and b from their graphs. Lower-achieving students could be given, for example, hint cards to provide support for the correct use of the laws of logarithms.

➤ Bring students together to discuss their findings. Discuss methods for finding the gradient and the y-intercept. Discuss finding the values of a and n and the accuracy of the values.

➤ Students can now do Exercise 7.2.

➤ Questions 1 and 4 provide opportunities for exploring straight-line graphs from experimental data.

➤ Questions 2 and 5 provide opportunities for finding equations.

➤ Questions 3 and 6 provide opportunities for problem solving in a real-life context.

PLENARY (10 mins)

Equipment: Mini whiteboards, or similar

Ask students 'show me' or similar questions to explore their understanding of the lesson. Cover all aspects of the learning outcome.

For example: *Show me a linearisation of $y = 7x^3$.*

Show me the y-intercept of the equation $\ln y = \ln k + n \ln x$.

➢ Working in pairs, students create a small set of data for variables y and x that are connected by the equation $y = ax^n$ or $y = ab^x$, where a, n, A and b are constants. The data can then be shared for manipulation to find the values of the constants. Answers can be returned to be checked.

Homework and answers: Resource sheets, homework and extension exercises can be found at the end of this chapter and in the downloadable materials. Answers can be found in the downloadable materials.

CHECKING PROGRESS	Use the responses to the plenary to check students' progress.

7 Straight-Line Graphs

TOPIC:
7.3 Transforming from linear form to given relationships

KEY WORDS:
coefficient

IGCSE MATHS PRIOR KNOWLEDGE:
Use and interpret equations of the form $y = mx + c$

Work out the gradient of a straight-line

Use simultaneous equations

Learning aims:
- Transform given relationships to and from straight-line form, including determining unknown constants by calculating the gradient or intercept of the transformed graph.

Resources:
- Student Book: pages 151–153
- Graphical calculators and apps
- Spreadsheet software, or similar

Common mistakes and remediation:

A common type of question covered in this section typically involves working out the equation of a straight-line passing through two points where the graph axes are not x and y. A common error for students is not using the axes labels when setting up their straight-line equation. Students should be encouraged to draw their own sketch of the graph and the given points including the axes labels to avoid this error. For those students who have difficulty working out the gradient, they can use the alternative method of simultaneous equations to work out the values of m and c for their straight-line equation. They can then use the gradient formula as a check.

Useful tips:

Remember:

- $\log_{10} x$ can be written as $\lg x$
- $\log_e x$ can be written as $\ln x$
- if $y = a^x$ then $\log_a y = x$
- if $y = 10^x$ then $\lg y = x$
- If $y = e^x$ then $\ln y = x$
- the laws of logarithms
  - Law 1: $\log_a AB = \log_a A + \log_a B$
  - Law 2: $\log_a \dfrac{A}{B} = \log_a A - \log_a B$
  - Law 3: $\log_a A^n = n\log_a A$

Guidance:

For the main activity, do not influence students' choices of logarithms for the first paired activity.

For the main activity, spreadsheet software provides the opportunity for data to be manipulated accurately, accurate graphs to be created, etc. Trend lines can be used to find, for example, y-intercepts.

For the main activity, as time allows, the second and third paired activities could be extended by students creating their own data for questions that can then be shared for others to manipulate.

As the students work in pairs, encourage them to discuss their mathematics and reflect upon their work.

Note: Encourage students to explore the nature of graphical functions using graphical calculators or relevant IT, but remind them that these aids may not be used in the examination.

STARTER (5–10 mins)

➢ Display these logarithmic and exponential equations.

$\ln y = 2\ln (x - 4)$ $\ln y = 2x^4 - 3$ $\ln y = 3\ln x + 5$ $e^{3y} = 4x^2 + 7$ $4e^{5y} = 2x^3 - 1$

➢ Ask students to use the relationship between logarithms and exponentials to rearrange each equation and write y as a function of x.

(Answers: $y = (x - 4)^2$ $y = e^{2x^4 - 3}$ $y = e^5 x^{-3}$ $y = \dfrac{1}{3} \ln(4x^2 + 7)$ $y = \dfrac{1}{5}\ln\left(\dfrac{2x^3 - 1}{4}\right)$)

MAIN LESSON ACTIVITY (40–45 mins)

Equipment: Graphical calculators and apps, spreadsheet software

➢ Display this question, but not the answers.

The variables x and y are related in such a way that when $\ln y$ is plotted against $\ln x$ a straight-line graph is obtained, as shown in the diagram. The line passes through the points (3, 4) and (9, 7).

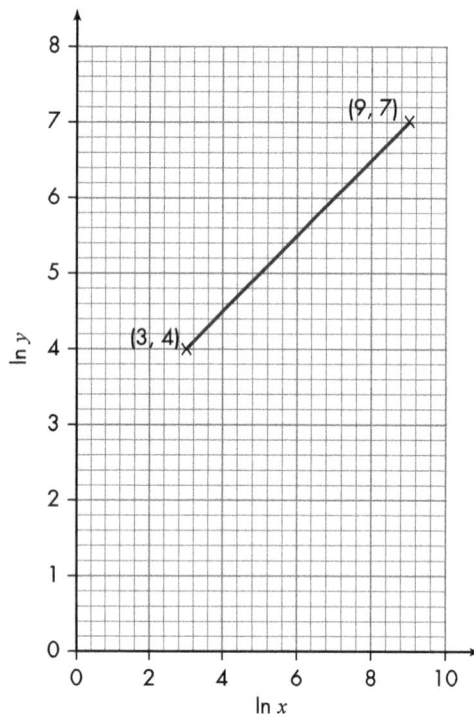

Show that x and y are connected by a relationship of the form $y = ab^x$ where a and b are constants.

$\left(\text{Answer: } b = \dfrac{1}{2}, a \approx 12, y = 12x^{\frac{1}{2}}\right)$

➢ Working in pairs, ask students to first write down a linear equation to connect $\ln y$ and $\ln x$ and compare with $y = mx + c$.

Point out that they can start by first linearising $y = ab^x$ or applying $Y = mX + c$ for the graph, where $Y = \ln y$ and $X = \ln x$

They can either use the coordinates of the points the line passes through with the gradient formula to find the value of m, or use them with simultaneous equations to find the values of m and c. They can then use the relationship between logarithms and exponentials to write the connection in the required form and identify the values of a and b. Lower-achieving students could be given, for example, hint cards to provide support for the correct use of the relationship between logarithms and exponentials. Encourage students to think about the accuracy to which the logarithms should be given. They can use graphical calculators and apps, spreadsheet software, or similar, to check their work.

➢ Bring students together to discuss their findings. Discuss methods for finding the gradient and the y-intercept from the straight-line graph including the use of simultaneous equations. Discuss comparing $\ln y = \ln a + x \ln b$ with $y = mx + c$, and identifying the vertical axis intercept as the constant term and the gradient as the coefficient of x. Discuss finding the values of a and b, and the accuracy of the values.

➢ Display this question but not the answer.

The relationship between experimental values of two variables, x and y, is given by $y = Ab^x$, where A and b are constants. The variables x and y are related in such a way that when $\ln y$ is plotted against x a straight-line graph is obtained, as shown in the diagram. The line passes through the points $(1, 4)$ and $(13, -2)$.

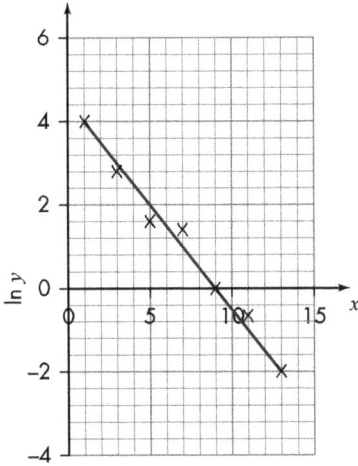

Work out the values of A and b

(Answer: $A \approx 90$, $b \approx 0.6$)

➢ Working in pairs, ask students to investigate finding the values of A and b. Remind them that $y = e^{mx+c}$ can be written as $y = e^{mx} \times e^c = e^m)^x \times e^c$ and the numerical values of e^m and e^c can be worked out on a calculator. Lower-achieving students could be given, for example, hint cards to provide support for the correct use of the relationship between logarithms and exponentials. Encourage students to think about the accuracy to which the exponentials should be given. They can use graphical calculators and apps, spreadsheet software, or similar, to check their work.

➢ Bring the students together to discuss their findings. Discuss methods for finding the gradient and the y-intercept from the straight-line graph including the use of simultaneous equations. Discuss comparing $\ln y = mx + c$ with $y = mx + c$ and identifying the vertical axis intercept as the constant term and the gradient as the coefficient of x. Discuss finding the values of A and b, and the accuracy of the values.

➢ Students can now do Exercise 7.3.

➢ Question 1 provides opportunities for transforming from straight-line form to relationships of the form $y^2 = Ax^3 + B$.

➢ Question 2 provides opportunities for transforming from straight-line form to relationships of the form $e^{2y} = Ax^2 + B$.

➢ Question 3 provides opportunities for transforming from straight-line form to relationships of the form $y^3 = A\ln x + B$.

➢ Question 4 provides opportunities for transforming from straight-line form to relationships of the form $y = e^p x^q$

➢ Question 5 provides opportunities for problem solving.

PLENARY (10 mins)

Equipment: Mini whiteboards, or similar

➢ Ask students 'show me' or similar questions to explore their understanding of the lesson. Cover all aspects of the learning outcome. For example: *Show me an equation for y in terms of x using the linear form ln y = 6 ln x − 2*

(Answer: $y = 0.14x^{-6}$)

Homework and answers: Resource sheets, homework and extension exercises can be found at the end of this chapter and in the downloadable materials. Answers can be found in the downloadable materials.

CHECKING PROGRESS	Use the responses to the plenary to check students' progress.

TOPIC:

7.4 Working with the mid-point and length of a straight-line

KEY WORDS:

mid-point, Pythagoras' theorem

IGCSE MATHS PRIOR KNOWLEDGE:

Draw straight-line graphs

Work out the gradient of a straight-line

Use Pythagoras' theorem

Learning aims:	**Resources:**
• Solve problems involving mid-point and length of a line, including finding and using the equation of a perpendicular bisector	• Student Book: pages 153–156

Common mistakes and remediation:

Students can have conceptual difficulties with ratio. It can be helpful to reinforce the relationship of ratio with fractions, for example if $a : b = m : n$ then $\dfrac{a}{b} = \dfrac{m}{n}$. Also, the relationship with division of lengths. For example, if the point P divides the line AB in the ratio $a : b$ then the length $AP = \dfrac{a}{a+b} AB$

Useful tips:

Remember, drawing a diagram can support visualising a question.

Remember, the square root of a number can be positive or negative.

Remember, giving the exact length of a line might mean leaving the answer in simplified surd form.

Be careful when manipulating negative values. Remember $- \times - = +$

Guidance:

The starter is revision of content from the IGCSE. The material will be revised in this lesson.

For the main activity, for the first discussion, include additional revision of finding the mid-point of a line and its length as necessary, for example, show that a right-angled triangle is formed by the points A(2, 7), B(0, 5) and C(3, 2). Find the mid-point of each side of the triangle.

For the main activity, encourage students to draw diagrams to help them visualise questions.

As the students work in pairs, encourage them to discuss their mathematics and reflect upon their work.

STARTER (5–10 mins)

➢ Display the diagram, but not the answer, on the board.

Ask students to find the equation of the straight-line, its exact length and the coordinates of its mid-point.

(Answer: $5y = 3x - 20$, $\sqrt{87}$, (5, –1))

➢ Working in pairs, students draw their own straight-line, find its exact length and the coordinates of its mid-point. Encourage students to include coordinates, etc. The straight-line can then be shared for another pair to evaluate. The answers can be returned to be checked.

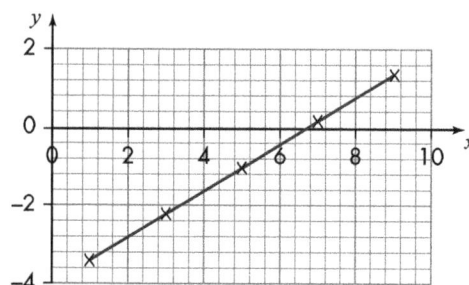

MAIN LESSON ACTIVITY (40–45 mins)

➤ Using one of the students' straight-line graphs, discuss the general method for finding a mid-point of a line, for example, $\left(\dfrac{x_1 + x_2}{2}, \dfrac{y_1 + y_2}{2}\right)$. Discuss the use of Pythagoras' theorem to find the length of a line, for example, $\sqrt{(x_2 - x_1)^2 + (y_2 - y_1)^2}$

➤ Display these questions, but not the answers, on the board.

The points $P(-3, 4)$, $Q(7, 1)$ and R lie on a straight-line such that Q is the mid-point of PR.

Find the coordinates of R.   (Answer: $(17, -2)$)

The points $R(-2, 3)$, $S(-7, 2)$ and T lie on a straight-line such that S is the mid-point of RT.

Find the coordinates of T.   (Answer: $(-12, 1)$)

The length of the line joining the points $A(3, 6)$ and $B(5, k)$ is 12.

Find the two possible values of k.   (Answer: $k = 17.8$ or $k = -5.83$)

The length of the line joining the points $C(-3, 6)$ and $D(-0.5, r)$ is 9.5.

Find the two possible values of r.   (Answer: $r = 15.2$ or $r = -3.17$)

➤ Working in pairs, ask the students to investigate the problems.

➤ Bring the students together to discuss their findings. Discuss the use of the general method for finding a mid-point of a line to the find the coordinates of R and T, for example using $\left(\dfrac{x_1 + x_2}{2}, \dfrac{y_1 + y_2}{2}\right)$.

Discuss the use of Pythagoras' theorem to find the values of k and r, for example using $\sqrt{(x_2 - x_1)^2 + (y_2 - y_1)^2}$.

➤ Display this question, but not the answers, on the board.

Given that P lies on the line AB, find the coordinates of P, when:

    a $A(-2, 5)$, $B(5, 14)$ and $AP = \dfrac{1}{3} AB$ $\left(\text{Answer:} \left(\dfrac{1}{3}, 8\right)\right)$

    b $A(-7, 4)$, $B(2, -2)$ and $AP = \dfrac{2}{5} AB$

        (Answer: $(-3.4, 1.6)$)

    c $A(3, 9)$, $B(8, 10)$ and $AP : PB = 7 : 2$

    $\left(\text{Answer:} \left(6\dfrac{8}{9}, 9\dfrac{7}{9}\right)\right)$

    d $A(-6, 2)$, $B(1, -4)$ and $AP : PB = 3 : 5$

        (Answer: $(-3.375, -0.25)$)

➤ Working in pairs, students investigate the problems.

➤ Bring students together to discuss their findings. Discuss methods for finding P when AP is stated as a fraction of AB and the ratio $AP : PB$ is given, for example, the use of algebraic methods.

➤ Students can now do Exercise 7.4.

➤ Questions 1 and 2 provide opportunities for investigating the mid-points of lines.

➤ Questions 3 to 6 provide opportunities for investigating the lengths of lines.

➤ Question 7 provides opportunities for investigating fractions and ratios applied to line segments.

PLENARY (10 mins)

Ask students to explain briefly what they have understood from the lesson to another person, who they did not work with on the problems.

Homework and answers: Resource sheets, homework and extension exercises can be found at the end of this chapter and in the downloadable materials. Answers can be found in the downloadable materials.

CHECKING PROGRESS	Use the verbal feedback to partners in the plenary to check students' progress.

7 Straight-Line Graphs

TOPIC:

7.5 Working with parallel and perpendicular lines

KEY WORDS:

parallel, perpendicular, negative reciprocal, bisector

IGCSE MATHS PRIOR KNOWLEDGE:

Identify parallel lines

Work out the gradient of a straight-line

Learning aims:

- Know and use the condition for two lines to be parallel or perpendicular

Resources:

- Student Book: pages 156–160
- A1/flipchart paper
- Mini whiteboards, or similar

Common mistakes and remediation:

Students often have difficulty when identifying equations of lines that are parallel and perpendicular when the equations are not given in the same format. Reinforce that the coefficient of x is the gradient of a straight-line only if the equation is written in the form $y = mx + c$ and that equations may first need to be rearranged, so that the coefficients of x can be compared.

Useful tips:

Remember, drawing a diagram can support visualising a question.

Remember, be careful not to reverse the values when substituting values for x and y into equations.

Remember, giving the exact answer might mean writing the answer as a fraction or mixed number.

Be careful when manipulating negative values. Remember $- \times - = +$

Two lines can be shown to be perpendicular if the product of their gradients is −1

A triangle can be shown to be right-angled in two ways:

- showing two of the sides are perpendicular
- using Pythagoras' theorem

Guidance:

The starter is revision of content from IGCSE. The material will be revised in this lesson.

For the for the first discussion in the main activity, include, if necessary, additional explanation and examples of how parallel lines and perpendicular lines are found.

For the main activity, after the discussion of the word problem, include, as necessary, additional problems to support student understanding.

For the main activity, students might need additional examples of word problems to support them in creating their own.

For the main activity, solved word problems could be displayed as posters.

For the main activity, encourage students to draw diagrams to help them visualise questions.

Consider questions that you could ask students as they work in groups, particularly those that encourage students to explain and justify their thinking. Also, encourage students to discuss their mathematics and reflect upon their work.

STARTER (5–10 mins)

➤ Display this diagram but not the answer.

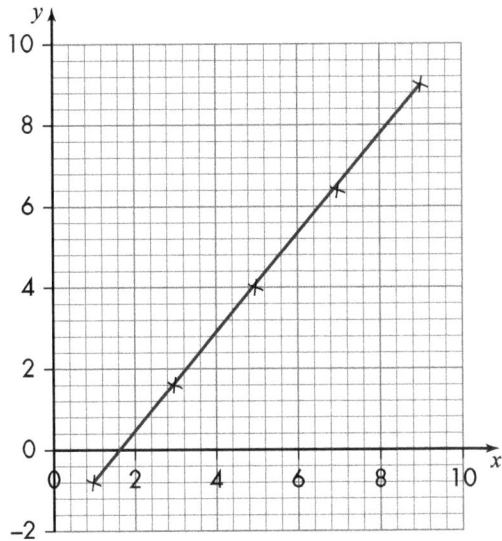

➤ Ask students to find an equation of the straight-line, its exact length and the coordinates of its mid-point.

➤ Ask students to find an equation of the line that is parallel to the first line and passes through the point (2, 6).

➤ Ask students to find an equation of the perpendicular bisector of the original line.

(Answers: $4y = 5x - 8$, $\sqrt{164}$, (5, 4.25) $4y = 5x + 14$ $5y = -4x + 41.25$)

MAIN LESSON ACTIVITY (40–45 mins)

Equipment: A1/flipchart paper

➤ Working in pairs, each student writes down an explanation of how they answered parts two and three of the starter. Then compare them with their partner's responses, seeking clarification where necessary.

➤ Working in pairs, students draw their own straight-line, find its exact length and the coordinates of its midpoint. Then choose a point that a parallel line can pass through and find the equation of this line. Ask them to create a line segment from the parallel line and find the equation of the perpendicular bisector of the line segment. The problem can then be shared for another pair to evaluate. The answers can be returned to be checked. Lower-achieving students can be encouraged to create lines that have positive gradients. Higher-achieving students can be encouraged to create lines with negative, fractional or decimal gradients. Encourage students to include coordinates on both the original line and the line segment.

➤ Bring students together to discuss their responses. Discuss parallel lines having the same gradient when their equations are in the form $y = mx + c$. Discuss methods for finding the equation of a parallel line, for example, the use of substitution of the given coordinates into an equation to support finding the equation. Discuss the gradient of a perpendicular line being the negative reciprocal of the original line, for example, if the gradient of a line is m then the gradient of a perpendicular line is $-\dfrac{1}{m}$. Discuss methods for finding the equation of a perpendicular line, for example, the use of substitution of the given coordinates into an equation to support finding the equation (See guidance above.)

➤ Display this question, but not the answer.

A line joins the points $A(4, -5)$ and $B(-2, 7)$. The perpendicular bisector of AB meets the line through A which is parallel to the y-axis, at the point P.

Find the area of the triangle ABP.   (Answer: Area of triangle $ABP = 22.5$)

➤ Working in pairs, students investigate the problem.

➤ Bring students together to discuss the problem. Discuss suggested steps needed to solve the problem: find the gradient of $AB \rightarrow$ find the mid-point of $AB \rightarrow$ find the equation of the perpendicular bisector $\rightarrow$ find the coordinates of $P \rightarrow$ find the area of the triangle. (See guidance above.)

➤ Working in groups of three or four, students create similar word problems that need mathematical techniques from lessons 7.4 and 7.5 to solve them, for example, finding gradients, mid-points, exact lengths, parallel lines, perpendicular bisectors. (See guidance above.)

➤ Working in groups of three or four, students investigate shared word problems, producing their solutions on A1/flipchart paper, with explanations of the steps that they used to solve the problem.

- Students can now do Exercise 7.5.
- Question 1 provides opportunities for investigating parallel lines.
- Question 2 provides opportunities for finding gradients of perpendicular lines.
- Questions 3 and 4 provide opportunities for investigating perpendicular lines.
- Questions 5 and 6 provide opportunities for word problems and problem solving.

PLENARY (10 mins)

Equipment: Mini whiteboards, or similar

- Ask students 'show me' or similar questions to explore their understanding of the lesson. Cover all aspects of the learning outcome.
- For example: *Show me a perpendicular bisector of 3y + 2x − 7 = 0. Show me the first step needed to solve …* (*a given problem*)

Homework and answers: Resource sheets, homework and extension exercises can be found at the end of this chapter and in the downloadable materials. Answers can be found in the downloadable materials.

CHECKING PROGRESS	Use the answers to the 'show me' questions to check students' progress.

7 Straight-Line Graphs

Resource sheet 7.1

Interpreting equations of the form $y = mx + c$

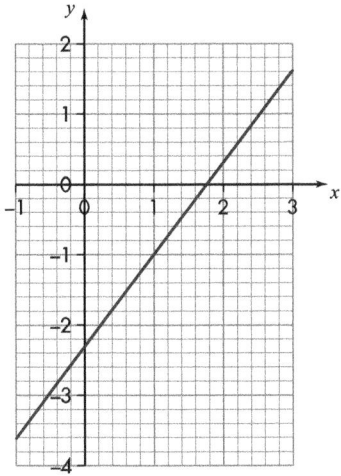	$4x - 3y = 7$
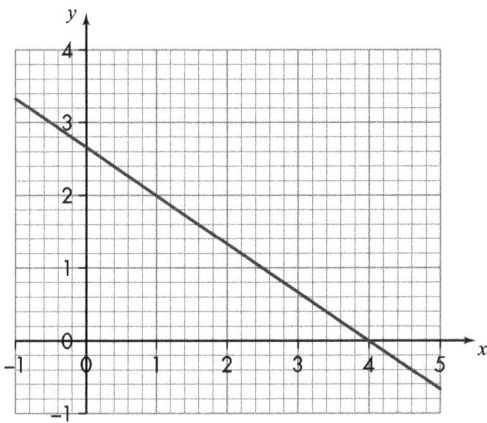	$8 = 2x + 3y$
Gradient $= 0.4$, y-intercept $= -1.2$	$2x - 5y = 6$
$AB = 6.4$	A is $(3, 4)$ B is $(7, 9)$
$AB = 10.2$	A is $(-2, 7)$ B is $(-4, -3)$
$3y + 9 + 6x = 0$	$y = -2x + 7$
$24y + 8x + 3 = 0$	$15y + 5x + 6 = 0$

Collins Cambridge IGCSE™ Additional Maths Teacher's Guide © HarperCollins*Publishers* 2023   121

7 Straight-Line Graphs

Homework

7.1 Interpreting equations of the form $y = mx + c$

Non-calculator

1 Find the gradient of the line joining the two points.

    a (3, 7) and (5, 9)   **b** (−3, 5) and (4, 8)

    c (−3, 5) and (2, −3)   **d** (−2, −4) and (−4, −7)

2 Find an equation of the line with the gradient $-\dfrac{3}{4}$ that passes through the point with coordinates (−2, −3).

3 The gradient of the line that passes through the points with coordinates $(4p, -2)$ and $(-1, -p)$ is $-\dfrac{7}{5}$. Find the value of p.

4 Find an equation of the line that passes through (3, 7) and (−7, 2).

5 Find an equation of each of the lines in question 1.

6 Investigate the use of real-world applications of linear graphs. For example, the cost of taxi fares related to journey distance.

Homework

7.2 Transforming relationships of the form $y = ax^n$ and $y = ab^x$ to linear form

1. Each set of data is connected by an equation of the form $y = ax^n$, where a and n are constants. For each data set:

    i   plot a graph of lg y against lg x

    ii use your graph to find the value of a and the value of n

    iii write the equation in the form $y = ax^n$

a

x	2	4	6	8
y	12	48	108	192

b

x	5	10	15	20
y	4	1	0.444 444	0.25

c

x	3	5	7	9	11
y	81	375	1029	2187	3993

d

x	3	5	7	9	11
y	162	1250	4802	13 122	29 282

2. Two variables x and y are connected by the relationship $y = ab^x$, where A and b are constants.

    a Transform the relationship $y = ab^x$ into linear form.

    An experiment was carried out measuring values of y for certain values of x. The values of ln y and x were plotted and a line of best fit was drawn. The graph is shown on the grid below.

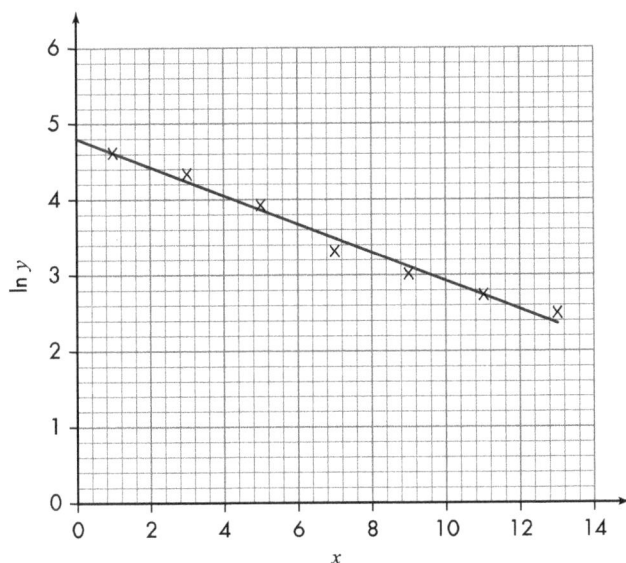

    b Use the graph to determine the value of A and the value of b, giving your answers to 2 significant figures.

    c Find x when $y = 125$.

7 Straight-Line Graphs

Homework

7.3 Transforming from linear form to given relationships

1 Variables x and y are such that when ln y is plotted against ln x a straight-line graph is obtained.

Transform the equation of the line which passes through each pair of coordinates into the form $y = ax^n$, where a and n are constants.

   a (1, 3) and (5, 9)   b (1.7, 4) and (4.7, 14)

   c (0.4, 3) and (5, 3.7)   d (0.7, 1.2) and (1.8, 2.4)

2 Variables x and y are such that when ln y is plotted against x a straight-line graph is obtained.

Transform the equation of the line which passes through each pair of coordinates into the form $y = Ab^x$, where A and b are constants. Give your values for A and b correct to 2 significant figures.

   a (1, 3.4) and (3, 5.6)   b (2, −1.2) and (4, −3.6)

3 Variables x and y are such that when y^2 is plotted against ln x a straight-line graph is obtained.

Transform the equation of the line which passes through each pair of coordinates into the form $y^2 = A\ln x + B$, where A and B are constants.

   a (2.5. 6) and (3, 10)   b (3, 1.4) and (5, 6.8)

4 Variables x and y are such that when ln y is plotted against x^3, a straight-line graph passing through the points (2, 9) and (7, 5) is obtained.

Find y as a function of x.

7 Straight-Line Graphs

Homework

7.4 Working with the mid-point and length of a straight-line

Non-calculator

1   Find the coordinates of the mid-point of the line joining the points:

    a (7, 3) and (−2, 4)   **b** (13, 10) and (−3, −7)

    c (1.5, 2.5) and (3.5, 4.7)   **d** (−8, −4) and (−10, −14)

2   P is the mid-point of the line joining the points A and B.

    Find the coordinates of B, given:

    a $A(−2, 3)$ and $P(−2, 4)$ **b** $A(3, 4)$ and $P(7, −10)$

    c $A(−10, 14)$ and $P(−1, 6)$ **d** $A(4, 9)$ and $P(10, 7)$

3   Find the exact length of each of the lines joining the points in question 1.

4   Given that P lies on the line joining A to B, find the coordinates of P, when:

    a $A(−3, 6)$, $B(6, 12)$ and $AP = \dfrac{1}{3} AB$ **b** $A(−7, 4)$, $B(8, 14)$ and $AP = \dfrac{1}{5} AB$

    c $A(3, 2)$, $B(7, 4)$ and $AP = \dfrac{1}{6} AB$ **d** $A(3, 2)$, $B(7, 14)$ and $AP = \dfrac{3}{5} AB$

    e $A(4, 7)$, $B(7, 8)$ and $AP : PB = 3:5$ **f** $A(−4, 11)$, $B(3, 7)$ and $AP : PB = 3 : 11$

Calculator

5   The length of the line joining the points $A(k, −4)$ and $B(3, 2)$ is 14.

    Find the two possible values of k.

6   The length of the line joining the points $A(3, 7)$ and $B(4, k)$ is 35.

    Find the two possible values of k.

Homework

7.5 Working with parallel and perpendicular lines

Non-calculator

1 Find an equation of the line that passes through the given point and is parallel to the line with the given equation. Write each equation in the form $ax + by + c = 0$, where a, b and c are integers:

a $(7, 3)$: $2y = 3x + 4$ b $(13, 10)$: $3y - 2x = 12$

c $(1.5, 2.5)$: $4y + 5x - 6 = 0$ d $(-8, -4)$: $3x - 7y + 1 = 0$

2 Find the gradient of a line that is perpendicular to a line with each gradient:

a 2   b 0.5

c $\dfrac{7}{8}$ d -3.7

3 Using the points and equations from question 1, find an equation of the line that passes through each given point and is perpendicular to each line with the given equation. Write each equation in the form $ax + by + c = 0$, where a, b and c are integers.

4 Find an equation of the perpendicular bisector of the line joining these points. Write the equations for part a and part b in the form $ax + by + c = 0$, where a, b and c are integers.

a $(7, 3)$, $(4, 6)$ b $(13, 10)$, $(-5, -4)$

c $(-8, -4)$, $(2, -10)$,   d $(-3, 7)$, $(-1, -5.4)$

5 The perpendicular bisector of the line joining the points $A(3, -7)$ and $B(-2, -9)$ meets the line, through B parallel to the y-axis, at P.

Find the area of triangle ABP.

6 Create your own word problem that needs mathematical techniques from lessons 8.4 and 8.5 to solve it. For example, finding gradients, mid-points, exact lengths, parallel lines, perpendicular bisectors.

Share with another student in your class.

Extension

7.2 Transforming relationships of the form $y = ax^n$ and $y = ab^x$ to linear form

1   Investigate the use of transforming exponential equations of the form $y = ax^n$ and $y = ab^x$ in subjects such as chemistry and in any real-world applications.

2   Produce a summary of your investigation in the form of a presentation, webpage, video or similar.

Extension

7.4 Working with the mid-point and length of a straight-line

1   Investigate the position of the centroid of a triangle, finding the general form for its coordinates.

2   Investigate the distance of a point from a straight line, finding any appropriate formulae.

3   Produce a summary of your investigation in the form of a presentation, webpage, video or similar.

Extension

7.5 Working with parallel and perpendicular lines

1   Investigate the equation of a circle.

2   Investigate the equation of a tangent to a circle.

3   Investigate orthogonal circles.

4   Investigate circles that touch.

5   Produce summaries of your investigations in the form presentations, webpages, videos or similar.

8 Coordinate Geometry of the Circle

TOPIC:
8.1 Equation of a circle, centre $(0, 0)$, radius r

KEY WORDS:
centre, radius, Pythagoras' theorem, tangent, gradient

IGCSE MATHS PRIOR KNOWLEDGE:
Use Pythagoras' theorem

Identify the gradient and equation of a straight-line

Learning aims:
- Know and use the equation of a circle with radius r and centre (a, b)
- Solve problems involving tangents to a circle

Resources:
- Student Book: pages 170–172
- Graph paper

Common mistakes and remediation:
Students often forget to square / square root the radius term of the equation of a circle. Encourage them to check solutions are sensible in the context of the question (perhaps by choosing a point on the circle and checking it fits the equation).

Occasionally students think they can apply a square root across the equation (e.g. if $x^2 + y^2 = 9$ then $x + y = 3$). Again, choosing a coordinate point on the circle to check will show this is an invalid approach.

Useful tips:
Students will have seen similar equations in Chapter 5.

Guidance:
Encourage students to consider negative as well as positive square roots (or a mixture) as possible solutions to equations of circles.

For able students this lesson could be combined with lesson 8.2.

STARTER (5–10 mins)
Equipment: Squared or graph paper

➤ Students work in pairs. Ask them to draw a pair of axes from −12 to +12 on both scales.

➤ Ask students to find all the points with integer coordinates that are exactly 10 units from the origin, and plot them on their axes.

➤ What do they notice about the points?

➤ Ask the students what would happen if you included **all** the coordinate points that are exactly 10 units from the origin – what shape would you get? Why? Explanations may include comments about the definition of a circle or loci.

MAIN LESSON ACTIVITY (45 mins)

- ➤ Leading directly on from the starter, what methods did they use to find their coordinate points? Recap the use of Pythagoras' theorem to find possible positive and negative values for x and y on the graph of $x^2 + y^2 = 25$, as well as $x = 0$ and $y = 0$ solutions.

- ➤ Ask students what they think the equation would be for a circle of centre $(0, 0)$ and radius 6. Encourage them to justify their answer. If possible, demonstrate or ask them to check with graphing software.

- ➤ Ask students if they have an equation of the form $x^2 + y^2 = c$, where c is a positive constant, what can they say about the graph? Lead to the generalisation $x^2 + y^2 = r^2$.

- ➤ Develop the topic (as in Example 2 in student book). If the point $(6, 1)$ is on a circle centre the origin, what is the equation of the circle? Give students a couple of minutes to try this, then work through method with them.

- ➤ Go back to the circle in the starter – what is its equation? $(x^2 + y^2 = 100)$. Draw the circle and a tangent at $(8, 6)$. Model the process of finding the equation of a tangent (or ask students how they would do it), as in Example 4 in the student book.

- ➤ Set students selected questions from Exercise 8.1, ensuring that they tackle a range of question types. Lower-achieving students may need more consolidation of earlier questions, whereas higher-achieving students could answer the early questions orally and be set the later questions as opportunities to record methods and solutions.

PLENARY (5–10 mins)

- ➤ Ask students to write down a common mistake they think other students might make with this topic.
- ➤ Share ideas and students' strategies to avoid these mistakes.

Homework and answers: Resource sheets, homework and extension exercises can be found at the end of this chapter and in the downloadable materials. Answers can be found in the downloadable materials.

CHECKING PROGRESS	Can students write instructions to find the equation of a circle centre $(0, 0)$ going through the point $(-4, 6)$? Can students explain in words how to find the equation of the tangent to the circle at this point?

8 Coordinate Geometry of the Circle

TOPIC:
8.2 Equation of a circle, centre (a, b), radius r

KEY WORDS:
radius, diameter, tangent, Pythagoras' theorem, mid-point

IGCSE MATHS PRIOR KNOWLEDGE:
Use Pythagoras' theorem

Identify the gradient and equation of a straight-line

Learning aims:
- Know and use the equation of a circle with radius r and centre (a, b)
- Solve problems involving tangents to a circle

Resources:
- Student Book: pages 172–175
- Resource sheet 8.1

Common mistakes and remediation:

Students sometimes make errors with signs when considering centres of circles with negative coordinates – encouraging them to substitute values then simplify (rather than substituting and simplifying in one step) avoids this error.

Useful tips:

Using graphing software during explanations in this topic can enable a focus on the concepts being explained rather than just the process of using an equation to draw a circle.

Guidance:

For able students, this lesson could be combined with either Lesson 8.1 or Lesson 8.3.

STARTER (5–10 mins)

Equipment: Resource Sheet 8.1 (optional)

➢ Give students a series of coordinate points: A(2, 4), B(4, –2), C(–3, –3), D(–6, 1), E(–2, 3), F(1, 1). To challenge, just give them the coordinates; if support is needed, use resource sheet 8.1.

➢ In pairs / threes, ask them to find:
- o Points that are an integer distant apart (CD and DF)
- o The two points that are closest together (A and F)
- o The two points that are furthest apart (B and D)

➢ Discuss methods used and the idea that in general to find the distance between two points (a, b) and (c, d) the calculation is $\sqrt{(c - a)^2 + (d - b)^2}$.

MAIN LESSON ACTIVITY (45 mins)

➢ Start with a diagram of a circle with centre (a, b), a point on the edge (x, y) and radius r (as in the Student Book). Ask students how they could find the radius of the circle.

➢ Demonstrate using Pythagoras' theorem to find the radius. Emphasise that the equation $(x - a)^2 + (y - b)^2 = r^2$ will be true for **every** point on the circle, so is the equation of the circle.

➢ If you have graphing software available, you might also wish to demonstrate how the centre of the circle impacts on the equation by graphing $(x - a)^2 + (y - b)^2 = 25$ and use sliders to show how the position of the circle changes as the values of a and b change.

➢ Check students' understanding by asking them to state the equation of a circle with centre $(2, 1)$ and radius 4.
(Answer $(x - 2)^2 + (y - 1)^2 = 16$)

➢ Ask students how they would find the equation of a circle if the only information they have is that a diameter of the circle goes from $(-6, -6)$ to $(0, 2)$. Follow process similar to Example 7 in student book:

     o   Find midpoint of diameter

     o   Use Pythagoras' theorem to find the radius

     o   Substitute centre and radius values into the equation for a circle

➢ Set students selected questions from Exercise 8.2. Question 1 could possibly be completed orally or with mini-boards.

PLENARY (5–10 mins)

➢ Give students a centre and a point on the circumference of a circle. For example $(2, -3)$ and $(5, 1)$. Students have a given time (2–3 mins) to find both the equation of the circle and of the tangent at that point.

(Answer: $(x - 2)^2 + (y + 3)^2 = 25$, $4x + 3y = 23$)

➢ Check solutions and review methods used to solve the problem.

Homework and answers: Resource sheets, homework and extension exercises can be found at the end of this chapter and in the downloadable materials. Answers can be found in the downloadable materials.

CHECKING PROGRESS	Students work in pairs to test each other. For example:
	One student gives the centre and radius, the other provides the equation.
	One student gives an equation, the other sketches the circle.
	One student sketches a circle, the other gives the equation.
	Solutions agreed by both students and/or checked using graphical software.

TOPIC:

8.3 General equation of a circle centre ($-g$, $-f$) and radius r

KEY WORDS:

tangent, normal, intersect, completing the square

IGCSE MATHS PRIOR KNOWLEDGE:

Use Pythagoras' theorem

Identify the gradient and equation of a straight-line

Learning aims:

- Know and use the general equation of a circle with radius r and centre (a, b)
- Solve problems involving the intersection of a circle and a straight-line
- Solve problems involving tangents to a circle

Resources:

- Student Book: pages 175–177
- Resource sheet 8.2

Common mistakes and remediation:

Students need to be careful with signs when manipulating equations. Encourage them to get into the habit of checking with simple values.

Useful tips:

Graphical software can help to demonstrate that different forms of an equation lead to the same circle.

Although questions are non-calculator, do not let arithmetic slow down the process too much.

Guidance:

Some students may prefer to use the entire completing the square process when solving this type of problem – for some students doing this may help them relate this section back to the previous one.

STARTER (5–10 mins)

Equipment: Resource sheet 8.2

➢ Resource sheet can be cut into cards or used as an entire sheet.

➢ Ask students to match the expressions into pairs as quickly as they can (they could work in pairs for this).

➢ Students swap sheets / positions (if the cards are matched on desks) to check each other's solutions.

➢ Ask students what process they are using (completing the square) and how this might relate to the work done in lesson 8.2 – can they see a link?

MAIN LESSON ACTIVITY (45 mins)

- Give students the general equation $(x - a)^2 + (x - b)^2 = r^2$ and ask them to expand the terms and rearrange it so that all the constant terms are on the right hand side – to get $x^2 + y^2 - 2ax - 2by = r^2 - (a^2 + b^2)$. Ask what the centre of the circle is and where those terms appears in the equation.

- Now ask students to do the same with $(x + g)^2 + (x + f)^2 = r^2$ to get $x^2 + y^2 + 2gx + 2fy = r^2 - (g^2 + f^2)$

- What is the centre of this circle? *(–g, –f)*

- Rearrange to put everything on the left-hand side $x^2 + y^2 + 2gx + 2fy + (g^2 + f^2) - r^2 = 0$

- Explain that as f, g and r are all constant values, this can be simplified to $x^2 + y^2 + 2gx + 2fy + c = 0$, where $c = (g^2 + f^2) - r^2$

- Demonstrate that c can be rearranged to find the radius: $r = \sqrt{(g^2 + f^2 - c)}$.

- Explain that this means that $x^2 + y^2 + 2gx + 2fy + c = 0$ is a general form of the equation of a circle centre $(-g, -f)$ and radius $\sqrt{(g^2 + f^2 - c)}$.

- Model how this form of the equation of a circle can be used either by using examples 8 and 9 in the student book or by selecting questions from Exercise 8.3 to work through with students (for example, one part of question 1, question 3 and question 4).

- Set students selected questions from Exercise 8.3. If time, encourage students to check their answers using graphical software.

PLENARY (5–10 mins)

- Discuss with students which form of the equation of a circle they find easier to work with.

- Are all equations of this form equations of circles? Why might they not be?

- Ask them to record two key pieces of advice to themselves when using this general form of the equation of a circle.

Homework and answers: Resource sheets, homework and extension exercises can be found at the end of this chapter and in the downloadable materials. Answers can be found in the downloadable materials.

CHECKING PROGRESS	Can students identify the centre and radius of a circle with equation $x^2 + y^2 - 8x - 4y + 4 = 0$? Explain their method to a partner. What about $x^2 + y^2 - 8x - 4y - 4 = 0$? Write instructions to find the equation of a circle with centre (1, –2) and tangent (–2, 2). Swap instructions with a partner and check each other's work.

8   Coordinate Geometry of the Circle

TOPIC:

8.4 Intersections of a circle

KEY WORDS:

intersection, chord, tangent, normal

IGCSE MATHS PRIOR KNOWLEDGE:

Use Pythagoras' theorem

Identify the gradient and equation of a straight-line

Learning aims:

- Solve problems involving the intersection of a circle and a straight-line
- Solve problems involving tangents to circles
- Solve problems involving the intersection of two circles

Resources:

- Student Book: pages 177–181
- Resource sheet 8.3

Common mistakes and remediation:

Students tend to make careless errors in manipulating algebraic equations or try to skip steps. Clear setting out of work and steps in working (as in the examples in the Student Book) tend to minimise these errors.

Useful tips:

Graphical software can be useful to demonstrate concepts, particularly when 'sliders' can be used to show how the graphs change as values change, and also to check solutions visually when students have completed problems.

Guidance:

Students need to be confident in the use of simultaneous equations for this section.

Encourage students to draw sketch diagrams for the questions, as this will help them check that their solutions 'look' right.

STARTER (5–10 mins)

Equipment: Resource sheet 8.3

➤ Give students the equations of two curves and two straight-lines:

$$y = x^2 - 4, y = -x^2 + 4x - 2, x + y = 2, y = 2x - 1$$

If you are using the resource sheet, ask students to match the equations to the curves / lines before continuing.

➤ Ask them to find the coordinates of the points of intersection between

- ○ The two straight-lines
- ○ Each curve and each of the straight-lines
- ○ The two curves

If you are using the resource sheet, ask students to justify their solutions algebraically rather than just by inspection.

➤ What can they say about the line $y = 2x - 1$ and the curve $y = -x^2 + 4x - 2$? How do they know?

MAIN LESSON ACTIVITY (45 mins)

➢ Leading on from the starter – how many times can a straight-line intersect a circle? Ask students to sketch their answers (mini-boards may be useful if you have them).

➢ Ask students to think about how they might use algebra to work out how many times a particular line and circle intersect. Relate back to work on simultaneous equations.

➢ Examples 10–12 in the Student Book demonstrate methods and approaches, but these should provide further support for students rather than be the only examples they see.

➢ Ask one student to provide a circle equation and another to provide the equation of a straight-line then work together as a class to see if they intersect, it is a tangent, or there is no intersection to demonstrate method.

➢ Complete an example of when a line does not intersect a circle. For example $x^2 + y^2 - 6x - 4y - 12 = 0$ and $y = 2x + 10$. Show the method of substitution and simplification that results in a quadratic equation which has a negative discriminant, therefore no real roots, therefore no intersection.

➢ Give the students an equation of a circle such as $x^2 + y^2 + 4y - 3 = 0$. Can they find the equation of a line that intersects the circle twice? A line that is a tangent? A line that does not intersect the circle at all? Encourage peer assessment of solutions.

➢ Now ask students to consider the intersection of two circles. They should be confident by now that there will be two, one or no intersections, but will need an example to be clear on the process. Use page 180 in the Student Book as a guide to the process – perhaps review Example 13 (or a similar one with your own equations) with the students to ensure they are clear as to the steps.

➢ Set students selected questions from Exercise 8.4. Ensure they complete a mix of calculator and non-calculator questions.

PLENARY (5–10 mins)

➢ Ask students to find the points of intersection (to 1 d.p.) of the circles with the equations $C_1: x^2 + y^2 - 6x + 8y = 0$ and $C_2: x^2 + y^2 + 4x - 4y - 32 = 0$ (Solution: $(-2, -4)$, $(3.9, 0.9)$)

➢ If time, ask students to find the equation of another circle that just touches the circle C_1 … then the equation of a circle that doesn't touch C_1 at all. Use peer assessment to check solutions.

Homework and answers: Resource sheets, homework and extension exercises can be found at the end of this chapter and in the downloadable materials. Answers can be found in the downloadable materials.

CHECKING PROGRESS	Give students the circles $C_1: x^2 + y^2 - 2x + 8y - 8 = 0$, $C_2: x^2 + y^2 - 10x + 8y + 37 = 0$ and the line L: $y = 2x - 1$.
	
	Ask them to find:
	
	○ The equation of the tangent to the circle C_1 at $(4, 0)$.
	   $(y = -0.75x + 3)$
	
	○ The points of intersection of C_1 and L.
	   $((1, 1)$ and $(-3, -7))$
	
	○ The points of intersection of C_1 and C_2.
	   $((5.6, -2.1)$ and $(5.6, -5, 9))$
	
	○ The points of intersection of C_2 and L.
	   (none)
	
	○ The common chord shared by C_1 and C_2.
	   $(x = 5.6)$

8   Coordinate Geometry of the Circle

Resource sheet 8.1

Starter activity

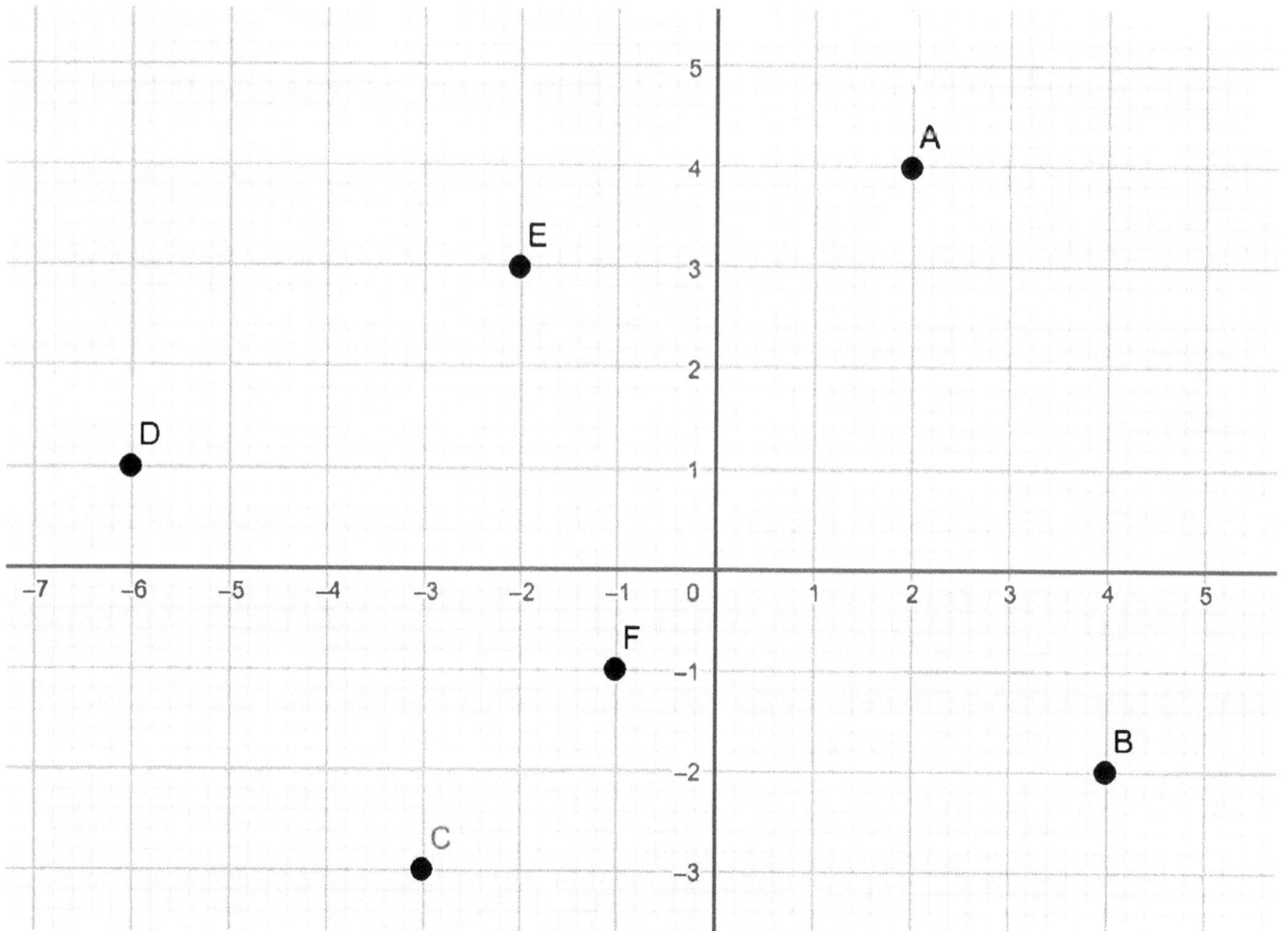

Resource sheet 8.2

Starter activity

$x^2 + 4x + 4$	$x^2 + 8x + 16$	$x^2 + 4x + 3$
$x^2 + 6x + 10$	$x^2 + 6x + 8$	$x^2 - 4x - 5$
$x^2 + 8x + 8$	$x^2 - 4x - 4$	$x^2 - 6x - 9$
$x^2 - 6x + 9$	$x^2 + 8x - 16$	$x^2 - 8x - 8$
$(x + 2)^2$	$(x - 3)^2$	$(x + 4)^2$
$(x - 2)^2 + 1$	$(x - 2)^2 - 8$	$(x + 2)^2 - 1$
$(x + 4)^2 - 8$	$(x + 3)^2 - 1$	$(x + 3)^2 + 1$
$(x - 3)^2 - 18$	$(x - 4)^2 - 8$	$(x - 4)^2 - 8$

Resource sheet 8.3

Starter activity

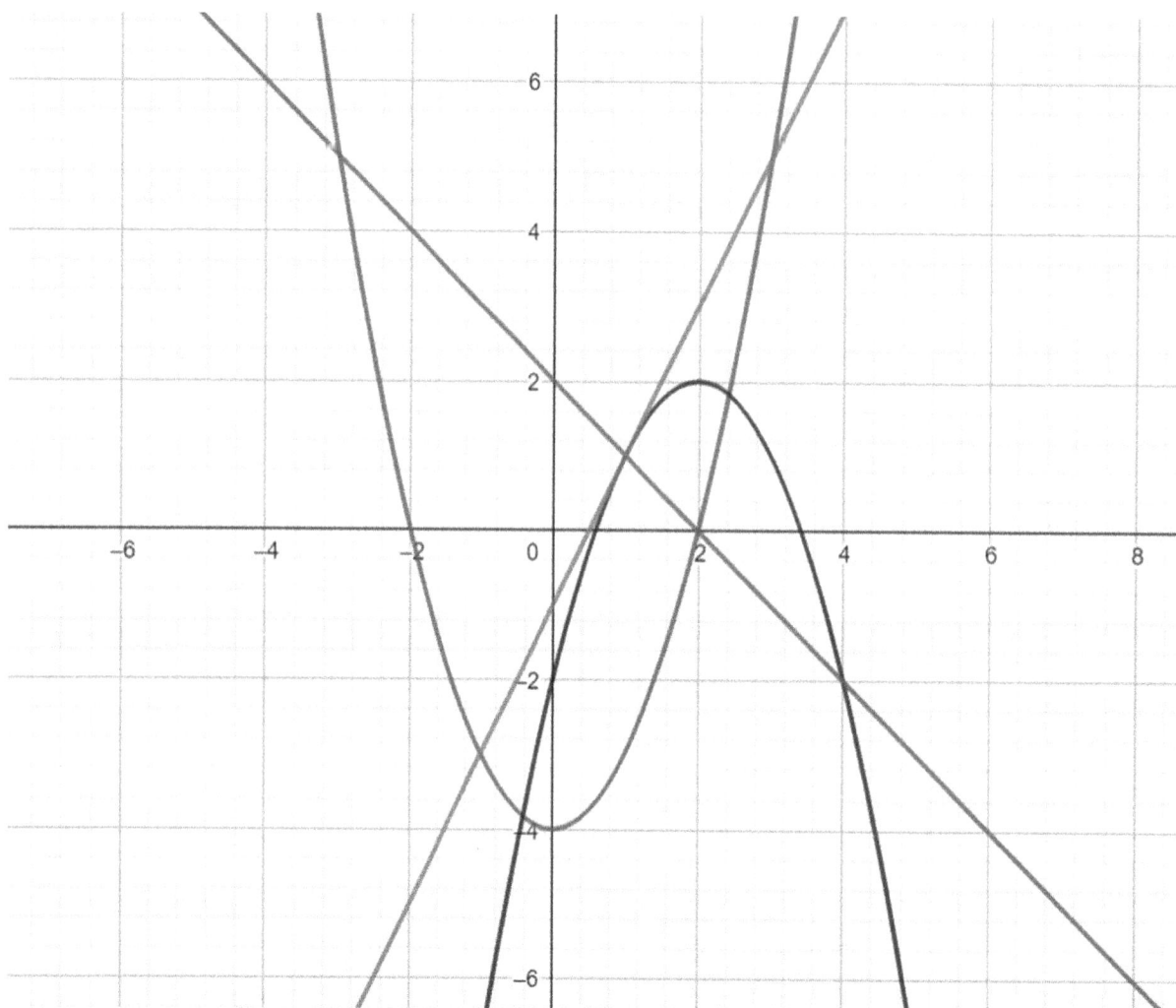

Homework

8.1 Equation of a circle, centre 0, 0), radius r

1   Write down the equation of the circle with:

   a   centre (0, 0) and radius 4

   b   centre (0, 0) and diameter 12

   c   centre (0, 0) and a point (9, 2)

   d   centre (0, 0) and a point (−3, 7)

2   State the equation of the circle that has a diameter from (−6, 2) to (6, −2).

3   State the equation of the tangent to the circle $x^2 + y^2 = 100$ at the point (8, 6).

4   State the equation of the tangent to the circle $x^2 + y^2 = 13$ at the point (3, −2).

5   A circle has equation $x^2 + y^2 = 49$. Does the point (4, 5) lie on the circle, inside it or outside of it? Justify your answer.

Homework

8.2 Equation of a circle, centre (a, b), radius r

1   State the equation of each of the following circles:

   a   centre (4, 5) and radius 3

   b   centre (−3, −5) and radius 8

   c   centre (−3, 0) and radius $\sqrt{12}$

2   State the equation of the circle with

   a   centre (4, 1) and the point (−2, 1) on the circumference

   b   centre (−2, −1) and the point (−2, 3) on the circumference

3   State the equation of a circle which has a diameter from (0, 2) to (6, −6).

4   A square has vertices at the points A (−1, 2), B (5, 8), C (11, 2), D (5, −4).
     What is the equation of the circle that circumscribes this square?

8 Coordinate Geometry of the Circle

Homework

8.3 General equation of a circle

1   State the coordinates of the centre and the radius of the circles with each of these equations

    a $x^2 + y^2 + 6x - 2y - 3 = 0$

    b $x^2 + y^2 - 5x + y - 2.5 = 0$

2   State whether these points are inside, outside or on the circumference of the circle $x^2 + y^2 - 10x - 2y + 1 = 0$

    a $(3, -3)$ **b** $(8, 5)$ **c** $(2, 6)$ **d** $(5, -4)$

3   Give the equation of the tangent to the circle $x^2 + y^2 - 4x - 8y - 5 = 0$ at the point $(-1, 8)$.

4   A circle has the equation $x^2 + y^2 - 4x + 8y - 80 = 0$

    a Give the equation of the tangent to the circle at the point $(-6, 2)$

    b Give the equation of the tangent to the circle at the point $(10, 2)$

    c Identify the coordinates of the point where these two tangents meet.

8 Coordinate Geometry of the Circle

Homework

8.4 Intersections of a circle

1   Calculate the points of intersection of

   a   The circle $x^2 + y^2 + 8x - 4y - 5 = 0$ and the line $y = \frac{1}{3}x - 1$.

   b   The circle $x^2 + y^2 - 6x - 4y - 87 = 0$ and the line $x - 7y + 61 = 0$.

2   a   Demonstrate that the line $4x - 3y + 18 = 0$ is a tangent to the circle $x^2 + y^2 - 8x - 6y = 0$.

   b   Calculate the coordinates of the point where the tangent touches the circle.

3   [NC] A circle with centre (9, 7) passes through the point A (5, 10).

   a   State the equation of the circle.

   b   State the equation of the tangent to the circle at the point A.

   Another tangent to the circle passes through the point B (6, 3) on the circumference of the circle.

   c   State the coordinates of the point where the two tangents meet.

4   Calculate the points of intersection of the circles $x^2 + y^2 + 6x - 4y + 4 = 0$ and $x^2 + y^2 - 2x + 2y - 23 = 0$.
Give your answers correct to 1 decimal place.

5   A triangle has vertices at the points A (−4, 3), B (1, 3) and C (1, 0).
The triangle is circumscribed by a circle.

   a   State the equation of the circle.

   The chord AB is also the diameter of another circle.

   b   State the equation of this circle.

Extension

8.1 Equation of a circle, centre (0, 0), radius r

A graphical calculator or graphing software could be used for this investigation.

The equation of a circle centre (0, 0), radius r is $x^2 + y^2 = r^2$.

1   Start with the equation $x^2 + y^2 = 1$.

What happens to the circle when you change the equation to $\dfrac{x^2}{a^2} + y^2 = 1$, where a is an integer?

What happens to the circle when you change the equation to $x^2 + \dfrac{y^2}{b^2} = 1$, where b is an integer?

2   What happens when you graph an equation such as $4x^2 + 9y^2 = 36$?

Show that this can be rearranged to $\dfrac{x^2}{9} + \dfrac{y^2}{4} = 1$.

3   Explore other equations of the form $\dfrac{x^2}{a^2} + \dfrac{y^2}{b^2} = 1$, where a and b are integers.

Can you make any general statements?

Extension

8.3 General equation of a circle

1 A circle has centre (1, 4) and two points on its circumference that do NOT form a diameter are (5, 7) and (−2, 8).
What is the equation of the circle?

2 Three points on the circumference of a circle are (14, 6), (2, 14) and (−10, −4).
One pair of points give a diameter of the circle.
What is the equation of the circle?

3 **a** Determine the equation of the tangent to the circle $x^2 + y^2 − 6x − 4y − 12 = 0$ at the point (0, 6).

This line is also the tangent to a point on a circle with centre (−7, 7) and radius 5.

b What is the equation of this second circle?

These two circles also have a vertical tangent in common.

c Determine the equation of the vertical tangent.

4 Write your own challenge question involving circles and tangents. Give to a partner to solve. Check their solution.

9 Circular Measure

TOPIC:

9.1 Radians

9.2 Arc length

KEY WORDS:

radians, arc, arc length, subtend

IGCSE MATHS PRIOR KNOWLEDGE:

Use a calculator efficiently

Understand how to find arc length, given the sector radius and angle of a sector in degrees

Learning aims:

- Solve problems involving the arc length and sector area of a circle, including knowledge and use of radian measure

Resources:

- Student Book: pages 186–188

Common mistakes and remediation:

Students often have their calculators set in the wrong mode. Ensure that they know how to change the mode from degrees to radians.

Useful tips:

Encourage students to learn the equivalents of common angles such as $30°\left(\dfrac{\pi}{6}\right)$, $45°\left(\dfrac{\pi}{4}\right)$, $60°\left(\dfrac{\pi}{3}\right)$, $90°\left(\dfrac{\pi}{2}\right)$ and $180°$ (π).

Guidance:

Ensure that students remember the arc length formula from IGCSE and that they are familiar with what a radian actually is.

Exercise 9.1 leads them from using the simple formula for finding arc length, through finding perimeters of compound shapes to working back to find the radius and the angle of the sector. They will need to work with their calculators in radian mode for questions 6 and 7.

Students need to become confident in tackling non-calculator questions in radians. The idea is that if a question is asked in terms of π, then then answer can also be written as a multiple of π.

STARTER (10 mins)

➢ Display on the board the sector diagram for part 1a of the starting point of Chapter 9 in the Student Book.

➢ Ask students how they would find the arc length.

➢ Elicit the principal of finding the fraction $\left(\dfrac{\theta}{360}\right)$ of the circumference and multiplying this by the circumference ($2\pi r$).

➢ Show how to calculate the arc length for an angle of 30° as 5.2 cm (1 d.p.).

➢ Ask students to calculate the arc length of the other two sectors in this question.

MAIN LESSON ACTIVITY (40 mins)

➢ Draw on the board a circle with a sector that has the same arc length, r, as the radius of the circle. Explain to students that the angle of this sector is 1 radian and that this is an important new unit that is often used in circular measure as well as trigonometry.

➢ Show that $r = \dfrac{1\,\text{radian}}{360} \times 2\pi r$.

➢ Rearrange to give $360r = 1\ \text{radian} \times 2\pi r$.

➢ Divide through by $2r$ to give $180° = 1\ \text{radian} \times \pi$.

➢ Show that this leads to the identities:

$\pi\,\text{radians} \equiv 180°$

and $1\ \text{radian} \equiv \dfrac{180°}{\pi}$

➢ Emphasise that θ radians $= \left(\dfrac{180\theta}{\pi} \right)$ degrees

Now talk about finding arc lengths for sectors with angles given in radians, leading students to find:

arc length $= \dfrac{\theta}{360} \times 2\pi r\ =\ \dfrac{180 \times \theta \times 2\pi r}{360 \times \pi}\ =\ \theta\, r\ = r\theta$

➢ Show clearly how the πs and the 360s cancel to give a very neat, simple formula.

➢ Go through Example 1 from the Student Book, showing use of the simple formulae.

➢ Demonstrate how using radians means that calculators are not necessarily needed to calculate arc lengths. For example r = 6 cm, q = 3 radians so arc length = 6 x 3 = 18 cm.

➢ Then go through Example 2, where students need to use trigonometry to find the angle, hence their calculators need to be in radian mode. Explain this carefully to students so that they are familiar with changing the mode on their calculators.

➢ Ensure that all students know how to change their calculator from degree mode to radian mode and vice versa. They will need to be able to do this in questions 6 and 7.

➢ Students start Exercise 9.1, making sure they do not use calculators for the non-calculator questions.

➢ Ensure that higher-achieving students attempt questions 6 and 7; they could leave out questions 2 and 3.

PLENARY (10 mins)

➢ Ask students for the formulae for arc length of a sector, given the angle in degrees.

➢ Ask students for the formula, given the angles in radians.

➢ Practise recognising the equivalences for common angles given in radians, starting by asking students to tell you what angle, in degrees, is equivalent to π radians (180°). Show how to obtain this from the conversion factor.

➢ Now ask for the equivalent angle, in degrees, for $\dfrac{\pi}{2}$ (90°), $\dfrac{\pi}{3}$ (60°) and 2π (360°).

➢ Now ask what 45° is, expressed in radians $\left(\dfrac{\pi}{4} \right)$, showing students how to work it out, if necessary.

➢ Now ask for the equivalents to 120° $\left(\dfrac{2\pi}{3} \right)$, 135° $\left(\dfrac{3\pi}{4} \right)$.

Homework and answers: Resource sheets, homework and extension exercises can be found at the end of this chapter and in the downloadable materials. Answers can be found in the downloadable materials.

CHECKING PROGRESS	Consider the replies to the plenary questions. Are all students able to contribute?

9 Circular Measure

TOPIC:

9.3 Sector area

KEY WORDS:

None

IGCSE MATHS PRIOR KNOWLEDGE:

Use a calculator efficiently

Understand how to find sector area, given the radius and angle of a sector in degrees

Learning aims:	Resources:
• Solve problems involving the arc length and sector area of a circle, including knowledge and use of radian measure	• Student Book: page 189 – 191

Common mistakes and remediation:

Students often have their calculators set to the wrong mode. Ensure they know how to change mode from degrees to radians and vice versa.

Useful tips:

Encourage students to learn the equivalents of common angles such as $30°\left(\dfrac{\pi}{6}\right)$, $45°\left(\dfrac{\pi}{4}\right)$, $60°\left(\dfrac{\pi}{3}\right)$, $90°\left(\dfrac{\pi}{2}\right)$ and

$180°$ (π) for ease of use in more stretching questions.

Guidance:

Ensure that students remember the sector area formula from IGCSE and that they are confident with what radians are. Exercise 9.2 leads them from using the formula to find sector areas to working back, to find the radius as well as the angle of the sector. They will need to work with their calculators in radian mode for questions 6, 7 and 8.

Students need to become confident in tackling non-calculator questions in radians. The idea is that if a question is asked in terms of π, then then answer can also be written as a multiple of π.

STARTER (10 mins)

➢ Display on the board the sector diagram for part 1b of the starting point of Chapter 9 in the Student Book.

➢ Ask students how they would find the area of the sector.

➢ Elicit the principle of finding the fraction $\left(\dfrac{\theta}{360}\right)$ of the area and multiplying this by the area of the circle, πr^2.

➢ Show how to calculate the sector area as 55.85 cm² (2 d.p.).

➢ Ask them to calculate the area of the other two sectors in this question.

➢ Remind the class of the identities:

π radians $\equiv 180°$

and 1 radian $\equiv \dfrac{180°}{\pi}$

➢ Check that they remember that θ radians $= \left(\dfrac{180\theta}{\pi}\right)$ degrees

MAIN LESSON ACTIVITY (40 mins)

➢ If you have not already done so, display the following on the board:

$$\text{sector area} = \frac{\theta}{360} \times \pi r^2$$

➢ Now talk about finding areas for sectors with angles given in radians, leading students to find sector

$$\text{area} = \frac{\theta \times 180}{360 \times \pi} \times \pi r^2 = \frac{1}{2} r^2 \theta$$

➢ Show clearly how the πs and the 180s cancel to give a neat, simple formula sector area $= \frac{1}{2} r^2 \theta$ where θ is an angle in radians

➢ Go through Example 3 from the Student Book, showing how to use this formula and that the calculation can be completed to get an exact answer without a calculator.

➢ Then go through Example 4, where students need to use trigonometry to find the angle, hence their calculators need to be in radian mode. Some will need reminding that they need their calculators to be in radian mode, but they should already be in that mode unless students have changed them.

➢ At this point, it is worth explaining to students that, when they are working with trigonometry or angle measures, since their calculators can operate in different modes, they should always check that the mode is appropriate for what they are calculating at the time – as this could change even during a single lesson!

➢ Students start Exercise 9.2.

➢ Ensure that higher-attaining students attempt questions 6, 7 and 8, even if they miss out questions 2 and 3.

PLENARY (10 mins)

Equipment: mini-boards (if available)

➢ Use mini-boards (if available) for students to display answers to the following questions as these provide a quick and easy way of seeing that all students understand the work covered during the lesson. Alternatively ask students to jot down answers and compare with a partner. No calculators to be used during plenary.

➢ Again, ask students for the formulae for arc length and area of a sector, given the angle in degrees.

➢ Ask students what these formulae are, given the angles in radians.

➢ See how many students remember how many degrees are the same as π radians (180°).

➢ Now ask what angle in radians equivalent to 90° $\left(\frac{\pi}{2}\right)$, 60° $\left(\frac{\pi}{3}\right)$, 270° $\left(\frac{3\pi}{2}\right)$

➢ Now ask them what $\frac{\pi}{4}$ radians is, expressed in degrees (45°).

➢ Now ask the equivalents to $\frac{3\pi}{4}$ radians (135°), $\frac{2\pi}{3}$ radians (120°), $\frac{\pi}{8}$ radians (22.5°).

➢ Ask students if they know what the approximate value of 1 radian is. Show how to find out by dividing $\frac{180}{\pi}$, which gives approximately 57°.

➢ Ask students if an angle of 2 radians will be obtuse or not. (Yes it is, as it is just under 120°.)

➢ On paper, ask students to sketch diagrams showing 1 radian, 2 radians, 3 radians, half a radian and one and a half radians.

Homework and answers: Resource sheets, homework and extension exercises can be found at the end of this chapter and in the downloadable materials. Answers can be found in the downloadable materials.

CHECKING PROGRESS	Ensure that all students are involved in answering the plenary questions, then collect all answers for the drawing of angles and check that they are all reasonable attempts.

9 Circular Measure

TOPIC:

9.4 Problems involving arcs and sector area

KEY WORDS:

None

IGCSE MATHS PRIOR KNOWLEDGE:

Use a calculator efficiently

Learning aims:
- Solve problems involving the arc length and sector area of a circle, including knowledge and use of radian measure

Resources:
- Student Book: pages 191–196

Common mistakes and remediation:

Students often have their calculators set to the wrong mode. Ensure they know how to change mode from degrees to radians and vice versa.

Useful tips:

Students need to understand when to use the cosine rule and when to use the sine rule. They should always use the sine rule, if possible, before trying the cosine rule.

Guidance:

Remind students about the sine rule and the cosine rule and ensure that they can apply them before they start looking at sector problems.

Remind students that answers may be written in terms of π, particularly for non-calculator questions.

STARTER (10 mins)

➤ Display on the board triangle ABC in which angle A is 70°, AC is 8 cm and BC is 10 cm.

➤ Ask the students if they can remember how to calculate the size of angle B. They may need some prompting before they suggest the sine rule.

➤ Remind them of the sine rule and how to apply it in this triangle to give $\dfrac{\sin B}{8} = \dfrac{\sin 70°}{10}$.

➤ Remind students that their calculators need to be in degree mode. Then they should get the answer that B = 48.7°.

➤ Rub out the 10 cm from BC and write 10 cm for AB, then ask the students if they can remember how to calculate the length of BC. Again they may need to be prompted before suggesting the cosine rule.

➤ Remind the class of the identity $\cos A = \dfrac{b^2 + c^2 - a^2}{2bc}$.

➤ Remind students how to manipulate this identity so that what they are trying to calculate becomes the subject of the formula, so for the current triangle this becomes $a^2 = b^2 + c^2 - 2bc \cos A \rightarrow BC^2 = 8^2 + 10^2 - 2 \times 8 \times 10 \times \cos 70°$ (where BC is now called a).

➤ Again, with calculators in degree mode, they should find that $BC^2 = 109.2768 \rightarrow BC = 10.45$ cm.

➤ Now ask students if they know how to find the area of this triangle ABC.

➤ You may need to prompt them to use the formula $\dfrac{1}{2} ab \sin C$, where a and b are the two sides of a triangle and C is the angle between them.

➤ Hence here the area will be $\dfrac{1}{2} \times 8 \times 10 \times \sin 70° = 37.6$ cm².

MAIN LESSON ACTIVITY (40 mins)

➢ Explain to the students that they are now going to look at some interesting problems involving sectors that may require the use of the sine rule or the cosine rule.

➢ Go through Example 5 in the Student Book, which does not need any trigonometry.

➢ Go through Example 6, where students need to use trigonometry to solve the problem. Remind them to set their calculators in radian mode so that the angle they find is in radians and is easier to use in the formula.

➢ Remind students again that they should always check that their calculator is in the appropriate mode for what they are calculating at that time, as this could change even during a single lesson.

➢ Students start Exercise 9.3.

➢ Higher-attaining students could start this exercise at question 5, while lower-attaining students start at question 1.

PLENARY (10 mins)

➢ Draw a sector, OAB, on the board with radius shown as 8 cm and arc length as 6 cm.

➢ Draw in the chord AB and shade in the top part of the sector, between the chord and the arc.

➢ Ask students how they could find the area of this shaded part.

➢ Students should respond with 'area of the sector OAB minus the area of the triangle OAB'.

➢ Ask them how they would find the area of the sector: 'Find the angle of the sector from the arc and radius as $8\theta = 6$, hence $\theta = \dfrac{6}{8}$ radians'.

➢ This gives the area of the sector OAB as $\dfrac{1}{2} \times 8^2 \times \dfrac{6}{8} = 24$ cm².

➢ Now ask them how they would find the area of the triangle OAB.

➢ With some prompting, lead them to the area using $\dfrac{1}{2} ab \sin C$ where a and b are the two sides of the included angle C.

➢ This gives area of OAB as $\dfrac{1}{2} \times 8 \times 8 \times \sin \dfrac{6}{8}$ where $\dfrac{6}{8}$ is in radians. This gives 21.8 cm².

➢ The area of the shaded part may now be found as $24 - 21.8 = 2.2$ cm².

➢ If students have completed Extension 9.3, did they use this method? What other methods could be used?

➢ Remind students that problem-solving questions can bring in other parts of mathematics they have studied elsewhere.

Homework and answers: Resource sheets, homework and extension exercises can be found at the end of this chapter and in the downloadable materials. Answers can be found in the downloadable materials.

CHECKING PROGRESS	Ensure that all students are answering plenary questions and involved in the discussions. If some are struggling, encourage higher-attaining students to articulate their answers so that lower-attaining ones can follow.

9 Circular Measure

Homework

9.2 Arc length

1 [NC] Calculate the arc length for each sector.

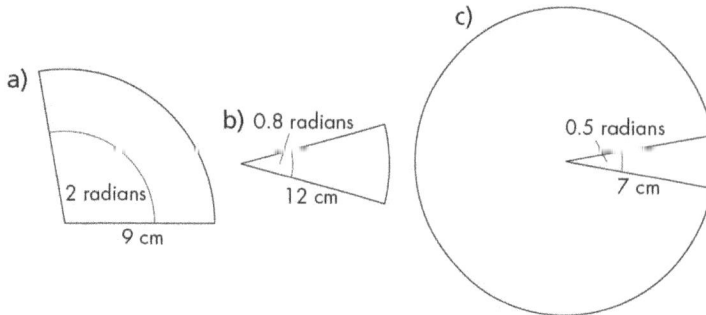

2 [NC] Calculate the arc length of a sector that has radius 10 cm and subtends an angle of:

a   120°

b   1.5 radians

c $\dfrac{\pi}{5}$ radians.

3 [NC] Calculate the total perimeter of each sector.

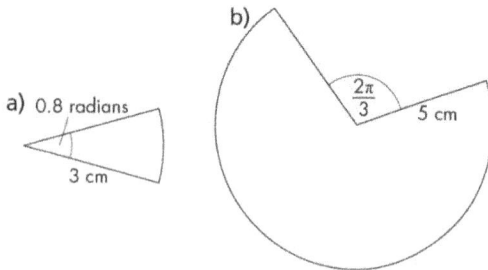

4 [NC] A sector of radius 10 cm has an arc of length 8 cm. Calculate the angle θ of the arc.

5 [NC] A sector has a perimeter of 30 cm. Calculate the angle θ subtended by the arc, given that the radius of the arc is 8 cm.

6 The diagram shows a sector of radius 7 cm and a chord of length 11 cm.

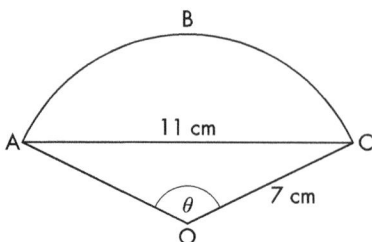

Calculate the arc length ABC.

9 Circular Measure

Homework

9.3 Sector area

1 [NC] Calculate the area of each sector.

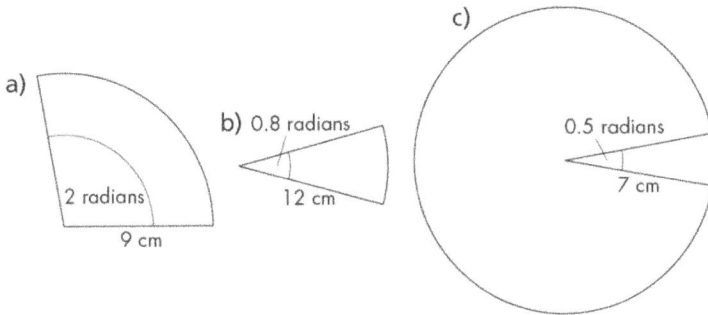

2 [NC] Calculate the area of a sector that has radius 5 cm and subtends an angle of:

a 1.6 radians

b 100°

c 0.4 radians.

3 Calculate the area of each sector.

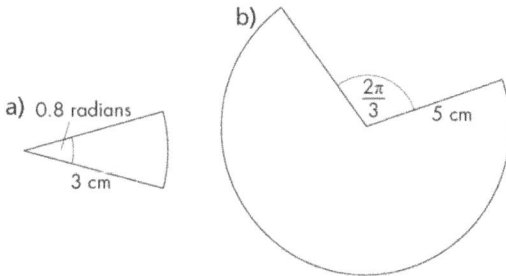

4 A sector of radius 9 cm has an area of 40.5 cm². Calculate the angle θ subtended by the arc, in radians.

5 A sector has an area of 48 cm². Calculate the angle θ, in radians, subtended by the arc, given that the radius of the arc is 8 cm.

6 The diagram shows a sector of radius 11 cm and a chord of length 7 cm.

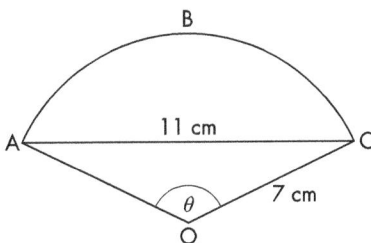

Calculate the area of the sector ABCO.

Homework

9.4 Problems involving arcs and sector area

1   The diagram shows a sector ABC, centre A, radius 10 cm.

The arc length BC is 12 cm.

Calculate the area of the shaded part of the diagram.

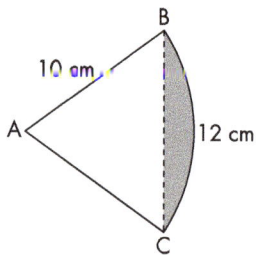

2   The diagram shows a sector ABC centre A, angle of 1.5 radians.

The shaded part of the sector is 5 cm^2.

Calculate the arc length BC.

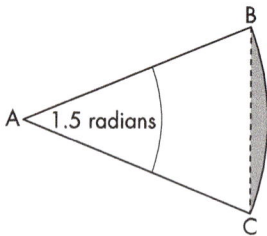

3   The diagram shows a circle of radius 8 cm, centre O.

A tangent DC of length 12 cm is drawn as shown.

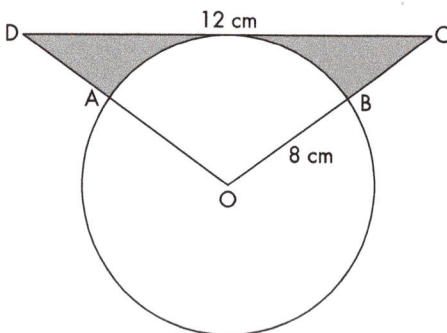

Calculate the area of the shaded part of the diagram.

4   The diagram show an arc AD of a circle, centre O, and an arc BC of a circle, centre O.

The arc length AD is 10 cm, arc length BC is 15 cm and length DC is 6 cm.

Calculate the area of the shape ABCD as shown.

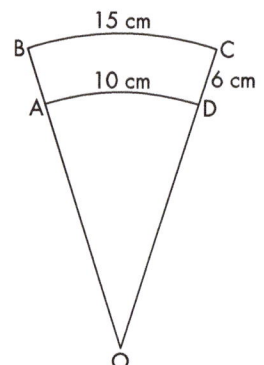

Extension

9.2 Arc length

1   The diagram shows a sector with radius 7 cm.
    Calculate the arc length AB.

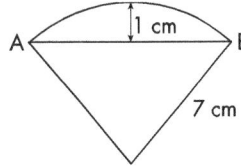

2   The diagram shows a sector with radius 5x and chord AB is 3x.
    The arc length AB is 4.57 cm. Calculate the value of x.

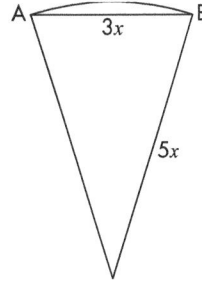

3   The diagram shows a sector with radius 5x and arc length 3x.

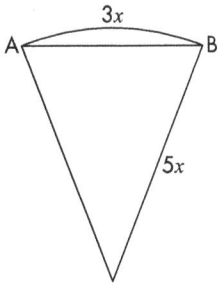

    The length of the chord AB is 7.68 cm. Calculate the value of x.

4   The diagram shows a sector with radius 8x and chord AB 6x.

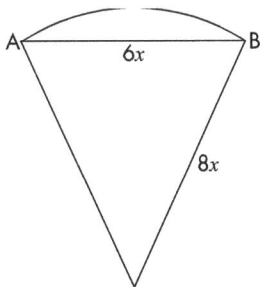

    The difference between arc length AB and chord AB is 0.271 cm. Calculate the value of x.

5   The diagram shows a sector with radius 6x.

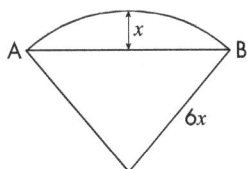

    The arc length AB is 10.54 cm. Calculate the value of x.

Extension

9.3 Sector area

1   The shape in the diagram is made up of two identical arcs.

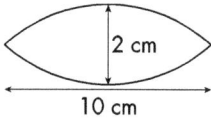

Calculate the perimeter of the shape.

2   The shape in the diagram is made up of two identical arcs.

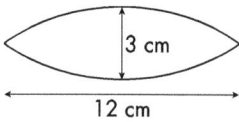

Calculate the area of the shape.

3   The shape in the diagram shown is made up of two identical arcs.

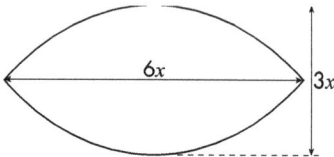

The perimeter of the shape is 48.884 cm. Calculate the value of x.

4   The shape in the diagram has two lines of symmetry.

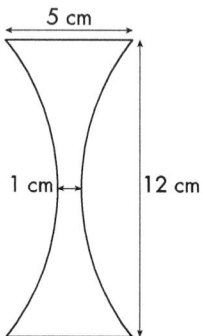

Calculate the area of the shape.

5   The diagram shown has four lines of symmetry.

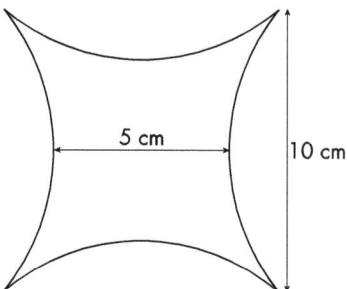

Calculate the area of the shape.

Extension

9.4 Problems involving arcs and sector area

1 The diagram shows a circle centre O, radius x cm. The line AC is a tangent to the circle.
   The length BC is 5 cm, the area of the shaded region is 7.1 cm². Find the value of x.

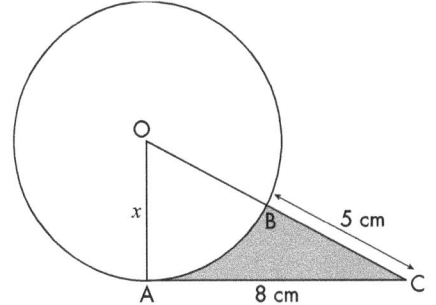

2 The diagram shows a circle centre O, radius x cm. The length AD is $x - 1$ cm.
   The length OD is 4 cm, the arc length AB is 18.37 cm. Find the length AC.

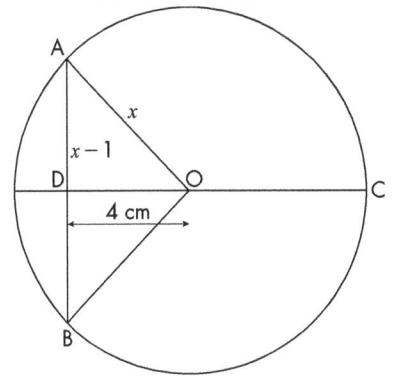

3 The diagram shows a circle centre O, radius x cm, with a sector AOB having sector angle x radians.
   The area of sector OAB is T cm². The length of arc AB is $4T$ cm. Find the value of x.

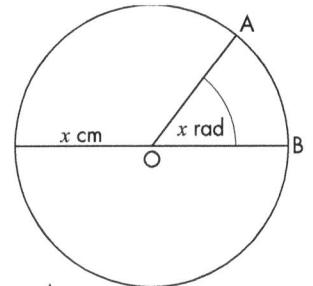

4 The diagram shows a circle centre O, radius 4 cm. The lines AC and BC are tangents to the circle.
   The shaded area is 2.9 cm².The length BC is 3.726 cm. Find the length of the arc AB.

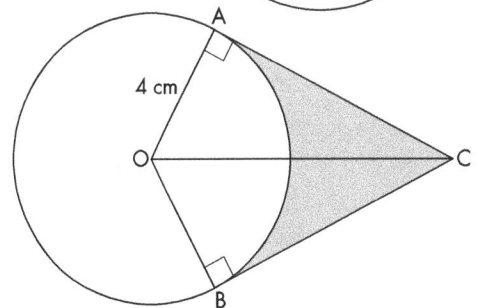

5 The diagram shows two arcs from different centres, radii 5 cm and 10 cm.
   Calculate the difference in the two arc lengths.

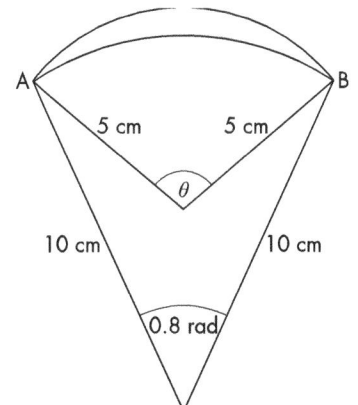

10 Trigonometry

TOPIC:

10.1 Trigonometrical values for angles of any magnitude

KEY WORDS:

quadrant, periodic, domain, range

IGCSE MATHS PRIOR KNOWLEDGE:

Use the sine, cosine and tangent functions

Learning aims:
- Know and use the six trigonometric functions of angles of any magnitude

Resources:
- Student Book: pages 202–212
- Resource sheet 10.1
- Interactive unit circle (if available)

Common mistakes and remediation:

Students often forget the relevance of a negative value of a trigonometric function and simply treat it as the same angle but negative. It is helpful for them to learn a suitable acronym to help them remember the quadrants in which negative values of trigonometric functions occur.

Useful tips:

Teach students the acronym ASTC (anticlockwise from the first quadrant). Alternatively, they could use ACTS (clockwise from the first quadrant) or CAST (anticlockwise from the fourth quadrant). Whichever form they choose, the letter tells them which ratio is positive (all, sine, tangent, cosine for ASTC).

Remind students that all trigonometric values should be written to 3 significant figures (but not rounded off in the middle of a calculation).

Guidance:

Make full use of the diagrams in the Student Book, to illustrate the graphs of each trigonometric function. It is important that students are familiar with the shapes of these graphs and can recognise the key points on them, where they cross axes and where the asymptotes are.

If available, an interactive unit circle with graph alongside can be very helpful in demonstrating these concepts.

STARTER (10 mins)

Equipment: Resource sheet 10.1, interactive unit circle (if available)

➤ Display on the board the diagram of the unit circle and the triangle used at the beginning of 10.1. (Use an interactive version of the unit circle if one is available.)

➤ Ask students to tell you which of the ratios of the sides gives each of sine, cosine and tangent of θ. Most should remember these, but some students will need reminding.

➤ Show that if P moves to the second quadrant, then θ becomes obtuse and the x-value will be negative, giving rise to negative cosine and tangent.

➤ Then show P moving to the third quadrant, which takes θ between 180° and 270° and makes the values of both x and y negative, making both sine and cosine negative but tangent positive.

➤ Then show P moving to the fourth quadrant, which takes θ between 270° and 360°. Now just y is negative, making both sine and tangent negative but cosine positive.

➤ Label each quadrant, anticlockwise from the first quadrant, as A, S, T, C, to illustrate the quadrant where each trigonometric function is positive: A – all, S – sine, T – tangent, C – cosine.

➤ Explain to students that they can use a phrase such as 'All Sun Tans Children' to help remember ASTC. Some prefer the other way round, giving 'Can All Schools Teach' – CAST. Many different mnemonics can be invented; for example, if you prefer ACTS, 'All Clever Teachers Smile'.

➤ Tell students that you will be using this mnemonic during the course of the next few lessons and that they will start to learn it (or another, if they prefer) as they use it over the coming weeks.

MAIN LESSON ACTIVITY (40 mins)

➢ Note: If you have graphical software available, this could be used throughout this exposition in addition to the diagrams and examples in the student book.

➢ Show students the sine curve, shown on page 203 in the Student Book.

➢ Explain that this graph is periodic, which means it will repeat itself every 360° and just keep on going – in both directions. Say that the graph has a period of 360°. You will also see that the domain of θ is any real number, as θ can have any value from $-\infty$ to ∞, but the range of sin θ is $-1 \leq \sin \theta \leq 1$, which means that the value of sin θ is always between −1 and 1. If you (or the students) have graphical software available, this can be used to show the continuing, periodic nature of the graph.

➢ Ask students to look at the symmetries of this graph: its rotational symmetry and line symmetry around 90° and 180°. This symmetry helps to clarify the values of sine for all angles between 0° and 360°.

➢ Use the second diagram to illustrate that 0.454 is the sine of 27° and is also the sine of (180° − 27°).

➢ Now ask students to look at the third diagram, which shows the sine of 34° is 0.559. Using the symmetries of the graph, students can see that −0.559 is also the sine of (180° + 34°) and (360° − 34°).

➢ Ask students to look at the graph of $y = \cos \theta$ on page 205. Let them discuss the symmetries and how they would find the cosines of angles between 0° and 360°.

➢ After a few minutes ask students to tell you what they have found. They should identify line symmetry about $y = 180°$ as well as rotational symmetry. They may even say, correctly, that the graph is the same as $y = \sin \theta$ but translated 90° to the right. Elicit from students how they can use the graph to find the cosines of all angles between 0° and 360°, along with the correct sign. You can use the diagram on page 206 to illustrate this.

➢ Discuss with students the period (360°) of the curve, the domain of θ (any real number) and the range of cosine θ ($-1 \leq \cos \theta \leq 1$). See if they can tell you that this is identical to the sine curve.

➢ Now ask students to look at the graph of $y = \tan \theta$ on page 208. Talk about the asymptotes at 90° and 270°, asking students to try to explain why they are there. If necessary, explain that at those points the ratio of opposite over adjacent approaches infinity and negative infinity and so, at these points the tangent of θ is undefined. Let students discuss with each other how they can use the graphs to determine the tangents of all angles between 0° and 360°.

➢ After a few minutes, refer to the second diagram and elicit from students how to use the graph to find the tangents of all these angles and ascertain whether they are negative or positive.

➢ Remind students of the diagram on 209 of the Student Book, showing all four quadrants and which trigonometric functions are positive. Then go through Example 4 with the students, using the symmetries of the graph as illustrated in the example.

➢ Students start Exercise 10.1.

➢ Ensure that higher-achieving students attempt questions 6 and 7, even if they leave out questions 2 and 3.

PLENARY (10 mins)

➢ Ask students to look at question 10 in Exercise 10.1.

➢ Ask if they can tell you what the period of this graph is (13 hours).

➢ Ask students to give the domain of the time and the range of the height. The domain is 0 to 24, repeated, but in practice it is all of time itself. The range of the height appears to be 2–7 but practically this will change as weather conditions change.

➢ Ask them for any similarities there may be with the sine and cosine curves.

➢ Discuss with students what other situations could give rise to a similar type of curve. Answers could vary from sound waves to Mexican waves.

Homework and answers: Resource sheets, homework and extension exercises can be found at the end of this chapter and in the downloadable materials. Answers can be found in the downloadable materials.

CHECKING PROGRESS	Ask students which mnemonic they prefer and check that they remember it.
	Ask students for a definition of a periodic graph and check they can give the domain, range and period for each of the three trigonometric graphs in this section.

10　Trigonometry

TOPIC:
10.2　Further trigonometric functions

10.3　Other trigonometric functions

KEY WORDS:
secant, cosecant, cotangent, tangent, cosine, sine, radians

IGCSE MATHS PRIOR KNOWLEDGE:
Use the sine, cosine and tangent functions

Learning aims:	Resources:
• Know and use the six trigonometric functions of angles of any magnitude • Solve, for a given domain, trigonometric equations involving the six trigonometric functions and the above relationships	• Student Book: pages 212–214 and 214–216

Common mistakes and remediation:

Students often mix up sec and cosec, as logically it looks as if the definitions should be the other way round. They need this to be pointed out so that they remember cosec is **not** $\dfrac{1}{\cos}$ but $\dfrac{1}{\sin}$, $\dfrac{1}{\sin x}$.

Useful tips:

Make sure that students learn the fact that cosec is **not** $\dfrac{1}{\cos}$, then the other two ratios are relatively easy to remember.

Guidance:

Some students will remember the surd form of the familiar angles 30°, 60° and 45°. They also need to be aware of the triangles they come from and remember them so that they can easily work the ratios out if they find it difficult to remember them. They need to become familiar with the larger angles associated with these surd form trigonometric ratios.

They also need to learn the other new trigonometric functions.

STARTER (15 mins)

➢ Display on the board a right-angled triangle with two 45° angles (unlabelled) and both shorter sides labelled 1. Ask students what the hypotenuse of this triangle is. They should be able to tell you $\sqrt{2}$. If any are unsure, let students discuss why this is so, from Pythagoras' theorem.

➢ Label one of the acute angles 45° and ask students if they can tell you the values of sin 45°, cos 45° and tan 45° without using their calculators. Discuss how you can get this information from the diagram and that $\sin 45° = \cos 45° = \dfrac{1}{\sqrt{2}}$, with tan 45° = 1. (Note: students should be familiar with the idea that $\dfrac{1}{\sqrt{2}} = \dfrac{\sqrt{2}}{2}$, and that it is neater not to have a surd on the bottom of a fraction)

➢ Now display on the board an equilateral triangle of side length 2. Draw a vertical line from the apex to the base to create a right-angled triangle with angles 30° and 60°, labelled as such. Ask students what the length of this vertical line is. They should all now be able to tell you it is $\sqrt{3}$, again from Pythagoras' theorem.

➢ Discuss with students what the trigonometric functions are for 30° and 60°, without using calculators but using the diagram.

➤ Write on the board π radians. Ask students for the equivalent angle in degrees (180°). Now ask what 360° will be (2π).

➤ Now ask what the degree equivalents are of $\frac{\pi}{2}$ (90°), $\frac{\pi}{4}$ (45°), $\frac{\pi}{3}$ (60°) and $\frac{\pi}{6}$ (30°).

➤ Let students do Exercise 10.2 without using a calculator.

MAIN LESSON ACTIVITY (40 mins)

➤ Explain that you are now going to introduce three new trigonometric functions that students will also be using through the rest of this chapter.

➤ Introduce secant, abbreviated to sec, and define it as secant $A = \frac{1}{\text{cosine } A}$ or $\sec A = \frac{1}{\cos A}$.

➤ Introduce cosecant, abbreviated to cosec, and define it as cosecant $A = \frac{1}{\text{sine } A}$ or cosec $A = \frac{1}{\sin A}$.

➤ Introduce cotangent, abbreviated to cot, and define it as cotangent $A = \frac{1}{\text{tangent } A}$ or cot $A = \frac{1}{\tan A}$.

➤ Now go through Example 5 on Student Book page 215, reminding them of ASTC.

➤ Go through Example 6.

➤ Students start Exercise 10.3.

➤ Ensure that higher-achieving students attempt questions 7, 8 and 9.

PLENARY (5 mins)

Equipment: mini-boards (optional)

➤ Ask students to close all their books. If mini-boards are available, students can use them to display answers (which gives you the opportunity to check that all students are responding correctly). No calculators to be used for this activity.

➤ Now ask if they can define each of cot θ, sec θ and cosec θ.

➤ Ask students if they can remember what 60° is in radians $\left(\frac{\pi}{3}\right)$.

➤ Now ask, what cot $\frac{\pi}{4}$ is $\left(\text{equivalent to cot } 45° \text{ and so } \frac{1}{1}, \text{which is } 1\right)$.

➤ Now ask what sec $\frac{\pi}{6}$ is $\left(\text{equivalent to sec } 30°, \text{which is } \frac{2}{\sqrt{3}}\right)$.

➤ Now ask what cot $\frac{\pi}{6}$ is $\left(\text{equivalent to cot } 30° \text{ and so } \frac{1}{\sqrt{3}} = \sqrt{3}\right)$.

Homework and answers: Resource sheets, homework and extension exercises can be found at the end of this chapter and in the downloadable materials. Answers can be found in the downloadable materials.

CHECKING PROGRESS	Check that students remember the triangles that the surd forms of key trigonometric functions are worked out from

10 Trigonometry

TOPIC:

10.4 Graphs of trigonometric functions

KEY WORDS:

amplitude, period

IGCSE MATHS PRIOR KNOWLEDGE:

Use the sine, cosine and tangent functions

Learning aims:

- Understand and use the amplitude and period of a trigonometric function, including the relationship between graphs of related trigonometric functions.
- Draw and use graphs of $y = a \sin bx + c$, $y = a \cos bx + c$ and $y = a \tan bx + c$

Resources:

- Student Book: pages 216–227
- Resource sheets 10.2, 10.3, 10.4, 10.5, 10.6, 10.7
- Graphing software if available

Common mistakes and remediation:

Many students are confused by the period of trigonometric functions, and the realisation that multiplying θ by a number greater than 1 will reduce the period, but multiplying by a fraction (a number less than 1) will increase the period. Take time to show students, especially lower-achieving ones, how this is manifesting itself on the graph from the equation. If graphing software is available, this can be used effectively to demonstrate the effect of different multipliers of θ on the resulting graph.

Useful tips:

Remind students that corresponding changes to sine and cosine graphs are the same, in relation to period and amplitude, and that the tangent curve has an infinite amplitude.

Encourage students to practice sketching trigonometric graphs. They should be aware of the difference between a sketch and an accurate graph.

Guidance:

Use of diagrams is important, as students will need to see exactly what is happening to the key points as the values in the equations change. Keep referring students to the diagrams both on your board and in the Student Book. Resource sheets 10.2, 10.3 and 10.4 provide copies of the three graphs for students to refer to. Resource sheets 10.5, 10.6 and 10.7 show some variations of these graphs.

Do not rush through this section: for students needing extra support this may take two lessons – one to introduce concepts and one to consolidate skills.

STARTER (15 mins)

Equipment: Resource sheets 10.2, 10.3, 10.4, graphing software if available.

➤ Display on the board a sketch of the graph of $y = \sin x$, as seen on page 216, in the Student Book, but without any labelling.

➤ Ask the students to tell you key points on the graph, the axis intercepts and greatest heights and depths.

➤ Ask them to tell you about the symmetries of the graph, talk about the amplitude being 1 and the period being 360°.

➤ Discuss with the class other scenarios that may lead to a graph of this shape but with different amplitudes and periods. Possibilities are daylight hours, tides and sound as well as Mexican waves in a sports crowd.

➤ Now repeat for $y = \cos x$ and $y = \tan x$ but do not ask where else you may see these graphs.

MAIN LESSON ACTIVITY (45 mins)

Equipment: Resource sheets 10.2, 10.3, 10.4, 10.5, 10.6, 10.7, graphing software if available.

➤ Leaving the graph of $y = \sin x$ on display, write $y = 3 \sin \theta$ on the board and ask students what shape this graph might have. Elicit from them how they can do this by thinking of the y-value for common θ values, such as $0°$, $90°$, $180°$.

➤ Slowly, using their responses, sketch the graph as seen on page 217 of the Student Book, explaining that the period will stay the same at $360°$ but the amplitude now becomes 3.

Discuss with students what the shape might be for $y = 5 \sin \theta$, $y = 7 \sin \theta$, leading to the generalisation of $y = A \sin \theta$ having amplitude of A and period of $360°$. Demonstrate with graphing software and a range of values. For students needing additional chalenge, ask what would happen if the amplitude A takes a negative value.

➤ Now go back to a graph of $y = \sin \theta$, with the labels, and write up on the board $y = \sin 2\theta$, asking what shape this graph might take.

➤ Again, using their responses to key points, show, for example, that where $\theta = 45°$ then 2θ will be $90°$ and hence there will be a peak of 1; similarly, when θ is $90°$, 2θ will be $180°$ and so the curve will need to cross the horizontal axis. Continue in this way and sketch the new graph of $y = \sin 2\theta$ as on page 218 of the Student Book, having an amplitude of 1 but this time 'squashed' to show a period of $180°$.

➤ Talk through the possible graph of $y = \sin \frac{1}{2}\theta$ in a similar way, showing that the graph is now stretched out with a period of $720°$, as on page 218 of the Student Book, near the foot of the page, or model with graphical software.

➤ Repeat the above activity, sketching $y = \sin \theta + 1$.

➤ Talk through the generalisation of sketching $y = A \sin b\, \theta + c$, where the amplitude will be A, the period will be $\frac{360°}{b}$ and the peaks and troughs translated vertically by c. Discuss whether students have seen graphs of this shape elsewhere.

➤ Show that, similarly, the sketches of $y = A \cos b\theta + c$ will have an amplitude of A, a period of $\frac{360°}{b}$ with peaks and troughs translated vertically by c.

➤ Starting from a sketch on the board of $y = \tan \theta$, talk through how to sketch, say, $y = 3 \tan \theta$, stretched up but still an amplitude of infinity with the period staying the same at $180°$. Then talk through the sketch of, say, $y = \tan 2\theta$, giving just a change of period to $\frac{180°}{b}$.

➤ If time and IT access allows, students could explore generalisations using graphical software.

➤ Talk the students through Example 7 on page 222 of the Student Book, and then Example 8 on page 223.

➤ Talk through the graphs of $y = |\sin \theta|$, $y = |\cos \theta|$ and $y = |\tan \theta|$, as on pages 223–224 of the Student Book.

➤ Students start Exercise 10.4.

➤ Try to ensure that the highest-achieving students try questions 12 and 13, maybe missing out questions 5 to 11.

PLENARY (5 mins)

➤ Refer to question 6 in Exercise 10.4.

➤ Discuss with students the shapes of the graphs and what they represent before asking about their amplitudes and periods.

➤ Ask students to think of a Mexican wave and to try to describe its possible amplitude, as well as its period, giving answers in contexts such as 'height difference from sitting to standing but adding some arm length, period being the arena circumference'.

Homework and answers: Resource sheets, homework and extension exercises can be found at the end of this chapter and in the downloadable materials. Answers can be found in the downloadable materials.

CHECKING PROGRESS	Check that all students are familiar with both basic shapes of trigonometric functions and are able to think through variations.

10 Trigonometry

TOPIC:

10.5 Trigonometric identities

KEY WORDS:

identities, prove

IGCSE MATHS PRIOR KNOWLEDGE:

Use the sine, cosine and tangent functions

Learning aims:

- Prove trigonometric relationships involving the six trigonometric functions

Resources:

- Student Book: pages 227–229
- Interactive unit circle diagram (if available)

Common mistakes and remediation:

Many students find it difficult to learn the later identities off by heart initially, so it is important that they fully understand how they can work them out for themselves from the basic identities learnt at IGCSE.

Useful tips:

Encourage students to prove the last two identities mentally without needing to write them down.

Encourage the students to get into the habit of putting the identities to be proved into sine and cosine, as this often makes it easier to see how to proceed with the proof.

Guidance:

Ensure that lower-attaining students fully understand how to work with the two basic identities to develop the other three and can then use them to prove other identities.

STARTER (10 mins)

Equipment: Interactive unit circle (if available)

➤ Display on the board a sketch of the unit circle with the triangle, as shown in the diagram at the beginning of section 10.5 in the Student Book. Ensure the vertical height of the triangle is labelled $\sin \theta$ and the horizontal length labelled $\cos \theta$, with the hypotenuse 1.

➤ Ask students what this diagram tells them about $\tan \theta$. You may need to lead them to see that it gives

$\tan \theta = \dfrac{\text{opposite}}{\text{adjacent}} = \dfrac{\sin \theta}{\cos \theta}$, so $\tan \theta = \dfrac{\sin \theta}{\cos \theta}$. Explain the use of the symbol $\equiv$ as being 'equivalent to'. Remind students

that they should have come across this in IGCSE and have learnt it already – if they've forgotten it they need to relearn it now.

➤ Tell students that this is what is called an identity and, as such, can be quoted as a result in proofs.

➤ Ask students what else the triangle tells them. (Note that these two points could come in either order; take them as they come.) You are expecting the students to recognise that they can apply Pythagoras' theorem to the triangle to get $\sin^2 \theta + \cos^2 \theta \equiv 1$. Again, this is an identity that they should remember from IGCSE and they still need to know it now.

➤ Tell students that this is another identity that is very useful in proving other identities.

➤ Ask students if they can now tell you what $\sin^2 \theta$ equals. Elicit from them $1 - \cos^2 \theta$.

➤ Ask students if they can now tell you what $\cos^2 \theta$ equals. Elicit from them $1 - \sin^2 \theta$.

MAIN LESSON ACTIVITY (45 mins)

➢ Leave the identities of tan $\theta \equiv \dfrac{\sin\theta}{\cos\theta}$ and $\sin^2\theta + \cos^2\theta \equiv 1$ on the board.

➢ Write cot θ on the board and ask students if they can say what this might be in terms of sin θ and cos θ.

➢ Draw from the students that they know $\cot\theta = \dfrac{1}{\tan\theta}$ and so that will give $\cot\theta = \dfrac{\cos\theta}{\sin\theta}$. Explain that this is another identity which they need to be familiar with.

➢ Ask students to look at the identity $\sin^2\theta + \cos^2\theta \equiv 1$ on the board.

➢ Explain that you are going to show them what happens when they divide this through by $\cos^2\theta$.

➢ This will give $\tan^2\theta + 1 \equiv \sec^2\theta$. Ensure that you go through this carefully, taking even the lowest-attaining students with you, as this is another identity which the students need to be familiar with, normally written as $1 + \tan^2\theta = \sec^2\theta$. Explain that they need to be able to prove this for themselves from that initial identity.

➢ Now take them back to the identity $\sin^2\theta + \cos^2\theta \equiv 1$ and explain that you are going to divide through by $\sin^2\theta$.

➢ Lead students carefully through to get $1 + \cot^2\theta \equiv \operatorname{cosec}^2\theta$, which is the last identity they need to be familiar with for the time being.

➢ Go through Example 9 in the Student Book with students, showing how they can start with the left-hand side and, using identities they already know, can follow this through to give a different result.

➢ Go through Example 10 in the Student Book with students, showing again the process of starting with the left-hand side and working through. Then show the approach of starting by assuming the identity is true and multiplying both sides by $(1 - \cos\theta)$ to give a known identity, which means your starting point must have been true. Ask students which method they prefer and which they would consider more mathematically reliable.

➢ Students start Exercise 10.5.

PLENARY (5 mins)

➢ With no books open in front of the students and a clean board, ask students if they can remember each of the five identities they have met today.

➢ The simplest you would expect to be given are the first two; tan $\theta \equiv \dfrac{\sin\theta}{\cos\theta}$ and $\sin^2\theta + \cos^2\theta \equiv 1$.

➢ Once students have identified them, these two can be written on the board.

➢ The next simplest will probably be $\cot\theta \equiv \dfrac{\cos\theta}{\sin\theta}$; write this on the board.

➢ Now ask for those that are most difficult to remember: given what is already on the board, students should be able to work them out in their heads.

➢ Lead them to $1 + \tan^2\theta \equiv \sec^2\theta$ and $1 + \cot^2\theta \equiv \operatorname{cosec}^2\theta$.

➢ Explain to students that they do not need to learn these last two off by heart, but rather know how to derive them easily.

Homework and answers: Resource sheets, homework and extension exercises can be found at the end of this chapter and in the downloadable materials. Answers can be found in the downloadable materials.

CHECKING PROGRESS	Students need to learn these identities by rote, so check that each student remembers them (or how to derive them), during the plenary.

10 Trigonometry

TOPIC:

10.6 Solving trigonometric equations

KEY WORDS:

None

IGCSE MATHS PRIOR KNOWLEDGE:

Use the sine, cosine and tangent functions

Learning aims:

- Solve, for a given domain, trigonometric equations involving the six trigonometric functions.

Resources:

- Student Book: pages 229–231

Common mistakes and remediation:

Students will need help in realising that you can add multiples of 360° (180° for tan) onto basic trigonometric solutions to give alternative solutions. Show them diagrammatically, either with the unit circle or the graphs. It may be necessary to take this very carefully and slowly with lower-achieving students.

Useful tips:

Encourage students to look for the smallest possible value that is too large for a final solution, then they know the full range they are working with.

Sketch graphs or the unit circle can be useful for students to check they have found all the solutions.

Guidance:

Ensure that lower-achieving students have had a chance to solve at least one sin, one cos and one tan equation successfully.

STARTER (10 mins)

➢ Display on the board a sketch of the unit circle with a set of axes, crossing at the centre, showing all four quadrants.

➢ Ask students to tell you how to label this diagram to help them remember which trigonometric functions have positive values. Draw from them ASTC or whichever suitable acronym you have taught them earlier.

➢ Write on the board: $\cos \theta = 0.5$.

➢ Ask students what value θ can take. Draw from them the simple answer of 60°, then the alternative answer (360° − 60°), which is 300°.

➢ Ask students if there are more solutions. Lead them to 360° + 60°, which is 420°, and also 360° + 300°, which is 660°.

➢ Ask students if there are any more, eliciting that in fact there is an infinite number of solutions to this, which is why they need some sort of boundary when they are asked for a solution.

➢ Ask students if they can now tell you all the solutions for $\sin \theta = 0.5$, where θ is less than 720°.

➢ Elicit the answers: 30°, 150°, 390° and 510°.

MAIN LESSON ACTIVITY (45 mins)

➢ Write on the board the equation from Example 11 in the Student Book, $\cos(5x + 25°) = 0.5$, and explain that they are looking for solutions between $0°$ and $180°$.

➢ Ask students what they could now say about $5x + 25°$.

➢ You need to draw from the students that this means that $5x + 25°$ could be $60°$ and $300°$.

➢ Students should also tell you that other possibilities could be $360° + 60°$ and $360° + 300°$ giving $420°$ and $660°$. But are there any more?

➢ Elicit that they could travel around the circle again to give possible solutions as $720°$ added to each, giving $780°$ and $1020°$.

➢ But where should they stop looking for more?

➢ Explain that students must remember that they are looking for the solutions to $5x + 25°$ = one of the suggested values, bearing in mind that the final solutions for x need only be between $0°$ and $180°$.

➢ Take the largest value suggested so far, $1020°$ and solve the equation $5x + 25° = 1020°$.

➢ Show that this solution is $199°$ and too large, so they only need to consider those values suggested that are less than $1020°$.

➢ Show that using the values of $60°$, $300°$, $420°$, $660°$ and $780°$ they get the solutions $x = 7°$, $55°$, $79°$, $127°$ and $151°$.

➢ Go through Example 12 in the Student Book with students, finding all the solutions in the range $0° \leq x \leq 360°$ that satisfy the equation $5 \tan x = 7 \sin x$.

➢ Show how this leads to the equation $\sin x(5 - 7 \cos x) = 0$, which gives two direct solutions of $\sin x = 0$ and $5 - 7 \cos x = 0$. They then need to find all the possible solutions of these equations in the given range for x.

➢ Go through Example 13 with students: this equation is in radians. The process is very similar, but they will need to bear in mind that they are dealing with radian values and use 2π instead of $360°$ for possible larger values than the basic ones.

➢ Students start Exercise 10.6 – ensure they have the opportunity to complete questions in radians as well as degrees.

PLENARY (5 mins)

➢ With no books open in front of the students, and a clean board, ask students to tell you all the solutions to $\tan \theta = 1$. These will be $45°$, $180° + 45°$, $360° + 45°$, etc.

➢ You may need to remind lower-achieving students that the period of the graph of tan is $180°$ and not $360°$, so they can add multiples of $180°$ to their basic value, not just multiples of $360°$.

➢ Now ask students to give some solutions to $\tan 2x = 1$.

➢ This time it is $2x$ that equals $45°$, $225°$, $405°$, so the solutions for x will be $22.5°$, $112.5°$, $202.5°$, ...

➢ Now ask for the solutions to $\tan 3x = 1$. Solutions will be $15°$, $75°$, $135°$ ...

Homework and answers: Resource sheets, homework and extension exercises can be found at the end of this chapter and in the downloadable materials. Answers can be found in the downloadable materials.

CHECKING PROGRESS	In the plenary, ensure that all students are able to answer questions; if some cannot, then ask higher-achieving students to explain their thinking.
	Ask students to write an equation of the form $A \sin x/3 = B$ (A an integer and $-1 \leq B \leq 1$), set a domain and swap with a partner to solve each other's equation. Share solutions. Students needing additional challenge could try to construct a more complex equation.

Resource sheet 10.1

Signs of trigonometric functions

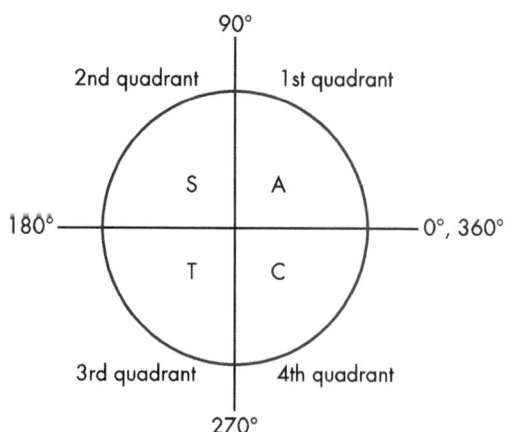

In the first (1st) quadrant, all trigonometric values are positive.

In the second (2nd) quadrant, only sine values are positive.

In the third (3rd) quadrant, only tangent values are positive.

In the fourth (4th) quadrant, only cos values are positive.

This can be summarised as:

1st quadrant	**A**ll
2nd quadrant	**S**ine
3rd quadrant	**T**angent
4th quadrant	**C**osine

starting with the first quadrant and counting anticlockwise.

Find a way to remember this, for example:

- ASTC reading **anticlockwise** from the first quadrant (you could remember this as **A**ll **S**un **T**ans **C**hildren)
- CAST reading **anticlockwise** from the fourth quadrant showing which quadrants have positive trigonometric values.

Use one of these, or make one up for yourself, as long as you remember this important rule.

Resource sheet 10.2

The sine curve

This is the graph of $f(\theta) = \sin \theta$ for θ from $0°$ to $360°$.

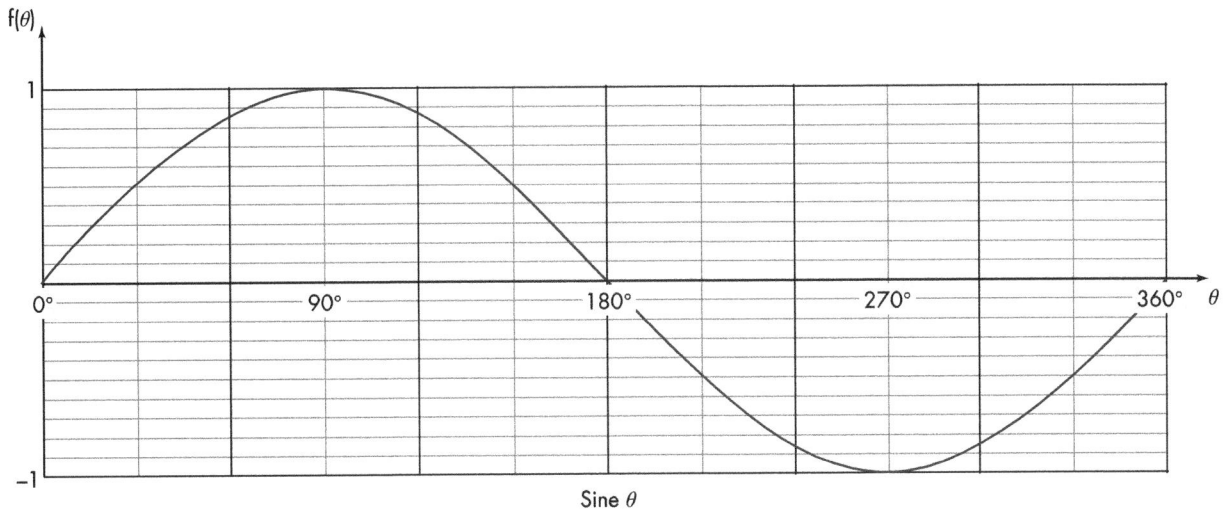

Sine θ

Resource sheet 10.3

The cosine curve

This is the graph of $f(\theta) = \cos \theta$ for θ from $0°$ to $360°$.

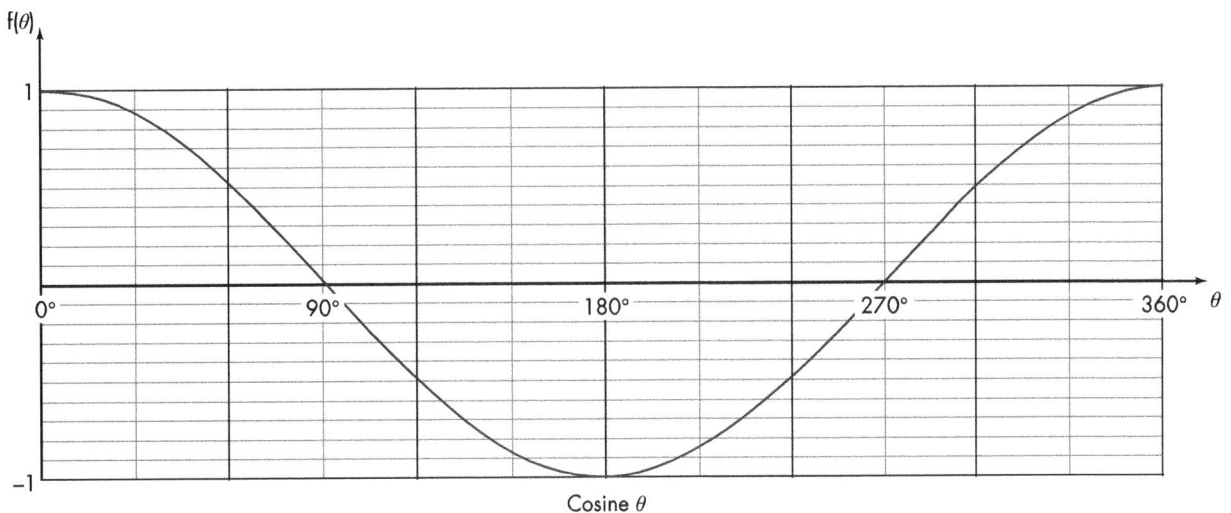

Cosine θ

Resource sheet 10.4

The tangent curve

This is the graph of f(θ) = tan θ for θ from 0° to 360°.

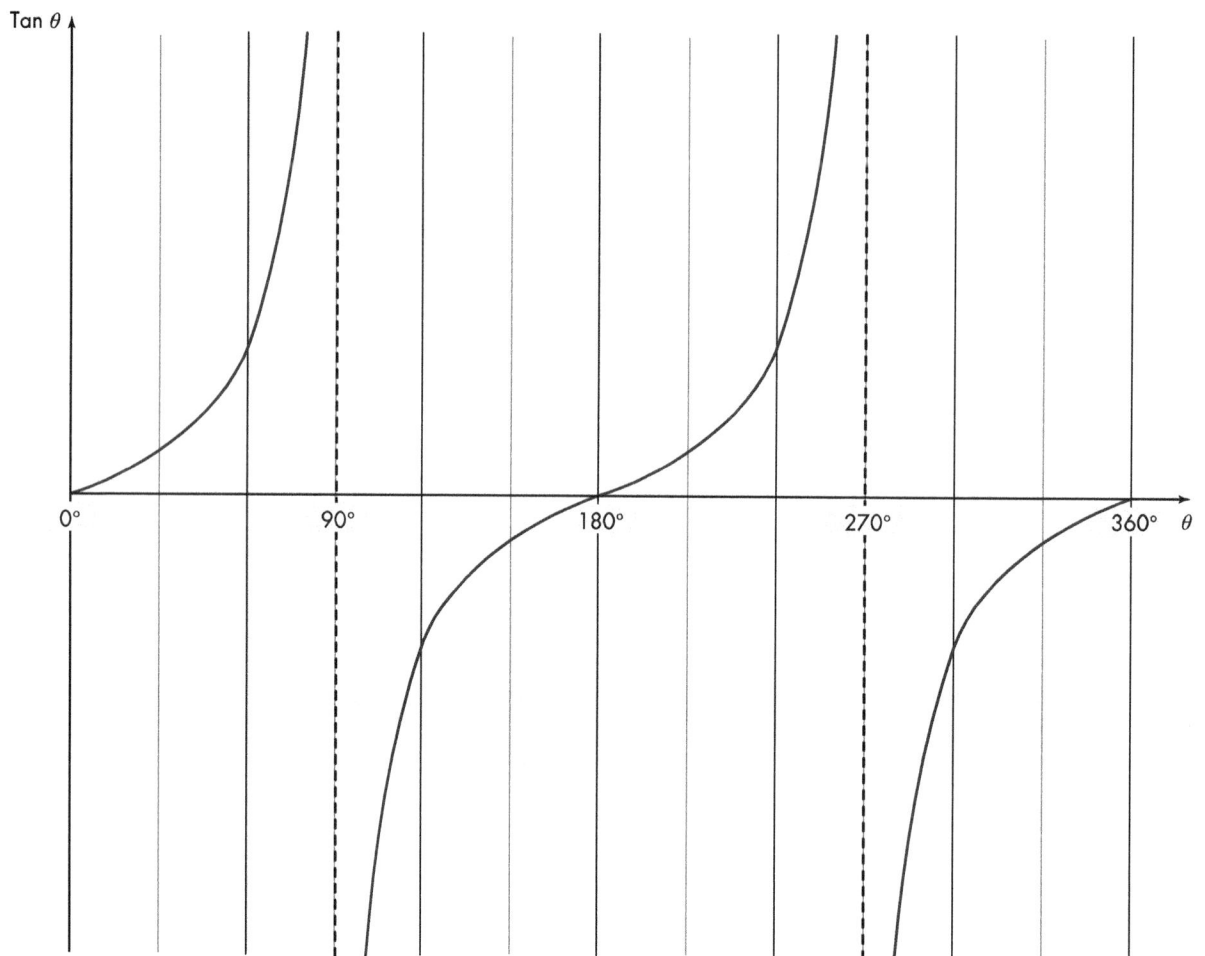

Resource sheet 10.5

Variations of $y = \sin \theta$

The graph of $y = A \sin b\theta + c$ will:

➤   be the same shape as $y = \sin \theta$

➤   have an amplitude of A

➤   have a period of $\dfrac{360°}{b}$

➤   move vertically by c (up if c is positive, down if c is negative).

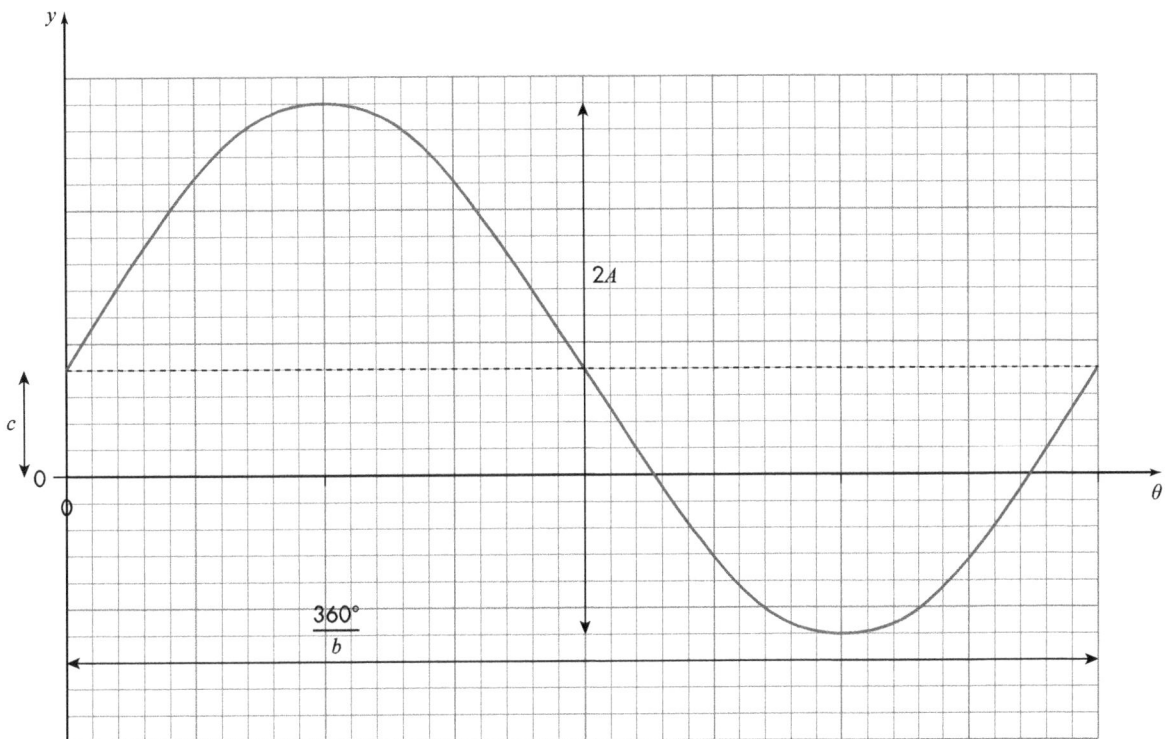

Resource sheet 10.6

Variations of $y = \cos \theta$

It is the same shape as the graph of $y = \sin \theta$ but it is translated 90° along the horizontal axis.

It also has amplitude of 1 and period of 360°.

The variations follow the same pattern as the sine curve.

The graph of $y = A \cos b\theta + c$ will:

➤ be the same shape as $y = \cos \theta$

➤ have an amplitude of A

➤ have a period of $\dfrac{360°}{b}$

➤ move vertically by c (up if c is positive, down if c is negative).

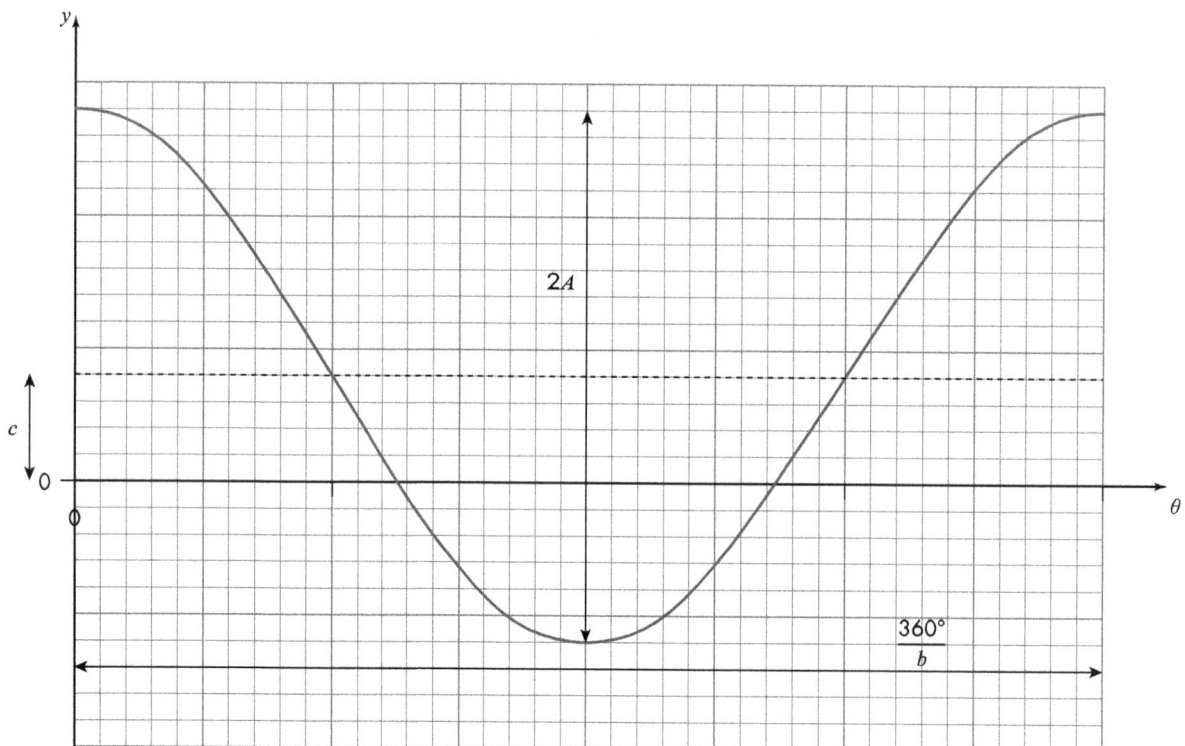

Resource sheet 10.7

Variations of $y = \tan \theta$

The graph of $y = A \tan b\theta + c$ will:

➢ be the same shape as $y = \tan \theta$

➢ have an infinite amplitude

➢ have a period of $\dfrac{180°}{b}$

➢ move vertically by c (up if c is positive, down if c is negative).

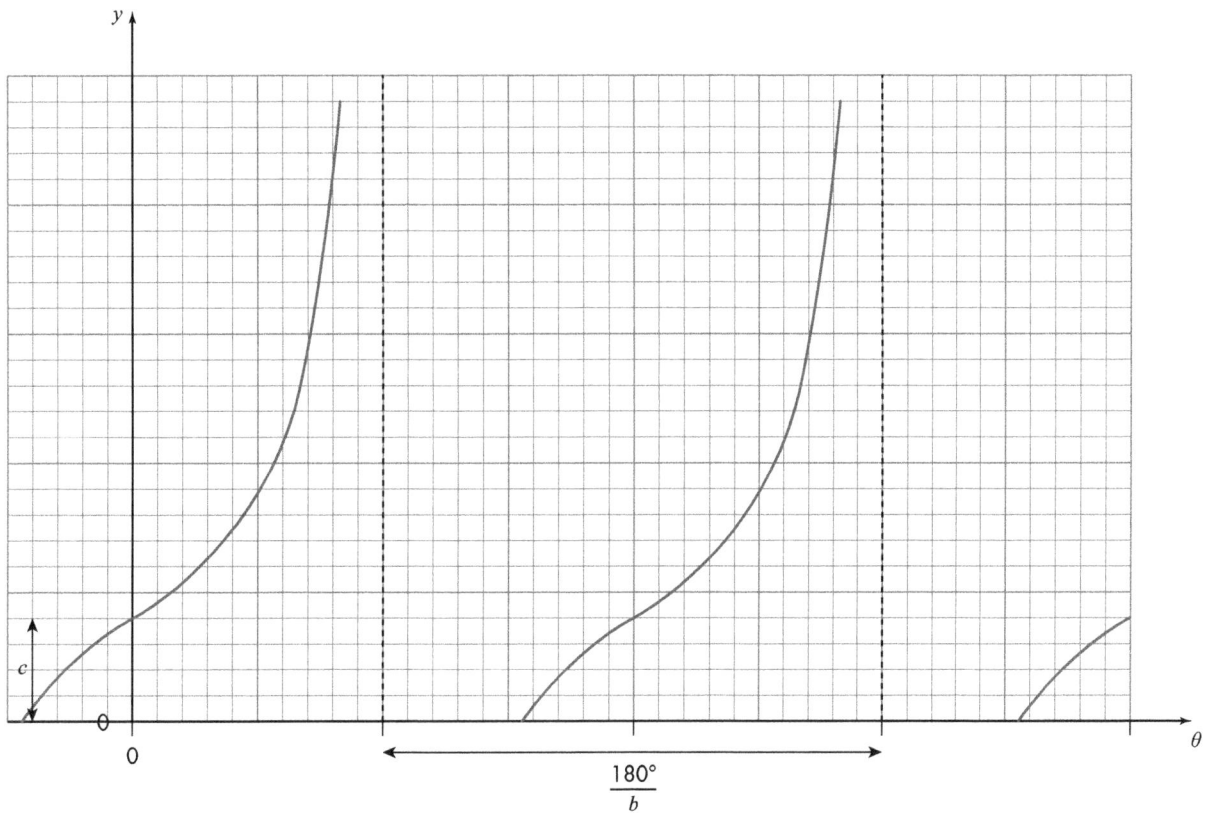

Homework

10.1 Trigonometric values for angles of any magnitude

1   State the two angles between $0°$ and $360°$ for each of these sine values.

    a 0.3   **b** −0.7

2   State the two angles between $0°$ and $360°$ for each of these cosine values.

    a 0.2   **h** −0.35

3   State the angles between $0°$ and $360°$ for each of these tangent values.

    a 0.85   **b** −1.35

4   **a**   A navigator was told he was on a bearing with a sine of 0.45. What bearing might the navigator be on?

    b   A pilot was on a bearing with a cosine of −0.45. What bearing might the pilot be on?

5   **[NC]** You are told that $\sin 37° = 0.602$.

    Without using a calculator, state:

    a   another angle whose sine has the value of 0.602

    b   two angles that have a sine of −0.602.

6   **[NC]** You are told that $\cos 46° = 0.695$.

    Without using a calculator, state:

    a   another angle whose cosine has the value of 0.695

    b   two angles that have a cosine of −0.695.

7   **[NC]** You are told that $\tan 27° = 0.510$.

    Without using a calculator, state:

    a   another angle whose tangent has the value of 0.510

    b   two angles that have a tangent of −0.510.

10 Trigonometry

Homework

10.2/10.3 Other trigonometric functions

1 [NC] $\sqrt{2}$ [OBJ] $\sqrt{3}$ [OBJ].

  a $\cos 30° + \sin 45°$ **b** $\tan 60° + \sin 30°$ **c** $\cos 45° - \tan 30°$

2 [NC] Solve giving your answers in terms of π: :

  a $\sec\theta = \sqrt{2}$, $0 \le \theta \le \pi$ **b** $\operatorname{cosec}\theta = 2$, $0 \le \theta \le 2\pi$

3 [NC] Solve giving your answers in terms of π: :

  a $\cot\theta = -\sqrt{3}$, $0 \le \theta \le \pi$ **b** $\sec\theta = -2$, $0 \le \theta \le 2\pi$

4 Solve:

  a $\operatorname{cosec} x + 5 = 0$, $0° \le x \le 360°$ **b** $4 - \sec x = 0$, $0° \le x \le 360°$

5 Solve:

  a $3\cot\theta = 4$ $0° \le \theta \le 360°$ **b** $5\sec\theta = 8$ $0° \le \theta \le 360°$

6 Solve:

  a $5\cot\theta = -2$ $0° \le \theta \le 360°$ **b** $4\operatorname{cosec} x = 6$ $0° \le \theta \le 360°$

7 Find all the solutions of $\sec^2 x = 4$, $0° \le x \le 360°$.

Homework

10.4 Graphs of trigonometric functions
Non-calculator

1 State the amplitude of each function.

   a $y = 5 \sin 3\theta + 4$

   b $y = 3 \cos 2\theta + 4$

2 State the period of each function.

   a $y = 2 \sin 4x + 1$

   b $y = 4 \cos 5x - 3$

   c $y = \cos \dfrac{1}{4} x$

3 State the period of each function.

   a $y = \tan 4\theta + 3$

   b $y = \tan 10\theta - 5$

   c $y = \tan \dfrac{1}{4} x$

4 Sketch the graph of each function for $0° \leq \theta \leq 360°$.

   a $y = 5 \sin \theta$

   b $y = 4 \cos \theta$

5 Sketch the graph of each function for $0° \leq \theta \leq \pi$.

   a $y = \sin 4\theta$

   b $y = \cos 2\theta$

6 Sketch the graph of each function for $-30° \leq \theta \leq 90°$.

   a $y = \tan 4\theta$

   b $y = \tan 4\theta + 1$

7 Sketch the graph of each function for $0 \leq \theta \leq 2\pi$.

   a $y = 4 \sin \theta + 3$

   b $y = 3 \cos \theta + 2$

   c $y = 2 \tan \dfrac{1}{2} \theta + 2$

8 a Sketch the graph of each function for $0 \leq \theta \leq \pi$.

      i $y = |\cos 3\theta|$

      ii $y = |\tan 2\theta|$

      iii $y = |\sin 4\theta|$

   b State the period of each graph in part **a**.

Homework

10.5 Trigonometric identities

Non-calculator

1 Prove that $\dfrac{\sec^2\theta - 1}{\sec^2\theta} = \sin^2\theta$.

2 Prove that $\cos\theta + \tan\theta\sin\theta \equiv \sec\theta$.

3 Show that $\tan\theta + \cot\theta \equiv \dfrac{\sec\theta}{\sin\theta}$.

4 Show that $2\tan\theta \equiv \dfrac{\cos\theta}{1-\sin\theta} - \dfrac{\cos\theta}{1+\sin\theta}$.

5 Prove that $\cos^2\theta - \sin^2\theta \equiv \dfrac{1-\tan^2\theta}{1+\tan^2\theta}$.

6 Prove that $\dfrac{\cos\theta - \sin\theta}{\cos\theta + \sin\theta} \equiv \dfrac{1-2\sin\theta\cos\theta}{1-2\sin^2\theta}$.

Homework

10.6 Solving trigonometric equations

1 Solve the equation $\sec 3x = 5$, $0° \le x \le 180°$.

2 Solve the equation $4\sin 2x = 3$, $0° \le x \le 360°$.

3 **[NC]** Solve the equation $2\sin\left(2x + \dfrac{\pi}{6}\right) = 1$, $0 \le x \le \pi$.

4 Solve the equation $\tan 2x = 2\sin 2x$, $0° \le x \le 360°$.

5 **[NC]** Solve the equation $\cos x - 3\sin^2 x = 1$, $0° \le x \le 360°$.

6 Solve the equation $4\cos^2 x + \sin x = 1$, $0° \le x \le 360°$.

7 Find all the angles between $0°$ and $360°$ that satisfy these equations.

   a $\cos(4x + 25) = -0.3$

   b $\cos x + 4\sin x = 0$

8 Find all the solutions to these equations between $0°$ and $180°$.

   a $\sec(5x - 10) = 2$

   b $3(\cos 3x - \sin 3x) = \sin 3x$

Extension

10.1 Trigonometric values for angles of any magnitude

Find all the angles between $0°$ and $360°$ that satisfy these equations.

1 $\cos 3x = 0.7$

2 $\sin 2x = -0.8$

3 $\tan 0.8x = -2.4$

4 $\sin 5x = 0.85$

5 $\cos \dfrac{1}{3}x = -0.27$

Extension

10.2/10.3 Other trigonometric functions

1 Find all the angles between $0°$ and $360°$ that satisfy the equation $\cos(2x + 20°) = 0.3$.

2 Find all the angles between 0 and π that satisfy the equation $\cos\left(2x - \dfrac{\pi}{4}\right) = -0.5$.

3 Find all the angles between $0°$ and $360°$ that satisfy the equation $\sin(3x - 30°) = -0.8$.

4 Find all the angles between 0 and π that satisfy the equation $\sin\left(2x + \dfrac{\pi}{3}\right) = 0.5$.

5 Find all the angles between $0°$ and $360°$ that satisfy the equation $\tan(3x - 50°) = 2$.

Extension

10.4 Graphs of trigonometric functions

Non-calculator

1 Sketch the graph of $y = \sin(2\theta + 90°)$ for $0° \leq \theta \leq 360°$.

2 Sketch the graph of $y = \cos\left(3\theta - \dfrac{\pi}{3}\right)$ for $0 \leq \theta \leq 2\pi$.

3 Sketch the graph of $y = \tan(2\theta + 45°)$ for $0° \leq \theta \leq 360°$.

4 Sketch the graph of $y = \left|\sin\left(\dfrac{1}{2}\theta + 60°\right)\right|$ for $0° \leq \theta \leq 360°$.

5 Sketch the graph of $y = \left|\cos\left(2\theta + \dfrac{\pi}{4}\right)\right|$ for $0 \leq \theta \leq \pi$.

Extension

10.5 Trigonometric identities

Non-calculator

Here are two more trigonometric identities.

$\sin (A + B) = \sin A \cos B + \cos A \sin B$

$\cos (A + B) = \cos A \cos B - \sin A \sin B$

These questions are a challenge. Please note trigonometric identities are **not** on
the syllabus, however will be useful for preparation for the study of mathematics at AS and A level

Use these to prove the following identities

1   $\sin (A - B) = \sin A \cos B - \cos A \sin B$

2   $\sin (A - B) + \sin (A + B) = 2 \sin A \cos B$

3   $\cos (A - B) = \cos A \cos B + \sin A \sin B$

4   $\cos (A - B) + \cos (A + B) = 2 \cos A \cos B$

5   $\cos 2A = \cos^2 A - \sin^2 A$

Extension

10.6 Solving trigonometric equations

These questions are a challenge. Please note trigonometric equations are **not** on
the syllabus, however will be useful for preparation for the study of mathematics at AS and A level.

Find all the angles between $0°$ and $360°$ that satisfy these equations.

1   $\sin 2\theta = \cos \theta$

2   $2 (\cos \theta - \sin \theta) = \sin \theta$

3   $8 \sin \theta + 3 \sec \theta = 0$

4   $3 \sin^2 \theta - 8 \sin \theta \cos \theta - 3 \cos^2 \theta = 0$

5   $\tan \theta = 3 \cot \theta$

11 Permutations and Combinations

TOPIC:

11.1 Permutations

KEY WORDS:

permutation, arrangement, factorial, selection, factorial notation

IGCSE MATHS PRIOR KNOWLEDGE:

Write down the number of possible events in a simple scenario in order to calculate a probability

Learning aims:

- Know and use the notation $n!$ and the expression for permutations and combinations of n items taken r at a time

Resources:

- Student Book: pages 238–240
- Two large foam dice
- Mini whiteboards or similar

Common mistakes and remediation:

Students often fail to use the factorial button and/or the ^nP_r button on the calculator correctly. Ensure every student is confident in using these buttons on their own calculator by encouraging them to use them in their calculations wherever possible to provide plenty of practice.

Useful tips:

The number of permutations for selecting r out of n items is given by $^nP_r = \dfrac{n!}{(n-r)!}$

Point out that, by definition, $0! = 1$

This can be related to the use of the formula to find the number of arrangements of n items $= {}^nP_n = \dfrac{n!}{(n-n)!} = \dfrac{n!}{0!} = n!$

Guidance:

Lower-achieving students will need more assistance in seeing the link between the number of items and the way in which the factorial pattern emerges. Emphasise that a permutation is a calculation of the number of ways items can be ordered or arranged. Also remind them that, for permutation calculations, the order of the arrangement is important so that they are able to differentiate between permutation and combination calculations.

Note

Remind the students that problems involving:

- repetition of objects
- objects arranged in a circle
- permutations and combinations

are beyond the scope of this specification and are not assessed in the examination.

However, some examples are included in this chapter as extension material. They are a useful preparation for students intending to study AS or A level mathematics.

STARTER (10 mins)

Equipment: 2 large foam dice

➤ Ask students what the probability is of tossing a coin and getting a head. They should all be comfortable with the answer of $\frac{1}{2}$. Discuss why the answer is a half. This is because there are only two possibilities and there is only one way of getting a head.

➤ Now ask students: *What is the probability of rolling a dice and getting a five?* The answer is $\frac{1}{6}$. Again discuss why this is – there are now six possibilities but there is only one way of getting 5.

➤ Now ask: *What is the probability of rolling a dice and getting a number larger than two?* Discuss with students how to find this out. Elicit how many possibilities there are (6) and then how many of these give a number larger than 2 (4), so the probability is $\frac{4}{6}$ which cancels to $\frac{2}{3}$.

➤ Ask students what the probability is of randomly choosing someone in this room aged over 30. (Change this age to suit your classroom scenario!) The answer is likely to be one out of how many people there are in the room, including yourself.

➤ If there are both boys and girls in the room, ask what the probability is of selecting a girl at random from the room, then the chance of a boy being selected.

➤ If there is only one sex in the classroom, then choose another way of categorising students by, say, those wearing blue, to ask a similar question.

MAIN LESSON ACTIVITY (40 mins)

➤ Write A on the board and tell the students: *There is only one way I can order this one letter.* Write A – 1.

➤ Now put AB on the board and ask: *How many ways can you order these two letters?* Show that the answer is 2, AB and BA. Write AB – 2.

➤ Continue with ABC. You will need to demonstrate the six different ways these letters can be arranged. Write ABC – 6.

➤ Discuss with the class how to calculate the number of ways by looking at the number of ways to select the first letter (3), then to select the second letter, after the first has been selected (2), then finally how many are left to select for the third letter (1). This gives a total of $3 \times 2 \times 1 = 6$ ways to arrange the three letters. Explain that this is the number of **permutations** for the order of these three letters. Ensure that lower-achieving students see the connection between three items and the calculation to find the answer 6.

➤ Now ask students to work out how many permutations there will be for four letters ABCD, without having to write them all down. Elicit that the answer will be $4 \times 3 \times 2 \times 1 = 24$. If it helps the lower-achieving students, then get them to write down all these different combinations in a logical order, to verify that this is a much quicker way to get to the solution.

➤ Now ask students to work out how many permutations there are for five letters ABCDE (120). Explain to students that permutation calculations often occur in mathematics problems and that the short way of writing $8 \times 7 \times 6 \times 5 \times 4 \times 3 \times 2 \times 1$ is 8! This is called 'eight factorial' and they can find a button for this on their calculators.

➤ Ask students to find the button labelled x! on their calculators. Check they can use this button by working out $3! = 6$ and $4! = 24$. Explain to students that using the factorial button will save them a lot of calculation time.

➤ Using the five letters ABCDE, ask the students how many ways they can select just two out of these five letters. Lead the discussion to 5×4 which is 20 ways. Then ask how many ways they could select three of these letters, leading them to $5 \times 4 \times 3$ which is 60.

➤ Show how the number of ways to select 'two from five' can be expressed as $\frac{5!}{3!} = \frac{5\times4\times3\times2\times1}{3\times2\times1}$.

➤ Lead students to see that, in general, the number of ways of selecting r items from a choice of n different items will be:

$$\frac{n!}{(n-r)!}$$

➤ Explain the notation students need to know for permutations. ^nP_r represents the number of permutations of r items selected from n.

➤ Talk through Example 11.3 with students.

➤ Students can now start Exercise 11A. Ensure that the highest-achieving students get the opportunity to work on question 13.

PLENARY (10 mins)

Equipment: Mini whiteboards

➤ Ask students how many ways the letters in DAD can be arranged. Discuss the fact that there are only three possibilities: DAD, DDA and ADD

➤ Explain to students that the next two exercises are a challenge but that finding the number of permutations of repeated letters in *LULL* and *OHHH* etc. is **not** on their syllabus. Ask students how many ways the letters LULL can be arranged. Lead the discussion to the answer of four possibilities: ULLL, LULL, LLUL, LLLU

➤ Ask students how many ways the letters OHHHH can be arranged. Lead discussion to five, eliciting that this can be seen quite simply as being how many places there are for the single letter to take.

➤ Now consider DADA, asking how many ways these letters can be arranged. There are six: DDAA, DAAD, AADD, ADDA, DADA, ADAD

➤ Explain to students that the topic of permutations expands in a variety of ways, which they will explore in the next few lessons.

Homework and answers: Resource sheets, homework and extension exercises can be found at the end of this chapter and in the downloadable materials. Answers can be found in the downloadable materials.

CHECKING PROGRESS	Check that all students are involved in the plenary and are able to offer solutions.

11 Permutations and Combinations

TOPIC:
11.2 Permutation problems

KEY WORDS:
None

IGCSE MATHS PRIOR KNOWLEDGE:
Write down the number of possible events in a simple scenario in order to calculate a probability

Learning aims:	**Resources:**
• Solve problems on arrangement and selection using permutations or combinations	• Student Book: pages 240–244

Common mistakes and remediation:
When solving problems that involve working out the number of permutations for a set of items that are not all different, students often forget to consider the number of ways that the items which are the same can be arranged. To address this, ask them to write out in full the possible order for examples using a small number of items and build up the number of items that are the same.

Show how each example relates to the formula for the number of permutations of n items in which there are k of one item, m of another item and r of another item which is $\dfrac{n!}{k!m!r!}$

Useful tips:
Students need to read questions carefully to be able to identify the method they need to use for each problem. For example, when groups of the same item need to be placed together within a set of items that are arranged, as illustrated in Example 11.4.

Guidance:
Lower-achieving students will need more assistance in identifying the different methods needed to deal with the number of permutations of a set of items that are not all different.

STARTER (10 mins)

➢ Set up the scenario with students, using the board to illustrate numbers, so that they are reminded as they work through the questions. Say that there is a small group of students, two boys and three girls.

➢ Ask: *What is the probability of randomly selecting two boys from the group?* Discuss with the class how they did this for IGCSE. The probability of selecting the first boy will be $\dfrac{2}{5}$ and the probability of selecting the second boy will be $\dfrac{1}{4}$ (lower-achieving students will need the 4 explaining: only four students are left after the first selection). Now multiply the two probabilities to get $\dfrac{2}{20}$, cancelling to $\dfrac{1}{10}$.

➢ Now ask: *What is the probability of selecting two girls from the same group of five students?* After some discussion, lead the class to $\dfrac{3}{5} \times \dfrac{2}{4} = \dfrac{6}{20} = \dfrac{3}{10}$.

➢ Now ask them about selecting one boy and one girl from the same group.

➢ You may have to remind them that there are two ways this may happen, as the first could be a boy or a girl. So you have to consider the chance of a boy selected then a girl and add this to the chance of a girl selected then a boy. This should lead to $\dfrac{2}{5} \times \dfrac{3}{4} + \dfrac{3}{5} \times \dfrac{2}{4} = \dfrac{12}{20} = \dfrac{3}{5}$.

➢ Ask students: *What links all three answers?* Lead the discussion to the fact that the sum of the probabilities is 1 as the three outcomes are exhaustive. The only possible outcomes are (boy, boy), (boy, girl), (girl, boy), (girl, girl).

MAIN LESSON ACTIVITY (45 mins)

➤ Set up the scenario, as on pages 240–241 in the Student Book, of a bookshelf holding five fiction books and six non-fiction books.

➤ Ask students how many possible permutations there are of arranging these books. They should be able to tell you 11!, which someone can find on their calculator as 39 916 800 different arrangements.

➤ Now ask students to consider what the answer might be if they decided to put all the fiction together and all the non-fiction together. Ask: *In how many ways can the five fiction books be arranged?* (5!) Then ask: *In how many ways can the non-fiction books be arranged?* (6!)

➤ Discuss with the class that as there are 5! arrangements of the fiction and 6! arrangements of the non-fiction, to find the total number of different arrangements they need to multiply these two figures to give 5! × 6!.

➤ But that is only if the fiction books come first – there is also the possibility that the non-fiction books come first, so there are two ways they can arrange the two sets. So, they must double the 5! × 6! to get 172 800 different possible arrangements.

➤ Now ask the students to consider the number of arrangements if all the fiction books were next to each other, but they could be placed anywhere amongst the non-fiction books.

➤ Lead the class to see that they can consider the fiction books as one item and so there are now 7 items to arrange, giving 7! arrangements. But as there are also 6! ways of arranging the fiction books, there are 7! × 6! arrangements altogether.

➤ Now write on the board the word 'parallelogram' and ask students to consider how many different arrangements there are of these letters, noting that there are three 'a's, three 'l's and two 'r's.

➤ Remind students that if they consider all letters as independent then there are 13! different arrangements, yet the three 'a's can occur in 3! ways, as can the three 'l's, and the two 'r's can appear in 2! ways and so the number of different arrangements will be $\dfrac{13!}{3!\,3!\,2!}$.

➤ Lead students to see that the number of permutations of n items of which k are the same is given by $\dfrac{n!}{k!}$.

➤ Lead students to see that, in general, the number of permutations of n items in which there are k of one item, m of another item and r of another item is given by $\dfrac{n!}{k!\,m!\,r!}$.

➤ Talk the students through Example 11.5 in the Student Book, carefully explaining to lower-achieving students how to deal with the problem of selecting numbers larger than 5000 and the odd numbers.

➤ Students can now start Exercise 11.2.

PLENARY (5 mins)

➤ Ask students how many ways they could arrange four books on a shelf. (4! = 24) You can use books from your room to illustrate this as a kinaesthetic example.

➤ Ask students how many ways these books can be put on the shelf, if two are large and must be at each end. The answer will be 2! × 2! = 4.

➤ Ask: *What if there were ten books with the four largest being equally placed at each end, so there were two at each end?* The answer is 4! × 6! = 17 280.

Homework and answers: Resource sheets, homework and extension exercises can be found at the end of this chapter and in the downloadable materials. Answers can be found in the downloadable materials.

CHECKING PROGRESS	Ensure that all students are involved in the plenary and offering suggestions. Get higher-achieving students to talk through their solutions for the benefit of the lower-achieving students.

TOPIC:

11.3 Combinations

KEY WORD:

combination

IGCSE MATHS PRIOR KNOWLEDGE:

Write down the number of possible events possible in a simple scenario in order to calculate a probability

Learning aims:	Resources:
• Recognise the difference between permutations and combinations and know when each should be used	• Student Book: pages 244–247
• Know and use the notation n! and the expressions for permutations and combinations of *n* items taken *r* at a time	

Common mistakes and remediation:

Many students are confused about the differences between permutations and combinations. This needs careful explanation and clear use of the correct vocabulary.

For example, when selecting two of the letters ABC:

- there are 6 permutations, AB, AC, BA, BC, CA, CB
- there are 3 combinations, AB, AC, BC

For combinations the order is unimportant, so AB is the same as BA, AC is the same as CA and BC is the same as CB.

Useful tips:

The number of combinations for selecting *r* out of *n* items is given by $^nC_r = \dfrac{^nP_r}{r!} = \dfrac{n!}{r!\,(n-r)!} = \dbinom{n}{r}$

Keep emphasising the difference between permutations and combinations from the start of the lesson.

For the number of **permutations**, the order of the items **is important**

For the number of **combinations**, the order of the items **is not important**

Guidance:

Lower-achieving students will need more assistance in being able to understand the difference between permutations and combinations. For example, in identifying combinations, if ABC is one possible selection, then this is the only possible selection containing these 3 letters

STARTER (10 mins)

➤ Write three letters A, B and C on the board and ask students: *In how many ways can you select a combination of two of these letters?*

➤ You will need to lead the discussion as to the difference between permutations and combinations here, stressing that combinations do not make any considerations for order. Hence, the different combinations will be A and B, A and C along with B and C, giving three combinations.

➤ Add the letter D to the previous three and ask the same question: *What combinations are possible?* Write them on the board as they are suggested; AB, AC, AD, BC, BD and CD, six in total. Show the students how they should be looking at this logically, selecting the combinations in a specific order so as not to miss any out.

➤ Now ask them to see if they can write for themselves all the different combinations of two letters from A, B, C, D and E. They should end up with ten.

➤ Ask students if they could look at the number pattern so far and suggest how many combinations there would be if they added another letter, F. The answer is 15.

➢ Ask students to tell you how they would find how many combinations of any two letters from the alphabet of 26 letters there will be, and why. The answer is $\frac{26 \times 25}{2} = 325$, found by looking at the number pattern derived so far of $N \times (N-1) \div 2$ where they select two items from N objects.

MAIN LESSON ACTIVITY (45 mins)

➢ Tell the students they need to be looking for a link between permutations and combinations.

➢ Going back to the starter activity, they have a starting point for selecting two items from N items of $N \times (N-1) \div 2$ combinations.

➢ Now look at selecting three from five items. Write the letters A, B, C, D and E on the board and ask students to write down all the different combinations of three letters, using the logical rules discussed in the starter. This will give ABC, ABD, ABE, ACD, ACE, ADE, BCD, BCE, BDE, CDE: ten altogether.

➢ Show that there are ten distinct combinations, but how many different permutations are there of each individual combination? Show that, for example, ABC has six different permutations from 3!.

➢ Show also that the number of permutations of three items selected from five would be $\frac{5!}{(5-3)!} = 60$.

➢ Now if they divide this by the number of permutations of each set of three items, $3! = 6$, they get 10, which is the number they found.

➢ The number of combinations of three different items taken from five items is $\frac{5 \times 4 \times 3}{3 \times 2 \times 1}$, which is denoted by the symbol $^{5}C_3$.

➢ So they have a rule for finding the number of combinations of selecting r items from N as the total number of combinations is given by: $^{n}C_r$ which is equal to $\frac{^{n}P_r}{r!}$. This means $^{n}C_r = \frac{n!}{r!\,(n-r)!}$

➢ Explain that $\frac{n!}{r!\,(n-r)!}$ can be written as $\binom{n}{r}$. This is also known as the Binomial Coefficient and students will meet this notation again in the next chapter.

➢ Talk the students through Example 6 in the Student Book, emphasising the link between combinations and permutations.

➢ Talk the students through Example 8 in the Student Book.

➢ Students can now start Exercise 11.3.

PLENARY (5 mins)

➢ Total the numbers of males and females in the room, putting these totals on the board. If it's a single-sex class, choose a suitable alternative such as 'those with long hair or not'.

➢ Ask students how many different combinations of four students can be selected from the room. The answer will be $^{N}C_4$ with N being the total number in the room.

➢ Ask students how many different combinations of four students can be selected from the room, where the four must contain two males and two females.

➢ Where there are M males and F females, this will give the result $\frac{M \times (M-1) \times F \times (F-1)}{2 \times 2}$.

Homework and answers: Resource sheets, homework and extension exercises can be found at the end of this chapter and in the downloadable materials. Answers can be found in the downloadable materials.

CHECKING PROGRESS	It is important that all students understand the difference between permutations and combinations. Check that all students are clear about this at various points in the lesson.

TOPIC:

11.4 Combinations problems

KEY WORD:

committee

IGCSE MATHS PRIOR KNOWLEDGE:

Write down the number of possible events in a simple scenario in order to calculate a probability

Learning aims:	Resources:
• Solve problems on arrangement and selection using permutations or combinations	• Student Book: pages 247–250

Common mistakes and remediation:

Students often have difficulty when working with combination problems that involve arranging a set of items which are not all different. Encourage students to read through the problem carefully to make sure they understand exactly what is required to find the solution.

Useful tips:

The number of combinations for selecting r out of n items is given by $^nC_r = \dfrac{n!}{r!\,(n-r)!}$

Encourage students to rewrite the numbers from the problem in a clear way before starting the solution.

Guidance:

Lower-achieving students will need assistance in interpreting some of the problems.

STARTER (10 mins)

Work through Example 10 in the Student Book. Write the five letters A, B, C, D and E on the board and set up the scenario about a security lock that has five buttons labelled with these letters. A code can be pre-set using the letters. The code can consist of 1 letter, 2 letters, 3 letters, 4 letters or 5 letters. The code letters can be entered in any order and cannot be repeated.

➢ Ask students how many codes there are using one letter. This should be straightforward, as 5.

➢ Ask students how many codes there are using two letters. This is $^5C_2$, which gives $\dfrac{5\times4}{2} = 10$ possible codes.

➢ Ask students how many codes there are using three letters. This is $^5C_3$, which gives $\dfrac{5\times4\times3}{3\times2} = 10$ possible codes.

➢ Ask the students how many codes there are with just four letters. This is $^5C_4$, which gives $\dfrac{5\times4\times3\times2}{4\times3\times2} = 5$ possible codes.

➢ Now ask students how many codes there are if all five letters are used. This should be straightforward as 1 code.

➢ Complete this activity by asking how many possible codes there are in total for this security lock. If you have kept the answers to each question above on the board then the students should be able to tell you the answer is 31.

➢ Now show the students an alternative way to find the solution to this problem.

Since you have the possibility of any combination, except using no letters at all, then consider that:

A can be used or not used – 2 possibilities

B can be used or not used – 2 possibilities

C can be used or not used – 2 possibilities

D can be used or not used – 2 possibilities

E can be used or not used – 2 possibilities.

➤ Hence altogether there are $2 \times 2 \times 2 \times 2 \times 2 = 2^5 = 32$ possibilities, but this includes the possibility that none of the letters is used, which is not a valid code. So again, the number of valid codes is $32 - 1 = 31$.

MAIN LESSON ACTIVITY (45 mins)

➤ Tell students they have just worked through one type of combination problem and you're going to work through another one with them. Work through an example similar to Example 11 (in the Student Book) as below.

➤ Set up the scenario of a manager needing to choose a team of eight players from a squad of 12 that consists of five men and seven women.

➤ Find the number of different teams that could be chosen if the team must include at least one woman.

➤ Discuss with the class the fact that as a team of eight must be chosen and there are only 5 men, then there must always be at least one woman in the selection, so our answer is simply the number of combinations of selecting eight people from the twelve $^{12}C_8$, which gives $\dfrac{12!}{4!\,8!} = 495$.

➤ Now ask them about the number of different teams that could be chosen if the team must include at least three men.

➤ Now they have to look at the different possibilities; they can have all 5 men and 3 women, 4 men and 4 women or 3 men and 5 women.

➤ Consider the first possibility of all 5 men and 3 women. There is only one way to select all 5 men, but there are $^7C_3$ ways of selecting the 3 women, giving $\dfrac{7 \times 6 \times 5}{3 \times 2} = 35$.

➤ Now consider the second possibility of 4 men and 4 women. There are $^5C_4$ ways to select 4 men, and there are $^7C_4$ ways of selecting the 4 women, giving a total number of combinations as $^5C_4 \times {}^7C_4$.

➤ This calculates as $\dfrac{5 \times 4 \times 3 \times 2}{4 \times 3 \times 2 \times 1} \times \dfrac{7 \times 6 \times 5 \times 4}{4 \times 3 \times 2 \times 1}$, which gives 175.

➤ Now consider the third possibility of 3 men and 5 women. There are $^5C_3$ ways to select 3 men, and there are $^7C_5$ ways of selecting the 5 women, giving a total number of combinations as $^5C_3 \times {}^7C_5 = 210$.

➤ Add up the possibilities $35 + 175 + 210 = 420$.

➤ Students can now start Exercise 11.4.

PLENARY (5 mins)

➤ Ask students to tell you the number of permutations of n items. Answer: $n!$

➤ Ask students to tell you the value of 0! Answer: 1

➤ Ask students to tell you the number of permutations of r items taken from n items. Answer: $^nP_r = \dfrac{n!}{(n-r)!}$

➤ Ask students to tell you the number of combinations of r items taken from n items. Answer: $^nC_r = \dfrac{n!}{r!\,(n-r)!} = \dbinom{n}{r}$

To aid learning, students could use whiteboards to hold up and show their answers.

Homework and answers: Resource sheets, homework and extension exercises can be found at the end of this chapter and in the downloadable materials. Answers can be found in the downloadable materials.

CHECKING PROGRESS	Do ensure that all students are involved in the discussions during the plenary, taking care that the weaker students are following the conversations.

Homework

11.1 Permutations

1   Write down all the permutations of the letters in the word 'owl'.

2   How many different ways can seven students sit next to each other in a line of seven chairs?

3   a   How many permutations are there for six books to be arranged on a shelf?

    b   Theo has eight books on his shelf. In how many different ways could he arrange them?

4   a   How many different permutations are there of the digits 5, 6, 7 and 8?

    b   How many three-digit numbers can you make with the numbers 5, 6, 7 and 8?

    c   How many three-digit numbers can you make with the numbers 1, 2, 3, 4, 5 and 6?

5   Write down the number represented by:

    a $\dfrac{7!}{5!}$ b $\dfrac{8!}{4!}$

    c $\dfrac{10!}{7!}$ d $\dfrac{8!}{5!}$

6   What is the value of:

    a $^{8}P_3$ b $^{11}P_6$

    c $^{9}P_3$ d $^{9}P_5$?

7   How many different ways are there of writing any three different letters from the word 'switch'?

8   A race involves eight runners. How many different ways are there for the first four runners finishing the race?

Homework

11.2 Combined permutations

1   A shelf contains five physics books and four chemistry books. In how many different ways can they be arranged on the shelf if:

    a   there are no restrictions

    b   they are grouped by subject

    c   only the physics books need to be grouped together?

2   A shelf contains 10 electronic games; six combat games and four strategy games. In how many different ways can they be arranged on the shelf if:

    a   there are no restrictions

    b   they are grouped by category

    c   the first game is a strategy game and the last one is a combat game?

3   a   How many different four-digit numbers can be formed from the digits 1, 2, 3, 4, 5 and 6 if no digit is repeated?
    b   How many of the four-digit numbers found in **part a** are odd?
    c   How many of the four-digit numbers found in **part a** are less than 3000?

4   In a group of students, five are aged eighteen, four are aged seventeen and three are aged sixteen. They are asked to stand in a straight line before they go into assembly.
    In how many different ways can the line be arranged if:
    a   all the sixteen-year-olds stand together
    b   all the eighteen-year-olds stand together, and all the seventeen-year-olds stand together
    c   the first in the line is an eighteen-year-old and last in the line is also an eighteen-year-old?

11   Permutations and Combinations

Homework

11.3 Combinations

1   How many combinations are there of the letters in the word 'eighty' if:
    a   any three of the letters are chosen
    b   any four of the letters are chosen?

2   a   How many combinations are there for arranging four of 10 books on a shelf?
    b   I have 12 books I have not read. I am going on holiday and want to take four of them with me to read. How many different combinations of these four books can I take?

3   Explain what $^{10}C_6$ means.

4   Work out the value of each number.
    a $^8C_5$ b $^8P_5$
    c $^7C_4$ d $^7P_4$

5   A teacher has to choose a quiz team of five students from a class of 16. How many different teams could she select?

6   A rugby team manager has a squad of 18 players. A team of seven players has to be chosen. How many different combinations of players could be chosen?

Homework

11.4 Problems with permutations and combinations

1   Eight different birthday cards are placed on a shelf. There are three cards from family and five cards from friends. Find the number of different arrangements of the cards if all the family cards are placed together.

2   A darts team of four people is to be chosen from a group of six men and four women. Find the number of different teams that can be chosen if at least two women must be on the team.

3   A committee of three people is to be chosen from a group of eight men and six women. Find the number of different committees that can be chosen if it must include at least one man and one woman.

4   A 6-character security code is to be chosen from the 12 characters shown below. At least one character from each category must be chosen. Each character may be used once only in any code.
   • Letters: A, B, C, D and E
   • Numbers: 1, 2, 3 and 4
   • Symbols: !, #, and *
   Find the number of different security codes that may be chosen if the security code must start and finish with a number.

5   The numbers 1, 2, 3, 4, 5 and 6 are placed in a line.
   a   How many different six-digit numbers could be shown?
   b   How many multiples of 5 can be made from these digits?
   c   How many even numbers can be made from these digits?

6   There are 12 boys and 8 girls in a club. Six of them are to be selected to go on a trip. In how many ways can the selection be made if there must be at least two boys and two girls on the trip?

7   A staff car park has space for 12 cars parked side by side. Six of the staff cars are black, four of the cars are red and two of them are white.
   a   Find the number of different ways the cars can be parked if there are no restrictions.
   b   Find the number of different ways the cars can be parked if all the same colour cars are together.

8   The numbers on the faces of a dice are 1, 2, 3, 4, 5 and 6. I roll three identical dice.
   How many different combinations are there of the three numbers I may roll?

Extension

11.1 Permutations

1   This question is a challenge; please note that arrangements in a circle are **not** on your syllabus. How many permutations are there for six people to sit in a circle?

2   How many permutations are there of the letters in the word 'madam'?

3   The digits in the number 115 599 get mixed up. How many different numbers can be made from these digits?

4   At a celebration, 10 blue flags, 10 white flags and 5 yellow flags are to be flown in a line. How many different permutations are there for these flags to be flown in a line?

5   At a school assembly, 14 of the 30 teachers are seated in a row on the stage. How many different permutations are there for the teachers in the row?

Extension

11.2 Combined permutations

1   At a family party, there are 10 females and eight males. They are seated in two teams of nine people.
How many different ways can this be done if:
   a   there are no restrictions
   b   each team must have at least two males and two females?

2   A teacher has 21 maths books and 8 statistics books to put on a shelf in his new classroom.
In how many different ways can they be arranged if:
   a   they are grouped by subject
   b   only the maths books need to be grouped together?

Questions 3 and 4 are challenge questions; please note that repetitions is **not** on the syllabus.

3   Are there more or less than a million permutations of the letters in the words 'one million?

4   Twenty children go into dinner and sit around five tables.
Each table seats four children.
How many different permutations are there for the seating arrangements?

Extension

11.3 Combinations

1 This question is a challenge; please note that arrangements in a circle are **not** on the syllabus.
There are eight chairs in a circle, for a group of eight people. Mr Spooner and Mrs Spooner are in the group.
In how many different ways can Mr Spooner and Mrs Spooner be seated in this circle?

2 A team manager has to choose 11 players from a squad of 18 players. How many different teams could she select?

3 Four students are to be chosen as representatives for a school of 60 students. How many combinations are there?

4 How many odd numbers less than 8000 can be formed using the digits 1, 4, 5, 6 and 9?
Each digit may be used only once in any number.

Extension

11.4 Problems with permutations and combinations

1 Three prizes, one for Mathematics, one for Physics and one for Chemistry, are to be awarded in a class of 20 students.
Find the number of different ways in which the three prizes can be awarded if:
a students may not win more than 1 prize
b students may not win all 3 prizes.

2 How many 5-digit numbers that are divisible by 3, can be formed using the digits 0, 1, 2, 3, 4, 5 (without repetition)?

3 Everyone in a room shakes hands with everyone else in the room. The total number of handshakes is 66.
How many people are in the room?

4 A polygon has 44 diagonals. How many sides does it have?

TOPIC:

12.1 Arithmetic progressions

KEY WORDS:

arithmetic progression, arithmetic sequence, arithmetic series, common difference

IGCSE MATHS PRIOR KNOWLEDGE:

Recognise patterns in sequences

Find the nth terms for linear and quadratic sequences

Learning aims:

- Recognise arithmetic and geometric progressions and understand the difference between them
- Use the formulae for the nth term and for the sum of the first n terms to solve problems involving arithmetic progressions

Resources:

- Student Book: pages 256–258

Common mistakes and remediation:

Students often mix up a, d and l in the formula for the nth term and the sum of the first n terms. Practicing substitution into these formulae can help overcome this. They can also confuse the notation u_n and S_n.

Introducing the terms of an AP in a table form can help students visualise the pattern of the terms and the connection between the position of the term and the coefficient of d, i.e. the coefficient of d is 1 less than its position. This will enable them to find the general form for u_n

Position	1	2	3	4	5	....	n
Term	a	$a+d$	$a+2d$	$a+3d$	$a+4d$	....	$a+(n-1)d$

Useful tips:

These formulae are on the formulae page of the exam papers:

$u_n = a + (n-1)d$

$$S_n = \frac{1}{2}n(a+l) = \frac{1}{2}n\{2a+(n-1)d\}$$

Encourage students to write the letter l in a loopy way, in their work, so that they don't misread it as a 1.

It is important to distinguish between the descriptors used in this section:

An **arithmetic progression** (AP) is a sequence of numbers in which the difference between successive terms is constant. The constant is known as the **common difference**, d.

An arithmetic progression is also known as an **arithmetic sequence**.

An **arithmetic series** is the sum of the terms in an arithmetic progression/sequence.

Guidance:

Lower-achieving students may need assistance in understanding and being able to reproduce the proof of the sum to n terms formulas.

STARTER (5 mins)

➢ Put the following sequence on the board: 4, 7, 10, 13.

➢ Ask students what the next term will be. (16)

➢ Now ask students to describe the sequence. (Adding 3 on each time, starting with 4.)

➢ Ask students swhat the nth term of the sequence will be. ($3n + 1$)

➢ Put the next sequence on the board: 1, 6, 11, 16.

➢ Ask what the nth term will be for this sequence. You may have to lead the discussion to find $5n - 4$.

MAIN LESSON ACTIVITY (45 mins)

➢ Tell students that the sequences they have just been looking at are called arithmetic progressions (or APs for short). Also known as arithmetic sequences. They are sequences in which the same numerical constant is added to form each subsequent term. This means the difference between consecutive terms is the same.

➢ Tell students that the difference between terms is normally called the common difference, represented by d, and the first term is usually denoted by a.

➢ Show students that, taking the first term as a, the second term will be $a + d$, the third term will be $a + 2d$, the fourth term will be $a + 3d$, and so on. You can set this up in a table so that they can see the connection between the position of each term and the coefficient of d.

➢ Show how this leads to the general form for the nth term of the AP as $u_n = a + (n - 1)d$.

➢ Now ask students what the nth term will be for the sequence: 7, 11, 15, 19…

➢ Lead the discussion to nth term as $u_n = 7 + (n - 1)4$ or, rearranging, $u_n = 7 + 4(n - 1)$.

➢ The following proof needs to be explained carefully, so that lower-achieving students have the chance to assimilate the steps between each stage, as they may be confused.

➢ Explain that the last term of an AP is commonly denoted by the letter l for last term. The sum of a sequence of terms in an AP is called an arithmetic series. If S_n denotes the sum of the first n terms of a sequence:

$S_n = a + (a + d) + (a + 2d) + … + (l - 2d) + (l - d) + l$

➢ Reversing this order gives:

$S_n = l + (l - d) + (l - 2d) + … + (a + 2d) + (a + d) + a$

➢ Adding these two lines gives:

$2S_n = (a + l) + (a + l) + (a + l) + … + (a + l) + (a + l) + (a + l)$

➢ As there are n terms, this will give the result $2S_n = n(a + l)$, giving $S_n = \frac{1}{2}n(a + l)$.

➢ Explain to students that they know that the last term, l, is also the nth term, given by $a + (n - 1)d$, substituting gives:

$S_n = \frac{1}{2}n\{a + a + (n - 1)d\}$

➢ Point out that $\frac{1}{2}n = \frac{n}{2}$ and the alternative forms $S_n = \frac{n}{2}(a + l) = \frac{n}{2}\{2a + (n - 1)d\}$ may also be used

➢ Students need to ensure they understand and can reproduce this proof.

➢ Go through the following example: In an AP, the 8th term is 26 and the sum of the first 8 terms is 124. Find the sum of the first 20 terms.

➢ Say: *Write down what we know: $n = 8$, $l = 26$ and $S_8 = 124$.*

➢ *Now use the formula $S_n = \frac{1}{2}n(a + l)$. You can see you know every term except a. Show how to substitute what you know to determine that $a = 5$*

➢ Now use $u_n = a + (n - 1)d$ for the 8th term, u_8 to determine that $d = 3$

➢ Note that you could also use $S_n = \frac{1}{2}n\{2a + (n - 1)d\}$

➢ Now again use $S_n = \frac{1}{2}n\{2a + (n - 1)d\}$ to find S_{20}, substitute to find the sum is 670.

➢ Students can now start Exercise 12.1.

PLENARY (10 mins)

- ➢ Write on the board the sequence 5, 7, 9, 11.
- ➢ Ask students what the 100th term will be; assist where needed to get to $5 + (10 + 99 \times 2)$ to arrive at 203.
- ➢ Ask students to find the number of terms of an AP that will give a sum of 690, when the first term is 3 and the common difference is 7. Lead the discussion to use of the formula $S_n = \frac{1}{2}n\{2a+(n-1)d\}$ to give $n = 20$.
- ➢ Now ask students to show you how to prove the formula $S_n = \frac{1}{2}n\{2a+(n-1)d\}$
- ➢ Get the students to lead this. You may need to prompt, but do not show them; let them to work it out for themselves.

Homework and answers: Resource sheets, homework and extension exercises can be found at the end of this chapter and in the downloadable materials. Answers can be found in the downloadable materials.

CHECKING PROGRESS	Ensure that all students are involved in the plenary discussions, especially when discussing the steps involved in the proof of the formula for S_n as this is a vital concept to grasp.

12 Series

TOPIC:

12.2 Geometric progressions

KEY WORDS:

geometric progression, geometric sequence, geometric series, common ratio

IGCSE MATHS PRIOR KNOWLEDGE:

Recognise patterns in sequences

Find the nth terms for linear and quadratic sequences

Learning aims:

- Recognise arithmetic and geometric progressions and understand the difference between them
- Use the formulae for the nth term and for the sum of the first n terms to solve problems involving geometric progressions

Resources:

- Student Book: pages 259–262

Common mistakes and remediation:

Students often forget to include the '−1' in the power of the nth term. Introducing the terms of a GP in a table form can help students visualise the pattern of the terms and the connection between the position of the term and the power of r i.e. the power of r is 1 less than its position. This will enable them to find the general form for u_n

Position	1	2	3	4	5	....	n
Term	a	ar	ar^2	ar^3	ar^4	....	ar^{n-1}

Useful tips:

These formulae are on the formulae page of the exam papers:

$u_n = ar^{n-1}$

$$S_n = \frac{a(1-r^n)}{(1-r)} \quad (r \neq 1)$$

The above formula for the sum of the first n terms gives negative values for the numerator and denominator if $|r| > 1$

Point out that $\dfrac{a(1-r^n)}{(1-r)}$ is equivalent to $\dfrac{a(r^n-1)}{(r-1)}$ (multiplying numerator and denominator by □1) and this form is easier to use for $|r| > 1$

Note:

$|r| < 1 \quad \Rightarrow -1 < r < 1$ and includes all positive and negative proper fractions

$|r| > 1 \quad \Rightarrow r < -1$ or $r > 1$

$r = 1 \quad \Rightarrow S_n = 0$ so the formula is not valid

Encourage students to always consider the value of r before deciding which version of the sum formula to use. This will avoid unnecessarily working with negative values.

It is important to distinguish between the descriptors used in this section:

A **geometric progression** (GP) is a sequence of numbers in which each successive term is found by multiplying the previous term by a constant value.

The constant is known as the **common ratio**, r, so called as it can be found by dividing any term in the sequence by the previous term.

A geometric progression is also known as a **geometric sequence**.

A **geometric series** is the sum of terms in a geometric progression/sequence.

Guidance:

Lower-achieving students may need assistance in understanding and being able to reproduce the proof of the sum to n terms formula.

STARTER (10 mins)

- Write on the board the sequence: 1, 3, 9, 27
- Ask students what the nth term will be for this sequence. (3^{n-1})
- Write on the board the sequence: 4, 8, 16, 32
- Ask students what the next term will be. (64)
- Now ask students to describe the sequence. (Starting with 4, multiply each term by 2 to find the next term.)
- Ask students what the nth term of the sequence will be. ($4 \times 2^{(n-1)} = 2^2 \times 2^{(n-1)} = 2^{(n+1)}$)
- Write on the board the sequence: 5, −10, 20, −40 and ask students what the nth term will be.
- Lead the class through discussion to identifying the multiplying factor is −2, the first term is 5 and they can derive the nth term as $5 \times (-2)^{(n-1)}$. Discussion should include properties of powers of negative numbers, i.e. odd powers are negative and even powers are positive, as well as $a^0 = 1$

MAIN LESSON ACTIVITY (45 mins)

- Tell students that the sequences they have just been looking at are called geometric progressions (GPs for short). They are sequences in which each term is multiplied by the same constant to form the subsequent term.
- Tell students that the constant multiplier is called the common ratio, represented by r, and the first term is usually denoted by a as in arithmetic progressions.
- Write on the board the general GP as a, ar, ar^2, ar^3, ...

  Noting the first term is a, the second term is ar, the third term is ar^2, the fourth term will be ar^3.
- Use the table form to show the terms relative to their position and ask students to tell you the general form for the nth term. This is $u_n = ar^{n-1}$.
- Now ask students to tell you what the nth term will be for the sequence: 3, 12, 48, 192...
- Lead the discussion to find the nth term as $3 \times 4^{(n-1)}$.
- Ask students to find the twelfth term. They should substitute, working on $3 \times 4^{(12-1)}$ giving 12 582 912.
- The following proof needs to be explained carefully, so that lower-achieving students have the chance to assimilate the steps between each stage, as it is a difficult concept for students to absorb.
- Show that the sum of the first n terms can be given by:

  $S_n = a + ar + ar^2 + ar^3 + ... + ar^{(n-2)} + ar^{(n-1)}$
- Multiplying each term by r gives:

  $rS_n = ar + ar^2 + ar^3 + ar^4 + ... + ar^{(n-1)} + ar^n$
- Show that, by subtraction:

  $S_n - rS_n = a - ar^n$
- This leads to $S_n (1 - r) = a(1 - r^n)$, giving the result $S_n = \dfrac{a(1 - r^n)}{1 - r}$.
- Again, tell students they need to be understand this proof as they could be asked to reproduce it themselves.
- Explain to students that if r is greater than 1, they can multiply the numerator and denominator on the RHS by −1, to give $r - 1$ as the denominator, giving $S_n = \dfrac{a(r^n - 1)}{r - 1}$.
- Go through the following example: In a GP, the third term is 1 and the sixth term is 64. Find the sum of the first 12 terms.
- Say: *Write down what we know.* The sixth term is $u_6 = ar^5 = 64$ and the third term is $u_3 = ar^2 = 1$.
- Show how to divide these to get $\dfrac{ar^5}{ar^2} = \dfrac{64}{1}$, which in turn gives $r^3 = 64$ and hence $r = 4$.

- ➤ Now substitute in, say, $ar^2 = 1$ to give $a \times 16 = 1$, giving $a = \dfrac{1}{16}$.

- ➤ Now use $S_n = \dfrac{a(r^n - 1)}{r - 1}$ to find S_{12}. Substitute to find the sum is 349 525.3125.

- ➤ You may wish also to go through Example 5 in the Student Book with lower-achieving students, to ensure they understand how to proceed.

- ➤ Students can now start Exercise 12.2.

PLENARY (5 mins)

- ➤ Write on the board the sequence 1, 10, 100, 1000 …

- ➤ Ask students what the 20th term will be; hopefully the students will quickly say 10^{19}

- ➤ Ask students which term will be equal to one million; lead them to recognise that one million is 10^6 and so it is the 7th term.

- ➤ Ask students to tell you which term is equal to one billion; lead them to recognise that one billion is 10^9 and so it is the 10th term.

- ➤ You could extend this to one trillion (13th term).

- ➤ You could even extend to one googol (101st term). Discuss with students other applications of this term, and why it is relevant.

Homework and answers: Resource sheets, homework and extension exercises can be found at the end of this chapter and in the downloadable materials. Answers can be found in the downloadable materials.

CHECKING PROGRESS	Ensure that all students can easily recognise and describe the differences between an AP and a GP.

12 Series

TOPIC:

12.3 Sum to infinity

KEY WORDS:

Sum to infinity, convergence, divergence,

IGCSE MATHS PRIOR KNOWLEDGE:

Recognise patterns in sequences

Find the nth term for linear and quadratic sequences

Learning aims:

- Recognise arithmetic and geometric progressions and understand the difference between them
- Use the condition for convergence of a geometric progression, and the formula for the sum to infinity of a convergent geometric progression

Resources:

- Student Book: pages 262–264

Common mistakes and remediation:

Students often struggle to understand that the sum to infinity can only exist for a convergent GP in which $|r| < 1$.

Ask them to investigate the values of r^n for $-1 < r < 1$ using increasing values of n, where n is a positive integer.

It can be shown that $r^n \rightarrow 0$ as $n \rightarrow \infty$

In the series $S_n = r + r^2 + r^3 + \dots r^n$, as $n \rightarrow \infty$ the value of $r^n \rightarrow 0$ which means adding this term will make little or no difference to the value of S_n

$$S_n = \frac{a(1-r^n)}{(1-r)} \text{, when } |r| < 1 \text{, as } n \rightarrow \infty, r^n \rightarrow 0 \text{ and } S_n \rightarrow S_\infty = \frac{a(1-0)}{(1-r)} = \frac{a}{1-r}$$

Useful tips:

These formulae are on the formulae page of the exam papers:

$u_n = ar^{n-1}$

$$S_n = \frac{a(1-r^n)}{(1-r)} \quad (r \neq 1)$$

$$S_\infty = \frac{a}{(1-r)} \quad (|r| < 1)$$

Guidance:

Lower-achieving students may need assistance with understanding the concept of the sum to infinity.

STARTER (10 mins)

➢ Ask students: *What is the biggest number there is?* You are initiating a discussion about infinity; there is no largest number as there is always one more than any suggested number!

➢ Sketch the tangent graph on the board to illustrate an asymptote, where a line tends to infinity as θ gets closer to 90°.

Ask: *Can you think of any other graph that has an asymptote?* Hopefully they will suggest $y = \dfrac{1}{x}$ or similar. Show the graph of

$y = \dfrac{1}{x}$ using available software and point out that as x gets closer to zero so y tends to infinity. This occurs as x approaches zero from the left or right side of the y-axis, so $y \to \pm\infty$. They should identify that the y-axis is an asymptote for this graph.

Now consider the shape of the graph as y gets closer to zero. The curve gets closer and closer to the x axis and x tends to infinity. This occurs as y approaches zero from above and below the x-axis, so $x \to \pm\infty$ and they should also identify the x-axis is an asymptote.

Now talk about the equation $y = \dfrac{1}{x}$; as x gets very large, y will tend to the value 0. This can be written, $y \to 0$ as $x \to \pm\infty$

As the equation can be rearranged and written as $x = \dfrac{1}{y}$, it is also true that $x \to 0$ as $y \to \pm\infty$

MAIN LESSON ACTIVITY (45 mins)

➢ Tell the students that the APs and GPs they have being looking at will carry on and are infinite. Ask: *Do you think we can find the sum of any of these infinite sequences?*

➢ The initial response will be 'no', because in most sequences they have looked at so far the terms have been increasing each time and so will get larger and larger, so their sum will be infinity as well. Tell students that these are called divergent sequences. Lead the discussion to consider possibilities if the terms are getting smaller.

➢ Put on the board a GP such as 1, $\dfrac{1}{4}$, $\dfrac{1}{16}$, $\dfrac{1}{32}$ .... As the number of terms increases, the values of the terms get smaller, so it should be possible to find the sum to infinity, as the sum of the sequence tends to some value as n tends to infinity. These sequences are convergent, as the sum converges to a particular value.

➢ Display this sequence: 1, $\dfrac{1}{4}$, $\dfrac{1}{16}$, $\dfrac{1}{32}$ ..., noting that $a = 1$ and $r = 0.25$.

➢ So using $S_n = \dfrac{a\left(1 - r^n\right)}{1 - r}$, when $n \to \infty$, $S_\infty = 1 \times \dfrac{\left(1 - 0.25^\infty\right)}{\left(1 - 0.25\right)}$.

Talk about the value of 0.25^n as n gets very large. Lower-achieving students may need the help of a calculator to see this for themselves, but as n gets large, then the value of 0.25^n tends to a very small number and so, as n tends to infinity, 0.25^n will tend to 0. This can be written, $0.25^n \to 0$ as $n \to \infty$

➢ This leads to the fact that $S_\infty = \dfrac{1 \times \left(1 - 0\right)}{\left(1 - 0.25\right)} = \dfrac{1}{0.75} = 1.33...$

➢ Talk about a general case, where $-1 < r < 1$ (or $|r| < 1$). Then the sequence will converge, as $r^n \to 0$ as $n \to \infty$

➢ Elicit that for $|r| < 1$ then $S_\infty = \dfrac{a}{1 - r}$.

➢ Write on the board the sequence 3, $\dfrac{9}{5}$, $\dfrac{27}{25}$ ... and ask students if they think it's possible to find the sum to infinity for this sequence. The answer is 'yes' because $r = \dfrac{3}{5}$ and $-1 < \dfrac{3}{5} < 1$

➢ Ask students to find this total. Show how to set up the formula to give $\dfrac{3}{\left(1 - 0.6\right)} = 7.5$.

➢ Go through Example 6 in the Student Book with lower-achieving students.

➢ Students can now start Exercise 12.3.

PLENARY (5 mins)

➢ Remind students that they have come across some interesting numerical sequences during these last few lessons and have a number of formulae that they need to be able to prove. They could write these out on a coloured record card, so they could use it for revision purposes.

The following questions could be answered by students writing their answers on mini whiteboards.

Ask students to write down:

➢ the general form for the nth term of an AP. $a + (n-1)d$

➢ a general form for the sum of the first n terms of an AP. $\frac{1}{2}n\{2a+(n-1)d\}$ or $\frac{1}{2}n(a+l)$

➢ the general form for the nth term of a GP. $ar^{(n-1)}$

➢ a general form for the sum of the first n terms of a GP. $\frac{a(r^n-1)}{(r-1)}$ or $\frac{a(1-r^n)}{(1-r)}$

➢ the values of r for which they would use their formula. $|r|>1$ or $|r|<1$

➢ the value of r for which neither sum formula is valid $r=1$

➢ the values of r for which GPs are divergent $|r|>1 \Rightarrow r<-1$ or $r>1$

➢ the values of r for which GPs are convergent $|r|<1 \Rightarrow -1<r<1$

➢ the formula for the sum to infinity of a convergent GP. $S_\infty = \frac{a}{1-r}$ where $|r|<1$

Homework and answers: Resource sheets, homework and extension exercises can be found at the end of this chapter and in the downloadable materials. Answers can be found in the downloadable materials.

CHECKING PROGRESS	Check that all students get involved in the plenary as a means of checking their understanding.

TOPIC:

12.4 Binomial expansions

KEY WORDS:

binomial expression, binomial expansion, Pascal's triangle, binomial theorem

IGCSE MATHS PRIOR KNOWLEDGE:

Find the nth term for quadratic sequences

Learning aims:

- Use the binomial theorem for expansion of $(a + b)^n$ for positive integer n

- Use the general term $\begin{pmatrix} n \\ r \end{pmatrix} a^{n-r} b^r$, $0 \leq r \leq n$

Resources:

- Student Book: pages 264–269

Common mistakes and remediation:

In applying the binomial theorem to powers of binomial expressions such as $(2x + 3y)^4$, students often forget to include the powers of the coefficients of x and y in the expansion. Encourage them to make use of brackets in expansions of this form, so that this mistake can be avoided i.e.

$$(2x + 3y)^4 = (2x)^4 + \begin{pmatrix} 4 \\ 1 \end{pmatrix}(2x)^3(3y) + \begin{pmatrix} 4 \\ 2 \end{pmatrix}(2x)^2(3y)^2 + \begin{pmatrix} 4 \\ 3 \end{pmatrix}(2x)(3y)^3 + (3y)^4$$

$$= 16x^4 + (4 \times 16x^3 \times 3y) + (6 \times 4x^2 \times 9y^2) + (6 \times 2x \times 27y^3) + 81y^4$$

$$= 16x^4 + \quad 192x^3y \quad + \quad 216x^2y^2 \quad + \quad 324xy^3 \quad + 81y^4$$

Useful tips:

The binomial theorem expansion is on the formulae page of the exam papers:

$$(a + b)^n = a^n + \begin{pmatrix} n \\ 1 \end{pmatrix} a^{n-1}b + \begin{pmatrix} n \\ 2 \end{pmatrix} a^{n-2}b^2 + \ldots\ldots + \begin{pmatrix} n \\ r \end{pmatrix} a^{n-r}b^r + \ldots\ldots + b^n$$

where n is a positive integer and $\begin{pmatrix} n \\ r \end{pmatrix} = \dfrac{n!}{(n-r)!r!}$

Remind students that they can also use Pascal's triangle to find the coefficients of the terms in a binomial expansion.

Students should be familiar with the general term for the binomial theorem: $\begin{pmatrix} n \\ r \end{pmatrix} a^{n-r}b^r$, $0 \leq r \leq n$

Point out that, in each term, the combined power of a and $b = n - r + r = n$

Students can use this fact to check they have used the binomial theorem correctly.

Remind them that they have already met the notation $\begin{pmatrix} n \\ r \end{pmatrix} = \dfrac{n!}{(n-r)!r!}$ in the previous chapter.

It is equivalent to ^nC_r and can be worked out using the ^nC_r button on the calculator.

Guidance:

Lower-achieving students may need assistance with the expansion of binomial expressions involving two variables with coefficients. .

STARTER (5 mins)

➤ Ask students if they remember Pascal's triangle.

➤ Illustrate Pascal's triangle on the board and leave it there for reference during the main lesson. Continue it as far as the sixth row, showing how the lines build up.

➤ Ask students if they can see any patterns in the diagonal rows of the triangle.

➤ They should be able to see the AP of 1, 2, 3, 4, … and the triangular numbers.

➤ Talk about the importance of Pascal's triangle to mathematics and explain that they will soon see its connection to the binomial expansion.

MAIN LESSON ACTIVITY (45 mins)

➤ Write on the board $x^2 + 4x$, $3 + x$, $5 - x^3$, $x + y$, and ask what is common about all these expressions. Draw from students that they all consist of the sum or difference of two terms and this makes each of them a binomial expression.

➤ Explain to students that they are going to look at the expansion of binomial expressions. Start with a very simple one, $1 + x$.

➤ Write on the board $(1 + x)^1$ and ask what this will expand to. $1 + x$

➤ Write on the board $(1 + x)^2$ and ask what this will expand to. $1 + 2x + x^2$

➤ Write on the board $(1 + x)^3$ and ask what this will expand to. You may need to help lower-achieving students, carefully showing how this expands to $1 + 3x + 3x^2 + x^3$.

➤ Write on the board $(1 + x)^4$ and ask if any student would like to predict what this will be. This will provoke a number of guesses that can be written on the board. You are trying to get them to spot the link with Pascal's triangle, still on display, in order to arrive at $1 + 4x + 6x^2 + 4x^3 + x^4$.

➤ Ensure that the lower-achieving students can visualise this link with Pascal's triangle and ask them to predict the expansion of $(1 + x)^5$, which will be $1 + 5x + 10x^2 + 10x^3 + 5x^4 + x^5$.

➤ Now write $a + b$ on the board and tell the students that this is a generalisation of any binomial expression. Ask them to tell you what $(a + b)^2$ is. $a^2 + 2ab + b^2$

➤ Now write $(a + b)^3$ on the board and ask if they can expand that. $a^3 + 3a^2b + 3ab^2 + b^3$

➤ You may have to demonstrate this clearly, especially to lower-achieving students.

➤ Ask if any student can see a link between this expansion and Pascal's triangle and a way in which they could now predict $(a + b)^4$.

➤ Show the link, explaining that $(a + b)^4 = a^4 + 4a^3b + 6a^2b^2 + 4ab^3 + b^4$.

➤ Introduce the students to the binomial theorem, which is given on the formulae page in the exam papers:

$$(a+b)^n = a^n + \binom{n}{1}a^{n-1}b + \binom{n}{2}a^{n-2}b^2 + \dots\dots + \binom{n}{r}a^{n-r}b^r + \dots\dots + b^n$$

where n is a positive integer and $\binom{n}{r} = \dfrac{n!}{(n-r)!r!}$

➤ Remind them that they have already met the notation $\binom{n}{r} = \dfrac{n!}{(n-r)!r!}$ in the previous chapter for working out combinations.

$\binom{n}{r}$ is equivalent to ^nC_r and can be worked out using the ^nC_r button on the calculator.

➤ Introduce students to the general term for the binomial theorem: $u_r = \binom{n}{r}a^{n-r}b^r$, $0 \le r \le n$

Point out that, in each term, the combined power of a and $b = n - r + r = n$

Students can use this fact to check they have used the binomial theorem correctly.

➤ Remind students that unless n is large, they may find it simpler to use Pascal's triangle to find the coefficients in the expansion.

➤ Work through an example of finding the first four terms of the expansion of $(2 + x)^9$.

- ➤ Show students how to use the binomial theorem with the ^nC_r button on their calculators to get:

  $(2 + x)^9 = 2^9 + (9 \times 2^8 \times x) + (36 \times 2^7 \times x^2) + (84 \times 2^6 \times x^3) + \dots$

  This can be shown to give $512 + 2304x + 4608x^2 + 5376x^3 + \dots$

- ➤ Tell students that for questions involving expansions using large values of n set on the non-calculator paper, they can use the factorial notation for $\binom{n}{r}$ in the general term, and work out $u_r = \dfrac{n!}{(n-r)!\, r!}\ a^{n-r} b^r$, for $r = 1, 2, 3, 4, \dots$

  to find the first four terms.

- ➤ Go through Examples 9 and 10 in the Student Book with students. Note that Example 10 illustrates the pattern where there is a negative sign in the binomial expression.

- ➤ Students can now start Exercise 12.4.

- ➤ The highest-achieving students could work through questions 2, 3 and 4 and then move on to look through Examples 11 and 12 in the Student Book before starting Exercise 12.5.

PLENARY (10 mins)

- ➤ Ask students to expand $(1 - x)^2$. $1 - 2x + x^2$

- ➤ Ask students to expand $(1 - x)^3$ without doing the actual expansion but using Pascal's triangle and thinking through the pattern.

  $1 - 3x + 3x^2 - x^3$

- ➤ Now ask students to expand $(1 - x)^4$, again without doing the actual expansion but using Pascal's triangle and thinking through the pattern.

  $1 - 4x + 6x^2 - 4x^3 + x^4$

- ➤ Ask students what they notice about the signs in the expansion. They should notice that the signs of the terms alternate from positive to negative.

- ➤ Finally, ask students to predict the expansion of $(1 - x)^5$

  $1 - 5x + 10x^2 - 10x^3 + 5x^4 - x^5$.

Homework and answers: Resource sheets, homework and extension exercises can be found at the end of this chapter and in the downloadable materials. Answers can be found in the downloadable materials.

CHECKING PROGRESS	Ensure that all students are involved in the discussions of the plenary, especially the point about alternating signs in the expansion involving a negative x.

Homework

12.1 Arithmetic progressions

1 Find the sum of the first 15 terms of each series.

   a $2 + 8 + 14 + 20 + \ldots$ **b** $3 + 8 + 13 + 18 + \ldots$

2 Find the sum of the first 20 terms of each series.

   a nth term $5 + 3n$ **b** nth term $1n \quad 5$

3 Find the sum of the first 20 terms of the AP with:

   a first term 6 and 12th term 50   **b** first term 3 and 11th term 73.

4 The sum of the first 20 terms in an AP is 1790 and the sum of the first 30 terms is 4035. Find:

   a the first term

   b the common ratio

   c the number of terms in the sequence for which the sum is 2800.

5 In an AP the first term is 2 and the 8th term is five times the second term.
Find the 12th term and the sum of the first 20 terms.

6 How many terms of the sequence $4x$, $7x$, $10x$, $13x$, … must be added for the sum to be $424x$?

7 In an AP, the 10th term is 35 and the 20th term is 185.
Find the sum of the first 100 terms of the sequence.

8 Find the sum of the first one hundred multiples of 9.

12 Series

Homework

12.2 Geometric progressions

1   Find the sum of the first 10 terms of each GP.

    a   1, 5, 25, 125 …   **b**   0.5, 1, 2, 4 …

2   Find the sum of the first 11 terms of each GP when:

    a   first term, $a = 6$, constant value, $r = -3$

    b   first term, $a = 100$, constant value, $r = 0.5$

3   The 5th term of a GP is 324 and the 10th term is 78 732. Find the sum of the first 12 terms.

4   The sum of the first five terms in a GP is 1042 and the sum of the first seven terms is 26 042. Find:

    a   the first term

    b   the common difference

    c   the number of terms in the sequence when the sum is −3 255 208.

5   The 6th term of a GP is 256 and the 10th term is 4096. Find the sum of the first 12 terms.

6   The first three terms of a GP are $x - 10$, x, $4x - 15$ and all the terms in the GP are positive. Find:

    a   the value of x

    b   the value of the 6th term

    c   the sum of the first 10 terms.

12 Series

Homework

12.3 Infinite sequences

1 State which of these sequences are **a** divergent and which are **b** convergent.
   Give clear reasons for your answers.

   i   5, 25, 125, 625, …   ii   5, 0.5, 0.05, 0.005, …

   iii 3072, 768, 192, 48, …   iv   2, 2.25, 2.5, 2.75, 3, …

2 Find the sum to infinity for each sequence:

   a   1, 0.2, 0.04, 0.008, …   b   5, 2, 0.8, 0.32, …   c   7, 2.1, 0.63, 0.189, …

3 The 4th term of a GP is 15 and the 6th term is 0.6. Find the sum to infinity.

4 The sum of the first two terms of a GP is 225 and the sum of the first four terms is 369. Find:

   a   the sum of the first 10 terms

   b   the sum to infinity.

5 The first term of a GP is 4 and the common ratio $r = 0.5$. Find:

   a   the sum of the first six terms

   b   the sum to infinity

   c   the least number of terms for which the sum is greater than 7.999.

6 The first term of a GP is 48 and the sum of the first three terms is 111. Find the sum to infinity.

12 Series

Homework

12.4 Binomial expansions

1   a   Find the expansion of $(1 + 2x)^5$. Simplify each term.

     b   Find the expansion of $(1 - 4x)^5$. Simplify each term.

2   a   Find the expansion of $(3 + 2x)^4$. Simplify each term.

     b   Find the expansion of $(5 - 3x)^4$. Simplify each term.

3   Find the coefficient of x^3 in the expansion of:

     a $(5 + 3x)^6$ b $(6 - 2x)^7$

4   The coefficient of x^2 in the expansion of $(2 + qx)^5$ is 2000.

     a   Find the value of the constant p.

     b   Using your value of p, find the coefficient of x^2 in the expansion of $(4 - x)(2 + px)^6$.

5   The first 3 terms in the expansion of $(4 - px)^q$ are $4096 - 24\,576x + rx^2$.

     Find the values of p, q and r.

6   a   Find the expansion of $(5 + x)^6$. Simplify each term.

     b   Find the expansion of $(5 - x)^6$. Simplify each term.

     c   Show how you can use your answers to **a** and **b** to calculate the exact value of $5.1^6 - 4.9^6$.

7   a   Find the expansion of $(3 + x^2)^4$. Simplify each term.

     b   Find the coefficient of x^4 in the expansion of:

        i $(1 - x^2)(3 + x^2)^4$ ii $\left(1 + \dfrac{1}{x^2}\right)(2 + x^2)^4$

Extension

12.1 Arithmetic progressions

1   The first three terms of an AP are 2, 5, 8....

     Find the value of n for which the sum of the first $2n$ terms is greater than the sum of the first n terms by 292.

2   The 9th term of an AP is -1 and the sum of the first 9 terms is 45. Find the sum of the first 15 terms.

3   The sum of the first n terms of an AP is $2n^2 + n$. Find the first term and the common difference.

4   The first three terms of an AP are $\dfrac{1}{b+c}$, $\dfrac{1}{a+c}$, $\dfrac{1}{a+b}$. Show that a^2, b^2, c^2 are also consecutive terms of an AP.

Extension

12.2 Geometric progressions

1   The first term of a geometric sequence is 3. The sum of the first n terms of the sequence converges to 4 as n tends to infinity. Find the sum of the first 10 terms.

     Give your answer to six decimal places.

2   The first three terms of an AP are 1, x, y. The first three terms of a GP are 1, x, $-y$. Find the first three terms of the GP in surd form.

3   How many terms of the GP 10, 8, 6.4 must be taken to make the sum greater than 49?

4   A one metre length of string is cut into 10 pieces. The lengths of the pieces of string are in geometrical progression.

     The length of the longest piece is eight times the length of the shortest piece.

     Calculate the length of the shortest piece of string.

Extension

12.3 Infinite sequences

1   Find a sequence that has a sum to infinity of 2.5.

2   The first term of a GP is 432 and the fourth term is 128. Find the sum to infinity for the GP.

3   Find a sequence with first term a, where $0 < a < 1$ and a sum to infinity of 10.

4   A GP has a first term of 1 and a common ratio of $\sin \theta$. The sum to infinity of the GP is 3.

     Find all possible values of θ, where $0° \leq \theta \leq 360°$.

Extension

12.4 Binomial expansion

These questions are a challenge. Please note that binomial expansions of the form $(a + b)^n$, where $n < 0$, are **not** on the syllabus, however will be useful for preparation for the study of mathematics at AS and A level.

> **Note**
>
> This form of the binomial theorem can be applied to expressions of the form $(1 + x)^n$
>
> where n is a negative number (or a fraction).
>
> $$(1+x)^n = 1 + nx + \frac{n(n-1)}{2!}x^2 + \frac{n(n-1)(n-2)}{3!}x^3 + \dots$$
>
> The expansion produces an infinite number of terms and is valid when $|x| < 1$.

1 Expand $(1 + 2x)^{-1}$ in ascending powers of x up to and including x^3. State the range of validity for x.

2 Expand $(1 - 3x)^{-2}$ in ascending powers of x up to and including x^3. State the range of validity for x.

3 Expand $(1 + 2x)^{-3}$ in ascending powers of x up to and including x^3. State the range of validity for x.

4 Expand $(1 + \sin \theta)^{-1}$ in ascending powers of $\sin \theta$ up to and including $\sin^3 \theta$. State the range of validity for θ.

13 Vectors

TOPIC:
13.1 Position and unit vectors

KEY WORDS:
position vector, column vector, unit vector, scalar, magnitude, modulus, component, collinear

IGCSE MATHS PRIOR KNOWLEDGE:
Recognise vectors given in a variety of forms

Add and subtract simple vectors

Calculate the magnitude of a vector

Learning aims:
- Understand and use vector notation
- Know and use position vectors and unit vectors
- Find the magnitude of a vector; add and subtract vectors and multiply vectors by scalars

Resources:
- Student Book: pages 276–280

Common mistakes and remediation:

Students often forget to underline vectors expressed as lower case letters such as $\underline{a}$, or draw arrows over vectors to indicate the direction between two points, e.g. $\overrightarrow{OP}$. They also forget that parallel vectors are exact multiples or factors of each other. Provide plenty of practice and remind them they will be penalised in their exams if they do not use correct vector notation.

Useful tips:

Encourage students to draw a diagram to help solve vector problems whenever possible. This will enable them to visualise the problem and it will assist their thinking.

Emphasise that scalar quantities have magnitude, but vector quantities have magnitude and direction. Remind students of the correct notation when working with vectors:

For vector $\overrightarrow{OP} = x\mathbf{i} + y\mathbf{j}$, the magnitude of $\overrightarrow{OP} = \left|\overrightarrow{OP}\right| = \sqrt{x^2 + y^2}$

In general, for any two-dimensional vector $\mathbf{a} = \begin{pmatrix} x \\ y \end{pmatrix} = x\mathbf{i} + y\mathbf{j}$, a unit vector in the direction of $\mathbf{a} = \dfrac{\mathbf{a}}{|\mathbf{a}|}$

Guidance:

Go through working out expressions for unit vectors carefully with lower-achieving students.

STARTER (5 mins)

➤ Ask students if they can recall what a position vector is. This should be revision from IGCSE but you need to ensure that lower-achieving students remember. Show students what a position vector is by displaying an example in a diagram on the board.

➤ Check students know how to add two position vectors. Ask them to display their answers to an examples on the board both diagrammatically and in column vector form. It is important that all students know how to add and subtract position vectors.

➤ Check that students remember what the magnitude of a vector is. Remind them pictorially that it is the value of the length of the vector. Use the vector $\begin{pmatrix} 3 \\ 4 \end{pmatrix}$ to illustrate a vector with magnitude 5.

➤ Introduce the notation $|\mathbf{a}|$ for the magnitude of vector $\mathbf{a}$. Tell them that this is also known as the modulus of vector $\mathbf{a}$.

MAIN LESSON ACTIVITY (45 mins)

➢ Introduce the idea of a unit vector as one having a magnitude of 1 unit. Use a diagram on the board to show $\overrightarrow{OP}$, a unit vector denoted as $\begin{pmatrix} i \\ j \end{pmatrix}$, where $i = \begin{pmatrix} 1 \\ 0 \end{pmatrix}$ and $j = \begin{pmatrix} 0 \\ 1 \end{pmatrix}$

➢ Explain to students that any position vector can also be expressed in the form $a = ix + jy$.

➢ Show that the unit vector in the direction of OP will be given by $\dfrac{ix + jy}{|\overrightarrow{OP}|}$ which is equal to $\dfrac{ix + jy}{\sqrt{x^2 + y^2}}$.

➢ Work through Example 2 in the Student Book to demonstrate how to work with unit vectors. Lower-achieving students need to be given a lot of guidance through the working in this example, as even the highest-achieving students will need to refresh their understanding and knowledge of vectors.

➢ Introduce the term 'collinear points', meaning 'points which lie on the same straight line'. Talk about the fact that vectors can be used to show that, in geometry, some points lie on the same straight line.

➢ Talk students through Example 3 in the Student Book. Draw clear diagrams on the board to illustrate the vectors in the question, clearly labelling each vector and explaining each step.

➢ It is vital that all students understand that vectors which are parallel and share a common point must lie on the same straight line. It is worth making this point carefully, going through the different vectors that can be used to prove that points are collinear. Ensure that lower-achieving students have grasped the concept before moving them on to the problems.

➢ Students can now start Exercise 13.1.

PLENARY (10 mins)

➢ Ask students to identify vectors with a magnitude of 5; they should suggest $\begin{pmatrix} 3 \\ 4 \end{pmatrix}$ and $\begin{pmatrix} 4 \\ 3 \end{pmatrix}$.

➢ Ask students to identify vectors with a magnitude of 13: $\begin{pmatrix} 12 \\ 5 \end{pmatrix}$ and $\begin{pmatrix} 5 \\ 12 \end{pmatrix}$.

➢ Now ask students to identify a vector with a magnitude of 2, saying that you will accept answers in surd form.
Ensure that you draw from students all three of these: $\begin{pmatrix} 1 \\ \sqrt{3} \end{pmatrix}$, $\begin{pmatrix} \sqrt{3} \\ 1 \end{pmatrix}$, $\begin{pmatrix} \sqrt{2} \\ \sqrt{2} \end{pmatrix}$.

➢ Ask students if they can now identify more vectors with a magnitude of 5, other than those they started with.
Examples may include, $\begin{pmatrix} \sqrt{5} \\ \sqrt{20} \end{pmatrix}$, $\begin{pmatrix} \sqrt{15} \\ \sqrt{10} \end{pmatrix}$ and $\begin{pmatrix} \sqrt{12} \\ \sqrt{13} \end{pmatrix}$.

Homework and answers: Resource sheets, homework and extension exercises can be found at the end of this chapter and in the downloadable materials. Answers can be found in the downloadable materials.

CHECKING PROGRESS	Check that students are using correct notation for vectors in their work, for example, underlining the vectors.

13 Vectors

TOPIC:

13.2 Vectors in geometry

KEY WORDS:

None

IGCSE MATHS PRIOR KNOWLEDGE:

Add and subtract simple vectors

Learning aims:

- Find the magnitude of a vector; add and subtract vectors and multiply vectors by scalars

Resources:

- Student Book: pages 280–284

Common mistakes and remediation:

Students may fail to link the fact that they can follow a route through a vector diagram by linking the letters describing the end points of the vectors. This is remedied by careful explanation, along with practice.

Useful tips:

Encourage students always to draw a diagram where possible to assist their thinking.

Guidance:

Go through these proofs very carefully with lower-achieving students.

STARTER (5 mins)

➢ Draw on the board a diagram showing vectors $\overrightarrow{OA}$ and $\overrightarrow{OB}$ labelled **a** and **b** respectively.

➢ Ask students how they could use **a** and **b** to describe the vector $\overrightarrow{AB}$. Look for the response **b** − **a.**

➢ Remind all students, especially lower-achieving ones, why this is so, showing the routes of −**a** + **b** on the diagram.

➢ Now mark on the diagram point M as the midpoint of AB.

➢ Ask students to describe the vector $\overrightarrow{AM}$ in terms of **a** and **b.**

Look for the result $\frac{1}{2}$ (**b** − **a**). Again, ensure that all students are confident with this.

➢ Now ask students to describe vector $\overrightarrow{BM}$. You may need to lead the discussion, especially with lower-attaining students, to the answer of $\frac{1}{2}$ (**a** − **b**).

➢ Ensure that students see the point that a vector $\overrightarrow{QP}$ is in the opposite direction to vector $\overrightarrow{PQ}$ and $\overrightarrow{QP}$ is negative $\overrightarrow{PQ}$.

MAIN LESSON ACTIVITY (45 mins)

➢ Go through Example 4 in the Student Book with the students.

➢ Make sure you display a clear diagram on the board and move carefully through each stage of the example. It can be helpful to use an interactive whiteboard or different colours at this point of vectors.

➢ As you go through the first answer in part (a), explain carefully to students the vital point that the letters should link as you go from A to C, making sure that the second letter of the first vector is the first letter of the second vector, and so on. This is a vital point and lower-attaining students do not see it as easily as higher-attaining students do.

➢ In part (b), talk about vectors being parallel if one is a multiple of the other, as in the case being shown.

➢ Explain that parallel vectors could be seen as $\mathbf{a} + 3\mathbf{b}$, $2(\mathbf{a} + 3\mathbf{b})$, $n(\mathbf{a} + 3\mathbf{b})$, etc.

➢ Go through Example 5 in the Student Book with the students.

➢ Use a clear diagram on the board to assist students in following the question and the solution.

➢ The point about BP and BM being parallel, and having a common point B, is vital and it needs to be made carefully, ensuring that lower-attaining students also appreciate that it is these two facts that show they must lie on the same straight line.

➢ Students can now start Exercise 13.2.

PLENARY (10 mins)

➢ Draw on the board a parallelogram labelled $ABCD$.

➢ Ask students to explain how they can use vectors to show that the diagonals of this parallelogram bisect each other.

➢ Lead the discussion, which should start by labelling two sides with a vector such as $\overrightarrow{AB} = \mathbf{p}$ and $\overrightarrow{AD} = \mathbf{q}$. Ensure that you use arrows on the diagram to show the direction of the vectors.

➢ Now develop the discussion to labelling the opposite sides to follow on, as $\overrightarrow{DC} = \mathbf{a}$ and $\overrightarrow{BC} = \mathbf{b}$.

➢ Ensure that the intersection of the diagonals is labelled as, say, M.

➢ Now lead them to express $\overrightarrow{AC}$ as $\mathbf{a} + \mathbf{b}$.

➢ Now lead to $\overrightarrow{AM} = \mathbf{a} + \overrightarrow{BM}$ ... (i) and $\overrightarrow{AM} = \mathbf{b} - \overrightarrow{BM}$ ... (ii).

➢ Adding (i) and (ii) gives $2\overrightarrow{AM} = \mathbf{a} + \mathbf{b}$, and so $\overrightarrow{AM} = \frac{1}{2}(\mathbf{a} + \mathbf{b})$, showing that M is halfway along AC.

➢ Now see if the students can lead you through a similar route, showing that $\overrightarrow{BD} = \mathbf{b} - \mathbf{a}$, then $\overrightarrow{BM} = \mathbf{b} + \overrightarrow{CM}$ ... (iii) and $\overrightarrow{BM} = -\mathbf{a} - \overrightarrow{CM}$ ... (iv). Adding (iii) to (iv) shows $2\overrightarrow{BM} = \mathbf{b} - \mathbf{a}$ and hence $\overrightarrow{BM} = \frac{1}{2}(\mathbf{b} - \mathbf{a})$ and M is halfway along BD.

➢ Hence they have proven that the two diagonals of a parallelogram bisect each other.

Homework and answers: Resource sheets, homework and extension exercises can be found at the end of this chapter and in the downloadable materials. Answers can be found in the downloadable materials.

CHECKING PROGRESS	Ensure that all students take part in this plenary, and that lower-attaining students are following the proof.

13 Vectors

TOPIC:

13.3 Compose and resolve velocities

KEY WORDS:

unit vector, velocity

IGCSE MATHS PRIOR KNOWLEDGE:

Recognise vectors given in a variety of forms

Add and subtract simple vectors

Calculate the magnitude of a vector

Learning aims:	Resources:
• Compose and resolve velocities	• Student Book: pages 284–292

Common mistakes and remediation:

When finding an expression for the velocity of a body when given its speed and direction, students sometimes do not correctly link the unit vector in the direction of motion with the speed to find the velocity. This needs careful explanation, especially to the lower-achieving students, emphasising the relationship:

modulus of velocity = speed

Useful tips:

It is useful to draw a diagram illustrating the directions of vectors given in questions and place all known information onto the diagram in order to visualise the problem. Ensure that students are familiar with the relationship between the column vector form of the resolved parts of a vector and **i-j** notation.

Guidance:

Lower-achieving students will need more assistance in creating their own labelled diagrams, as well as working their way through the stages of more complex problems.

STARTER (5 mins)

➢ Put on the board a right-angled triangle showing smaller sides of length, 3 km and 4 km. Tell students that a car drives along a road represented by the hypotenuse in 10 minutes. How fast is the car travelling?

Draw from the students that the road being driven on must be 5 km long (Pythagoras), and that 5 km in 10 minutes means 6×5 km will be driven in one hour. So the speed is 30 km h^{-1}.

➢ Draw another right-angled triangle on the board and label the coordinates of the vertices as (5, 3), (10, 3) and (10, 15). Tell students that a bike drives along the length represented by the hypotenuse in 15 minutes. Ask: *How fast is it travelling?*

Draw from the students that the small roads shown are of length 5 km and 12 km, and so the length of the road being driven on must be 13 km (Pythagoras). As 13 km in 15 minutes means 4×13 km will be driven in one hour, the speed is 52 km h^{-1}.

MAIN LESSON ACTIVITY (40 mins)

- ➤ Talk to the students about velocity being speed in a particular direction and that this is a vector, having magnitude as speed and direction.
- ➤ Draw the below figure on the board.

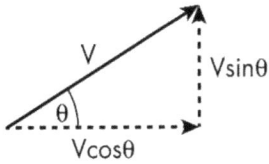

- ➤ Explain to students that the vector, V, can be resolved, using trigonometry, into two components as shown. The horizontal component is $V \cos \theta$ and the vertical component is $V \sin \theta$.

- ➤ Show how this can be expressed as a vector in different ways, one with position vector such as $\begin{pmatrix} V \cos \theta \\ V \sin \theta \end{pmatrix}$ or using unit vectors in *i* - *j* form as ($V \cos\theta\, \textbf{\textit{i}} + V \sin\theta\, \textbf{\textit{j}}$).

- ➤ Draw a vector on the board, telling students that this represents the motion of a vehicle travelling at 60 km h^{-1} in the direction given by position vector $\begin{pmatrix} 4 \\ 3 \end{pmatrix}$ relative to an origin O. In order to express the velocity of the vehicle as a vector you need to resolve its components. You can see that the modulus of the vector showing direction is $\sqrt{(4^2 + 3^2)} = 5$. Explain that you can now express the velocity as $\frac{60}{5} \times \begin{pmatrix} 4 \\ 3 \end{pmatrix}$ giving the vector $\begin{pmatrix} 48 \\ 36 \end{pmatrix}$.

- ➤ Go through Example 2 in the Student Book with the students, emphasising that vector expressions in **i-j** form can only be equal if the coefficient of **i** and the coefficient of **j** are the same in both vectors.

- ➤ Go through Example 4 in the Student Book with the students, emphasising that vectors are parallel when one is a multiple of the other, or both can be written as a multiple of the same vector.

- ➤ Now go through Example 5 part **a** with the students very carefully, making sure that lower-achieving students understand how to find the velocity of the lorry given its speed, as well as the position vectors to enable them to find its direction vector.

- ➤ Explain that part **b** is best approached with the use of a diagram, so that they can use the **i-j** form with **i** as the unit vector east and **j** the unit vector north to work out the angle the lorry's direction makes with the **i** vector. This will enable them to work out the bearing.

- ➤ Examples 6 and 7 cover the concepts of resultant velocity and the velocity of one body relative to another. It is worth discussing with the students the real-life applications of these two concepts before moving onto Example 8. For example, the velocity of a boat crossing a river against the flow of water; a plane landing against a cross wind; how the motion of someone walking on a train appears to someone standing on a platform as the train pulls out from the station.

- ➤ Example 8 leads into the more complex question Example 9. Ensure that students are comfortable with finding a general equation for a position vector in terms of time, *t*, for a body that moves from a given point with constant velocity as this is essential for Example 9 part **a**.

- ➤ For part **b**, show that the time given equates to $t = 2$, and you substitute this into the general position vector equations to find the position vector of each boat and hence find the distance between them.

- ➤ This should lead into part **c** where you need to set up a general equation in terms of *t*, for the distance between the two boats using Pythagoras' theorem. Carefully explain to the students that they can remove the square root complexity by simply squaring both sides.

- ➤ Show students how you expand both parts and combine them, taking care with the minus signs and arithmetic. Explain why they can ignore the negative solution as we do not use negative time as it starts from $t = 0$, so this only gives one solution for *t*.

- ➤ Ensure that you explain carefully to lower-achieving students why you need to multiply the decimal part of the time by 60 to find the minutes part of the time.

- ➤ Students can now start Exercise 13.3.

PLENARY (15 mins)

➤ Set up a problem about a ship leaving a port at 9 a.m.

➤ Explain that you will use i as a unit vector in the direction of east and j in the direction of north.

➤ Tell the students that the ship leaves port at 9 a.m. travelling at a speed of 26 km h^{-1} in the direction of $12i + 5j$.

➤ Ask students to work out the velocity of the ship.

➤ Draw from the students that they need to find the unit vector in the direction of travel, which will be given by $\dfrac{\overrightarrow{PS}}{|\overrightarrow{PS}|}$

where P is the position of the port and S is the position of the ship: $|\overrightarrow{PS}| = \sqrt{(12^2 + 5^2)} = \sqrt{169} = 13$.

➤ Now draw from the students that they can express the velocity of the ship as $\dfrac{26}{13}$ $(12i + 5j) = 24i + 10j$.

➤ Ask students what the position vector of the ship will be at 12 noon.

➤ Get them to establish that this is 3 hours travelling at $24i + 10j$ per hour and so using $s = vt$, the position vector will be $72i + 30j$.

➤ Repeat the questions, but this time with a speedboat travelling at 51 km h^{-1} in the direction $15i + 8j$.

➤ The resulting answers will be velocity of $(45i + 24j)$ km h^{-1} and a position vector of $(135i + 72j)$ m.

Homework and answers: Resource sheets, homework and extension exercises can be found at the end of this chapter and in the downloadable materials. Answers can be found in the downloadable materials.

CHECKING PROGRESS	Ensure that all students take part in the discussion of the plenary and that lower-achieving students are able to draw suitable diagrams to assist in solving the problems.

13 Vectors

Homework

13.1 Position and unit vectors

1 $\mathbf{m} = \begin{pmatrix} -5 \\ -2 \end{pmatrix}$ and $\mathbf{n} = \begin{pmatrix} 2 \\ -1 \end{pmatrix}$

Write down the column vectors that represent:

a $\mathbf{m} + \mathbf{n}$

b $\mathbf{m} - \mathbf{n}$

c $\mathbf{n} - \mathbf{m}$

d $5\mathbf{n}$

2 a On a copy of the grid shown, mark the points C to H such that:

$\overrightarrow{OC} = 2\mathbf{a} + 3\mathbf{b}$, $\overrightarrow{OD} = 2\mathbf{a} + \mathbf{b}$, $\overrightarrow{OE} = 3\mathbf{a} + 4\mathbf{b}$,

$\overrightarrow{OF} = \mathbf{a} + 2\mathbf{b}$, $\overrightarrow{OG} = 3\mathbf{a} + 2\mathbf{b}$, $\overrightarrow{OH} = 3\mathbf{a}$

b What can you say about points B, E, C and F?

c How could you tell this by looking at their position vectors?

d Complete these statements.

   i M is another point on the extended straight line OF

   $\overrightarrow{OM} = 2\mathbf{a} + \dots \mathbf{b}$

   ii N is another point on the extended straight line OD.

   $ON = \dots \mathbf{a} + 3\mathbf{b}$

   iii P is another point on the extended straight line OC.

   $OP = \dots \mathbf{a} - 3\mathbf{b}$

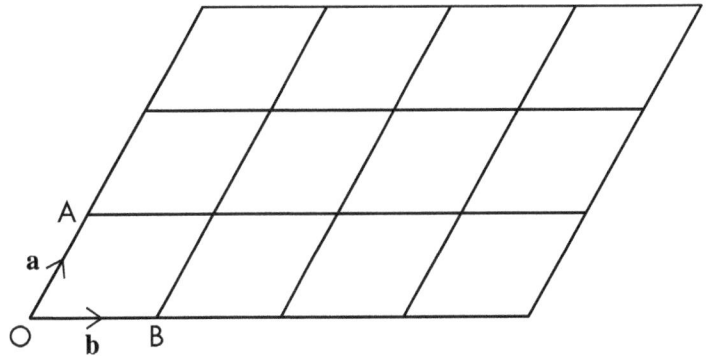

3 The points C, D and E are collinear. The vector $\overrightarrow{CD} = 2\mathbf{a} + \mathbf{b}$.

Which of the vectors below could represent $\overrightarrow{CE}$?

$\mathbf{a} + 2\mathbf{b}$, $6\mathbf{a} + 3\mathbf{b}$, $4\mathbf{a} - 2\mathbf{b}$, $-2\mathbf{a} - \mathbf{b}$

4 The position vectors of three points P, Q and R, relative to an origin O, are $4\mathbf{i} + \mathbf{j}$, $2\mathbf{i} + 5\mathbf{j}$ and $8\mathbf{i} - 7\mathbf{j}$.

$\overrightarrow{OR} = m\overrightarrow{OP} + n\overrightarrow{OQ}$

a Find the values of m and n.

b Find the unit vector in the direction of PQ.
Give your answer in its simplest surd form.

c Find the position vector of the mid-point of QR.

5 Vectors $\mathbf{a}$, $\mathbf{b}$ and $\mathbf{c}$ are such that $\mathbf{a} = \begin{pmatrix} 3 \\ 3 \end{pmatrix}$, $\mathbf{b} = \begin{pmatrix} -1 \\ -5 \end{pmatrix}$, $\mathbf{c} = \begin{pmatrix} 2 \\ 8 \end{pmatrix}$.

Given that $\lambda\mathbf{a} + \mu\mathbf{b} = 4\mathbf{c}$, find the value of λ and μ.

6 Vectors $\mathbf{p}$, $\mathbf{q}$ and $\mathbf{r}$ are such that $\mathbf{p} = \begin{pmatrix} 8 \\ 15 \end{pmatrix}$, $\mathbf{q} = \begin{pmatrix} 10 \\ 9 \end{pmatrix}$, $\mathbf{r} = \begin{pmatrix} -5 \\ 1 \end{pmatrix}$.

Show that $|\mathbf{p}| = |\mathbf{q} - \mathbf{r}|$.

Homework

13.2 Vectors in geometry

1   In the diagram, vectors $\overrightarrow{PQ} = \mathbf{a}$ and $\overrightarrow{PR} = \mathbf{b}$.

   M and N are the mid-points of PQ and PR respectively.

   a   Write these vectors in terms of $\mathbf{a}$ and $\mathbf{b}$.

       i $\overrightarrow{QR}$ ii $\overrightarrow{PM}$ iii $\overrightarrow{PN}$ iv $\overrightarrow{MN}$

   b   Show that MN is parallel to QR.

   c   What can you say about the lengths of MN and QR?

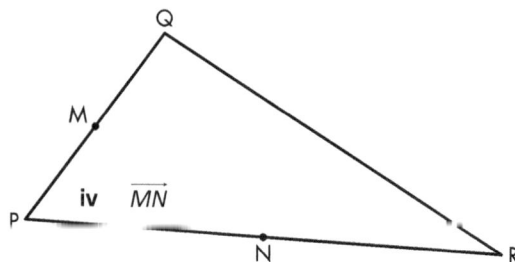

2   The diagram shows $\overrightarrow{AB} = \mathbf{b}$, $\overrightarrow{AE} = \overrightarrow{BC} = \mathbf{a}$ and $\overrightarrow{CD} = \mathbf{a} - \mathbf{b}$.

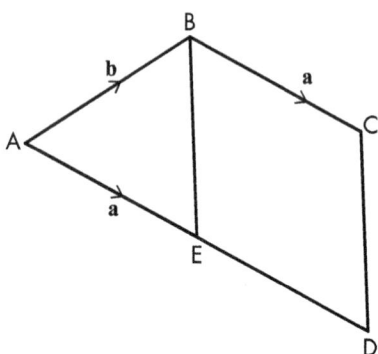

   a   Find $\overrightarrow{BE}$ and $\overrightarrow{AD}$ in terms of $\mathbf{a}$ and $\mathbf{b}$.

   b   What kind of quadrilateral is $BCDE$?

   c   What can be said about points A, E and D?

3   $ABCD$ is a parallelogram. P, Q, R and S are the mid-points of AB, BC, CD and DA respectively.

   a   Prove that $PQRS$ is also a parallelogram.

   b   What can you say about the areas of the two parallelograms?

4   $OABC$ is a parallelogram.

   E and F are mid-points of the sides AB and BC respectively; D is the intersection of AF and OE. Find the ratios:

   a $AD : DF$

   b $OD : DE$.

13 Vectors

Homework

13.3 Compose and resolve velocities

1   **a**   Calculate the magnitude, to 3 significant figures, and the bearing, to 1 decimal place, of the resultant velocity of 15 m s^{-1} on a bearing of 210° and 12 m s^{-1} due north.

2   A particle A is initially at the point with position vector $\begin{pmatrix} 20 \\ 10 \end{pmatrix}$ and moves with a constant speed of 5 m s^{-1} in the same

     direction as $\begin{pmatrix} 3 \\ -4 \end{pmatrix}$

   a   Find the position vector of A after t seconds.

     As A starts moving, a particle B starts to move such that its position vector after t seconds is given by $\begin{pmatrix} 90 \\ -80 \end{pmatrix} + \begin{pmatrix} 12 \\ 9 \end{pmatrix} t$

   b   Write down the speed of B.

   c   Find the exact distance between A and B when t = 10, giving your answer in its simplest surd form.

3   **a**   A particle P travels with a speed of 7.5 m s^{-1} in the direction $-9\mathbf{i} -12\mathbf{j}$. Find the velocity, $\mathbf{v}_P$, of P.

   b   A particle Q travels with velocity $\mathbf{v}_B = 12\mathbf{i} - 5\mathbf{j}$. Find the speed, in m s^{-1}, of Q.

     Particle P starts moving from the point with position vector $20\mathbf{i} -36\mathbf{j}$. At the same time particle Q starts moving from the point with position vector $-10\mathbf{i} - 40\mathbf{j}$.

   c   Find $\mathbf{r}_P$, the position vector of P after t seconds, and $\mathbf{r}_Q$, the position vector of Q after t seconds.

   d   Find the time when the particles collide and the position vector of the point of collision.

Extension

13.1 Position and unit vectors

The dot product between two vectors **a** and **b** is written as **a.b** and defined as: $\mathbf{a.b} = |\mathbf{a}| \times |\mathbf{b}| \times \cos\theta$ where θ is the angle between the two vectors. **Note** dot product is not on the syllabus, however it is useful for preparation for the study of mathematics at AS and/ A level

1   What is the dot product of two parallel vectors **a** and **b**?

2   What is the dot product of two perpendicular vectors **a** and **b**?

3   Given that $(m\mathbf{i} + n\mathbf{j}).(p\mathbf{i} + q\mathbf{j}) = mp\mathbf{i.i} + mq\mathbf{i.j} + np\mathbf{j.i} + nq\mathbf{j.j}$, explain why $(m\mathbf{i} + n\mathbf{j}).(p\mathbf{i} + q\mathbf{j}) = mp + nq$.

4   Find the angle between **a** and **b**, where $\mathbf{a} = 3\mathbf{i} - \mathbf{j}$ and $\mathbf{b} = 2\mathbf{i} + \mathbf{j}$.

5   What can you say about vectors **a** and **b** where $\mathbf{a} = 3\mathbf{i} - 2\mathbf{j}$ and $\mathbf{b} = 4\mathbf{i} + 6\mathbf{j}$?

Extension

13.2 Vectors in geometry

1   The vertices of a convex quadrilateral have position vectors **a, b, c** and **d,** relative to an origin O.
Each statement below indicates a particular geometrical property. State the property in each case.

   a $\mathbf{b} - \mathbf{a} = \lambda(\mathbf{c} - \mathbf{d})$ where λ is a constant not equal to 0 or 1.

   b $\mathbf{b} + \mathbf{d} = \mathbf{c} + \mathbf{a}$

   c $|\mathbf{a} - \mathbf{c}| = |\mathbf{b} - \mathbf{d}|$

2   The dot product between two vectors **a** and **b** is written as **a.b** and defined as:
$\mathbf{a.b} = |\mathbf{a}| \times |\mathbf{b}| \times \cos\theta$ where θ is the angle between the two vectors.

   The vector $\begin{pmatrix} x \\ y \end{pmatrix}$ has a magnitude of 1 and is perpendicular to $\begin{pmatrix} 2 \\ 1 \end{pmatrix}$.

   Use the dot product to find x and y, where x is positive.

3   Three non-collinear points P, Q and R have position vectors **p, q** and **r,** relative to an origin O.

   The point T is such that $\lambda\overrightarrow{PT} = \mu\overrightarrow{PQ}$.

   The point S is such that PTSR is a parallelogram.

   State, in terms of some or all **p, q, r,** λ and μ the position vectors of:

   a   T

   b   S

   c   the point of intersection of the diagonals of PTSR.

4   The position vectors of A, B and C are $2\mathbf{q} - \mathbf{p}$, $3\mathbf{p} - \mathbf{q}$ and $5\mathbf{p} + \lambda\mathbf{q}$, relative to an origin O.

   a   Find the value of λ for which ABC is a straight line and hence find the ratio of AB : BC.

   b   Find, in terms of **p** and **q**, the position vector of the point D such that AD = 3BD.

13 Vectors

Extension

13.3 Compose and resolve velocities

1   A barge needs to be pulled along a canal by two horses, one on each side of the canal. Horse A can pull with a force of 5.5 N, horse B can pull with a force of 5 N. Horse A is set up to pull the barge at an angle of 30° to the canal. At what angle must horse B be set up to pull so that the barge moves straight along the canal, parallel to each edge?

2   A boat can travel at 30 km h^{-1} in still water. It heads due west at 30 km h^{-1} and there is a 15 km h^{-1} wind blowing in a north-west direction. The tide flows at 25 km h^{-1} due south. In what direction and with what speed will the boat travel?

3   Andrew is on the back of a truck travelling at 54 km h^{-1} due north, when he throws a ball due east with an initial speed of 10 m s^{-1}. There is a 7.2 km h^{-1} wind blowing in a south-east direction. What is the speed and the direction of the ball immediately after it leaves Andrew's hand?

4   A plane is flying at 200 km h^{-1} due west. Eve jumps out of the plane with a jet pack which has a speed of 17 m s^{-1} due south. There is an 80 km h^{-1} wind blowing in a north-east direction. What is Eve's resultant speed and her direction of flight?

14 Calculus: Differentiation

TOPIC:

14.1 The idea of a derived function

KEY WORDS:

coordinates, gradient, chord, function, small increment, first principles, derived function, derivative

IGCSE MATHS PRIOR KNOWLEDGE:

Expand products of algebraic expressions

Manipulate algebraic fractions

Understand surds and indices

Draw graphs for functions of the form ax^n

Estimate gradients of curves by drawing tangents

Use function notation such as $f(x) = 3x^2 + 2x - 6$ or $f(x) = \sin(4x - 9)$

Realise $gf(x)$ means $g(f(x))$

Form composite functions

Understand the idea of a derived function

Use the derivatives of functions of the form ax^n where a is a rational constant and n is a positive whole number or zero

---

Learning aims:

- Understand the idea of a derived function
- Use the notations $f'(x)$, $f''(x)$, and $\frac{dy}{dx}$ and $\frac{d^2y}{dx^2}$ $\left[= \frac{d}{dx}\left(\frac{dy}{dx}\right)\right]$

Resources:

- Student Book: pages 298–301
- Graphing calculator (optional)
- Graph paper (optional)

Common mistakes and remediation:

Students often make errors in the algebra. Take care that they expand brackets correctly and are confident in subtracting expressions that contain a negative term.

Make sure the students write $\frac{dy}{dx}$ carefully. Some tend to use $\frac{\delta y}{\delta x}$, thinking it looks nice, but that is mathematically incorrect and is covered in Chapter 16.

Useful tips:

Think about using dynamic geometry software, or graph-drawing software, to show students how a tangent at a point on the curve changes as the point moves along the curve. The visualisation of the chord approaching the tangent is very powerful and the dynamism helps students understand what is happening. Graphing calculators allow students to draw the graphs and trace a point along the curve. They can also work out the numerical value of the gradient at that point, which is a useful check for students.

Guidance:

This topic can be difficult for students who are less secure in their mathematics and, since it is not tested, you might consider skimming over it fairly quickly. However, it is important for capable and motivated students, especially those going on to study mathematics further, to understand this first introduction to a limit, as this is a powerful method.

STARTER (5 mins)

Equipment: Graphing calculator and graph paper (both optional)

➤ Since the example in the Student Book uses $y = 3x^2$ you might want to use $y = 2x^2$ or a different coefficient of x^2 to show students the method.

Students will have met the differentiation of simple polynomials in the IGCSE Mathematics course, so will be aware of the results, but proving it by small increments lays good foundations for the future.

MAIN LESSON ACTIVITY (50 mins)

Equipment: Graphing calculator and graph paper (both optional)

➤ Wherever possible, introduce the topic by using some dynamic geometry software, or graph-drawing software, to show students how a tangent at a point on the curve changes as the point moves along the curve. The visualisation of the chord approaching the tangent is very powerful and the dynamism helps students understand what is happening.

After working through the table of functions and illustrations it is important to let students know that the result is a conjecture, not a proof, as it has not yet been shown to be true for all n. Exercise 14.1 allows students to practise the skills taught. The first three questions are proofs, so that students have the results against which they can check their answers; the next two are problem-solving questions, as the derived function is not given.

➤ Let students who have graphing calculators use them to see the graphs. They may need to be able to adjust the settings of the window to see the graph clearly and this encourages students to be aware of the domain and range of the graph.

Each question will take some time as the algebra can be rather intimidating for some students. Encourage them to use the correct notation and not to omit the $h \rightarrow 0$ underneath the lim.

➤ Do not push this section with lower-achieving students; it is meant to provide the foundations for those who may go on to study mathematics beyond the course. With lower-achieving students, you may wish just to consolidate what they learnt about differentiation in IGCSE Mathematics.

PLENARY (5 mins)

➤ Give students a few minutes to tell the person next to them something they have learnt in the lesson. Then ask one or two students to tell the class what that person said to them. This allows students to recap on what they learnt, and also develops listening and relaying mathematical information skills.

Homework and answers: Resource sheets, homework and extension exercises can be found at the end of this chapter and in the downloadable materials. Answers can be found in the downloadable materials.

CHECKING PROGRESS	Ask students to use the method of small increments to find $\dfrac{dy}{dx}$ when $y = x^2 - x$.

14 Calculus: Differentiation

TOPIC:
14.2 Differentiating polynomials

KEY WORDS:
integer, composite function, function of a function, chain rule, second derivative

IGCSE MATHS PRIOR KNOWLEDGE:
Expand products of algebraic expressions

Manipulate algebraic fractions

Understand surds and indices

Draw graphs for functions of the form ax^n

Estimate gradients of curves by drawing tangents

Use function notation such as $f(x) = 3x^2 + 2x - 6$ or $f(x) = \sin(4x - 9)$

Realise $gf(x)$ means $g(f(x))$

Form composite functions

Understand the idea of a derived function

Use the derivatives of functions of the form ax^n where a is a rational constant and n is a positive whole number or zero

---

Learning aims:
- Use the notations $f'(x)$, $f''(x)$, and $\frac{dy}{dx}$ and $\frac{d^2y}{dx^2} \left[= \frac{d}{dx}\left(\frac{dy}{dx}\right) \right]$
- Know and use the derivatives of the standard functions x^n (for any rational n), $\sin x$, $\cos x$, $\tan x$, e^x, $\ln x$
- Differentiate the products and quotients of functions

Resources:
- Student Book: pages 301–305
- CAS calculator (optional)
- A5 paper

Common mistakes and remediation:
Students sometimes forget that x can be written as x^1.

One source of error is when multiplying by a negative power; another is forgetting that $x^{-n} = \dfrac{1}{x^n}$.

Useful tips:
Make sure that students realise that $\sqrt{x}$ can be written as $x^{\frac{1}{2}}$. It is worthwhile spending a few minutes revising the use of indices to represent surds.

Guidance:
Students will have met differentiation of simple powers of x in their IGCSE Mathematics course so, for some, parts of this topic will be familiar. However, they may not have met the second derivative, or function of a function, and so this lesson contains a lot of new material.

The last two learning aims are incomplete as students are dealing only with polynomials here.

STARTER (5 mins)
Equipment: None essential, though a CAS calculator might be a useful tool for students to check answers

➤ Remind students about what they learnt in the IGCSE Mathematics course by showing them a few simple polynomials and asking them to differentiate them.

A. For example, 'Five quick questions': differentiate the following with respect to x: x^4, $8x - 9$, $6x^7$, $2x^3 - 3x^4$, πx^2.

MAIN LESSON ACTIVITY (50 mins)

Equipment: None essential, though a CAS calculator might be a useful tool for students to check answers

➤ Introduce the f, and f' notation as alternative ways of writing $y = ...$ and $\dfrac{dy}{dx} = ...$. Complete some examples similar to those in the Student Book, or one from Exercise 14.2.

B. There is nothing in the exercise on finding the second derivative because this is used more in Chapter 15, and this lesson already contains plenty of material.

➤ Follow this by showing students how to differentiate composite functions, which saves them a lot of work by avoiding the need to expand brackets with powers.

C. Encourage students to set their work out as shown in the examples, showing the substitution and writing the chain rule each time, as this helps fix it in their memory.

➤ In Exercise 14.2, the first three questions give students the substitution to use; in the problem-solving questions, the students have to decide on an appropriate substitution themselves.

PLENARY (5 mins)

Equipment: Sheets of A5 paper

➤ Give each student a sheet of paper. Ask them to write down a suitable composite function and then give it to someone else to differentiate. The students should have worked out the answer themselves so that they can check the solution that is returned to them, adding some feedback. Any discrepancies in the answers should be reconciled.

Homework and answers: Resource sheets, homework and extension exercises can be found at the end of this chapter and in the downloadable materials. Answers can be found in the downloadable materials.

CHECKING PROGRESS	Collect in the results of the plenary activity so you can see the progress your students have made. Since they will have marked the results themselves, this is not labour intensive on your behalf!

TOPIC:

14.3   Differentiating trigonometric functions

KEY WORDS:

sine, cosine, tangent

IGCSE MATHS PRIOR KNOWLEDGE:

Expand products of algebraic expressions

Manipulate algebraic fractions

Understand surds and indices

Draw graphs for functions of the form ax^n

Estimate gradients of curves by drawing tangents

Use function notation such as $f(x) = 3x^2 + 2x - 6$ or $f(x) = \sin(4x - 9)$

Realise $gf(x)$ means $g(f(x))$

Form composite functions

Understand the idea of a derived function

Use the derivatives of functions of the form ax^n where a is a rational constant and n is a positive whole number or zero

Learning aims:	Resources:
• Know and use the derivatives of the standard functions x^n (for any rational n), $\sin x$, $\cos x$, $\tan x$, e^x, $\ln x$	• Student Book: pages 305–308 • Graphing calculator (optional) • A5 paper

Common mistakes and remediation:

Students sometimes forget to put their calculators into radian mode.

Sources of error occur when $\sin ax + b$ is interpreted as $\sin(ax + b)$ and vice versa; $\sin^2 x$ may be interpreted as $\sin 2x$ and similar errors arise with any trigonometric functions.

Useful tips:

Think about using BODMAS, rather than BIDMAS, where O stands for 'other' in the sense that this includes trigonometric, logarithmic, exponential and any other operations. For example, for $\sin^2 x$ the student needs to do the sine operation before squaring. You might need to remind students that $\sin^2 x$ is a way of writing $(\sin x)^2$, which is different from $\sin x^2$.

Guidance:

Students will have been differentiating simple powers of x in their IGCSE Mathematics course, so they should be familiar with that part of the process. From their work in Chapter 10 they should be capable of working with the trigonometric functions and the shapes of their graphs, mentioned at the start of the relevant section in the Student Book.

The last two learning aims are incomplete as students are dealing only with polynomials and trigonometric functions here.

STARTER (5 mins)

Equipment: None essential, though a graphing calculator will be a very useful tool

➢   Remind students how they differentiated composite functions in the last section, as they will be using that technique here.

D.   For example, 'Five quick questions': write down five values of x where $\sin x = 0$ $\left(\text{or 1, or } \dfrac{1}{2}, \text{ or } \dfrac{\sqrt{3}}{2}, \text{etc} \right)$. Of course, this can be repeated with $\cos x$ or $\tan x$.

MAIN LESSON ACTIVITY (50 mins)

Equipment: None essential, though a graphing calculator will be a very useful tool for students. The use of dynamic geometry or graphing software with a beamer can have a big impact on showing students how the tangent changes as a point moves on a trigonometric curve. If data capture is part of that package then the values of the gradient of the tangent can be captured and graphed to show the connection between the graph and its derivative.

➤ If there is time, split the students into pairs and give each pair an interval (for example $0 \leq x < 0.2$, $0.2 \leq x < 0.4$). They should draw the graph of $\sin x$ (or $\cos x$) in that interval and then, by drawing a tangent at a point, find its gradient. You can then collect the results in a spreadsheet and graph those results so the students can see the graph of the gradients of the tangents.

E. There is nothing in the exercise on finding the second derivative because some of the derivatives contain a product and that will be dealt with in Topic 14.5.

➤ Follow the first activity by showing students how to use the process for differentiating composite functions, which they met in the previous section.

F. Encourage students to set their work out as shown in the examples.

➤ In Exercise 14.3 the first three questions develop students' skills; in the problem-solving questions the students have to decide on an appropriate substitution to use to find the result.

PLENARY (5 mins)

Equipment: Sheets of A5 paper

➤ Give each student a sheet of paper. Ask them to write down a suitable trigonometric function and then give it to someone else to differentiate. The students should have worked out the answer themselves so that they can check the solution that is returned to them, adding some feedback. Any discrepancies in the answers should be reconciled.

Homework and answers: Resource sheets, homework and extension exercises can be found at the end of this chapter and in the downloadable materials. Answers can be found in the downloadable materials.

CHECKING PROGRESS	Collect in the results of the plenary activity so you can see the progress your students have made. Since they will have marked the results themselves, this is not labour intensive on your behalf!

14 Calculus: Differentiation

TOPIC:

14.4 Differentiating exponential and logarithmic functions

KEY WORDS:

exponential function, logarithmic function

IGCSE MATHS PRIOR KNOWLEDGE:

Expand products of algebraic expressions

Manipulate algebraic fractions

Understand surds and indices

Draw graphs for functions of the form ax^n

Estimate gradients of curves by drawing tangents

Use function notation such as $f(x) = 3x^2 + 2x - 6$ or $f(x) = \sin(4x - 9)$

Realise $gf(x)$ means $g(f(x))$

Form composite functions

Understand the idea of a derived function

Use the derivatives of functions of the form ax^n where a is a rational constant and n is a positive whole number or zero

Learning aims:
- Differentiate products and quotients of functions

Resources:
- Student Book: pages 309–313
- Graphing calculator (optional)
- A5 paper

Common mistakes and remediation:

Students sometimes get confused between $\ln x$ and $\log x$.

Sources of error occur when students fail to insert brackets in their answers. They need to be reminded that $\ln ax + b$ is not the same as $\ln(ax + b)$.

Useful tips:

Encourage all students to show their working, using one $=$ sign per line, aligning subsequent $=$ signs beneath the first one. That way, if they check their answers and find a discrepancy it is easier for them to identify where the mistake has been made.

Guidance:

Students will have been differentiating simple powers of x in their IGCSE Mathematics course, so they should be familiar with that part of the process. From their work in Chapter 7 they should be capable of working with the exponential and logarithmic functions and the shapes of their graphs, mentioned at the start of the relevant section in the Student Book.

The last two learning aims are incomplete as students are dealing only with the functions they have met so far.

STARTER (5 mins)

Equipment: None essential, though a graphing calculator will be a very useful tool

➢ Remind students about how they differentiated composite functions in the previous sections, as they will be using that technique here.

➢ For example, 'Five quick questions': write down five values of x where $e^{f(x)} = 1$, where $f(x) = \sin x$, or $x^2 - 5x + 6$, etc. Any function that has a zero consolidates equation solving. This can be repeated for $\ln f(x) = 1$.

MAIN LESSON ACTIVITY (50 mins)

Equipment: None essential, though again a graphing calculator will be a very useful tool for each student. The use of dynamic geometry or graphing software with a beamer can have a big impact on showing students how the tangent changes as a point moves on an exponential or logarithmic curve. If data capture is part of that package then the values of the gradient of the tangent can be captured and graphed to show the connection between the graph and its derivative.

➤ If there is time, split the students into pairs and give each pair an interval (for example $-0.5 \leq x < 0$, $0 \leq x < 0.5$). They should draw the graph of e^x (or ln x if you keep the intervals positive) in that interval and then, by drawing a tangent at a point, find its gradient. You can then collect the results in a spreadsheet and graph the results so the students can see the graph of the gradients of the tangents.

➤ Part of the exercise is about finding the second derivative because that can be done with some of the first derivatives. Those that contain a product will be dealt with in Topic 14.5 and those that contain a product will be dealt with in Topic 14.6.

➤ Follow the first activity by showing students how to use the process for differentiating composite functions, which they met in the previous sections.

➤ Make sure that students appreciate the fact that ln x and e^x are inverse functions and so their graphs are reflections of each other in the line $y = x$. To see this clearly the axes will need to have equal scales as shown in the diagram on page 311.

➤ In Exercise 14.4 the first three questions develop students' skills; in the problem-solving questions the students have to decide on an appropriate substitution to use, to find the result, as well as dealing with the range of values.

➤ Remind students that ln $x^a = a$ ln x and ln $Ax =$ ln $A +$ ln x. This often simplifies results considerably and also reminds students about the logarithmic laws.

PLENARY (5 mins)

Equipment: Sheets of A5 paper

➤ Give each student a sheet of paper. Ask them to write down a suitable exponential function or a logarithmic function and then give it to someone else to differentiate. The students should have worked out the answer themselves so that they can check the solution that is returned to them, adding some feedback. Any discrepancies in the answers should be reconciled.

Homework and answers: Resource sheets, homework and extension exercises can be found at the end of this chapter and in the downloadable materials. Answers can be found in the downloadable materials.

CHECKING PROGRESS	Collect in the results of the plenary activity so you can see the progress made by your students. Seeing how they have done should guide you for the next lesson on whether they need more practice or can move on.

TOPIC:

14.5 Differentiating products of functions

KEY WORDS:

product, product rule

IGCSE MATHS PRIOR KNOWLEDGE:

Expand products of algebraic expressions

Manipulate algebraic fractions

Understand surds and indices

Draw graphs for functions of the form ax^n

Estimate gradients of curves by drawing tangents

Use function notation such as $f(x) = 3x^2 + 2x - 6$ or $f(x) = \sin(4x - 9)$

Realise $gf(x)$ means $g(f(x))$

Form composite functions

Understand the idea of a derived function

Use the derivatives of functions of the form ax^n where a is a rational constant and n is a positive whole number or zero

Learning aims:	Resources:
• Differentiate products and quotients of functions	• Student Book: pages 314–316

Common mistakes and remediation:

Students sometimes forget the results of the previous topic, so they should be recapped at the start of the lesson.

Again, sources of error occur when students fail to insert brackets in their answers. They need to be reminded that this is essential so that, for example, $(3 + x) \sin x$ is not written as $3 + x \sin x$.

Useful tips:

Encourage all students to write the product rule in full each time. They might find this tedious, but the repetition ensures it is not forgotten!

Students often fail to make any connection with mathematics they have studied before; they tend to think in small pieces and do not see the big picture. Now that they have the basic skills, some of the questions bring in some of the mathematics they have met in earlier chapters, such as the trigonometric identities and properties of logarithms (for example, $\ln x^n = n \ln x$). This is useful revision as well as practice with the product rule.

Guidance:

By now students will be proficient in differentiating polynomials and gaining in confidence with trigonometric, exponential and logarithmic functions.

The answers may not be in the form a student reaches, so they may need to do some algebraic manipulation to check that they do have the correct answer.

The last two learning aims are incomplete as students are dealing only with the functions they have met so far combined with the product rule.

STARTER (5 mins)

➤ Remind students about the basic results in the table at the start of the topic.

➤ For example, 'Five quick questions': write down the derivative of simple functions such as x^{10}, $\cos x$, e^x, $\ln 4x$ …. They should be able to recall simple derivatives very quickly.

MAIN LESSON ACTIVITY (50 mins)

➢ The best strategy here is to do a couple of examples and then let the students do the exercise.

➢ In Exercise 14.5 the first two questions develop students' skills; in the problem-solving questions the students have to decide on an appropriate strategy, as well as doing some algebraic manipulation.

➢ Again, remind students that $\ln x^a = a \ln x$ and $\ln Ax = \ln A + \ln x$. This often simplifies results considerably and also reminds students about the logarithmic laws.

PLENARY (5 mins)

➢ This time the objective of the plenary is to ensure that students remember the product rule. Ask students to recite the product rule to someone else, so they can check it. They should also write it down somewhere so the other student can check it is written down correctly.

➢ Now ask then to write down the derivative of the product of sin x and $\ln x$.

Homework and answers: Resource sheets, homework and extension exercises can be found at the end of this chapter and in the downloadable materials. Answers can be found in the downloadable materials.

CHECKING PROGRESS	Collect in the results of the plenary activity so you can see the progress your students have made. Seeing how they have done should guide you for the next lesson on whether they need more practice or can move on.

14 Calculus: Differentiation

TOPIC:

14.6 Differentiating quotients of functions

KEY WORDS:

quotient, quotient rule

IGCSE MATHS PRIOR KNOWLEDGE:

Expand products of algebraic expressions

Manipulate algebraic fractions

Understand surds and indices

Draw graphs for functions of the form ax^n

Estimate gradients of curves by drawing tangents

Use function notation such as $f(x) = 3x^2 + 2x - 6$ or $f(x) = \sin(4x - 9)$

Realise $gf(x)$ means $g(f(x))$

Form composite functions

Understand the idea of a derived function

Use the derivatives of functions of the form ax^n where a is a rational constant and n is a positive whole number or zero

---

Learning aims:

- Differentiate products and quotients of functions

Resources:

- Student Book: pages 317–319

Common mistakes and remediation:

Remembering the quotient rule is the hardest part!

Useful tips:

Encourage all students to write the quotient rule in full each time. They might find this tedious, but the repetition ensures it is not forgotten.

It is worthwhile repeating that students often fail to make any connection with mathematics they have studied before; they tend to think in small pieces and do not see the big picture. Now that they have the basic skills, some of the questions bring in pieces of mathematics they will have met in earlier chapters, such as the trigonometric identities and properties of logarithms. This is useful revision as well as practice with the quotient rule.

Guidance:

By now students will be proficient in differentiating polynomials and gaining in confidence with trigonometric, exponential and logarithmic functions.

The answers may not be in the form a student reaches, so they may need to do some algebraic manipulation to check that they do have the correct answer.

The last two learning aims should now be complete as students have learnt how to deal with differentiating all types of function that they need for this course.

STARTER (5 mins)

➢ Remind students about the product rule.

➢ For example, 'Three fairly quick questions': write down the derivative of simple products such as $x \cos x$, $e^x \ln x$ …. They should be able to recall simple derivatives very quickly.

MAIN LESSON ACTIVITY (50 mins)

➢ Again, the best strategy here is to complete a couple of examples and let the students do the exercise.

➢ In Exercise 14.6 the first four questions develop students' skills; in the problem-solving questions the students have to do quite a bit of algebraic manipulation. The last two questions involve showing results, which is useful because it means students check their answers, and may pick up algebraic slips.

➢ Again, remind students that $\ln x^a = a \ln x$ and $\ln Ax = \ln A + \ln x$. This often simplifies results considerably and also reminds students about the logarithmic laws.

➢ Consider moving students on to tackle the chapter review, though you might want to keep this as an end-of-chapter test, or for revision purposes.

PLENARY (5 mins)

➢ This time the objective of the plenary is to ensure that students remember the quotient rule. Ask students to recite the quotient rule to someone else, so they can check it. They should also write it down somewhere so the other student can check it is written down correctly.

➢ Now ask them to work out the derivative of $\dfrac{x^2}{\ln x}$.

Homework and answers: Resource sheets, homework and extension exercises can be found at the end of this chapter and in the downloadable materials. Answers can be found in the downloadable materials.

CHECKING PROGRESS	Collect in the results of the plenary activity so you can see the progress your students have made. Seeing how they have done should guide you for the use of the problem-solving questions and chapter review.

Homework

14.1 The idea of a derived function

Non-calculator

For this homework, use the method of small increments in each question.

1   If $y = 4x - 6$, prove $\dfrac{dy}{dx} = 4$.

2   If $y = x^2$, prove $\dfrac{dy}{dx} = 2x$.

3   If $y = 2x^2 - 1$, prove $\dfrac{dy}{dx} = 4x$.

4   If $y = \dfrac{1}{x+2}$, $(x \neq -2)$, prove $\dfrac{dy}{dx} = -\dfrac{1}{(x+2)^2}$.

5   If $y = \dfrac{1}{2x-3}$, $(x \neq -1.5)$, prove $\dfrac{dy}{dx} = -\dfrac{2}{(2x-3)^2}$.

6   If $y = (x-3)x$, find $\dfrac{dy}{dx}$.

7   If $y = \dfrac{x+4}{x^2}$, $(x \neq 0)$, find $\dfrac{dy}{dx}$.

Homework

14.2 Differentiating polynomials

Non-calculator

1   If $f(x) = 4x^2 - 3x + 2$, find $f'(x)$ and $f''(x)$.

2   If $y = 5x^5 - 4x^3 + 3x - 1$, find $\dfrac{dy}{dx}$ and $\dfrac{d^2y}{dx^2}$.

3   If $y = u^4$ and $u = 2x^3 + 3$, find $\dfrac{dy}{du}$ and $\dfrac{du}{dx}$.

   Use your answers to find $\dfrac{dy}{dx}$ when $y = (2x^3 + 3)^4$.

4 If $y = 2u^3$ and $u = x^4 - 5x + 1$, find $\dfrac{dy}{du}$ and $\dfrac{du}{dx}$.

Use your answers to find $\dfrac{dy}{dx}$ when $y = 2(x^4 - 5x + 1)^3$.

5 If $f(x) = (2x + 7)^4$, use the substitution $u = 2x + 7$ to find $f'(x)$.

6 If $f(x) = (6x^2 - 7x - 3)^4$, find $f'(x)$.
Explain why your answer is the same as $4(12x - 7)(3x + 1)^3(2x - 3)^3$.

7 Differentiate $3\sqrt{x^2 - 4}$ with respect to x.

14 Calculus: Differentiation

Homework

14.3 Differentiating trigonometric functions

Non-calculator

1 Differentiate each function with respect to x.

a $\dfrac{1}{2}\sin x$

b $\pi \cos x$

c $-\dfrac{\tan x}{3}$

d $3\cos x - \sin x$

e $4\tan x - 3\cos x$

2 Find $\dfrac{dy}{dx}$ when:

a $y = \tan 7x$

b $y = 3x - \cos 3x$

c $y = 2x^3 + 5\sin x$

d $y = 3x^2 - \tan\dfrac{x}{2}$

3 Differentiate each function with respect to x.

a $\sin(5x + 3)$

b $\cos(2x - 3)$

c $\tan(10 - 7x)$

4 Find $\dfrac{dy}{dx}$ when:

a $y = \cos 3x^2$

b $y = \tan(2x - x^3)$

c $y = 4\sin(3x - x^5)$

5 Show that if $f(x) = 4\sin 3x$, $9f(x) + f''(x) = 0$.

6 Show that if $y = \sin 2x°$, $\dfrac{dy}{dx} = \dfrac{\pi}{90}\cos 2x°$.

7 Show that if $y = \tan 3x°$, $\dfrac{dy}{dx} = \dfrac{\pi}{60\cos^2 3x°}$.

14 Calculus: Differentiation

Homework

14.4 Differentiating exponential and logarithmic functions

Non-calculator

1 Differentiate the following functions with respect to x.

  a $y = x^3 - 2e^x$

  b $f(x) = 3x^3 - 5 + 4\ln x$

  c $y = \cos x + \dfrac{\ln x}{5}$

2 Find $\dfrac{dy}{dx}$ when:

  a $y = e^{x^2}$

  b $y = 3e^{(x^4 - 3x)}$

  c $y = e^{\sin x}$

3 If $y = \ln x^5$, explain, in two different ways, why $\dfrac{dy}{dx} = \dfrac{5}{x}$.

4 If $f(x) = \ln \tan x$ show that $\dfrac{dy}{dx} = \dfrac{2}{\sin 2x}$.

5 Find $\dfrac{dy}{dx}$ when $y = \ln(3x^2 - 12)$. For what values of x is your result valid?

6 Show that if $y = e^{\cos x^2}$, $\dfrac{dy}{dx} = -2xe^{\cos x^2} \sin x^2$.

7 Show that if $f(x) = \ln \sin x°$ for $0 < x < 180$, $f'(x) = \dfrac{\pi \cot x°}{180}$.

Homework

14.5 Differentiating products of functions

Non-calculator

1.   Use the product rule to differentiate these functions with respect to x.

    a $x \tan x$ **b** $e^x \cos x$

    c $x^2 e^x$ **d** $x \ln x$

2.   Find $f'(x)$ if:

    a $f(x) = 6x^2 - x^2 \sin x$ **b** $f(x) = (x^3 - 3) \ln x^2$

3.   Calculate $\dfrac{dy}{dx}$ when $y = x^2 \sin x + x \cos 2x$.

4.   Calculate $\dfrac{d^2y}{dx^2}$ if $y = x^5 \ln x^2$.

5.   Find $f''(x)$ if $f(x) = x \cos x \sin x$.

6.   By writing $\dfrac{1}{\sqrt{x}}$ as $x^{-0.5}$, differentiate $\dfrac{\ln x}{\sqrt{x}}$.

7.   Show that if $y = \cos x \sin^2 x$, $\dfrac{dy}{dx} = (2 - 3\sin^2 x)\sin x$.

Homework

14.6 Differentiating quotients of functions

Non-calculator

1   Use the quotient rule to differentiate each function with respect to *x*.

Simplify your answers as far as possible.

a $\dfrac{e^x}{x}$ **b** $\dfrac{2x+1}{4-3x}$ **c** $\dfrac{3x^2-1}{e^x}$

2   Find f′(*x*) if:

a $f(x)=\dfrac{4-3x}{2x+1}$ **b** $f(x)=\dfrac{e^{-2x}}{x^2-1}$ **c** $f(x)=\dfrac{\ln x}{\sqrt{x}}$

Express your answers in their simplest, factorised form where appropriate.

3   Calculate $\dfrac{d^2y}{dx^2}$ when $y=\dfrac{2x^2}{x+1}$.

4   Calculate f″(*x*) when $f(x)=\dfrac{2x}{x-1}$.

5   Calculate $\dfrac{dy}{dx}$ when $y=\dfrac{\tan x}{x^2}$ and when $y=\dfrac{x^2}{\tan x}$.

6   If $y=\sec x$ show that $\dfrac{d^2y}{dx^2}=\dfrac{1+\sin^2 x}{\cos^3 x}$.

7   If $f(x)=\dfrac{\ln x^3}{x^3}$ show that $f''(x)=\dfrac{36\ln x-21}{x^5}$.

Extension

14.1 The idea of a derived function

Non-calculator

For these extension questions, use the method of small increments each time.

1   If $y = \dfrac{x}{x+2}$, $(x \neq -2)$, find $\dfrac{dy}{dx}$.

2   If $y = \dfrac{x^2 + 3x}{x+3}$, $(x \neq -3)$, find $\dfrac{dy}{dx}$. (Think carefully!)

3   If $y = 5x^3 - x$, find $\dfrac{dy}{dx}$.

4   If $y = x^4 - x^2$, find $\dfrac{dy}{dx}$.

5   If $y = \dfrac{x-2}{x^3}$, $(x \neq 0)$, find $\dfrac{dy}{dx}$.

Extension

14.2 Differentiating polynomials

Non-calculator

1   If $f(x) = \sqrt{(x^2 + 4)}$, use an appropriate substitution to find $f'(x)$.

2   If $f(x) = \sqrt[3]{(x^2 - 3x)}$, use an appropriate substitution to find $f'(x)$.

3   If $f(x) = (3x - 2)^6$, use an appropriate substitution to find $f'(x)$ and $f''(x)$.

4   If $y = (2x - 4)^3$, use a substitution to show that $(x-2)\dfrac{d^2y}{dx^2} - 2\dfrac{dy}{dx} = 0$.

5   If $y = (5x + 3)^4$, find the value of k such that $(5x+3)\dfrac{d^2y}{dx^2} - k\dfrac{dy}{dx} = 0$.

Extension

14.3 Differentiating trigonometric functions
Non-calculator

1   If $f(x) = \sqrt{\sin x}$, use an appropriate substitution to find $f'(x)$.

2   If $f(x) = \sqrt{\tan x}$, find $f'(x)$.

3   If $f(x) = \sqrt[3]{\cos x}$, find $f'(x)$.

4   If $f(x) = 3\sin 2x$, show that $4f(x) + f''(x) = 0$.

5   If $y = \sec x$, show that $\dfrac{dy}{dx} = \tan x \sec x$.

14 Calculus: Differentiation

Extension

14.4 Differentiating exponential and logarithmic functions
Non-calculator

1   If $y = 4\ln x + \dfrac{25}{2x^2}$, show that $\dfrac{dy}{dx}$ can be written as $\dfrac{dy}{dx} = \dfrac{(2x-5)(2x+5)}{x^3}$.

2   If $e^y = x^2$, find $\dfrac{dy}{dx}$.

3   If $\ln y = \sin x$, find $\dfrac{dy}{dx}$.

4   If $f(x) = (x-2)^2 + e^x$, show that $2f''(x) + f'(x) - 2f(x) = 2(1-x)(x-4) + e^x$.

5   Find $f''(x)$, if $f(x) = 2\ln(x-4) - 2\ln(x+4)$.

Extension

14.5 Differentiating products of functions

Non-calculator

1 If $y = e^{x^2} \ln x$, find $\dfrac{dy}{dx}$.

2 If $y = xe^x \cos x$, find $\dfrac{dy}{dx}$.

3 If $f(x) = e^{2x}(1 + 2x)^5$, show $f'(x) = 4(x + 3)(1 + 2x)^4 e^{2x}$.

4 Show that 2^x can be written as $e^{x \ln 2}$ and hence find $\dfrac{dy}{dx}$ if $y = 2^{x \sin x}$.

5 Find $f'(x)$, if $f(x) = (3x - 2)^4 \sin(x \ln x)$.

Extension

14.6 Differentiating quotients of functions

Non-calculator

1 If $y = \dfrac{\sin x}{x}$, find $\dfrac{dy}{dx}$.

2 Find $f'(x)$, if $f(x) = x \sin x + \dfrac{x}{\tan x}$.

3 If $y = \ln\left(\dfrac{x}{\sin x}\right)$, use two different methods to find $\dfrac{dy}{dx}$.

4 If $y = \dfrac{6 - \ln x}{\cos x}$, find $\dfrac{dy}{dx}$.

5 If $e^{f(x)} = \dfrac{x}{x - 1}$, show $f'(x) = \dfrac{1}{x(1 - x)}$.

TOPIC:

15.1 Calculating gradients, tangents and normals

KEY WORDS:

gradient, function, tangent, normal, bisect

IGCSE MATHS PRIOR KNOWLEDGE:

Expand products of algebraic expressions

Manipulate algebraic fractions

Understand surds and indices

Draw graphs for functions of the form ax^n

Find the equation of straight line graphs in the form $y = mx + c$

Find the equation of a straight line through a given point

Find the gradient of parallel and perpendicular lines

Use function notation such as $f(x) = 3x^2 + 2x - 6$ or $f(x) = \sin(4x - 9)$

Understand the idea of a derived function

Use the derivatives of functions of the form ax^n where a is a rational constant and n is a positive whole number or zero

Apply differentiation to gradients and turning points (stationary points)

Discriminate between maxima and minima by any method

Learning aims:
- Use differentiation to find gradients, tangents and normals

Resources:
- Student Book: pages 324–326
- Resource sheet 15.1

Common mistakes and remediation:

Students sometimes mistake the mathematical meaning of 'normal' with its normal meaning! This is always a problem when the same word has two different meanings. However, it is used in a mathematical sense in this chapter.

Useful tips:

Consider using dynamic geometry software, or graph-drawing software, to show students how a tangent and normal relate to each other as a point moves along a curve. Remind students that the product of perpendicular gradients is –1.

Guidance:

This section is relatively straightforward as students should have met the equation of a straight line before. This chapter provides more practice in differentiating functions, so is best done after Chapter 14, to consolidate what they learnt there.

STARTER (5 mins)

Equipment: Resource sheet 15.1

➢ Give out Resource sheet 15.1 and ask students to draw in the tangents and normal at the points shown. Insist that they use rulers.

Students can check their results with each other.

MAIN LESSON ACTIVITY (50 mins)

➢ Wherever possible, introduce the topic by using some dynamic geometry software, or graph-drawing software, to show students how the tangent and normal at a point on the curve change as the point moves along the curve.

Show a fairly simple example such as a polynomial – this makes it easier for students to understand, as they should be familiar with differentiating simple powers of x. They may need reminding about the equation of a straight line and the property of perpendicular gradients.

➢ Exercise 15.1 allows students to practise the skills taught. The first two questions are relatively simple. The others build on skills students should have acquired from earlier chapters, particularly Chapters 3 and 5.

If students have graphing calculators, let them use them to see the graphs. They may need to be able to adjust the settings of the window to see the graph clearly and this encourages students to be aware of the domain and range of the graph.

➢ Question 6 involves quite a bit of algebra, so it would be best not to ask lower-achieving students to do this; it is meant to provide a challenge for the higher achievers.

PLENARY (5 mins)

➢ Give the students a few minutes to describe to the person next to them what the normal will look like if the tangent has a gradient of 0. Then ask them to sketch a curve where the tangent has a gradient of 0 and ask them to write down the general equation of the normal in that case ($x = $ constant).

Homework and answers: Resource sheets, homework and extension exercises can be found at the end of this chapter and in the downloadable materials. Answers can be found in the downloadable materials.

CHECKING PROGRESS	Ask students to find the equation of the normal to the curve $y = 2x^2$ where $x = 1$. Follow this up with asking them why the normal can be expressed as $4y + x = 9$.

15 Calculus: Applications of Differentiation

TOPIC:

15.2 Stationary points

KEY WORDS:

stationary point, maximum, minimum, second derivative, rate of change

IGCSE MATHS PRIOR KNOWLEDGE:

Expand products of algebraic expressions

Manipulate algebraic fractions

Understand surds and indices

Draw graphs for functions of the form ax^n

Find the equation of straight line graphs in the form $y = mx + c$

Find the equation of a straight line through a given point

Find the gradient of parallel and perpendicular lines

Use function notation such as $f(x) = 3x^2 + 2x - 6$ or $f(x) = \sin(4x - 9)$

Understand the idea of a derived function

Use the derivatives of functions of the form ax^n where a is a rational constant and n is a positive whole number or zero

Apply differentiation to gradients and turning points (stationary points)

Discriminate between maxima and minima by any method

Learning aims:

- Use differentiation to find a stationary point
- Apply differentiation to practical problems involving maxima and minima

Resources:

- Student Book: pages 326–328
- Resource sheets 15.2 and 15.3
- A5 paper

Common mistakes and remediation:

Students might confuse maxima and minima. Emphasise the difference with, for example, clear diagrams.

Useful tips:

Make sure that students write down the conditions for maxima and minima and that they check, using gradients either side of the stationary point, or use the second derivative. The former method is useful if the second derivative cannot be found.

Guidance:

Students will have been able to distinguish between maxima and minima for their IGCSE Mathematics, but now need to move to more formal methods. They may not have met the use of the second derivative.

STARTER (5 mins)

Equipment: Resource sheet 15.2.

➢ Remind students about what they learnt in the IGCSE Mathematics course about maxima and minima.

➢ Ask them to identify the points on the resource sheet and write, on either side of each one, whether

$\frac{dy}{dx} > 0$, $\frac{dy}{dx} = 0$ or $\frac{dy}{dx} < 0$.

MAIN LESSON ACTIVITY (50 mins)

Equipment: Resource sheets 15.2 and 15.3.

➢ Go through the conditions for maxima and minima, and check students' answers to Resource sheet 15.2

➢ Question 1 of Exercise 15.2 is on Resource sheet 15.3. Students can write their answers on the sheet and keep it as a reference, rather than miss out by not having the curves recorded in their exercise books.

➢ Encourage students to set their work out as shown in the examples.

➢ In Exercise 15.2 the first four questions are fairly standard; in the problem-solving questions, the students are faced with some more involved algebra.

PLENARY (5 mins)

Equipment: Sheets of A5 paper

➢ Give each student a sheet of paper. Ask them to sketch a suitable curve, then give it to someone else to mark on any stationary points. The students should have worked out the answer themselves so that they can check the solution that is returned to them, adding some feedback. Any discrepancies in the answers should be reconciled.

Homework and answers: Resource sheets, homework and extension exercises can be found at the end of this chapter and in the downloadable materials. Answers can be found in the downloadable materials.

CHECKING PROGRESS	Collect in the results of the plenary activity so you can see the progress your students have made. Since they will have marked the results themselves, this is not labour intensive on your behalf!

TOPIC:

15.3 Connected rates of change

KEY WORDS:

rate of change, rate of increase, chain rule

IGCSE MATHS PRIOR KNOWLEDGE:

Expand products of algebraic expressions

Manipulate algebraic fractions

Understand surds and indices

Draw graphs for functions of the form ax^n

Find the equation of straight line graphs in the form $y = mx + c$

Find the equation of a straight line through a given point

Find the gradient of parallel and perpendicular lines

Use function notation such as $f(x) = 3x^2 + 2x - 6$ or $f(x) = \sin(4x - 9)$

Understand the idea of a derived function

Use the derivatives of functions of the form ax^n where a is a rational constant and n is a positive whole number or zero

Apply differentiation to gradients and turning points (stationary points)

Discriminate between maxima and minima by any method

Learning aims:

- Apply differentiation to connected rates of change, small increments and approximations

Resources:

- Student Book: pages 328–330
- A5 sheets of paper

Common mistakes and remediation:

Students sometimes make mistakes in manipulating algebra – practice makes perfect!

Useful tips:

Encourage the drawing of a diagram when students solve problems.

Encourage the completion of all algebraic simplification before any substitution takes place.

Guidance:

Decide upon a suitable strategy for students to follow as they attempt a problem. For example:

- Determine the constants and variables given in the problem
- Write down relevant equations and derivatives
- Identify the connected rates of change needed to solve the problem

Important:

The extension questions take students further into the topic, challenging them to consider different, practical examples. Questions 4 and 5, in particular, will need careful thought by students.

STARTER (5 mins)

➤ Remind students how they differentiated composite functions in the previous section, emphasising the importance of the chain rule.

➤ For example, 'Three quick questions': write down the derivatives of three composite functions of your own choice. The composite functions must include exponential, log and trigonometric functions.

MAIN LESSON ACTIVITY (50 mins)

➤ Start by reminding your students that a graph can describe a rate of change; emphasise how a quantity changes with respect to time. Discuss how differentiation can be used to find a rate of change and, consequently, describe it.

➤ Use the example of the circle, shown in the Student Book, to show how rates of change can be connected by a common variable, time; emphasise the importance of the chain rule and how the reciprocal of a rate of change is sometimes needed.

➤ Go through Examples 5 and 6 with your students, explaining that a rate of change is found for a particular point in time; emphasise the importance of a strategy to solve the problems.

➤ In Exercise 15.3 the first four questions develop students' skills, with the third and fourth questions needing the reciprocal of a rate of change to be used; the problem-solving questions expect the students to look deeper into the problem to see the connections between different rates of change.

PLENARY (5 mins)

Equipment: Sheets of A5 paper

➤ Ask the students to work in pairs and give each pair a sheet of paper. Using question number 6 in Exercise 15.3 as a model, ask the students to create a similar problem-solving question, where the relationship between the base radius and the perpendicular height is given using a ratio. The question can then be given to another pair of students to solve. The students should have worked out the answer themselves so that they can check the solution that is returned to them, adding some feedback. Any discrepancies in the answers should be reconciled.

Homework and answers: Resource sheets, homework and extension exercises can be found at the end of this chapter and in the downloadable materials. Answers can be found in the downloadable materials.

CHECKING PROGRESS	Collect in the results of the plenary activity so you can see the progress your students have made. Since they will have marked the results themselves, this is not labour intensive on your behalf!

15 Calculus: Applications of Differentiation

TOPIC:

15.4 Small increments and approximations

KEY WORDS:

small increment, small change, approximation

IGCSE MATHS PRIOR KNOWLEDGE:

Expand products of algebraic expressions

Manipulate algebraic fractions

Understand surds and indices

Draw graphs for functions of the form ax^n

Find the equation of straight line graphs in the form $y = mx + c$

Find the equation of a straight line through a given point

Find the gradient of parallel and perpendicular lines

Use function notation such as $f(x) = 3x^2 + 2x - 6$ or $f(x) = \sin(4x - 9)$

Understand the idea of a derived function

Use the derivatives of functions of the form ax^n where a is a rational constant-and n is a positive whole number or zero

Apply differentiation to gradients and turning points (stationary points)

Discriminate between maxima and minima by any method

Learning aims:	Resources:
• Apply differentiation to connected rates of change, small increments and approximations	• Student Book: pages 331–333

Common mistakes and remediation:

Students often mix up $\dfrac{dy}{dx}$ and $\dfrac{\delta y}{\delta x}$. Make sure they practise writing these so that they are recognisably different and distinct.

Useful tips:

Mention that students need to read the questions carefully; sometimes it asks for the increase in y to be found, sometimes the increase in x. Since finding the increase in x involves a bit more manipulation and is not asked for as often as the increase in y, students sometimes get this wrong.

Guidance:

This is not the easiest of topics; lower-achieving students sometimes struggle with it.

STARTER (5 mins)

➤ Remind students how they differentiated composite functions in the previous section as they will be using that technique here.

➤ For example, 'Five quick questions': write down the derivative of y where y = a polynomial of your choice, a simple trigonometric or logarithmic function.

MAIN LESSON ACTIVITY (50 mins)

➤ Go through one or two examples, making sure that students note and understand the difference between $\frac{dy}{dx}$ and $\frac{\delta y}{\delta x}$.

➤ Stress the tips to the students.

➤ Encourage students to set their work out as shown in the examples.

➤ In Exercise 15.4 the first four questions develop students' skills; in the problem-solving questions, the students have to find the approximate change in x rather than y and this will be more challenging for lower-achieving students.

PLENARY (5 mins)

➤ Give the students a few minutes to tell the person next to them something they have learnt in the lesson. Then ask one or two students to tell the class what that person said to them. They can also (if time permits) write any new information on sticky notes and attach them to a display. This allows students to recap on what they learnt and also develops listening and relaying mathematical information skills.

Homework and answers: Resource sheets, homework and extension exercises can be found at the end of this chapter and in the downloadable materials. Answers can be found in the downloadable materials.

CHECKING PROGRESS	Make sure all students have completed question 1 correctly by checking their answers during the lesson.

TOPIC:

15.5 Practical applications

KEY WORDS:

None

IGCSE MATHS PRIOR KNOWLEDGE:

Expand products of algebraic expressions

Manipulate algebraic fractions

Understand surds and indices

Draw graphs for functions of the form ax^n

Find the equation of straight line graphs in the form $y = mx + c$

Find the equation of a straight line through a given point

Find the gradient of parallel and perpendicular lines

Use function notation such as $f(x) = 3x^2 + 2x - 6$ or $f(x) = \sin(4x - 9)$

Understand the idea of a derived function

Use the derivatives of functions of the form ax^n where a is a rational constant and n is a positive whole number or zero

Apply differentiation to gradients and turning points (stationary points)

Discriminate between maxima and minima by any method

Learning aims:	Resources:
• Apply differentiation to practical problems involving maxima and minima	• Student Book: pages 333–337 • A piece of string about 30 cm long

Common mistakes and remediation:

Students sometimes make mistakes in manipulating algebra – practice makes perfect!

To help, many of the questions are split up into parts, leading students through them. Students should check their results frequently, to avoid spending too much time manipulating incorrect algebra.

Useful tips:

Encourage all students to show their working using one = sign per line, aligning subsequent = signs beneath the first one. That way, if they check their answers and find a discrepancy it is easier for them to identify where the mistake has been made. Remember, students should check their results often to avoid spending too much time manipulating incorrect algebra; this cannot be stressed often enough!

Guidance:

Students need plenty of time for these questions; they can be lengthy and it is better for them to do a few correctly rather than rush through, making errors.

STARTER (5 mins)

Equipment: A piece of string about 30 cm long

➢ Ask students to use all the string to make a rectangular enclosure, one side of the rectangle being part of the straight side of the table. They should try to find the position of the string that encloses the maximum area (basically recreating the situation in question 1 of Exercise 15.5).

➢ Ask students to measure the sides of the rectangle; they will check their results in the plenary.

MAIN LESSON ACTIVITY (50 mins)

➤ Start by going through Example 9 with your students. Take it step by step, just as described before Example 9 in the Student Book.

➤ Reinforce the step-by-step method, as these questions are quite complex. It is important for students to acquire the necessary technique.

➤ Example 8 is more complex and it is best to leave this until students have mastered questions 1 to 4.

➤ In Exercise 15.5 the first three questions develop students' problem-solving skills.

PLENARY (5 mins)

Equipment: Students' results from the starter

➤ Students can now work out whether the result they got in the starter by trial and improvement fit the theoretical model. If they started with string of length x, their rectangle should have dimensions $\dfrac{x}{2}$ by $\dfrac{x}{4}$, but they should prove their result – question 1 will help them.

Homework and answers: Resource sheets, homework and extension exercises can be found at the end of this chapter and in the downloadable materials. Answers can be found in the downloadable materials.

CHECKING PROGRESS	Provided that students have managed at least the first three questions from Exercise 15.5 they will have made reasonable progress, good progress if they have done the first four and excellent progress if they have finished or nearly finished.

Resource sheet 15.1

Draw the tangents and normals on these curves at the points shown.

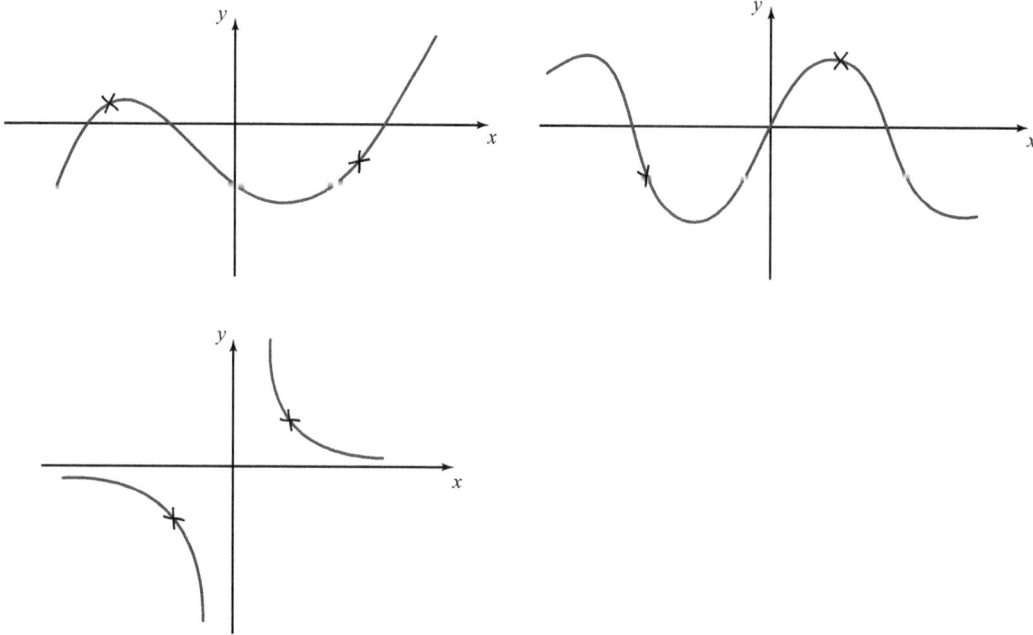

Resource sheet 15.2

State whether each lettered point is a maximum, a minimum or neither of these.

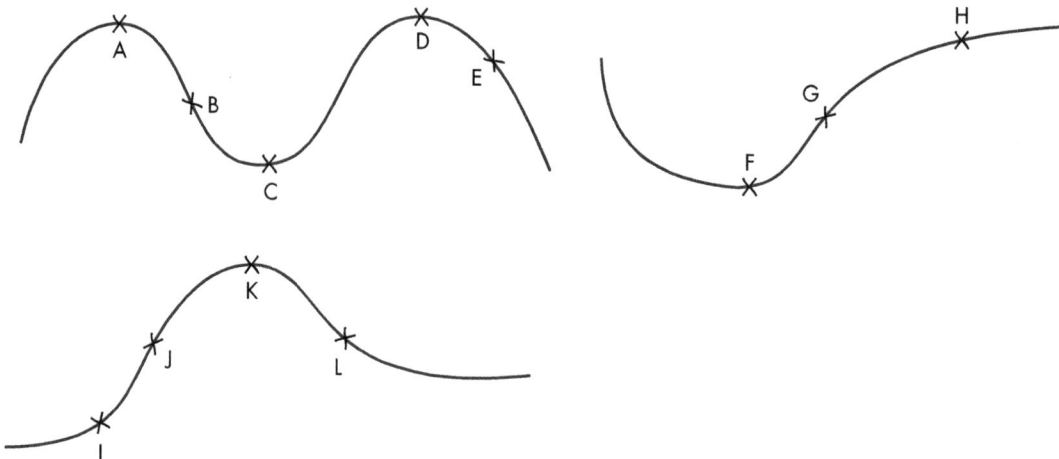

Resource sheet 15.3

Exercise 15.2, Question 1

For the graphs shown, state the sections of the curve where $\dfrac{dy}{dx} > 0$ and where $\dfrac{dy}{dx} < 0$. Identify the points where $\dfrac{dy}{dx} = 0$ and state whether each is a maximum or a minimum.

a

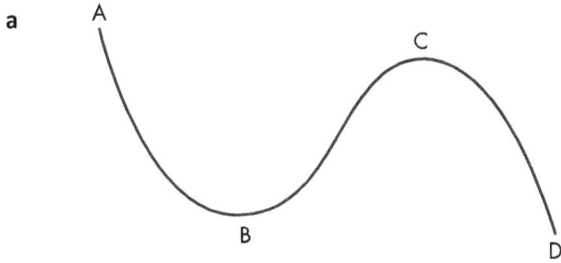

b

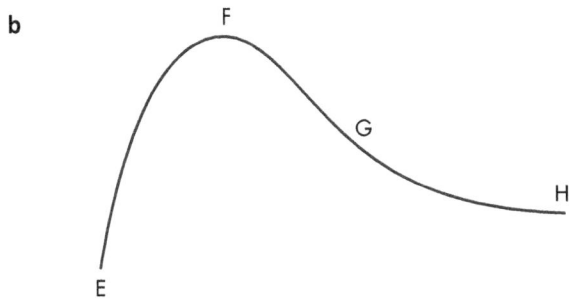

Homework

15.1 Calculating gradients, tangents and normals

1 [NC] Find the equations of the tangents to these curves where $x = 0$.

    a $y = 3x^2 + 2x$ **b** $y = e^x$ **c** $y = (x + 1)^5$

2 [NC] Find the equations of the normals to these curves where $x = 1$.

    a $y = \sqrt{x}$ **b** $y = \dfrac{1}{x}$

3 [NC] Find the equations of the tangents and normals to these curves at the given points.

    a $y = x^3 + 2x^2 - 3$, where $x = 1$.   **b** $y = \sin 3x$, where $x = \dfrac{\pi}{6}$.

4 [NC] **a**   Find the equations of the tangents to the curve $y = (x + 2)(x - 4)$ where the curve cuts the x-axis.

    b   Now find the equations of the normals at these points.

    c   What is the area of the shape enclosed by the two tangents and two normals, below both normals?

5 A curve is given by the equation $f(x) = \ln \cos x$ for $0 \le x < \dfrac{\pi}{2}$.

    Find the equation of the normal when the gradient of the tangent is -1.

6 [NC] Find the coordinates of the point of intersection of the normal at $(-1, 2)$ to the curve $y = 3x^2 + x$ and the normal at the point $(1, 0)$ to the curve $y + \ln x = 0$.

7 [NC] A curve is such that $y = \dfrac{3x^2}{2} - \ln(x + 2)$ for $x > -2$.

    Find the equation of the normal to the curve at the point where $x = -1$.

Homework

15.2 Stationary points

1 [NC] Sketch a curve with two maxima and one minimum.

2 [NC] Describe and sketch the stationary point where $\dfrac{dy}{dx} = 0$ and $\dfrac{d^2y}{dx^2} > 0$.

3 Find any stationary points on $y = x^3 - 6x^2 + 33$ and determine whether each is a maximum or a minimum.

4 [NC] Find any stationary points on $f(x) = x - \ln x$ and determine whether each is a maximum or a minimum.

5 [NC] Find the stationary point on f(x) = $\dfrac{4x\sqrt{x}}{3} - \sqrt{x}$ for $x > 0$ and determine its nature.

6 [NC] The curve $y = ax^2 + bx + c$ passes through the points (0, 10) and (5, 0).

It has a minimum point when $x = 3$.

Find the values of a, b and c.

7 The curve $y = \cos x^2$ has one maximum and one minimum, for $0 \leq x \leq \sqrt{1.5\pi}$.

Determine the coordinates of these two stationary points.

15 Calculus: Applications of Differentiation

Homework

15.3 Connected rates of change

1 [NC] A circle has a radius of x cm. x is increasing at a rate of 1.5 cm min^{-1}.

Find the rate of change of the area of the circle when the radius is 13 cm. Give your answer in terms of π.

2 [NC] A cube has a side length of x cm. x is increasing at a rate of 1.25 cm min^{-1}.

When the side length of the cube is exactly 12 cm, find:

a the rate of increase of the volume of the cube

b the rate of increase of the surface area of the cube.

3 The surface area of a sphere is given by $4\pi r^2$. The rate of change of the radius of a sphere is 3.5 mm s^{-1}.

Work out the rate of change of the surface area of this sphere when the radius is 85 mm.

4 The area of a circle is increasing at 7.5 cm^2 min^{-1}.

Find the rate of increase in the radius of the circle when the radius is 14 cm.

5 [NC] A sphere has a volume of V cm^3 and a surface area of S cm^2. $V = \frac{4}{3}\pi r^3$ and $S = 4\pi r^2$.

V is increasing at a rate of 55 mm^3 s^{-1}.

Find the rate of change of the surface area of the sphere when the radius is 105 mm.

6 The volume of a cube is increasing at a rate of 25.5 cm^3 min^{-1}.

Show that the rate of change of the surface area of the cube is 15.7 cm^2 min^{-1} when the side length is 6.5 cm.

7 A cone has a volume of V cm^3 which can be found using $V = \frac{1}{3}\pi r^2 h$. V is increasing at a rate of 9.8 cm^3 s^{-1}.

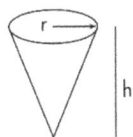

If the ratio of r to h is 2 : 11, find the rate of increase of h when r is 4.5 cm.

15 Calculus: Applications of Differentiation

Homework

15.4 Small increments and approximations

1 **[NC]** For $y = x^2 - x$ and x changing from 2 to 2.05, find the value of $\dfrac{dy}{dx}$ and hence the approximate value of $\dfrac{\delta y}{\delta x}$ and δy.

2 **[NC]** If $y = (x - 3)^3$ and x changes from 1 to 1.02, find the value of $\dfrac{dy}{dx}$ and hence the approximate value of $\dfrac{\delta y}{\delta x}$ and δy.

3 **[NC]** For each of these functions and values of y, find the values of $\dfrac{dy}{dx}$ and hence the approximate values of $\dfrac{\delta y}{\delta x}$ and δx.

   a $y = x^2 - 3x - 4$ for y changing from 0 to -0.01.

   b $y = 8x + \dfrac{1}{x^2}$ for y changing from 0 to 0.06.

4 **[NC]** Given that $y = x^4 - 2x - 2$, find the approximate change in y if x increases from 3 to 3.01.

5 **[NC]** Given that $y = (x^3 - 2)^4$, find the approximate change in y if x increases from 1 to 1.005.

6 Given that $y = 2 - \sin x$ in the domain $\pi < x < \dfrac{3\pi}{2}$ and y increases from 2.5 to 2.55, find the approximate change in x.

7 Given that $y = 5 - \ln x$ for $e < x$ and y changes from 4.7 to 4.71, find the approximate change in x.

Homework

15.5 Practical applications

1   **[NC]** Two quantities x and y have a difference of 6.

Find the turning points of x^2y and determine whether they are maxima or minima.

2   **[NC]** A cuboid is made from a thin sheet of metal, the cuboid length being twice its width.

If the box has a capacity of 9000 cm³, show that its surface area is $4x^2 + \dfrac{27000}{x}$ cm².

Hence find the dimensions of the box that has the least surface area.

3   A right-angled isosceles triangular prism is made so that its volume is 1000 cm³.

Show that its surface area is $x^2 + \dfrac{2000\left(2+\sqrt{2}\right)}{x}$ cm² where x cm is the length of one of the equal sides of the triangle.

Hence find the dimensions of the prism that has the least surface area.

4   If the capacity of a cylinder is 1 litre, show that its total surface area is $2\pi x^2 + \dfrac{2000}{x}$ if x cm is the radius of the base.

What value of x minimises the total surface area?

5   **[NC]** An open rectangular desktop waste paper bin has a square base. If the capacity of the bin is 4 litres, find its dimensions assuming the surface area is a minimum.

6   An open cylindrical waste paper bin has a circular base. If the capacity of the bin is 60 litres, find its dimensions assuming the surface area is a minimum.

7   A stained-glass window maker has 5 m of metal strip, which is enough to make the border of the Norman window shown, which consists of a semi-circle on a rectangle.

If the window's area has to be the largest possible to let in the maximum amount of light, find the dimensions of the rectangle.

Extension

15.1 Calculating gradients, tangents and normals

1   Find the equations of the tangents and normals to these curves at the given points.

[NC] a $y = x + \ln x$, where $x = 1$ **b** $y = \tan 3x$, where $x = \dfrac{\pi}{4}$

2   **[NC] a**   Find the equations of the tangents to the curve $y = (x + 3)(x - 5)$ where the curve cuts the x-axis.

     [NC] b   Now find the equations of the normals at these points.

     c   What is the perimeter of the quadrilateral enclosed by the two tangents and two normals?

3   A curve is given by the equation $f(x) = \sin^2 x$ for $x > 0$.

     Find the equation of the tangent at the first time when the gradient of the normal is -1.

4   **[NC]** Find the coordinates of the point of intersection of the normal at $(-1, -1)$ to the curve $y = 2x^3 - x$ and the normal at the point $(1, 0)$ to the curve $y + \ln x^2 = 0$.

5   **[NC] a** Find the equations of the tangents to the curve $y = (x + a)(x - a)$ where the curve cuts the x-axis.

     b   Now find the equations of the normals at these points.

     c   What is the value of a such that the area enclosed by the two tangents and two normal is a square?

15   Calculus: Applications of Differentiation

Extension

15.2 Stationary points

1   Find and identify the stationary points on the curve $y = 8x^2 + \dfrac{1}{2x^2}, x \neq 0$.

2   Find the stationary point on $f(x) = \dfrac{e^x}{(x-3)^3}$ for $x \neq 3$ and determine its nature.

3   Find and identify all the stationary points on the curve $y = \cos^2 x \sin x$ for $0 < x < \pi$.

Extension

15.3 Connected rates of change

1   A spherical balloon is being filled with gas at a rate of 15 cm³ sec⁻¹.
       Work out the rate of increase of the surface area of the balloon when the volume is 120 cm³.

2   [NC] A water trough is 3 m long, 1 m wide and 0.5 m deep. The cross-section of the trough is an isosceles triangle:

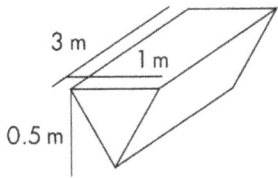

   Water is filling the trough at a rate of 5 litres min⁻¹.
   How fast is the level of the water in trough changing when the water is 30 cm deep? Give the answer in cm min⁻¹.

3   Gravel is being dumped by a mining conveyor onto a conical-shaped pile at a rate of 3 m³ min⁻¹.
       The diameter of the base of the pile is always 6 times the height of the pile.
       Find how fast the height of the pile is increasing when the height is 3.5 m. Give the answer in cm min⁻¹.

4   A storage tank is in the shape of an inverted cone, where d is 8 m and h is 10 m.
       Water is leaking out of the tank at a rate of 7 litres min⁻¹.
       When the height of the water in the tank is 0.15 m, the level of the water is dropping at a rate of 20 cm min⁻¹.

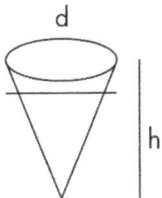

Find the rate at which water is flowing into the tank. Give the answer in litres min⁻¹.

5   [NC] A 13 m ladder is slipping down a wall. The base is moving at 3 m sec¹.
       When the base of the ladder is 5 m from the wall, how fast is the top of the ladder moving?

15 Calculus: Applications of Differentiation

Extension

15.4 Small increments and approximations

1   Given that $y = \dfrac{\sin x}{\ln x}$, find the approximate change in y if x increases from 2 to 2.01.

2   [NC] Given that $y = (x^2 - 3)^5$, find the approximate change in x if y increases from 1 to 1.02.

3   Given that $y = \dfrac{1 - \tan x}{x}$ in the domain $0 < x < \dfrac{\pi}{2}$ and y increases from 0 to 0.1, find the approximate change in x.

4   [NC] Given that $y = \ln(x^3 - 7)$ for $x > 2$ and y increases from 0 to 0.12, find the approximate change in x.

5   One side of a rectangle is five times the side of the other. Given that the perimeter increases from 18 cm to 18.12 cm, use the method of small increments to find the approximate change in the area.

Extension

15.5 Practical applications

1 **[NC]** A right-angled triangular prism has its two shorter sides in the ratio 3 : 4 and has a volume of 600 cm^3.
   Find the dimensions of the prism that has the least surface area.

2 If the capacity of a prism with a regular hexagon as its base and top is 1 litre, find its dimensions that make the total
   surface area a minimum.

3 **[NC]** The perimeter of this sector is 160 cm.
   Work out the maximum area of the sector and show that your answer is a maximum.

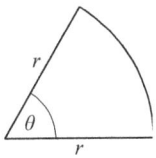

4 **[NC]** The cost of running an economy car, in dollars per hour, is given by the formula $R = 0.5 + \dfrac{x^2}{100}$, where x is the speed

   in km h^{-1}. Find the most economical speed for a journey of 300 km.

5 A chef wants to pack food in a metal prism with an isosceles triangular cross-section as shown. She wants the sides of
   the triangle to be in the ratio 5 : 5 : 6. The volume of the container has to be 972 cm^3. Find the dimensions of the prism
   that minimises the amount of material used.

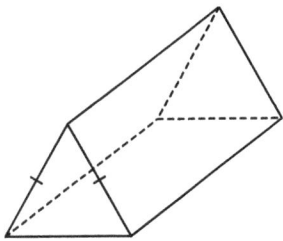

16 Calculus: Integration

TOPIC:

16.1 Integration as anti-differentiation

KEY WORDS:

integration, anti-differentiation, anti-differentiation, differential equation, (arbitrary) constant of integration

IGCSE MATHS PRIOR KNOWLEDGE:

Expand products of algebraic expressions

Manipulate algebraic fractions

Understand surds and indices

Substitute numbers into equations and work out their values

Use function notation such as $f(x) = 3x^2 + 2x - 6$ or $f(x) = \sin(4x - 9)$

Understand the idea of a derived function

Use the derivatives of functions of the form ax^n where a is a rational constant and n is a positive whole number or zero

---

Learning aims:

- Understand integration as the reverse of process of differentiation

Resources:

- Student Book: pages 344–349
- Resource sheet 16.1
- A5 paper
- Coloured pens

Common mistakes and remediation:

The content of this chapter will be totally new to students, so any mistakes will come from them forgetting some of what they have learnt when differentiating. One common error is forgetting the negative sign when integrating the sine function (or differentiating the cosine function).

Useful tips:

Remind students that they can check their answers by differentiating their results; this should take them back to the function they are integrating.

Guidance:

This section is relatively straightforward, provided that students are secure with differentiation. It pays dividends to remind them of the standard results of differentiation.

STARTER (5 mins)

➢ Remind students about the results of differentiation: 'Five quick questions' such as: Differentiate x^3. What would I have started with if, after I had differentiated, I ended with $5x^4$?

MAIN LESSON ACTIVITY (50 mins)

Equipment: Resource sheet 16.1

➢ The idea of this lesson is that there is an inverse operation to differentiation, which is called integration. Just as subtraction is the inverse of addition and division is the inverse of multiplication, integration can be thought of as the inverse of differentiation. However, this time the inverse operation doesn't quite revert to the original unless further information is provided because of the loss of the constant term when differentiating.

The differential equation diagrams (or 'iron filing diagrams') can be used as an introductory exercise, reminding students that the differential equation gives the equation of the gradient of the tangent at any point on the curve. You could start by looking at Example 1 in the Student Book and asking students to draw the diagram where $\frac{dy}{dx} = x$ or $\frac{dy}{dx} = \frac{1}{2}$.

➢ Exercise 16.1 allows students to practise 'anti-differentiation'. The first four questions are relatively simple, as students will probably be able to deduce the results without the need to differentiate first. The others build on problem-solving skills and students will need to find ways of integrating such functions more directly if they proceed to study A Level Mathematics

PLENARY (5 mins)

Equipment: Sheets of A5 paper, one between two students

➢ Give each pair of students a sheet of A5 paper. Allow them a few minutes to work together to produce a mini-poster on the connection between integration and differentiation. Then they pass this to another pair to check and receive feedback. Contributions to the poster can be made by students using different coloured pens.

Homework and answers: Resource sheets, homework and extension exercises can be found at the end of this chapter and in the downloadable materials. Answers can be found in the downloadable materials.

CHECKING PROGRESS	Collect in the checked mini-posters. A glance at these should provide enough feedback on whether or not students understand the concepts of integration and anti-differentiation.

16 Calculus: Integration

TOPIC:
16.2 Integrating polynomials

KEY WORD:
polynomials

IGCSE MATHS PRIOR KNOWLEDGE:
Expand products of algebraic expressions

Manipulate algebraic fractions

Understand surds and indices

Substitute numbers into equations and work out their values

Use function notation such as $f(x) = 3x^2 + 2x - 6$ or $f(x) = \sin(4x - 9)$

Understand the idea of a derived function

Use the derivatives of functions of the form ax^n where a is a rational constant and n is a positive whole number or zero

Learning aims:
- Integrate functions of the form $(ax + b)^n$ for any rational n, $\sin(ax + b)$, $\cos(ax + b)$, $\sec^2(ax + b)$, $e^{ax + b}$

Resources:
- Student Book: pages 349–351
- A5 paper

Common mistakes and remediation:
Students often forget to include the constant of integration and need to be reminded about it!

Useful tips:
Ask students to check their answers by differentiating so that they avoid silly mistakes.

Guidance:
Students generally have no problem when integrating positive integral powers of x, but they need to take care when the powers are negative or fractional, so a reminder of that is useful. The starter activity covers this.

STARTER (5 mins)
➢ Remind students about differentiating powers of x and how to differentiate polynomials.

➢ Ask them to differentiate $x^{\frac{3}{2}}$ and then to integrate the result to see what happens.

➢ Then set 'Five quick questions' on differentiating and integrating with fractional powers.

MAIN LESSON ACTIVITY (50 mins)
➢ Go through some examples before students try Exercise 16.2.

➢ In Exercise 16.2 the first four questions are fairly standard; in the problem-solving questions, the students are faced with some more involved algebra and need to divide out the fractions first; don't tell them what to do, however, as this is part of the problem-solving process.

➢ Check to ensure that in questions 5 to 7 students are not just integrating each term.

PLENARY (5 mins)

Equipment: Sheets of A5 paper

➢ Give each student a sheet of A5 paper. Ask them to draw a flowchart explaining how to integrate a simple polynomial. After three or four minutes, they should pass the paper to a partner to check that their flowchart works. If it does not, the partner should indicate where it has gone wrong.

Homework and answers: Resource sheets, homework and extension exercises can be found at the end of this chapter and in the downloadable materials. Answers can be found in the downloadable materials.

CHECKING PROGRESS	Collect in the results of the plenary activity so you can see the progress your students have made. Since they will have been checked by a partner, this should not be intensive on your behalf!

16 Calculus: Integration

TOPIC:
16.3 Integrating trigonometric functions

KEY WORDS:
trigonometric functions

IGCSE MATHS PRIOR KNOWLEDGE:
Expand products of algebraic expressions

Manipulate algebraic fractions

Understand surds and indices

Substitute numbers into equations and work out their values

Use function notation such as $f(x) = 3x^2 + 2x - 6$ or $f(x) = \sin(4x - 9)$

Understand the idea of a derived function

Use the derivatives of functions of the form ax^n where a is a rational constant and n is a positive whole number or zero

---

Learning aims:
- Integrate functions of the form $(ax + b)^n$ for any rational n, $\sin(ax + b)$, $\cos(ax + b)$, $\sec^2(ax + b)$, $e^{ax + b}$

Resources:
- Student Book: pages 352–354

Common mistakes and remediation:

Students often forget the negative sign when integrating sine functions and include it when integrating cosine functions.

Useful tips:

Make students aware that double negatives can occur, as in Example 6c.

Remind students they should write out all their working.

Guidance:

Provided students have learnt the results when differentiating, from Chapter 14, they should make reasonable progress with this topic.

STARTER (5 mins)

➢ Remind students about differentiating $\sin x$ and $\cos x$.

➢ Ask them to differentiate $\sin x$ and then to integrate the result to see what happens.

➢ Then 'Five quick questions' on differentiating and integrating simple trigonometric functions such as $\sin 2x$ and $\cos 3x$.

MAIN LESSON ACTIVITY (50 mins)

➢ Go through one or two examples, then allow the students to try Exercise 16.3.

➢ Encourage students to set their work out as shown in the examples.

➢ In Exercise 16.3 the first four questions develop students' skills; in the problem-solving questions, students need to do some involved differentiation and this will be more challenging for lower-achieving students.

PLENARY (5 mins)

➢ Give the students a few minutes to tell the person next to them something they have learnt in the lesson. Then ask one or two students to tell the class what their partner said to them. This allows students to recap on what they have learnt and also develops skills in listening and relaying mathematical information.

Homework and answers: Resource sheets, homework and extension exercises can be found at the end of this chapter and in the downloadable materials. Answers can be found in the downloadable materials.

CHECKING PROGRESS	Make sure all students have completed question 1 correctly by checking their answers during the lesson.

TOPIC:

16.4 Integrating exponential and other functions

KEY WORDS:

exponential function, logarithmic function

IGCSE MATHS PRIOR KNOWLEDGE:

Expand products of algebraic expressions

Manipulate algebraic fractions

Understand surds and indices

Substitute numbers into equations and work out their values

Use function notation such as $f(x) = 3x^2 + 2x - 6$ or $f(x) = \sin(4x - 9)$

Understand the idea of a derived function

Use the derivatives of functions of the form ax^n where a is a rational constant and n is a positive whole number or zero

---

Learning aims:

- Integrate functions of the form $(ax + b)^n$ for any rational n, $\sin(ax + b)$, $\cos(ax + b)$, $\sec^2(ax + b)$, $e^{ax + b}$

- Integrate functions of the form $\dfrac{1}{x}$ and $\dfrac{1}{ax + b}$

Resources:

- Student Book: pages 354–358
- Resource sheet 16.1 (optional)

Common mistakes and remediation:

As before, students sometimes make mistakes in manipulating the algebra – practice makes perfect!

Students should check their results frequently to avoid spending too much time manipulating incorrect algebra.

Useful tips:

Encourage all students to show their working using one = sign per line, aligning subsequent = signs beneath the first one. That way, if they check their answers and find a discrepancy it is easier for them to identify where the mistake has been made. Remember: students should check their results often to avoid spending too much time manipulating incorrect algebra.

Guidance:

Students need plenty of time to answer these questions; they are not as familiar with exponentials and logarithms as they are with polynomials or trigonometry, and processes in this section can be lengthy. It is better to do a few correctly rather than rush through making errors.

STARTER (5 mins)

➢ Remind students about differentiating e^x and $\ln x$.

➢ Then 'Five quick questions' on differentiating and integrating simple exponential and logarithmic functions such as e^{2x} and $\ln 3x$.

MAIN LESSON ACTIVITY (50 mins)

Equipment: Resource sheet 16.1 (optional), whiteboards (optional)

➤ The differential equation diagrams (or 'iron filing diagrams') can be used as an introductory exercise to this section, reminding students that the differential equation gives the equation of the gradient of the tangent at any point on the curve. You could start by looking at the diagram before Example 8 in the *Student Book* and asking students to draw the diagram where $\dfrac{dy}{dx} = \dfrac{1}{x}$ or $\dfrac{dy}{dx} = e^x$.

➤ Reinforce the fact that by writing the constant of integration as the logarithm of a constant, the final expression can be simplified as more than just '$+ c$', though they will not lose marks for not doing so.

➤ There is an opportunity to revise the laws of logarithms here.

➤ Students sometimes need reminding that $\ln 1 = 0$, $e^0 = 1$, $e^{\ln x} = x$, and $\ln e = 1$.

➤ In Exercise 16.4 the first four questions develop students' skills; problem-solving question 6 provides extra challenge.

PLENARY (5 mins)

➤ Students should write a fairly simple integral of the type studied in the lesson and pass it to a partner to work out. This could be done as a mini whiteboard activity. They can then check the answer, which they should have worked out in advance.

Homework and answers: Resource sheets, homework and extension exercises can be found at the end of this chapter and in the downloadable materials. Answers can be found in the downloadable materials.

CHECKING PROGRESS	Collect in and sift through the questions they have set and marked in the plenary activity. This should give you some feedback on how well they have done and whether more time is needed on this section.

16 Calculus: Integration

TOPIC:
16.5 Evaluating definite integrals

KEY WORDS:
indefinite integration, definite integral

IGCSE MATHS PRIOR KNOWLEDGE:
Expand products of algebraic expressions

Manipulate algebraic fractions

Understand surds and indices

Substitute numbers into equations and work out their values

Use function notation such as $f(x) = 3x^2 + 2x - 6$ or $f(x) = \sin(4x - 9)$

Understand the idea of a derived function

Use the derivatives of functions of the form ax^n where a is a rational constant and n is a positive whole number or zero

---

Learning aims:
- Evaluate definite integrals and apply integration to the evaluation of plane areas

Resources:
- Student Book: pages 358–361
- Graph paper

Common mistakes and remediation:

Sometimes students substitute the limits the wrong way round; mention that the top limit is the first limit to be substituted. Remind them that the 'top of the list' is generally the 'first in the list'.

Useful tips:

Encourage all students to show their working in detail, using one = sign per line, then aligning = signs in subsequent rows beneath the one in the first line. That way, if they check their answers and find a discrepancy it is easier for them to identify where the mistake has been made. Too many mistakes are made by students not using brackets when subtracting negatives in the lower bounds.

After continually being reminded about including the constant of integration, students now need to be aware that they should not include it when calculating definite integrals because it will cancel itself out.

Guidance:

Students need plenty of time with these questions; they should be familiar with the sines, cosines and tangents of simple fractions of π as these occur often when the trigonometric functions are involved in definite integration.

STARTER (5 mins)
➤ Remind students about all the techniques they have met so far in this chapter.
➤ Then give them five minutes to write down as many standard results as they can remember – these can be checked by their partners.

MAIN LESSON ACTIVITY (50 mins)

Equipment: Graph paper

➢ Students can then follow the examples given. Watch out for simple arithmetical errors!

➢ Most graphing calculators allow students to find the areas under curves, so let students use these to check their answers, making sure they are aware that such calculators may not be allowed in the examination.

PLENARY (5 mins)

➢ Ask students to work out $\int_{-1}^{1} x^3 \, dx$ and similar definite integrals with odd powers and limits of $+a$ and $-a$ and ask them to explain to a partner why their answer is always 0.

Homework and answers: Resource sheets, homework and extension exercises can be found at the end of this chapter and in the downloadable materials. Answers can be found in the downloadable materials.

CHECKING PROGRESS	Ask a student to present their answer to the plenary to the rest of the class. This should give some indication of whether they have understood the process.

16 Calculus: Integration

TOPIC:

16.6 Integrating to evaluate plane areas

KEY WORDS:

plane areas

IGCSE MATHS PRIOR KNOWLEDGE:

Expand products of algebraic expressions

Manipulate algebraic fractions

Understand surds and indices

Substitute numbers into equations and work out their values

Use function notation such as $f(x) = 3x^2 + 2x - 6$ or $f(x) = \sin(4x - 9)$

Understand the idea of a derived function

Use the derivatives of functions of the form ax^n where a is a rational constant and n is a positive whole number or zero

---

Learning aims:
- Evaluate definite integrals and apply integration to the evaluation of plane areas

Resources:
- Student Book: pages 362–367
- Graph paper
- Graphing calculators

Common mistakes and remediation:

Students often arrive at a wrong answer because they do not have a picture in their mind about the areas and the position of the curve on the grid axes. It is important that they sketch the curves first as otherwise the area between the curve and the x-axis under the x-axis can reduce the actual area – see Example 16.

Useful tips:

Encourage students always to sketch the curves and check their results frequently to avoid spending too much time manipulating incorrect algebra.

Guidance:

Students need plenty of time with these questions; they lead into the type of questions frequently asked in the examinations.

STARTER (5 mins)

➢ Remind students about integrating with limits.

➢ Then set 'Five quick questions' on differentiating and integrating simple basic functions.

MAIN LESSON ACTIVITY (50 mins)

Equipment: Graph paper, graphing calculators

➤ To enable students to assimilate the concept of the area under a curve, the first part of this lesson deals with the area under a straight-line graph passing through the origin.

➤ Reinforce the concept by giving them the task of calculating the area under a straight line that does not pass through the origin, for example $y = \frac{1}{2}x + 3$ between $x = 2$ and $x = 6$. They should not use integration for this, but get them to draw the graph and use the area of a trapezium to calculate the area between the line and the x-axis.

➤ They can then integrate the equation to check their answer.

➤ Students can then follow the examples given. As mentioned earlier, it is important that they sketch the curves first as otherwise the area between the curve and the x-axis under the x-axis can reduce the actual area – see Example 16.

➤ Most graphing calculators allow students to find the areas under curves, so let students use these to check their answers. However, it is important that students know what type of graphing calculators can and cannot be used in the examination.

PLENARY (5 mins)

➤ Students should write a fairly simple integral of the type studied in the lesson and pass it to a partner to work out. They can then check each other's answers, which they should have worked out in advance.

Homework and answers: Resource sheets, homework and extension exercises can be found at the end of this chapter and in the downloadable materials. Answers can be found in the downloadable materials.

CHECKING PROGRESS	Collect in and sift through the questions they have set and marked in the plenary activity. This should give you some feedback on how well they have done and whether more time is needed on this section.

16 Calculus: Integration

Resource sheet 16.1

Use this grid to draw tangents to invisible curves and hence sketch in a family of curves that satisfy a given differential equation.

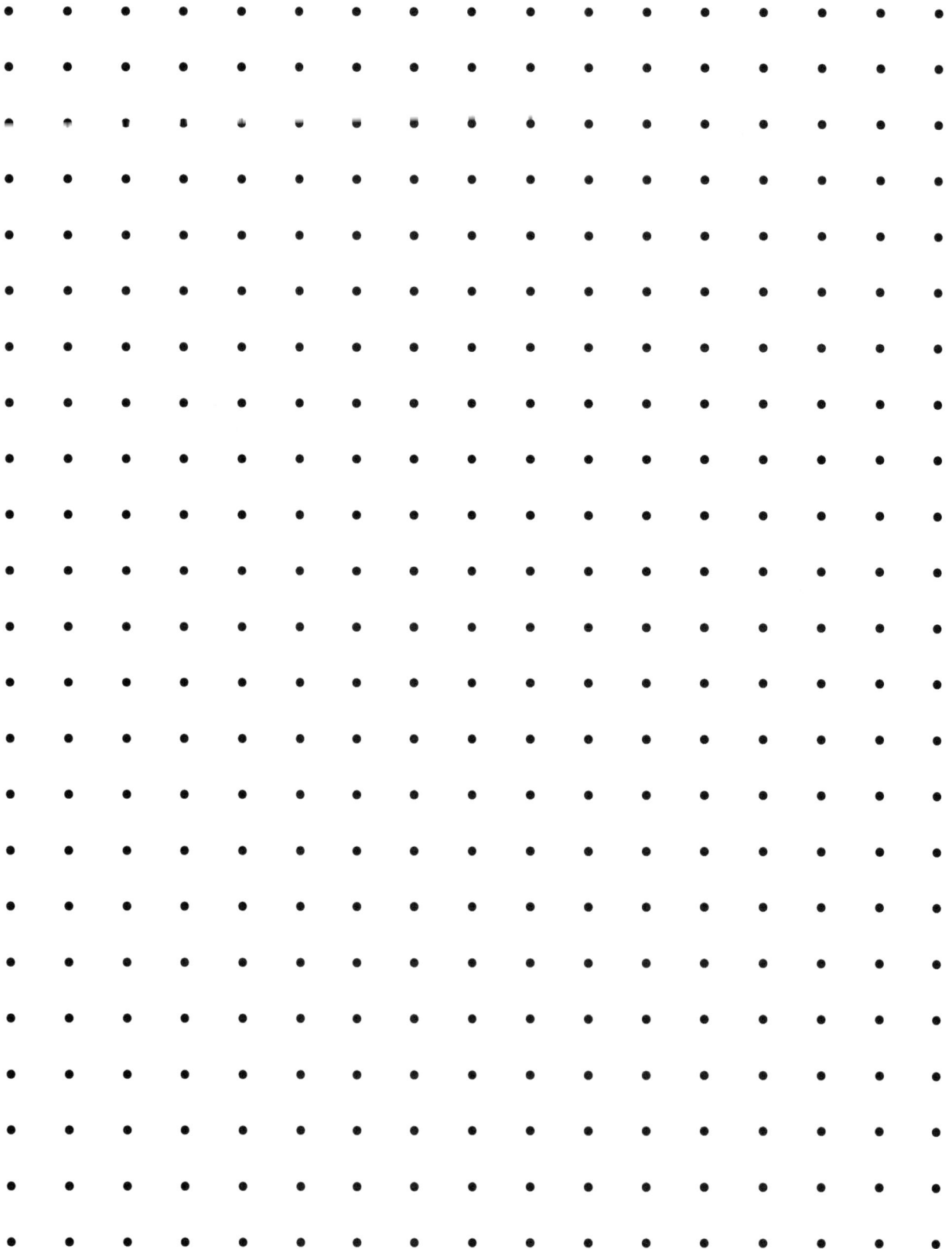

16 Calculus: Integration

Homework

16.1 Integration as anti-differentiation

Non-calculator

1   Using what you learnt in Chapter 14, copy and complete this table.
    The first column is done for you.

	a	b	c	d
$\dfrac{dy}{dx}$	$2x$	$5x$	-6	$\dfrac{2}{3}$
$y =$	$\int 2x\,dx$			
$y =$	$x^2 + c$			

2   a   Prove that $y = 2x^2 - \dfrac{1}{x^2}$ is a solution of the differential equation $\dfrac{dy}{dx} = 4x + \dfrac{2}{x^3}$.

    b   What is the most general solution of $\int \left(4x + \dfrac{2}{x^3} \right) dx$?

    c   Find the equation of the curve with gradient $4x + \dfrac{2}{x^3}$ that passes through (1, 3).

3   $y = 3x^4 - 5$

    a   Find $\dfrac{dy}{dx}$.

    b   Explain why, if $\dfrac{dy}{dx} = 12x^3$, this does not imply $y = 3x^4 - 5$.

    c   If $\dfrac{dy}{dx} = 12x^3$ and $y = 1$ when $x = 1$, find y in terms of x.

4   $f(x) = 4 \cos x$
    a   Write down $f'(x)$.
    b   Explain why, if $f'(x) = 4 \sin x$, this does not imply $f(x) = -4 \cos x$.
    c   If $f'(x) = 4 \sin x$, find $f(x)$ if $f\left(\dfrac{1}{2}\pi \right) = 3$.

5   $y = e^{2x^2}$

    a   Work out $\dfrac{dy}{dx}$.

    b   Use your result from part **a** to work out $f(x)$ where $f(x) = \int xe^{2x^2}\,dx$.

    c   If $f(0) = 1$, work out the value of the constant of integration.

6 $f(x) = \dfrac{1}{\sin x}$.

    a Work out f′(x).

    b Use your result from part **a** to work out y where $\int \operatorname{cosec} x \cot x \, dx$.

    c Work out the equation of the curve with gradient cosec x cot x that passes through the point $\left(\dfrac{\pi}{6}, 1 \right)$.

7   **a** If $y = x^3 \ln x^2$, find $\dfrac{dy}{dx}$.

    b Work out $\int x^2 (1 + 3\ln x) \, dx$.

    c Work out the equation of the curve with gradient x^2 (1 + 3 ln x) that passes through the point (1, 2).

16 Calculus: Integration

Homework

16.2 Integrating polynomials

Non-calculator

1 a Work out $y = \int \left(x^4 - 4x^3 \right) dx$.

   b Given that $y = \int \left(x^4 - 4x^3 \right) dx$ passes through (1, 0), find the value of the arbitrary constant of integration.

2 a Work out $\int \sqrt[4]{x} \, dx$.

   b If $f(x) = \int \sqrt[4]{x} \, dx$ and f(16) = 25, evaluate f(0).

3 Express $\int \left(x - \dfrac{1}{x} \right)^2$ in terms of x.

4 Express $\int \left(\sqrt{x} + \dfrac{3}{x} \right) \left(\sqrt{x} - \dfrac{3}{x} \right) dx$ in terms of x.

5 Work these out.

   a $\int (6x - 1)^5 \, dx$

   b $\int (3 - 2x)^9 \, dx$

6 Work out $\int \left(\dfrac{3x^3 - 4x^2 + 5x}{x} \right) dx$.

7 Work out $\int \left(\dfrac{x^3 - \dfrac{3}{x^3}}{x^2} \right) dx$.

Homework

16.3 Integrating trigonometric functions

Non-calculator

1   Work these out.

   a $\int \cos 8x \, dx$ **b** $\int \sin \dfrac{x}{3} \, dx$ **c** $\int 5 \sec^2 2x \, dx$

2   Work out

   a $\int (2 - \cos 0.5x) \, dx$ **b** $\int (x + 2 \sin (0.25x)) \, dx$

3   Work these out.

   a $\int (4 \cos x - 5 \sec^2 x) \, dx$ **b** $\int (\cos(2x - 3) + \sin(3 - 2x)) \, dx$

4   Work these out.

   a $\int (3x - \sin(2x + 1)) \, dx$ **b** $\int (4x^3 - \cos(3 + x)) \, dx$

5   Work out $\int (2 \cos 2x + 1) \, dx$ and $\int (2 \cos(2x + 1)) \, dx$, and explain the difference between the two integrals.

6 $f(x) = \int \sin \left(\dfrac{1}{3}x + \pi \right) dx$ and $f(\pi) = 1$.

   Find $f(x)$ in terms of x and hence work out $f(0)$.

7 $y = \int \cos(\pi - 3x) \, dx$ and $y = 1$ when $x = \dfrac{\pi}{2}$.

   Show that y can be written as $y = \dfrac{2 - \sin 3x}{3}$.

Homework

16.4 Integrating exponential and other functions[nc]

Non-calculator

For questions 1 to 6, work out the integrals.

1 **a** $\int e^{10x}\, dx$ **b** $\int e^{3x-2}\, dx$

2 **a** $\int \dfrac{1}{x-5}\, dx$ **b** $\int \dfrac{dx}{3x-3}$

3 **a** $\int \dfrac{1}{e^{3x}}\, dx$ **b** $\int \dfrac{dx}{\sqrt{e^{4x}}}$

4 **a** $\int \left(\sqrt{e^x} + \dfrac{2}{\sqrt{e^x}} \right)^2 dx$ **b** $\int \dfrac{1}{\dfrac{x}{3}+6}\, dx$

5 **a** $\int \dfrac{1}{5-4x}\, dx$ **b** $\int \dfrac{dx}{8-\dfrac{x}{4}}$

6 **a** $\int \dfrac{1}{(5-4x)^2}\, dx$ **b** $\int \dfrac{dx}{\left(3-\dfrac{x}{2}\right)^3}$

7 **a** Show that $y = a^x$ can be written as $y = e^{x \ln a}$, where a is a constant.

    b Hence work out $\dfrac{dy}{dx}$.

    c Use your result from part **b** to evaluate $\int a^x dx$.

Homework

16.5 Evaluating definite integrals

1   [NC] Evaluate these definite integrals.

    a $\int_0^1 \left(x^2 + 1 \right) dx$ **b** $\int_{-1}^1 \dfrac{dx}{x^5}$

2   [NC] Work out $\int_0^2 f(x)\, dx$ where:

    a $f(x) = 3x - 2$ **b** $f(x) = (x + 4)(x - 1)$.

3   [NC] Evaluate these definite integrals.

    a $\int_0^{\frac{\pi}{6}} \cos x \, dx$ **b** $\int_0^{\frac{\pi}{6}} \sin\left(2x - \dfrac{\pi}{3} \right) dx$

4   Work out $\int_1^3 f(x)\, dx$ to 3 significant figures where:

    a $f(x) = e^{2x - 3}$ **b** $f(x) = e^{5 - x}$.

5   [NC] Evaluate these definite integrals.

    a $\int_1^8 \dfrac{dx}{x + 6}$ **b** $\int_1^2 \dfrac{5\, dx}{10x - 2}$.

6   [NC] Evaluate these definite integrals.

    a $\int_3^4 \dfrac{dx}{2x - 4}$ **b** $\int_{-9}^{-3} \dfrac{dx}{8 - \dfrac{1}{3}x}$.

7   [NC] If $y = 2x + \dfrac{1}{2x}$, work out $\int_1^3 y^2 \, dx$.

16   Calculus: Integration

Homework

16.6 Integrating to evaluate plane areas

1   [NC] Find the area bounded by these curves, the x-axis and the lines given.

    a $y = 2x^3$, $x = 0$ and $x = 2$

    b $y = (x - 2)^2$, $x = 1$ and $x = 3$

2   Find the area bounded by these trigonometric curves, the x-axis and the lines given.

    a $y = \cos x - \sec^2 x$, $x = 0$ and $x = \dfrac{\pi}{3}$

    b $y = \sin 3x - \cos 4x$, $x = 0$ and $x = \dfrac{\pi}{3}$

3 Find the area bounded by these functions, the *x*-axis and the lines given.

Give your answers to 3 significant figures.

a $f(x) = x - e^{2x}$, $x = 0$ and $x = 2$

b $f(x) = e^x - \dfrac{1}{x-2}$, $x = 5$ and $x = 3$

4 Find the area bounded by $f(x) = x^3 + \dfrac{1}{3x+1}$, the *x*-axis, $x = 1$ and $x = 2$.

5 [NC] Find the area bounded by $y = -x^2 + 6x - 5$ and $y = 2x - 2$.

6 Find the area bounded by the curve $y = e^{0.5x}$ and the lines $x = 3$ and $y = 1$.

7 [NC] Find the area enclosed by the curve $y = (x-1)(x-2)(x-3)$ and the *x*-axis.

Extension

16.1 Integration as anti-differentiation

1 **[NC]** $f(x) = \sin x - x \cos x$

    a   Work out $f'(x)$.

    b   Use your result from part **a** to work out y where $y = \int x \sin x \, dx$.

    c   Work out the equation of the curve with gradient $x \sin x$ that passes through the point $(\pi, 2\pi)$.

2 **[NC] a**   If $y = e^x(x-1)$, find $\dfrac{dy}{dx}$.

    b   Work out $\int xe^x \, dx$.

    c   Work out the equation of the curve with gradient $2xe^x$ that passes through the point $(1, 1)$.

3 **[NC] a**   If $y = \dfrac{x^2(2\ln x - 1)}{4}$, find $\dfrac{dy}{dx}$.

    b   Work out $\int x \ln x \, dx$.

    c   Work out the equation of the curve with gradient $x \ln x$ that passes through the point $(1, 1)$.

4 **[NC] a**   Given that $y = \dfrac{1}{2}(\ln x)^2$, find $\dfrac{dy}{dx}$.

    b   Use your answer to part **a** to find $\int \left(\dfrac{\ln x}{x}\right) dx$.

    c   Work out the equation of the curve with gradient $\dfrac{\ln x}{x}$ that passes through the point $(e, 1)$.

5   **a**   Given that $f(x) = \ln\left(\dfrac{1+\sqrt{x}}{1-\sqrt{x}}\right)$ for $0 < x < 1$, show that $f'(x) = \dfrac{1}{(1-x)\sqrt{x}}$.

    b   Hence find $\int \dfrac{dx}{(1-x)\sqrt{x}}$.

    c   Work out the equation of the curve with gradient $\dfrac{1}{(1-x)\sqrt{x}}$ that passes through the point $\left(\dfrac{1}{2}, 1\right)$.

Extension

16.2 Integrating polynomials

Non-calculator

1   Work these out.

   a $\int \left(1 - \sqrt{x}\right)^2 dx$ **b** $\int \left(\dfrac{1+x}{x^3}\right) dx$

2   Work out $\int \left(\dfrac{5x^5 - 4x^4 + 6x^2}{x}\right) dx$.

3   Work out $\int \left(\dfrac{x - \dfrac{3}{x}}{x}\right)^2 dx$.

4   If $f\left(x\right) = \int 3x\left(1 - x^2\right) dx$ and $f(2) = 0$, find $f(x)$.

5   A curve is such that $\dfrac{dy}{dx} = \dfrac{1}{\sqrt{x-4}}$ for $x > 4$.

   The curve passes through the point (8, 2).

   a   Find the equation of the curve.

   b   Find the x-coordinate of the point on the curve where $y = 6$.

Extension

16.3 Integrating trigonometric functions
Non-calculator

1   Work out $\int \left(4x - \cos(3x-2) \right) dx$.

2   Work out $\int \left(12x^5 + \sin(2-5x) \right) dx$.

3 $f(x) = \int \sec^2 (\pi - 2x)\, dx$ and $f(\pi) = 1$.

    Find f(x) in terms of x and hence work out $f\left(\dfrac{3\pi}{8} \right)$.

4 $y = \int \sin \left(\dfrac{\pi}{2} - 4x \right) dx$ and $y = 1$ when $x = \dfrac{\pi}{8}$.

    Show that y can be written as $y = \dfrac{3 + \sin 4x}{4}$.

5   If $y = \cos (3 - 2x^4)$, find $\dfrac{dy}{dx}$.

    Use your result to work out $\int x^3 \sin(3 - 2x^4)\, dx$.

Extension

16.4 Integrating exponential and other functions
Non-calculator

In questions 1 to 3, work out the integral.

1 $\int \dfrac{1}{5 - \dfrac{x}{2}}\, dx$

2 $\int \left(\dfrac{3x^2 - 3}{x^3 - 3x} \right) dx$

3 $\int \left(\dfrac{4 + \sin 2x}{8x - \cos 2x} \right) dx$

4   Work out $\int 10^x\, dx$.

5 a   By writing $y = x^x$ as $\ln y = \ln x^x$, show that y can be written as $y = e^{x \ln x}$.

    b   Now find $\dfrac{dy}{dx}$ and use your result to work out $\int x^x (1 + \ln x)\, dx$.

Extension

16.5 Evaluating definite integrals

Non-calculator

1 Evaluate $\int_0^1 \left(e^{2x} - e^{-2x} \right) dx$.

2 Show that $\dfrac{3x-1}{x+2} = 3 - \dfrac{7}{x+2}$ and hence evaluate $\int_{-1}^1 \left(\dfrac{3x-1}{x+2} \right) dx$.

3 Evaluate $\int_0^2 \dfrac{x^3}{x+1}\, dx$.

4 If $xy = e$, evaluate $\int_1^e y\, dx$.

5 Given that $\sqrt{xy^{\frac{3}{2}}} = k$, where k is a constant, work out $\int_{0.5}^1 x\, dy$.

Extension

16.6 Integrating to evaluate plane areas

1 **[NC] a** Using integration, find the area enclosed by $2x + 3y + 12 = 0$ and the axes.
   b Use an alternative method to check your answer.

2 **[NC]** Find the area bounded by $y = -12$ and the curve $y = (x + 1)(x - 7)$.

3 A curve passes through the point $(1, -1)$ and the gradient of its normal at any point (x, y) is $\dfrac{1}{5-3x}$.

   Find the area bounded by the curve and the x-axis.

4 The region enclosed by the curve $y = 3\cos 2x$, the x-axis and the line $x = a$, where $0 < a < 0.7$ radian, lies entirely above the x-axis. Given that the area of this region is $\dfrac{1}{2}$ square unit, find the value of a.

5 Find the area enclosed by the curve $y = (x+1)^2 (x-3)$ and the x-axis.

TOPIC:

17.1 Applying differentiation to kinematics

KEY WORDS:

differentiation, first derivative, second derivative, distance, position, displacement, speed, velocity, acceleration, equation of motion, point, particle, body, variable, kinematics

IGCSE MATHS PRIOR KNOWLEDGE:

Expand products of algebraic expressions

Factorise and solve quadratic equations

Understand surds and indices

Substitute numbers into equations and work out their values

Use function notation such as $f(x) = 3x^2 + 2x - 6$ or $f(x) = \sin(4x - 9)$

Understand the idea of a derived function

Use the derivatives of functions of the form ax^n

Discriminate between maxima and minima

Apply the idea of rate of change to simple kinematics involving distance–time and speed–time graphs and acceleration

Calculate distance travelled as area under a speed–time graph

---

Learning aims:

- Apply differentiation and integration to kinematics problems that involve displacement, velocity and acceleration of a particle moving in a straight line with variable or constant acceleration

Resources:

- Student Book: pages 372–375
- A5 paper
- Coloured paper (optional)
- Coloured pens

Common mistakes and remediation:

Students will have some familiarity with kinematics through their work in physics or on the IGCSE Mathematics course, so any mistakes may come from them forgetting some of what they have learnt when differentiating. One common error is forgetting the negative sign when integrating the sine function (or differentiating the cosine function).

Useful tips:

Remind students that drawing a diagram often helps them visualise the problem. It gives the brain time to assimilate and think about the problem while it is engaged in the hand–eye coordination of drawing a diagram.

Also remind students that if a body is at rest, its velocity is 0.

Guidance:

This section is relatively straightforward provided that students are secure with differentiation. It pays dividends to remind them of the standard results of differentiation.

STARTER (5 mins)

➤ Remind students about the results of differentiation: 'Five quick questions', such as: Differentiate x^3. What would I have started with if, after I had differentiated, I ended with $5x^4$?

MAIN LESSON ACTIVITY (50 mins)

➢ The aim of this lesson is to consolidate the fact that differentiating the distance equation gives the velocity equation, and differentiating the velocity equation gives the acceleration equation.

As far as possible, try to avoid the word 'deceleration' as it is not often used in mathematics. Always write acceleration and use the sign of the acceleration, together with the sign of the velocity, to decide whether the body is slowing down or speeding up at any particular instant.

➢ In Exercise 17.1, students need to apply their differentiation skills to kinematics. The first five questions are relatively simple though students may need reminding that when an article hits the ground, it implies that $s = 0$, if s is measured from ground level. The last three questions build on problem-solving skills and lower-attaining students may not progress that far.

PLENARY (5 mins)

Equipment: Sheets of A5 paper, one shared between two students, coloured paper (optional), coloured pens

➢ Give students a few minutes to work with a partner to produce a mini-poster about the connection between the distance, velocity and acceleration equations. Coloured paper can be used, or ask pupils to use different coloured pens. Then they pass this to another pair to check and receive feedback.

Homework and answers: Resource sheets, homework and extension exercises can be found at the end of this chapter and in the downloadable materials. Answers can be found in the downloadable materials.

CHECKING PROGRESS	Collect in the mini-posters after they have been checked. A glance at these should provide enough feedback as to whether students understand the concept of differentiation to obtain the various kinematics equations.

TOPIC:

17.2 Applying integration to kinematics

KEY WORDS:

integration, limits, kinematics

IGCSE MATHS PRIOR KNOWLEDGE:

Expand products of algebraic expressions

Factorise and solve quadratic equations

Understand surds and indices

Substitute numbers into equations and work out their values

Use function notation such as $f(x) = 3x^2 + 2x - 6$ or $f(x) = \sin(4x - 9)$

Understand the idea of a derived function

Use the derivatives of functions of the form ax^n

Discriminate between maxima and minima

Apply the idea of rate of change to simple kinematics involving distance–time and speed–time graphs and acceleration

Calculate distance travelled as area under a speed–time graph

Learning aims:	Resources:
• Apply differentiation and integration to kinematics problems that involve displacement, velocity and acceleration of a particle moving in a straight line with variable or constant acceleration	• Student Book: pages 375–378 • A5 paper • Coloured pens

Common mistakes and remediation:

Students often forget to include the constant of integration, so may need to be reminded about it. A mark can be given in examinations for the constant of integration for indefinite integrals. The boundary conditions given in the questions allow the constant of integration to be determined. Sometimes students do not pick up on the subtle ways that the boundary conditions are hidden.

Useful tips:

Ask students to check their answers by differentiating so that they avoid silly mistakes.

Guidance:

Students generally have no problem when integrating positive integral powers of x, but may need reminding about the trigonometric and exponential functions.

STARTER (5 mins)

➢ Remind students about integrating powers of x and how to deal with trigonometric and exponential functions.

➢ Ask them to state the boundary conditions implicit within such statements as: 'Initially the particle is at rest.' 'After three seconds the particle is 2 metres from the origin.' 'The velocity is 5 m s^{-1} when the acceleration is 0.'

➢ Then ask 'Five quick questions' on integrating simple functions.

MAIN LESSON ACTIVITY (50 mins)

➢ Go through some examples, then students can try Exercise 17.2.

➢ In Exercise 17.2 the first three questions are fairly standard; in the problem-solving questions, the students are faced with some more subtle situations.

➢ For question 4, check to ensure that students are aware that as t tends to infinity, e^{-t} tends to 0.

➢ In question 5 the train arrives in London when its velocity is 0, so setting the velocity to 0 means $t = 0$ or 2. Therefore the distance is found by a definite integral with limits 0 and 2.

PLENARY (5 mins)

Equipment: Sheets of A5 paper, one shared between two students, coloured pens

➢ Give the students a few minutes to work with a partner to produce another mini-poster, this time in the form of a flowchart on the connection between the distance, velocity and acceleration equations and integration as well as differentiation. Then they pass this to another pair to check and receive feedback.

Homework and answers: Resource sheets, homework and extension exercises can be found at the end of this chapter and in the downloadable materials. Answers can be found in the downloadable materials.

CHECKING PROGRESS	Collect in the results of the plenary activity so you can see the progress that students have made. Since they will have been checked by other students, this should again not be intensive on your behalf!

TOPIC:

17.3 Using x–t, v–t and a–t graphs

KEY WORDS:

x–t graphs, v–t graphs, a–t graphs

IGCSE MATHS PRIOR KNOWLEDGE:

Expand products of algebraic expressions

Factorise and solve quadratic equations

Understand surds and indices

Substitute numbers into equations and work out their values

Use function notation such as $f(x) = 3x^2 + 2x - 6$ or $f(x) = \sin(4x - 9)$

Understand the idea of a derived function

Use the derivatives of functions of the form ax^n

Discriminate between maxima and minima

Apply the idea of rate of change to simple kinematics involving distance–time and speed–time graphs and acceleration

Calculate distance travelled as area under a speed–time graph

Learning aims:	Resources:
• Apply differentiation and integration to kinematics problems that involve displacement, velocity and acceleration of a particle moving in a straight line with variable or constant acceleration • Make use of the relationships in Chapter 14 to draw and use the following graphs: displacement–time distance–time velocity–time speed–time acceleration–time	• Student Book: pages 378–384 • Graph paper

Common mistakes and remediation:

Students often forget to look at the units on the graph axes: make sure they do not assume the units are always consistent! (Some speeds may be in km h^{-1}, yet the time may be in minutes rather than hours.)

Useful tips:

Make students aware that distance–time graphs can be used to find velocity–time graphs.

Guidance:

Provided that students have managed the work on distance–time graphs for their IGCSE Mathematics, this section should be relatively straightforward.

STARTER (5 mins)

➤ To remind students about distance–time graphs, sketch one on the board for them to describe to a partner. This could be one like Bradley's graph at the start of Section 17.3 in the Student Book.

MAIN LESSON ACTIVITY (50 mins)

Equipment: Graph paper

➤ Go through one or two examples, then allow the students to tackle Exercise 17.3.

➤ In Exercise 17.3 the first five questions develop students' skills; for the problem-solving questions, the students need to do some involved calculations, which will be more challenging for the lower-achieving students.

➤ A graphing calculator may be an aid to seeing the graphs in Exercise 17.3. Pupils will find this grabs their interest and provides a visual aid.

PLENARY (5 mins)

➤ Give the students a few minutes to tell the person next to them something they have learnt in the lesson. Then ask one or two students to tell the class what that person said to them. This allows students to recap on what they have learnt and also develops listening and relaying mathematical information skills. Alternatively, provide each student with a sticky note and ask them to write down what they have learnt and stick it onto the whiteboard. See how many students have picked up the same concepts and who has been ultra-perceptive.

Homework and answers: Resource sheets, homework and extension exercises can be found at the end of this chapter and in the downloadable materials. Answers can be found in the downloadable materials.

CHECKING PROGRESS	Make sure all students have completed questions 1 to 5 correctly by checking their answers during the lesson.

17 Calculus: Applications of Kinematics

Homework

17.1 Applying differentiation to kinematics

1   An observational rocket on the moon is projected vertically upwards at 50 m s^{-1}.

Its height, s, above the moon t seconds later is given by $s = 1 + 50t - 0.8t^2$.

Find its position, velocity and acceleration after 1 second.

When does the rocket hit the moon?

2   **[NC]** A particle moves along a straight line such that its distance from a fixed point, O, on the line is x m where $x = e^t - e^3t$.

    a   Where is the particle initially?

    b   Work out when its velocity is 0 and find the acceleration at that instant.

3   **[NC]** A particle moves along a straight line such that its distance from a fixed point, O, on the line is s m where $s = (t - 1)^6$.

    a   When is the particle at O?

    b   Calculate its velocity and acceleration at these times.

4   **[NC]** A particle moves along a straight line such that its distance from a fixed point, O, on the line is s m where $s = 2t^3 - 9t^2 + 4t$.

    a   When is the particle at O?

    b   Calculate its velocity and acceleration at these times.

5   A stone is thrown vertically down a well at 18 m s^{-1}. It is s metres from the rim of the well after t seconds, where $s = 18t + 4.9t^2$.

If it hits the water at the bottom of the well with a velocity of 67 m s^{-1} calculate:

    a   how long it took to hit the water

    b   the depth of the well.

6   A particle moves in a straight line from a fixed point, O, such that its distance, x cm from O after t seconds is given by $x = (t^2 + 3)(t - 5)$.

    a   Calculate its velocity and acceleration at time t.

    b   Use your answers to part **a** to find the position of the particle when it is instantaneously at rest.

    c   What is the velocity when the acceleration is zero?

7   A sky-diver is dropped from a plane. The distance h m above the ground is given by $h = 800 - 2\sqrt{t}$, where t is the time in seconds. What will be the velocity of the sky-diver when they land?

Homework

17.2 Applying integration to kinematics

1 **[NC]** A body moves in a straight line with velocity $10 - 2t$ m s^{-1}.
   Find an expression for its position if, after 2 seconds, the body is at the origin.

2 **[NC]** A body moves in a straight line with velocity $8 - 4t$ m s^{-1}.
   Find an expression for its position if, after 1 second, the body is 10 m from the origin.

3 **[NC]** A particle moves in a straight line with acceleration $12t - 4$ m s^{-2}.
   It starts at the origin with a velocity of 3 m s^{-1}.
   a Find an expression for its velocity, v, in terms of the time, t.
   b Find an expression for its position, x, in terms of the time, t.
   c Calculate its acceleration, velocity and position when $t = 1$.

4 **[NC]** A particle moves in a straight line with acceleration $15\sqrt{t} + 2$ m s^{-2}.
   It starts 2 m from the origin with a velocity of 5 m s^{-1}.
   a Find an expression for its velocity, v, in terms of the time, t.
   b Find an expression for its position, x, in terms of the time, t.
   c Calculate its acceleration, velocity and position when $t = 4$.

5 **[NC]** After 1 second a particle moving in a straight line has a velocity of 1 m s^{-1} and is 3 m along the positive direction from the origin. It moves with an acceleration of $\dfrac{1}{t^3}$ m s^{-2}.
   a Find an expression for its velocity at time t.
   b Find an expression for its position at time t.
   c Work out the particle's position and speed after half a second.

6 **[NC]** After 9 seconds a particle moving in a straight line has a velocity of 3 m s^{-1} and is 3 m along the positive direction from the origin. It moves with an acceleration of $\dfrac{1}{\sqrt{t}}$ m s^{-2}.
   a Find an expression for its velocity at time t.
   b Find an expression for its position at time t.
   c Work out the particle's position and speed after 4 seconds.

7 The velocity of a particle after time t seconds is given by $v = 3 + e^{-t}$ m s^{-1}.
   If the particle moves in a straight line and is initially at the origin, find its position at time t.
   Use your answer to find out where it will be after:
   a 1 second
   b 100 seconds
   c 1 000 000 seconds.
   d What can you deduce about its motion?

Homework

17.3 Using *x–t*, *v–t* and *a–t* graphs

1   **[NC]** A particle moves with a velocity of 3 m s^{-1} for 4 seconds, and then accelerates by 1 m s^{-2} for 3 seconds. It then moves with its new velocity for 3 seconds.

    Draw the velocity–time graph and use it to calculate how far the particle has travelled.

2   **[NC]** A particle starts with a velocity of 10 m s^{-1} for 1 second, and then accelerates by -2 m s^{-2} for 3 seconds. It then moves with a new constant acceleration until its velocity is reduced to 0 in the next 4 seconds.

    Draw the velocity–time graph and use it to calculate how far the particle has travelled.

3   The velocity, *v*, in m s^{-1}, of a certain particle varies with the time, *t*, in seconds, such that $v = \sqrt{49 - t^2}$.

    a   Draw a velocity–time graph for the first 7 seconds of motion.

    b   Determine the distance covered in the first 7 seconds.

    c   Work out the acceleration when $t = 4$.

4   **[NC]** A particle moves along a straight line for 3.5 seconds, such that its displacement from a fixed point O on the line is *x* cm, where $x = 2t^3 - 7t^2 + 2t + 4$ and *t* is the time in seconds.

    Sketch the particle's displacement–time graph, velocity–time graph and acceleration–time graph.

5   **[NC]** The diagram shows a velocity–time graph of a body moving in a straight line with velocity *v* km h^{-1} at time *t* minutes after leaving a fixed point.

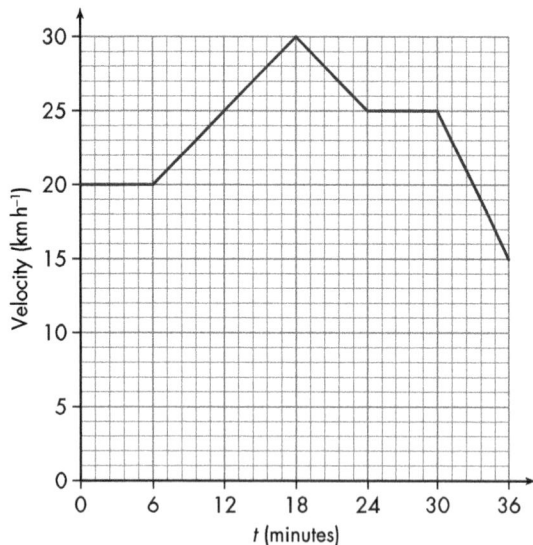

Find the distance travelled by the body.

6 [NC] This diagram shows the displacement–time graph of a car being driven along a French motorway.

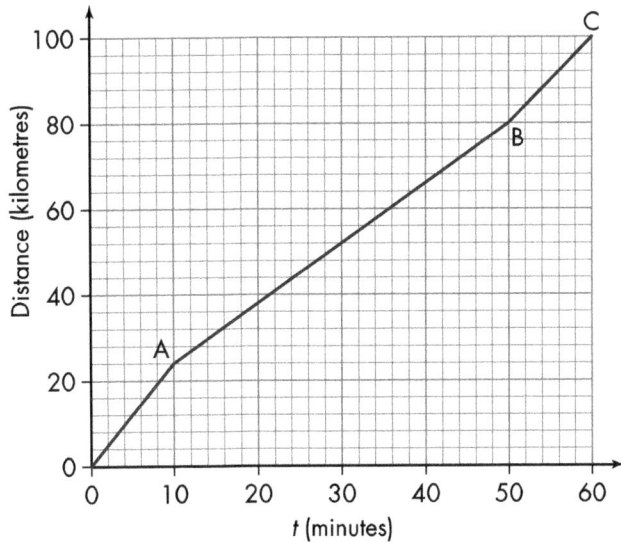

a Calculate the car's velocity for each part of the journey. The speed limit when it is raining is 110 km h^{-1}, otherwise it is 130 km h^{-1}. Comment on whether the driver broke the speed limit.

b Plot the velocity–time graph for the car.

7 A particle starts from rest and moves in a straight line with velocity v m s^{-1}, where t is the time in seconds and

- $v = 2t$ for the first 3 seconds
- $v = 5 + e^{2t-6}$ for the following 2 seconds.

Draw the velocity–time graph and calculate the distance covered.

Extension

17.1 Applying differentiation to kinematics

1   **[NC]** A particle moves along a straight line such that its distance from a fixed point on the line is x cm, where $x = 3 - \cos t$ and t is the time in seconds.

    a   Find its velocity and acceleration after t seconds.

    b   Where is the particle when it is first at rest?

    c   Where is the particle when it is next at rest?

    d   Where is the particle when it is first travelling fastest?

2   A bead is threaded on a vertical rod and moves in a straight line such that its distance from a fixed point, O, after a time t seconds is given by $x = \ln (t^3 - 5.5t^2 + 6t)$ where $0.1 < x < 1.4$.

    a   Find an expression for the velocity of the bead in terms of t.

    b   Find the position of the bead when the particle is first at rest.

3   A particle falls through a liquid such that its distance, d, from the top of the liquid, in cm, is given by the formula $d = 16t^2 - t^4$, where t is the time in seconds.

    a   Find the initial velocity and the velocity after 2 seconds.

    b   What is the acceleration when $t = 2$?

    c   When does the body come instantaneously to rest?

    d   The particle's acceleration is 0 m s^{-2} just as it reaches the bottom of the liquid.
        How deep is the liquid?

4   **[NC]** The displacement x m of a particle P, which is moving in a straight line, from a fixed point at time t s is given by $x = \dfrac{t^2}{\ln t}$. Find the value of t for which the particle P is instantaneously at rest.

5   **[NC]** The displacement s m of a particle R, which is moving in a straight line, from a fixed point at time t s, is given by $s = 3t - 12 \ln (t + 3) + \pi$.

    a   Find the value of t for which the particle R is instantaneously at rest.

    b   Find the value of t for which the acceleration of the particle R is $\dfrac{1}{3}$ m s^{-2}.

17 Calculus: Applications of Kinematics

Extension

17.2 Applying integration to kinematics

1   The velocity of a particle after time t seconds is given by $v = \dfrac{1}{t+1} - e^{-t} \, \text{m s}^{-1}$.

   If the particle moves in a straight line and is initially 2 m to the right of the origin, find its position at time t.
   Use your answer to find out where it will be after 3 seconds.

2   [NC] A train travels non-stop from Durham to York and its velocity t hours after leaving Durham is $420t(1 - t)$ miles per hour. Find:

   a   the distance between Durham and York

   b   the acceleration at time t

   c   the train's maximum speed.

3   [NC] A point, P, moves in a straight line with an acceleration of $\sin(\pi - 3t) \, \text{m s}^{-2}$, where t is the time in seconds.
   Initially its speed is 1 m s^{-1} and its position is 3 m from the origin.
   Describe how its position and speed change with time.

4   [NC] Given that $\dfrac{dx}{dt} = 9 \cos 3t$ represents the motion of a particle from an origin, O, where t is the time in seconds and

   that $x = 1$ cm initially, find x in terms of t and hence show that $\dfrac{d^2x}{dt^2} + 9x - 9 = 0$.

5   Two beads are threaded on a smooth straight wire. One bead, P, starts at the origin, O, with a velocity $v_p = 8t + e^{0.5t}$.
   The other bead, Q, starts at A, which is 30 m in the positive direction from O, with a velocity $v_q = -e^{0.5t}$.

   a   Find formulae for the displacements x_p and x_q of each bead from O at time t.

   b   Show that, where they meet, $t^2 + e^{0.5t} = 8.5$.

   c   The solution to the equation in part **b** is $t = 2.31$.
       How far has Q travelled in this time?

17 Calculus: Applications of Kinematics

Extension

17.3 Using x–t, v–t and a–t graphs

1   The diagram shows a velocity–time graph of a body moving in a straight line with velocity v m h^{-1} at time t minutes after leaving a fixed point.

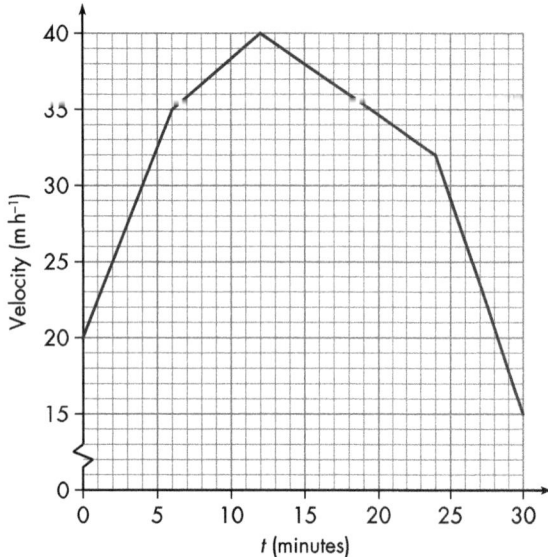

Find the distance travelled by the body.

2   **[NC]** A toy electric car is put on a straight track.

It accelerates with a constant acceleration for 3 seconds until it reaches a velocity of 12 m s^{-1}. It then slows down with a constant acceleration of -1.5 ms^{-2} for 2 seconds.

Finally, it slows down uniformly, coming to a stop 3 seconds later.

a   Draw a velocity-time graph.

b   How far did the car travel?

3   The velocity, v, in m s^{-1}, of a certain particle varies with the time, t, in seconds, such that $v = 64 - t^2$.

a   Draw a velocity–time graph for the first 8 seconds of motion.

b   Determine the distance covered in the first 8 seconds.

c   Work out the acceleration when $t = 5$.

4   A particle moves in a straight line with velocity $20 - 3.2t^2$ m s^{-1} for $0 \leq t \leq 2.5$, where t is the time in seconds.

a   Sketch the velocity–time graph and acceleration–time graph.

b   Find the distance travelled by the particle in the 2.5 seconds.

5   A particle starts from rest and moves in a straight line with velocity v m s^{-1}, where t is the time in seconds and

• $v = 6t$ for the first 3 seconds

• $v = 19 - e^{0.4t - 1.2}$ for the following 5 seconds.

Draw the velocity–time graph and calculate the distance covered.

Scheme of Work

Timings are based on an approximate allocation of 2 hours teaching time per section. This Scheme of Work is provided as an aid to planning, it is not intended to be prescriptive, nor complete. Availability of resource, time and individual school calendars will all impact on what is practical and achievable; the Scheme of work as offered here is presented to provide ideas on which teachers can build. Timings are indicative only.

Topic(s)	Learning outcomes	Student's Book pages	Key words
1.1 Mappings, functions and notation	Understand the terms: function, domain, range (image set), one – one function, many – one function, inverse function, and composition of functions Find the domain and range of functions	pp. 4 to 13	mapping diagram, one-one, many-one, one-many, many-many, function, domain, range
1.2 Composite functions	Understand the terms: function, domain, range (image set), one – one function, many – one function, inverse function, and composition of functions Form and use composite functions Find the domain and range of functions	pp. 13 to 14	Composite function
1.3 Inverse functions	Understand the terms: function, domain, range (image set), one – one function, many – one function, inverse function, and composition of functions Find the inverse of a one-one function	pp. 15 to 17	Inverse function, self-inverse function
1.4 Graphs of a function and its inverse	Use sketch graphs to show the relationship between a function and its inverse	pp. 17 to 20	
1.5 Modulus functions	Understand the relationship between $y = f(x)$ and $y = |f(x)|$, where f(x) may be linear quadratic, cubic or trigonometric	pp. 20 to 22	Modulus, absolute function
1.6 Graphs of $y = |f(x)|$ where $f(x)$ is linear	Understand the relationship between $y = f(x)$ and $y = |f(x)|$, where f(x) may be linear quadratic, cubic or trigonometric	pp. 19 to 22	
1.7 Graphs of $y = |f(x)|$ where $f(x)$ is quadratic	Understand the relationship between $y = f(x)$ and $y = |f(x)|$, where f(x) may be linear quadratic, cubic or trigonometric	pp. 26 to 31	Roots, turning point, stationary point
11.1 Permutations	Know and use the notation $n!$ and the expression for permutations and combinations of n items taken r at a time	pp. 238 to 240	Permutation, arrangement, factorial, selection
11.2 Permutation problems	Solve problems on arrangement and selection using permutations or combinations	pp. 240 to 244	
11.3 Combinations	Recognise the difference between permutations and combinations and know when each should be used Know and use the notation n! and the expressions for permutations and combinations of n items taken r at a time	pp. 244 to 247	Combination

Topic(s)	Learning outcomes	Student's Book pages	Key words
11.4 Combinations problems	Solve problems on arrangement and selection using permutations or combinations	pp. 247 to 250	Committee
2.1 The quadratic function	Find the maximum or minimum value of the quadratic function $f : x \mapsto ax^2 + bx + c$ by completing the square or by differentiation Use the maximum or minimum value of $f(x)$ to sketch the graph of $y = f(x)$ or determine the range for a given domain	pp. 34 to 39	Parabola, y-intercept, roots, minimum value, maximum value, turning point, stationary point
2.2 Completing the square	Find the maximum or minimum value of the quadratic function $f(x) = ax^2 + bx + c$ by completing the square Solve quadratic equations for real roots	pp. 39 to 42	Completing the square
2.3 The quadratic formula	Know the conditions for $f(x) = 0$ to have: (i) two different real roots, (ii) two equal roots, (iii) no real roots Solve quadratic equations for real roots	pp. 43 to 47	factorising, discriminant
2.4 Intersection of a line and a curve	Know the conditions for $f(x) = 0$ to have: (i) two real roots, (ii) two equal roots, (iii) no real roots and the related conditions for a given line to: (i) intersect a given curve, (ii) be a tangent to a given curve, (iii) not intersect a given curve Solve quadratic equations for real roots	pp. 47 to 49	
2.5 Quadratic inequalities	Find the solution set for a quadratic inequality either graphically or algebraically Know the conditions for $f(x) = 0$ to have: (i) two real roots (ii) two equal roots (iii) no real roots Solve quadratic equations for real roots	pp. 50 to 52	
12.1 Arithmetic progressions	Recognise arithmetic progressions Use the formulae for the nth term and for the sum of the first n terms	pp. 256 to 258	Arithmetic progression, arithmetic sequence, arithmetic series, common difference
12.2 Geometric progressions	Recognise arithmetic progressions Use the formulae for the nth term and for the sum of the first n terms	pp. 259 to 262	Geometric progression
12.3 Sum to infinity	Recognise arithmetic and geometric progressions and understand the difference between them Use the condition for convergence of a geometric progression, and the formula for the sum to infinity of a convergent geometric progression	pp. 262 to 264	Sum to infinity, divergence, convergence
12.4 Binomial expansions	Use the binomial theorem for expansion of $(a + b)^n$ for positive integer n Use the general term $\binom{n}{r} a^{n-r} b^r$, $0 \leq r \leq n$	pp. 264 to 269	Binomial expression, binomial expansion, Pascal's triangle, binomial theorem

Topic(s)	Learning outcomes	Student's Book pages	Key words
3.1 The factor theorem	Know and use the factor and remainder theorem Find factors of polynomials Solve cubic equations	pp. 58 to 64	Polynomial, variable, cubic, factor theorem, quotient, divisor, long division method, grid method
3.2 The remainder theorem	Know and use the factor and remainder theorem	pp. 64 to 67	Remainder, remainder theorem, dividend
5.1 Simultaneous equations	Solve simultaneous equations in two unknowns by elimination or substitution	pp. 104 to 107	Simultaneous equation, substitution, linear, non-linear, quadratic
5.2 Interpreting and solving simultaneous equations graphically	Solve simultaneous equations in two unknowns by elimination or substitution	pp. 108 to 112	Intersection, points of intersection, tangent, graphically
8.1 Equation of a circle, centre (0, 0), radius r	Know and use the equation of a circle with radius r and centre (a, b) Solve problems involving tangents to a circle	pp. 170 to 172	centre, radius, Pythagoras' theorem, tangent, gradient
8.2 Equation of a circle, centre (a, b), radius r	Know and use the equation of a circle with radius r and centre (a, b) Solve problems involving tangents to a circle	pp. 172 to 175	radius, diameter, tangent, Pythagoras' theorem, mid-point
8.3 General equation of a circle centre $(-g, -f)$ and radius r 8.4 Intersections of a circle	Know and use the general equation of a circle with radius r and centre (a, b) Solve problems involving the intersection of a circle and a straight-line Solve problems involving tangents to a circle Solve problems involving the intersection of a circle and a straight-line Solve problems involving tangents to circles Solve problems involving the intersection of two circles	pp. 175 to 177 pp. 177 to 181	tangent, normal, intersect, completing the square intersection, chord, tangent, normal
9.1 & 9.2 Radians and arc length	Solve problems involving the arc length and sector area of a circle, including knowledge and use of radian measure	pp. 186 to 187	Radians, arc, arc length, subtend
9.3 Sector area	Solve problems involving the arc length and sector area of a circle, including knowledge and use of radian measure	pp. 189 to 190	
9.4 Problems involving arcs and sector area	Solve problems involving the arc length and sector area of a circle, including knowledge and use of radian measure	pp. 191 to 192	
10.1 Trigonometric values for angles of any magnitude	Know and use the six trigonometric functions of angles of any magnitude	pp. 202 to 212	Quadrant, periodic, domain, range

Topic(s)	Learning outcomes	Student's Book pages	Key words
10.2 & 10.3 Further and other trigonometric functions	Know and use the six trigonometric functions of angles of any magnitude Solve, for a given domain, trigonometric equations involving the six trigonometric functions and the above relationships	pp. 212 to 216	Secant, cosecant, cotangent, tangent, cosine, sine, radians
10.4 Graphs of trigonometric functions	Understand and use the amplitude and period of a trigonometric function, including the relationship between graphs of related trigonometric functions. Draw and use graphs of $y = a \sin bx + c$, $y = a \cos bx + c$ and $y = a \tan bx + c$	pp. 216 to 227	Amplitude, period,
10.5 Trigonometric identities	Prove trigonometric relationships involving the six trigonometric functions	pp. 227 to 229	Identities, prove
10.6 Solving trigonometric equations	Solve, for a given domain, trigonometric equations involving the six trigonometric functions	pp. 229 to 231	
4.1 Solving absolute-value linear equations	• Solve equations of the type $\|ax + b\| = c \ (c \geqslant 0)$ $\|ax + b\| = cx + d$ $\|ax + b\| = \|cx + d\|$ $\|ax^2 + bx + c\| = d$ using algebraic or graphical methods	pp. 72 to 77	Absolute value, modulus
4.2 Solving absolute-value linear inequalities	• Solve graphically or algebraically inequalities of the type $k\|ax + b\| > c \ (c \geqslant 0)$ $k\|ax + b\| \leqslant c \ (c > 0)$ $k\|ax + b\| \leqslant \|cx + d\|$ where $k > 0$ $\|ax + b\| \leqslant \|cx + d$ $\|ax^2 + bx + c\| > d$ $\|ax^2 + bx^2 + c\| \leqslant d$	pp. 74 to 894	critical values
4.3 Solving cubic inequalities graphically	Solve graphically cubic inequalities of the form: $f(x) > d$, $f(x) \leqslant$ and $f(x) < d$ where $f(x)$ is a product of three linear factors and d is a constant	pp. 84 to 89	derivative, differentiation, turning points
4.4 Graphs of polynomials and their moduli	Sketch the graphs of cubic polynomials and their moduli, when given as a product of three linear factors	pp. 89 to 95	Polynomial
4.5 Solving quadratic equations by substitution	Use substitution to form and solve a quadratic equation	pp. 72 to 75	Quartic equation, radical equation

Topic(s)	Learning outcomes	Student's Book pages	Key words
6.1 Properties of exponential functions and their graphs	Work with simple properties and graphs of the exponential functions including e^x and $ke^{nx} + a$ where n, k and a are integers	pp. 118 to 121	The number e, domain, range, asymptote, growth, exponential growth, decay, exponential decay, half-life, exponential functions, base
6.2 Properties of logarithmic functions and their graphs	Know and use simple properties and graphs of the logarithmic and exponential functions, including $\ln x$ and e^x	pp. 121 to 126	the number e, domain, range, asymptote, base, exponent, power, index, exponential form, logarithmic form, Naperian or natural logarithm, common logarithm, inverse
6.3 Laws of logarithms	Know and use the laws of logarithms, including change of base of logarithms	pp. 126 to 129	Base, power
6.4 Changing the base of a logarithm	Know and use the laws of logarithms, including change of base of logarithms	pp. 129 to 130	Base
6.5 Equations of the form $a^x = b$	Solve equations of the form $a^x = b$	pp. 131 to 132	Taking logs
7.1 Interpreting equations of the form $y = mx + c$	Use the equation of a straight-line	pp. 138 to 142	Cartesian, coordinates, variable, constant, y-intercept, gradient
7.2 Transforming relationships of the form $y = ax^n$ and $y = ab^x$ to linear form	Transform given relationships to and from straight-line form, including determining unknown constants by calculating the gradient or intercept of the transformed graph	pp. 143 to 150	Transform, take logs, linearisation, plot, experimental data
7.3 Transforming from linear form to given relationships	Transform given relationships to and from straight-line form, including determining unknown constants by calculating the gradient or intercept of the transformed graph	pp. 151 to 153	Coefficient
7.4 Working with the mid-point and length of a straight line	Solve problems involving mid-point and length of a line, including finding and using the equation of a perpendicular bisector	pp. 153 to 156	mid-point, Pythagoras' theorem

Topic(s)	Learning outcomes	Student's Book pages	Key words
7.5 Working with parallel and perpendicular lines	Know and use the condition for two lines to be parallel or perpendicular	pp. 156 to 160	parallel, perpendicular, negative reciprocal, bisector
13.1 Position and unit vectors	Understand and use vector notation Know and use position vectors and unit vectors Find the magnitude of a vector; add and subtract vectors and multiply vectors by scalars	pp. 276 to 280	position vector, column vector, unit vector, scalar, magnitude, modulus, component, collinear
13.2 Vectors in geometry	Find the magnitude of a vector; add and subtract vectors and multiply vectors by scalars	pp. 280 to 284	
13.3 Compose and resolve velocities	Compose and resolve velocities	pp. 298 to 301	Unit vector, velocity
14.1 The idea of a derived function	Use the notations $f'(x)$, $f''(x)$, and $\frac{dy}{dx}$ and $\frac{d^2y}{dx^2} \left[= \frac{d}{dx}\left(\frac{dy}{dx}\right)\right]$	pp. 274 to 277	coordinates, gradient, chord, function, small increment, first principles, derived function, derivative
14.2 Differentiating polynomials	Use the notations $f'(x)$, $f''(x)$, and $\frac{dy}{dx}$ and $\frac{d^2y}{dx^2} \left[= \frac{d}{dx}\left(\frac{dy}{dx}\right)\right]$ Know and use the derivatives of the standard functions x^n (for any rational n), $\sin x$, $\cos x$, $\tan x$, e^x, $\ln x$ Differentiate the product of functions	pp. 301 to 305	Integer, composite function, function of a function, chain rule, second derivative
14.3 Differentiating trigonometric functions	Know and use the derivatives of the standard functions x^n (for any rational n), $\sin x$, $\cos x$, $\tan x$, e^x, $\ln x$	pp. 305 to 308	sine, cosine, tangent
14.4 Differentiating exponential and logarithmic functions	Differentiate products and quotients of functions	pp. 309 to 313	exponential function, logarithmic function
14.5 Differentiating products of functions	Differentiate products and quotients of functions	pp. 315 to 316	product, product rule
14.6 Differentiating quotients of functions	Differentiate products and quotients of functions	pp. 317 to 319	quotient, quotient rule

Topic(s)	Learning outcomes	Student's Book pages	Key words
15.1 Calculating gradients, tangents and normals	Use differentiation to find gradients, tangents and normals	pp. 324 to 326	gradient, function, tangent, normal, bisect
15.2 Stationary points	Use differentiation to find a stationary point Apply differentiation to practical problems involving maxima and minima	pp. 326 to 328	Stationary point, maximum, minimum, second derivative, rate of change
15.3 Connected rates of change	Apply differentiation to connected rates of change, small increments and approximations	pp. 328 to 330	rate of change, rate of increase, chain rule
15.4 Small increments and approximations	Apply differentiation to connected rates of change, small increments and approximations	pp. 331 to 333	small increment, small change, approximation
15.4 Practical applications	Be able to solve practical problems using differentiation	pp. 333 to 337	
16.1 Integration as anti-differentiation	Understand integration as the reverse of process of differentiation	pp. 344 to 349	integration, anti-differentiation, differential equation, integrals, (arbitrary) constant of integration
16.2 Integrating polynomials	Integrate functions of the form $(ax + b)n$ for any rational n, $\sin(ax + b)$, $\cos(ax + b)$, $\sec^2(ax + b)$, e^{ax+b}	pp. 349 to 351	Polynomials
16.3 Integrating trigonometric functions	Integrate functions of the form $(ax + b)n$ for any rational n, $\sin(ax + b)$, $\cos(ax + b)$, $\sec^2(ax + b)$, e^{ax+b}	pp. 352 to 354	Trigonometric functions
16.4 Integrating exponential and other functions	Integrate functions of the form $(ax + b)n$ for any rational n, $\sin(ax + b)$, $\cos(ax + b)$, $\sec^2(ax + b)$, e^{ax+b} Integrate functions of the form $\dfrac{1}{x}$ and	pp. 354 to 358	Exponential function, logarithmic function
16.5 Evaluating definite integrals	Evaluate definite integrals and apply integration to the evaluation of plane areas	pp. 358 to 361	Definite integral, indefinite integral
16.6 Integrating to evaluate plane areas	Evaluate definite integrals and apply integration to the evaluation of plane areas	pp. 362 to 367	Plane areas

Topic(s)	Learning outcomes	Student's Book pages	Key words
17.1 Applying differentiation to kinematics	Apply differentiation and integration to kinematics problems that involve displacement, velocity and acceleration of a particle moving in a straight line with variable or constant acceleration	pp. 372 to 375	differentiation, first derivative, second derivative, distance, position, displacement, speed, velocity, acceleration, equation of motion, point, particle, body, variable, kinematics
17.2 Applying integration to kinematics	Apply differentiation and integration to kinematics problems that involve displacement, velocity and acceleration of a particle moving in a straight line with variable or constant acceleration	pp. 375 to 378	Integration, limits, kinematics
17.3 Using x–t, v–t and a–t graphs	Apply differentiation and integration to kinematics problems that involve displacement, velocity and acceleration of a particle moving in a straight line with variable or constant acceleration Make use of the relationships in Chapter 14 to draw and use the following graphs: displacement–time distance–time velocity–time speed–time acceleration–time	pp. 378 to 384	x–t, v–t graphs, a–t graphs